600
BASIC
JAPANESE
VERBS

日本語
基本動詞
600語

600
BASIC
JAPANESE
VERBS

日本語
基本動詞
600語

Compiled by **HIRŌ JAPANESE CENTER**

TUTTLE Publishing

Tokyo | Rutland, Vermont | Singapore

Published by Tuttle Publishing, an imprint of Periplus Editions (HK) Ltd.

www.tuttlepublishing.com

ISBN 978-4-8053-1237-7
ISBN 978-4-8053-1825-6 (For sale in Japan only)

Distributed by:

North America, Latin America and Europe
Tuttle Publishing
364 Innovation Drive, North Clarendon
VT 05759-9436 USA.
Tel: 1(802) 773-8930
Fax: 1(802) 773-6993
info@tuttlepublishing.com
www.tuttlepublishing.com

Japan
Tuttle Publishing
Yaekari Building 3rd Floor
5-4-12 Osaki Shinagawa-ku
Tokyo 1410032, Japan
Tel: (81) 3 5437 0171
Fax: (81) 3 5437 0755
sales@tuttle.co.jp
www.tuttle.co.jp

Asia Pacific
Berkeley Books Pte. Ltd.
3 Kallang Sector #04-01, Singapore 349278
Tel: (65) 6741-2178
Fax: (65) 6741-2179
inquiries@periplus.com.sg
www.tuttlepublishing.com

26 25 24 23   11 10 9 8 7   2311VP
Printed in Malaysia

CONTENTS

ACKNOWLEDGMENTS

We wish to thank the following people for their help with the publication of this revised book: first, our students, who in one way or another have both guided and prodded us to seek new and better approaches to teaching Japanese; and second, Thomas Manson and Tara Tudor, who were all kind enough to help out with the tedious job of proofreading. Special gratitude is due to Sandra Korinchak, senior editor of Tuttle Publishing for offering the opportunity to revise our original book published in 1989.

Hitoshi Watanabe, Naomi Watanabe
Takae Watanabe

Hirō Japanese Center:

Phone: +81-3-3444-3481
Fax: +81-3-3444-3483
E-mail: hjc@cb.wakwak.com
URL: http://www.japaneselanguage.net

INTRODUCTION TO THE REVISED EDITION

Although there have been many changes made in this revised edition, there are a few we find of particular importance.

In the prior edition, we used only the Roman alphabet to transcribe the example sentences. We found that our intermediate and advanced students prefer to use the native script. Therefore this edition includes example sentences in Hiragana, Katakana and Jōyō-Kanji, the 2,136 Chinese characters recommended for daily use.

The second notable change is the revision to the compound verb section. The prior edition only provided examples of select compound verbs. The revised edition supplies the reader with verb endings that can be used with the pre-*masu* form as a stem to create customized compounds, allowing for flexibility in the student's learning method.

There are also many minor changes, such as the inclusion of Katakana-based loanwords (a very popular trend in Japanese speech in recent years) used as *suru*-verbs; we also revised the example sentences to better reflect the many changes made in modern-day society.

INTRODUCTION

Fluency in a language cannot be attained without a solid understanding of that language's verbs and their usages. Especially with Japanese, it is crucial for the student to master verbs in order to be able to communicate effectively.

In Japanese, the importance of the subject-verb relationship is not stressed as it is in Indo-European languages such as English. In English, verb forms change depending on whether the subject is singular or plural, first person or second person, and so on. Thus, for the verb "to go," one says "I *go*" and "He *goes*." More complicated are some of the many languages whose verb forms change depending on whether the subject is feminine or masculine.

In Japanese, however, verbs are not affected by their subjects in this manner; it does not make any difference whether the subject is singular or plural, or first person or second person. This, plus the fact that there are relatively few exceptions to the rules, makes Japanese verbs relatively less complicated to learn than those of many other languages. Once the students master certain rules for making such forms as the *masu*, imperative, *te*, and conditional forms, they will be able to apply these rules to almost any verb.

Of course, the students should be aware that while any form can in theory be made from any verb, forms of some verbs are seldom used in ordinary situations. Along with the main entries and their example sentences, this introduction will help students learn both the conjugation and the usage of Japanese verbs.

VERB GROUPINGS

One way to approach Japanese verbs is to classify them into three major groupings according to the way they are conjugated when spelled with Roman letters. (This classification method does not apply when they are written in the Japanese syllabary.) These groups are:

> Group 1: The *u*-dropping conjugation
> Group 2: The *ru*-dropping conjugation
> Group 3: Irregular conjugation

Knowing which group a verb belongs to enables one to determine the stem of a verb.

Group 1: (the *u*-dropping conjugation)

Most of the verbs in Group 1 are easy to recognize. With the exception of *suru* and *kuru*, if the ending of the plain (dictionary) form of a verb is anything but *-eru* or *-iru*, the verb belongs to this group. As shown below, to determine the stem, simply drop the final *-u* ending. The *masu* forms are then made by attaching *-imasu/-imasen* to the stem.

VERB	MEANING	STEM	MASU FORM	MASEN FORM
aru ある	to have	*ar-*	*arimasu* あります	*arimasen* ありません
dasu[1] 出す	to take out	*dash-*	*dashimasu* 出します	*dashimasen* 出しません
isogu 急ぐ	to hurry	*isog-*	*isogimasu* 急ぎます	*isogimasen* 急ぎません
iu 言う	to say	*i-*	*iimasu* 言います	*iimasen* 言いません
kaku 書く	to write	*kak-*	*kakimasu* 書きます	*kakimasen* 書きません
kau 買う	to buy	*ka-*	*kaimasu* 買います	*kaimasen* 買いません
matsu[1] 待つ	to wait	*mach-*	*machimasu* 待ちます	*machimasen* 待ちません
nuru 塗る	to paint	*nur-*	*nurimasu* 塗ります	*nurimasen* 塗りません
omou 思う	to think	*omo-*	*omoimasu* 思います	*omoimasen* 思いません
shinu 死ぬ	to die	*shin-*	*shinimasu* 死にます	*shinimasen* 死にません
tobu 飛ぶ	to fly	*tob-*	*tobimasu* 飛びます	*tobimasen* 飛びません
toru 取る	to take	*tor-*	*torimasu* 取ります	*torimasen* 取りません
yomu 読む	to read	*yom-*	*yomimasu* 読みます	*yomimasen* 読みません

[1] Verbs ending in *-su* and *-tsu* have a *sh* stem and *ch* stem respectively.

If the ending of a verb is either *-eru* or *-iru*, one must consult a reference source to determine if it belongs to Group 1 or Group 2. A small percentage of verbs ending in *-eru* and *-iru* do belong to Group 1, and likewise form their stem by dropping the final *-u* ending. Confusion may arise when words spelled the same have different meanings. For example, the word *kiru,* accenting the *ki* syllable, means "to cut" and belongs to Group 1; its stem is *kir-*. On the other hand, the *kiru* that accents the *ru* syllable means "to wear" and belongs to Group 2; its stem is *ki-*. In the same manner, the word *kaeru,* accenting the *ka* syllable, means "to return" and belongs to Group 1; its stem is *kaer-*. The *kaeru* that accents the *e* syllable, however, means "to change" and belongs to Group 2; its stem is *kae-*. Sometimes, there are no pronunciation differences, as exemplified by *iru.* Thus, while the word *iru* meaning "to need" belongs to Group 1, *iru* meaning "to exist" belongs to Group 2. Both are pronounced the same.

Examples of Group 1 verbs whose endings are *-eru* or *-iru* are listed below. The stem is formed by dropping the final *-u* ending; the *masu* forms, by attaching *-imasu/-imasen* to the stem.

VERB	MEANING	STEM	MASU FORM	MASEN FORM
hairu 入る	to enter	*hair-*	*hairimasu* 入ります	*hairimasen* 入りません
kaeru 帰る	to return	*kaer-*	*kaerimasu* 帰ります	*kaerimasen* 帰りません
shiru 知る	to know	*shir-*	*shirimasu* 知ります	*shirimasen* 知りません

Group 2: (the *ru*-dropping conjugation)

Most verbs ending in *-eru* or *-iru* belong to this group. The stem is formed by dropping the *-ru* ending, and the *masu* forms are made by adding *-masu/-masen* to the stem.

VERB	MEANING	STEM	MASU FORM	MASEN FORM
ageru 上げる	to raise, give	*age-*	*agemasu* 上げます	*agemasen* 上げません
dekiru できる	to be able	*deki-*	*dekimasu* できます	*dekimasen* できません
iru いる	to be	*i-*	*imasu* います	*imasen* いません
kangaeru 考える	to think	*kangae-*	*kangaemasu* 考えます	*kangaemasen* 考えません
miru 見る	to see	*mi-*	*mimasu* 見ます	*mimasen* 見ません
taberu 食べる	to eat	*tabe-*	*tabemasu* 食べます	*tabemasen* 食べません

Group 3: (irregular conjugation)

This group has only two verbs, *kuru* (来る) "to come" and *suru* (する) "to do." Their verb forms are shown in their respective entries in the main text of this book (pages 143 and 255, respectively).

Verb stem + adjuncts

Many adjuncts are attached to the verb stem to alter the verb's original meaning. Some of the more common examples are listed below.

a. *Kare no Nihon-go wa wakari-yasui.*
   彼の日本語は分かりやすい。
   His Japanese is easy to understand.

b. *Kanojo no Nihon-go wa wakari-nikui.*
   彼女の日本語は分かりにくい。
   Her Japanese is difficult to understand.

c. *Watashi wa benkyō shi-tai desu. Shigoto wa shi-takunai desu.*
   私は勉強したいです。仕事は、したくないです。
   I want to study. I don't want to work.

d. *Kare wa Nihon e iki-tagatte imasu.*
   彼は日本へ行きたがっています。
   He wants to go to Japan.

e. *Terebi o mi-nagara, shokuji shimashita.*
   テレビを見ながら、食事しました。
   I ate while watching television.

f. *Ame ga furi-sō desu.*
   雨が降りそうです。
   It looks like it will rain.

g. *Kanojo wa eiga o mi ni ikimashita.*
   彼女は映画を見に行きました。
   She went to see a movie.

h. *Kono kanji no yomi-kata ga wakarimasen.*
   この漢字の読み方が分かりません。
   I don't know how to read this kanji.

i. *Isogi-nasai*
   急ぎなさい。
   Hurry up.

EXPLANATIONS OF VERB FORMS

The following are explanations and examples of each of the verb forms listed in the main entries.

The Plain Form

The plain form—including the plain forms of the present, past, conditional, presumptive, volitional, potential, passive, causative, and causative passive forms—is used in everyday conversation among friends, family, and other close relationships. The present tense of the plain form of verbs is sometimes called the "dictionary form."

Note that there is a slight change regarding the conjugation of the negative forms of verbs such as *kau*, *iu*, and *omou*—Group 1 verbs that have the final *-u* preceded by a vowel. Instead of attaching *-anai/-anakatta* to the stem of these Group 1 verbs, *-wanai/-wanakatta* is attached to make the negative forms. Thus, *kau* becomes *kawanai*, *iu* becomes *iwanai*, and *omou* becomes *omowanai*.

The plain form generally is used as follows.

1. In informal conversations:

   a. *Ashita tomodachi ni au?*
      明日、友達に会う？
      Will you meet your friend tomorrow?

   b. *Un, au.*
      うん、会う。
      Yes, I will.

   c. *Uun, awanai.*
      ううん、会わない。
      No, I won't.

   d. *Kinō tomodachi ni atta?*
      昨日、友達に会った？
      Did you meet your friend yesterday?

   e. *Uun, awanakatta.*
      ううん、会わなかった。
      No, I didn't.

2. Within a clause of a complex sentence:

   a. *Kare wa ashita kuru to iimashita.*
      彼は明日来ると言いました。
      He said he would come tomorrow.

b. *Kare wa ashita iku ka dō ka wakarimasen.*
彼は明日行くかどうか分かりません。
I don't know whether he will go or not tomorrow.

c. *Kare wa aruku'n desu ka.*
彼は歩くんですか。
Will he walk?

d. *Kare ga oshieru no wa Getsuyōbi desu.*
彼が教えるのは月曜日です。
He teaches on Mondays.

e. *Kare ni ashita hanasanai yō ni itte kudasai.*
彼に明日話さないように言ってください。
Tell him not to talk tomorrow.

f. *Gakkō e kuru toki tomodachi ni aimashita.*
学校へ来るとき、友達に会いました。
I met a friend of mine on my way to school.

3. Before adjuncts:

a. *Raishū tegami o kaku tsumori desu.*
来週手紙を書くつもりです。
I intend to write a letter next week.

b. *Kare wa mata kuru hazu desu.*
彼はまた来るはずです。
He is supposed to come again.

c. *Kare wa Amerika e kaetta sō desu.*
彼はアメリカへ帰ったそうです。
I heard he went back to the United States.

d. *Tomodachi ni denwa shita hō ga ii desu yo.*
友達に電話したほうがいいですよ。
You should call your friend.

e. *Igirisu ni itta koto ga arimasu ka.*
イギリスに行ったことがありますか。
Have you been to England?

f. *Pātii de nonda-ri tabeta-ri shimashita.*
パーティーで飲んだり食べたりしました。
I ate and drank at the party.

g. *Koko de tabako o suwanai de kudasai.*
ここでタバコを吸わないでください。
Please don't smoke here.

The *Masu* Form

The *masu* form is often referred to as the "polite form." Suitable for a wide range of circumstances, the *masu* form is considered a polite, conventional way of speaking. Note that the present *masu* form covers both the English present and future tenses. The present *masu* form is made by attaching -*imasu*/-*imasen* to the stem of Group 1 verbs, or -*masu*/-*masen* to the stem of Group 2 verbs. The *masu* forms for the potential, passive, causative, and causative passive forms are made by dropping the final -*ru* syllable, and attaching -*masu*/-*masen*. For the *masu* forms for the humble and honorific forms, refer to the entries for *naru, nasaru, suru,* and *itasu.*

a. *Ashita dekakemasu ka.*
   明日出かけますか。
   Will you go out tomorrow?

b. *Iie, dekakemasen.*
   いいえ、出かけません。
   No, I won't.

c. *Kesa shinbun o yomimashita ka.*
   今朝新聞を読みましたか。
   Did you read the newspaper this morning?

d. *Iie, yomimasen deshita.*
   いいえ、読みませんでした。
   No, I didn't.

e. *Piano o hikimasu ka.*
   ピアノを弾きますか。
   Do you play the piano?

f. *Ame ni furaremashita.*
   雨に降られました。
   I was caught in the rain.

g. *Mō ichido yaraseraremashita.*
   もう一度やらせられました。
   They made me do it one more time.

The *Te* Form

The *te* form can be considered to be the Japanese equivalent of the English gerund. For most verbs, the *te* forms are made as follows:

Group 1 verbs: 1. Change the -*ku* ending to -*ite*. *

                  aku (to open)   *aite*

---

* One exception is *iku* (to go); the *te* form is not *iite*, but *itte*.

2. Change the *-gu* ending to *-ide*.
   sawagu (to be noisy)   *sawaide*

3. Change the *-su* ending to *-shite*.
   hanasu (to speak)   *hanashite*

4. Change the *-bu*, *-mu*, and *-nu* endings to *-nde*.
   tobu (to fly)   *tonde*
   yomu (to read)   *yonde*
   shinu (to die)   *shinde*

5. Change the *-ru* and *-tsu* endings to *-tte*.
   kaeru (to return)   *kaette*
   katsu (to win)   *katte*

6. Change the *-u* ending when preceded by a vowel to *-tte*.
   kau (to buy)   *katte*
   iu (to say)   *itte*

Group 2 verbs: Change the *-ru* ending to *-te*.
   miru (to see)   *mite*

Group 3 verbs: See the individual entries for **suru** and **kuru**. (pages 143 and 255, respectively).

To make the **te** forms of the potential, passive, causative, and causative passive forms of verbs, change the *-ru* ending to *-te*.

1. State of Doing

The **te** form, when combined with *iru/imasu*, indicates a state of doing; in other words, a state where the action is continuous.

a. *Ima, nani o shite imasu ka.*
   今、何をしていますか。
   What are you doing now?

b. *Nihon-go o benkyō shite iru.*
   日本語を勉強している。
   I'm studying Japanese.

c. *Yūbe hachi-ji goro watashi wa tegami o kaite imashita.*
   夕べ、8時ごろ私は手紙を書いていました。
   I was writing a letter at about eight o'clock last night.

2. Present Perfect

The present perfect tense is also indicated by the **te** form. It is made by combining the **te** form with *iru/imasu*. Note that the **te iru** form is often used in Japanese for conditions that are not always indicated in English by the present perfect tense.

a. *Eiga wa mō hajimatte imasu ka.*
映画はもう始まっていますか。
Has the movie started yet?

b. *Iie, mada hajimatte imasen.*
いいえまだ始まっていません。
No, it has not started yet.

c. *Ame wa yande iru.*
雨はやんでいる。
The rain has stopped.

d. *Michi wa migi ni magatte iru.*
道は右に曲がっている。
The road curves to the right.

e. *Kare wa futotte imasu.*
彼は太っています。
He is fat.

f. *Kare wa chichi-oya ni nite imashita.*
彼は父親に似ていました。
He looked like his father.

g. *Tanaka-san o shitte imasu ka.*
田中さんを知っていますか。
Do you know Mr. Tanaka?

   Iie, shirimasen.
   いいえ、知りません。
   No, I don't.

h. *Kanojo no namae o oboete imasu.*
彼女の名前を覚えています。
I remember her name.

i. *Nihon-go no jisho o motte imasu.*
日本語の辞書を持っています。
I have a Japanese dictionary.

j. *Kissaten de matte imasu.*
喫茶店で待っています。
I'll wait for you at the coffee shop.

3. Recording Events
   The *te* form is used when recording events according to a time sequence.
   In some cases, where one action stops and another starts is not always clear.

   a. *Resutoran ni haitte, kōhii o nonda.*
   レストランに入って、コーヒーを飲んだ。
   I went into a restaurant and had some coffee.

b. *Roku-ji ni okite, ie o dete, hachi-ji ni kaisha ni tsuita.*
６時に起きて、家を出て、８時に会社に着いた。
I got up at six, left the house, and reached the company at eight.

c. *Tomodachi ni atte, eiga o mite kara, ie ni kaerimashita.*
友達に会って、映画を見てから家に帰りました。
I met a friend, saw a movie, and then went home.

d. *Kaban o motte kimasu.*
カバンを持ってきます。
I'll bring my briefcase.

e. *Pātii ni tomodachi o tsurete ikimasu.*
パーティーに友達を連れて行きます。
I'll take my friend to the party.

4. Something Caused Something

The *te* form is used to indicate that something happened, something that caused something else (often an emotion).

a. *Tegami o yonde, anshin shimashita.*
手紙を読んで、安心しました。
Having read the letter, I was relieved.

b. *Nyūsu o kiite, bikkuri shimashita.*
ニュースを聞いて、びっくりしました。
I was surprised to hear the news.

c. *Byōki ga naotte, ureshii desu.*
病気が治って、うれしいです。
I'm glad you got well.

5. Giving and Receiving

The *te* form is used with verbs such as *ageru* and *morau* to indicate giving and receiving. The level of politeness required for a particular situation dictates which verbs follow the *te* form; for instance, a person of lower status rarely would use *ageru* to a superior. In the examples below, notice how the verb following the *te* form changes according to the degree of politeness. (See also pages 24–26 for an explanation of honorific and humble speech.)

a. *Tomodachi wa shashin o misete kuremashita.*
友達は写真を見せてくれました。
My friend showed me some photos.

b. *Sensei wa shashin o misete kudasaimashita.*
先生は写真を見せてくださいました。
My teacher (kindly) showed me some photos.

c. *Tomodachi ni shashin o misete moraimashita.*
友達に写真を見せてもらいました。
I got my friend to show me some photos.

d. *Sensei ni shashin o misete itadakimashita.*
先生に写真を見せていただきました。
I got my teacher to show me some photos.

e. *Tomodachi ni shashin o misete agemashita.*
友達に写真を見せてあげました。
I showed some photos to my friend.

f. *Sensei ni shashin o misete sashiagemashita.*
先生に写真を見せてさしあげました。
I showed some photos to my teacher.

g. *Tanaka-san wa haha ni shashin o misete kuremashita.*
田中さんは母に写真を見せてくれました。
Mr. Tanaka showed my mother some photos.

h. *Shachō wa chichi ni shashin o misete kudasaimashita.*
社長は父に写真を見せてくださいました。
The president of the company showed my father some photos.

i. *Haha wa Tanaka-san ni shashin o misete moraimashita.*
母は田中さんに写真を見せてもらいました。
My mother got Mr. Tanaka to show her some photos.

j. *Chichi wa shachō ni shashin o misete itadakimashita.*
父は社長に写真を見せていただきました。
My father got the president of the company to show him some photos.

k. *Imōto wa tomodachi ni shashin o misete agemashita.*
妹は友達に写真を見せてあげました。
My younger sister showed some photos to her friend.

l. *Imōto wa sensei ni shashin o misete sashiagemashita.*
妹は先生に写真を見せてさしあげました。
My younger sister showed some photos to her teacher.

6. With Other Verbs and Adjuncts
The *te* form is also used with other verbs and adjuncts.

a. *Haitte mo ii desu ka.*
入ってもいいですか。
May I come in?

b. *Sawatte wa ikemasen.*
触ってはいけません。
Don't touch.

c. *Doa o nokku shite mimashita.*
ドアをノックしてみました。
I tried knocking on the door.

d. *Ashita jū-ji ni kite hoshii desu.*
明日10時に来てほしいです。
I want you to come at ten o'clock tomorrow.

e. *Heya o sōji shite okimashita.*
部屋を掃除しておきました。
I cleaned the room (to have it ready in advance).

f. *Gohan o tabete shimaimashita.*
ご飯を食べてしまいました。
I finished the meal.

The Conditional Form

One way to make the conditional form for all verbs is to drop the final *-u* and add *-eba*. Thus *furu* becomes *fureba*. The negative conditional form is made by dropping the final *-i* of the plain negative form and adding *-kereba*; therefore, *furanai* becomes *furanakereba*.

Another way to make the conditional form is to add the adjunct *ra* to the past plain forms or past *masu* forms, such as *futta ra, fura-nakatta ra, furimashita ra*, or *furimasen deshita ra*. In this book, to help students understand how to make this *ra* conditional form, it is written as two separate words (*futta ra*). Students should be aware, however, that it conventionally is written as one word (*futtara*).

While there are slight changes in nuance between the forms using *ra* and the forms using *-eba*, in many cases, they can be used interchangeably with little difference in meaning.

a. *Ame ga fureba, ie ni imasu.*
雨が降れば、家にいます。
Ame ga futta ra, ie ni imasu.
雨が降ったら、家にいます。
Ame ga furimashita ra, ie ni imasu. (polite)
雨が降りましたら、家にいます。
If it rains, I'll stay home.

b. *Jisho o mireba, wakarimasu.*
辞書を見れば、わかります。
Jisho o mita ra, wakarimasu.
辞書を見たら、わかります。
If you check the dictionary, you will understand.

Generally speaking, when a specific request follows the conditional clause, or if the sentence has the meaning "when something happens, I will do this," the form using *ra* is preferred over the form using *-eba*.

a. *Kare ni atta ra, yoroshiku to itte kudasai.* (correct)
   彼に会ったら、よろしくと言ってください。
   If you meet him, please say hello for me.
   Kare ni aeba, yoroshiku to itte kudasai. (incorrect)

b. *Nyū Yōku ni tsuita ra, renraku suru tsumori desu.* (correct)
   ニューヨークに着いたら、連絡するつもりです。
   When I reach New York, I intend to get in touch with you.
   Nyū Yōku ni tsukeba, renraku suru tsumori desu. (incorrect)

The Volitional Form

This form indicating volition is made by adding *-ō/-imashō* to the stem of Group 1 verbs, and by adding *-yō/-mashō* to the stem of Group 2 verbs. One should note that for some verbs, the volitional form conventionally is not used; students should avoid using this form if it has been set inside parentheses in the main entries.

a. *Rainen, Nihon e ikō to omoimasu.*
   来年、日本へ行こうと思います。
   I think I'll go to Japan next year.

b. *Saifu o kaeshimashō.*
   財布を返しましょう。
   Let's return the wallet.

c. *Nichiyōbi ni eiga o miyō to omou.*
   日曜日に映画を見ようと思う。
   I think I'll see a movie on Sunday.

d. *Yamemashō.*
   やめましょう。
   Let's quit.

e. *Benkyō shimashō.*
   勉強しましょう。
   Let's study.

The Imperative Form

The imperative (command) form is said by a superior to an inferior. This form is made by adding *-e* to the stem of Group 1 verbs, and by adding *-ro* to the stem of Group 2 verbs. For negative imperatives, add the adjunct *na* to the plain present form of the verb. Note that with some verbs, the imperative form conventionally is not used; students should avoid using this form if it has been set inside parentheses in the main entries.

   a. *Suware.*
     座れ。
     Sit down.

   b. *Okane o tamero.*
     お金をためろ。
     Save your money.

   c. *Shizuka ni shiro.*
     静かにしろ。
     Be quiet.

   d. *Dare ni mo iu na.*
     誰にも言うな。
     Don't say this to anyone.

A less harsh way to make a command is to use *nasai*. Add *-i* + *nasai* to the stem of Group 1 verbs, and *-nasai* to the stem of Group 2 verbs. *Shi-nasai* and *ki-nasai* are for *suru* and *kuru*.

   a. *Suwari-nasai.*
     座りなさい。
     Sit down.

   b. *Kaku no wa yame-nasai.*
     書くのはやめなさい。
     Stop writing.

The Potential Form

This form, expressing possibility or capability, is made by adding *-eru/-emasu* to the stem of Group 1 verbs, and by adding *-rareru/-raremasu* to the stem of Group 2 verbs. The negative form is made by adding *-enai/-emasen* to the stem of Group 1 verbs, and *-rarenai/-raremasen* to the stem of Group 2 verbs. For the potential forms of the honorific and humble forms, refer to the entries for *naru*, *nasaru*, *suru*, and *itasu*. Recently, the potential forms of Group 2 verbs have come to be constructed like Group 1 verbs; since this is considered unacceptable by many, in the main entries, this more colloquial form is listed underneath the standard form.

Also note that for some verbs, the potential form rarely is used; students should avoid using this form if it has been set inside parentheses in the main entries.

a. *Ashita jū-ji goro aemasu ka.*
明日10時ごろ会えますか。
Can I meet you about ten o'clock tomorrow?

b. *Ashita aenakereba, asatte wa dō desu ka.*
明日会えなければ、あさっては、どうですか。
If I cannot meet you tomorrow, how about the day after?

c. *Nan-ji goro deraremasu ka.*
何時ごろ出られますか。
About what time can you go out?

The Passive Form

The passive form conveys the idea that something was done to you and you were adversely affected. It is formed by adding *-areru/-aremasu* to the stem of Group 1 verbs (*-wareru/-waremasu* for verbs ending in two vowels such as *omou*), and *-rareru/-raremasu* to the stem of Group 2 verbs. The negative form is made by adding *-arenai/-aremasen* to the stem of Group 1 verbs (*-warenai/-waremasen* for verbs ending in two vowels), and *-rarenai/-raremasen* to the stem of Group 2 verbs. Note that the potential and passive forms of Group 2 verbs are identical and that both transitive and some intransitive verbs can be used in a passive sentence. Also note that for some verbs, the passive form is rarely used; students should avoid using this form if it has been set inside parentheses in the main entries.

a. *Dorobō ni okane o nusumaremashita.*
泥棒にお金を盗まれました。
My money was stolen by the thief.

b. *Ie ni kaeru tochū de, ame ni furaremashita.*
家に帰る途中で、雨に降られました。
On my way home, I was caught in the rain.

c. *Minna ni mitsumerarete, komatta.*
みんなに見つめられて、困った。
I didn't know what to do because everyone was staring at me.

The Causative Form

This form, conveying the idea of making someone do something, is formed by adding *-aseru/-asemasu* (*-asenai/-asemasen* for negative forms) to the stem of most Group 1 verbs. For Group 1 verbs that end in two vowels, such as *utau*, the causative is formed by adding *-waseru/-wasemasu* (*-wasenai/-wasemasen* for the negative forms) to the stem. For Group 2 verbs, the causative is formed by adding

-saseru/-sasemasu to the stem (*-sasenai/-sasemasen* for negative forms). Note that with some verbs, the causative form rarely is used; students should avoid using this form if it has been set inside parentheses in the main entries.

a. *Kare wa musuko o kaimono ni ikaseta.*
   彼は息子を買い物に行かせた。
   He made his son go shopping.

b. *Kanojo wa kodomo ni piano o narawasemashita.*
   彼女は子どもにピアノを習わせました。
   She made her child learn to play the piano.

c. *Watashi ni harawasete kudasai.*
   私に払わせてください。
   Please let me pay.

d. *Sono koto wa mō sukoshi kangaesasete kuremasen ka.*
   そのことはもう少し考えさせてくれませんか。
   Could you please let me think it over some more?

The Causative Passive Form

This form conveys the idea of "I was made to do something and was adversely affected by it." It is formed by adding *-aserareru/-aseraremasu* (*-aserarenai/-aseraremasen* for negative forms) to the stem of most Group 1 verbs, and *-saserareru/-saseraremasu* (*-saserarenai/-saseraremasen* for negative forms) to the stem of Group 2 verbs. For Group 1 verbs that end in two vowels, such as *utau*, the causative passive form is made by adding *-waserareru/-waseraremasu* (*-waserarenai/-waseraremasen* for negative forms) to the stem. As with the potential forms, in colloquial speech, causative passive forms of Group 2 may be formed similarly to the Group 1 verbs. In the main entries, this non-standard form is listed below the conventional forms. Also, for some verbs, the causative passive form is rarely used—such cases are marked off by parentheses in the main entries.

a. *Shigoto de Hon Kon ni ikaseraremashita.*
   仕事で香港に行かせられました。
   I was made to go to Hong Kong on business.

b. *Watashi-tachi wa uta o utawaseraremashita.*
   私たちは歌を歌わせられました。
   We were made to sing a song.

c. *Kare wa sensei ni takusan benkyō saserareta.*
   彼は先生にたくさん勉強させられた。
   He was made to study a lot by his teacher.

POLITE LANGUAGE: HONORIFIC AND HUMBLE SPEECH

The use of polite language, that is, of honorific and humble forms, is an integral part of the Japanese language, and it is recommended that the student be at least familiar with it. In general, honorific speech is used when the subject is, or is related to, someone else, and humble speech is used when the subject concerns yourself or that which is associated with yourself. Basically, there are three situations which require the use of polite language.

1. A speaker uses polite language to an in-group member (such as someone in his school or company) when that person is senior in age or status. Thus, a worker uses both honorific and humble speech (depending on the subject) when speaking to his boss, as does a student to his teacher. Also, a worker would generally use honorific language when speaking to a fellow worker when the subject is their boss.

If, however, a worker is talking about either himself or his boss to a person who does not belong to his in-group, humble language is used. Thus, a worker would use humble language to describe his boss's actions if he were talking to someone in a different company.

2. In general, a speaker uses polite language to a non-in-group person, unless that person is clearly junior in age or status to him. Thus, a worker uses polite language to a president of another company, as well as to a worker at another company when speaking about that worker's president.

If the speaker is of the same social status as the person he is talking to, whether polite language is used or not depends on how well the two people know each other. If they are just casual acquaintances, honorific and humble speeches usually are used.

3. When the speaker is not sure of the social status of the person he is talking to, usually he will opt for polite language. Thus, people meeting for the first time tend to use polite language with each other.

How to Make Honorific and Humble Verb Forms

Note that many verbs have special honorific and humble verb counterparts. One example is the verb *iku* (to go), whose humble form is the verb *mairu*, and whose honorific form is the verb *irassharu*. These special counterparts are listed in the main entries.

For those verbs not having such counterparts, the honorific and humble forms can be made as follows:

1. HONORIFIC: *o* + verb stem + *ni naru*
    The most common way to make an honorific form out of a verb is to add *o* to the verb stem, and then follow it with *ni naru*.

    a. *Sensei wa hon o o-yomi ni narimasu.*
       先生は本をお読みになります。
       The teacher reads the book.

    b. *Tegami o o-kaki ni narimashita ka.*
       手紙をお書きになりましたか。
       Have you written the letter?

    Though used with less frequency, a politer honorific form can be made by replacing *ni naru* with *nasaru: o* + verb stem + *nasaru*.

    a. *Ano e o o-kai nasaimashita ka.*
       あの絵をお買いなさいましたか。
       Did you buy that painting?

    b. *Futari no kekkon no koto o o-kiki nasaimashita ka.*
       二人の結婚のことをお聞きなさいましたか。
       Did you hear about their marriage?

2. HONORIFIC: passive form
    The passive form of verbs also is used to express politeness.

    a. *Tanaka-san, kinō hon' ya ni ikaremashita ka.*
       田中さん、昨日、本屋に行かれましたか。
       Mr. Tanaka, did you go to the bookstore yesterday?

    b. *Sensei wa denwa de sugu kotaeraremashita.*
       先生は電話ですぐ答えられました。
       The teacher answered immediately by telephone.

3. HONORIFIC: *dōzo* + *o* + verb stem + *kudasai*
    A polite way of making a request is to add *dōzo* and *kudasai* around the *o* + verb stem.

    a. *Dōzo o-kake kudasai.*
       どうぞ、おかけください。
       Please have a seat.

    b. *Dōzo o-meshiagari kudasai.*
       どうぞ、お召し上がりください。
       Please start eating.

4. HUMBLE: *o* + verb stem + *suru*

With most verbs, the humble form can be made by adding *o* to the verb stem, and then following it with *suru*.

   a. *Ashita, shachō-shitsu ni o-kaeshi shimasu.*
   明日、社長室にお返しします。
   I will return it to the president's office tomorrow.

   b. *Mina-sama ni kyūryō ni tsuite o-hanashi shitai to omoimasu.*
   皆様に給料についてお話したいと思います。
   I would like to talk with everyone about salaries.

Suru generally can be replaced with *itasu*: *o* + verb stem + *itasu*.

   a. *Sūtsu-kēsu o o-mochi itashimasu.*
   スーツケースをお持ちいたします。
   Let me carry your suitcase.

   b. *Sū-fun-kan no uchi ni, o-yobi itashimasu.*
   数分間の内に、お呼びいたします。
   I will call for you in a few minutes.

TRANSITIVE AND INTRANSITIVE

In Japanese, verbs classified as transitive take a direct object, and thus use the particle *o*.

   a. *Watashi wa tegami o kakimashita.*
   私は手紙を書きました。
   I wrote a letter.

   b. *Mado o shimete kudasai.*
   窓を閉めてください。
   Please close the windows.

A verb classified as intransitive does not take a direct object, and *usually* does not use an *o* as a particle.

   a. *Kyūryō ga agarimashita.*
   給料が上がりました。
   Our salaries went up.

   b. *Kabe ni e ga kakatte iru.*
   壁に絵がかかっている。
   There is a picture hanging on the wall.

In Japanese, some intransitive verbs use the particle *o*, as shown below. These intransitive verbs tend to have meanings referring to motion, and used with *o*, give the idea of "going through a defined area."

a. *Watashi wa kōen o hashirimashita.*
   私は公園を走りました。
   I ran at the park.

b. *Watashi wa go-fun de kōsu o hashirimashita.*
   私は五分でコースを走りました。
   I ran the course in five minutes.

In cases where a verb has both a transitive form and an intransitive form, the form more commonly used is listed first; for instance, (intrans. and trans.). Note the change in meanings of such verbs, as shown below

a. *Shigoto ni isogu.*
   仕事に急ぐ。
   To hurry to work.

b. *Shigoto o isogu.*
   仕事を急ぐ。
   To work faster.

c. *Mise ga hiraku.*
   店が開く。
   The shop opens.

d. *Mise o hiraku.*
   店を開く。
   We open a shop.

Note:
The Romanization system used in this book is a modification of the Hepburn system. Macrons are used for double vowels (*ā, ō, ū*), and *n* (rather than *m*) is used before *b, m,* or *p*. Also, all characters used here are part of the list of 2,136 characters prescribed for everyday use by the Ministry of Education, Culture, Sports, Science and Technology in Japan. Those verbs with characters not in that list are written in *hiragana*.

KEY TO SYMBOLS AND ABBREVIATIONS

( ) The verb forms enclosed in parentheses are rarely used in modern Japanese, and thus it is advisable that the reader avoid using them.

PLAIN FORM	*aru*
IMPERATIVE	*(are)*
TE FORM	*atte*

, The comma is used in the example sentences to help the student understand the meaning of the sentence. Its usage in some sentences may differ from conventional grammatical usage.

; In the verb definitions, a semi-colon differentiates a) more than two different verbs pronounced similarly, or b) the transitive and intransitive cases of a verb.

a) 話す to speak; 離す to keep away; 放す to set free, let go: (all trans.)

b) 出す to put out, send, pay, submit: (trans.); begin doing: (intrans.)

: The colon is used to indicate that all preceding verbs are either transitive or intransitive.

開ける to open; 空ける to empty, keep the day open: (both trans.); 開ける the day breaks: (intrans.)

* The asterisk is used in the verb definitions to indicate that the student should refer to the note at the bottom of the page.

trans. transitive
intrans. intransitive
lit., literally
caus. causative

A GUIDE TO JAPANESE VERBS

agaru あがる

上がる to go up, rise, get nervous, to finish, enter: (intrans.)

		Affirmative	*Negative*
PLAIN FORM	PRESENT	agaru	agaranai
	PAST	agatta	agaranakatta
MASU FORM	PRESENT	agarimasu	agarimasen
	PAST	agarimashita	agarimasen deshita
TE FORM		agatte	agaranakute
CONDITIONAL	PLAIN	agareba/agatta ra	agaranakereba agaranakatta ra
	FORMAL	agarimashita ra	agarimasen deshita ra
VOLITIONAL	PLAIN	agarō	–
	FORMAL	agarimashō	–
IMPERATIVE		agare	agaru na

	Affirmative		*Affirmative*
POTENTIAL	agareru	**CAUS. PASSIVE**	agaraserareru/ agarasareru
PASSIVE	agarareru	**HONORIFIC**	oagari ni naru/ agarareru
CAUSATIVE	agaraseru	**HUMBLE**	(oagari suru)

Examples:

1. *Kyūryō ga agarimashita.*
   給料が上がりました。
   My salary went up.

2. *Kaze de netsu ga 39do made agatta.*
   風邪で熱が39度まで上がった。
   My temperature went up to 39° because of cold.

3. *Supiichi o suru toki, itsumo agarimasu.*
   スピーチをするとき、いつも上がります。
   When I make a speech, I always get nervous.

4. *Ame ga agatta ra, dekakemashō ka.*
   雨が上がったら、出かけましょうか。
   When it stops raining, let's go out.

5. *Enryo shinaide, dōzo oagari kudasai.*
   遠慮しないで、どうぞお上がりください。
   Don't hesitate. Come in please.

ageru あげる

上げる to raise, lift, give, (attached to a verb) finish; 挙げる to raise; 揚げる to fly: (all trans.)

		Affirmative	Negative
PLAIN FORM	PRESENT	ageru	agenai
	PAST	ageta	agenakatta
MASU FORM	PRESENT	agemasu	agemasen
	PAST	agemashita	agemasen deshita
TE FORM		agete	agenakute
CONDITIONAL	PLAIN	agereba ageta ra	agenakereba agenakatta ra
	FORMAL	agemashita ra	agemasen deshita ra
VOLITIONAL	PLAIN	ageyō	–
	FORMAL	agemashō	–
IMPERATIVE		agero	ageru na

	Affirmative		Affirmative
POTENTIAL	agerareru/agereru	**CAUS. PASSIVE**	agesaserareru
PASSIVE	agerareru	**HONORIFIC**	oage ni naru/ agerareru
CAUSATIVE	agesaseru	**HUMBLE**	oage suru

Examples:

1. *Kaban o tana ni agemasu.*
   かばんを棚に上げます。
   I'll put my bag on the shelf.

2. *Tomodachi no tanjōbi ni purezento o agemashita.*
   友達の誕生日にプレゼントをあげました。
   I gave a present to my friend on his birthday.

3. *Shitsumon ga atta ra, te o agete kudasai.*
   質問があったら、手を挙げてください。
   Please raise your hand if you have a question.

4. *Nihon-go o oshiete agemashō ka.*
   日本語を教えてあげましょうか。
   Shall I teach you Japanese?

5. *Ronbun o kaki-ageta ra renraku shimasu.*
   論文を書き上げたら、連絡します。
   When I finish writing my thesis, I'll contact you.

akeru あける

開ける to open; 空ける to empty, keep the day open: (both trans.);
明ける the day breaks: (intrans.)*

		Affirmative	*Negative*
PLAIN FORM	PRESENT	akeru	akenai
	PAST	aketa	akenakatta
MASU FORM	PRESENT	akemasu	akemasen
	PAST	akemashita	akemasen deshita
TE FORM		akete	akenakute
CONDITIONAL	PLAIN	akereba/ aketa ra	akenakereba/ akenakatta ra
	FORMAL	akemashita ra	akemasen deshita ra
VOLITIONAL	PLAIN	akeyō	–
	FORMAL	akemashō	–
IMPERATIVE		akero	akeru na

	Affirmative		*Affirmative*
POTENTIAL	akerareru/akereru	**CAUS. PASSIVE**	akesaserareru
PASSIVE	akerareru	**HONORIFIC**	oake ni naru/ akerareru
CAUSATIVE	akesaseru	**HUMBLE**	oake suru

Examples:

1. *Mado o akete mo ii desu ka.*
   窓を開けてもいいですか。
   May I open the window?

2. *Doa ni kagi ga kakatteite, akeraremasen.*
   ドアに鍵がかかっていて、開けられません。
   I can't open the door because it is locked.

3. *Ryokō ni iku node, shibaraku ie o akemasu.*
   旅行に行くので、しばらく家を空けます。
   Since we are going on a trip, we'll be away from home for a while.

4. *Kondo no Nichiyōbi o akete oite kudasai.*
   今度の日曜日を空けておいてください。
   Please keep this Sunday open.

5. *Akemashite omedetō gozaimasu.*
   明けましておめでとうございます。
   A Happy New Year.

---

* The intransitive *akeru* 明ける, meaning "the day breaks," generally has no imperative, volitional, potential, passive, causative, causative passive, honorific, or humble forms.

akirameru あきらめる

あきらめる to give up: (trans.)

		Affirmative	Negative
PLAIN FORM	PRESENT	akirameru	akiramenai
	PAST	akirameta	akiramenakatta
MASU FORM	PRESENT	akiramemasu	akiramemasen
	PAST	akiramemashita	akiramemasen deshita
TE FORM		akiramete	akiramenakute
CONDITIONAL	PLAIN	akiramereba/ akirameta ra	akiramenakereba/ akiramenakatta ra
	FORMAL	akiramemashita ra	akiramemasen deshita ra
VOLITIONAL	PLAIN	akirameyō	–
	FORMAL	akiramemashō	–
IMPERATIVE		akiramero	akirameru na

	Affirmative		Affirmative
POTENTIAL	akiramerareru/ akiramereru	**CAUS. PASSIVE**	akiramesaserareru
PASSIVE	akiramerareru	**HONORIFIC**	oakirame ni naru/ akiramerareru
CAUSATIVE	akiramesaseru	**HUMBLE**	(oakirame suru)

Examples:

1. *Nebō shita node, asagohan o taberu no o akiramemashita.*
   寝坊したので、朝御飯を食べるのをあきらめました。
   I gave up eating breakfast because I overslept.

2. *Kono kikaku wa mikomi ga nai. Akirameyō.*
   この企画は見込みがない。あきらめよう。
   This plan has no chance of success. Let's give it up.

3. *Akiramete wa ikemasen.*
   あきらめてはいけません。
   You must not give it up.

4. *Gōru wa mō sukoshi da. Akirameru na.*
   ゴールはもう少しだ。あきらめるな。
   The goal is just an inch. Do not give it up.

5. *Nani o iwarete mo, watashi wa akiramenakatta.*
   何を言われても、私はあきらめなかった。
   Even though I was told something, I did not give it up.

akiru あきる

飽きる to be tired of, fed up with: (intrans.)

		Affirmative	Negative
PLAIN FORM	PRESENT	akiru	akinai
	PAST	akita	akinakatta
MASU FORM	PRESENT	akimasu	akimasen
	PAST	akimashita	akimasen deshita
TE FORM		akite	akinakute
CONDITIONAL	PLAIN	akireba/akita ra	akinakereba/ akinakatta ra
	FORMAL	akimashita ra	akimasen deshita ra
VOLITIONAL	PLAIN	akiyō	–
	FORMAL	akimashō	–
IMPERATIVE		akiro	akiru na

	Affirmative		Affirmative
POTENTIAL	akirareru/akireru	CAUS. PASSIVE	akisaserareru
PASSIVE	akirareru	HONORIFIC	oaki ni naru/ akirareru
CAUSATIVE	akisaseru	HUMBLE	(oaki suru)

Examples:

1. *Mainichi onaji shigoto o suru no ni akimashita.*
   毎日同じ仕事をするのに飽きました。
   I'm tired of doing the same work everyday.

2. *Musuko wa sono omocha ni mō akita yō da.*
   息子はそのおもちゃにもう飽きたようだ。
   Already my son seems to be fed up with the toy.

3. *Benkyō ni akita ra, sanpo shimasu.*
   勉強に飽きたら、散歩します。
   When I'm tired of studying, I take a walk.

4. *Sugu ni akiru no wa anata no warui kuse da.*
   すぐに飽きるのはあなたの悪い癖だ。
   It is your bad habit to get tired immediately.

5. *Sonna sekkyō wa kiki-akita.*
   そんな説教は聞き飽きた。
   I'm fed up with listening to that lecture.

aku あく

開く to open, begin; 空く to become vacant, be free: (both intrans.)

		Affirmative	Negative
PLAIN FORM	PRESENT	aku	akanai
	PAST	aita	akanakatta
MASU FORM	PRESENT	akimasu	akimasen
	PAST	akimashita	akimasen deshita
TE FORM		aite	akanakute
CONDITIONAL	PLAIN	akeba/aita ra	akanakereba/ akanakatta ra
	FORMAL	akimashita ra	akimasen deshita ra
VOLITIONAL	PLAIN	akō	–
	FORMAL	akimashō	–
IMPERATIVE		ake	aku na

	Affirmative		Affirmative
POTENTIAL	akeru	**CAUS. PASSIVE**	akaserareru
PASSIVE	akareru	**HONORIFIC**	oaki ni naru/akareru
CAUSATIVE	akaseru	**HUMBLE**	(oaki suru)

Examples:

1. *Kono botan o osu to, doa ga akimasu.*
   このボタンを押すと、ドアが開きます。
   The door will open when you press this button.

2. *Kagi ga kowarete ite, mado ga akanai.*
   鍵が壊れていて、窓が開かない。
   Since the key is broken, the window won't open.

3. *Ginkō wa ku-ji ni aku sō desu.*
   銀行は9時に開くそうです。
   I heard the bank opens at nine o'clock.

4. *Sono seki wa aite imasu ka.*
   その席は空いていますか。
   Is that seat vacant?

5. *Doyōbi wa isogashii kedo, Nichiyōbi nara aite imasu.*
   土曜日は忙しいけど、日曜日なら空いています。
   I'll be busy on Saturday, but I'll be free on Sunday.

arasou あらそう

争う to fight, compete, dispute, contend: (trans.)

		Affirmative	Negative
PLAIN FORM	PRESENT	arasou	arasowanai
	PAST	arasotta	arasowanakatta
MASU FORM	PRESENT	arasoimasu	arasoimasen
	PAST	arasoimashita	arasoimasen deshita
TE FORM		arasotte	arasowanakute
CONDITIONAL	PLAIN	arasoeba/arasotta ra	arasowanakereba/ arasowanakatta ra
	FORMAL	arasoimashita ra	arasoimasen deshita ra
VOLITIONAL	PLAIN	arasoō	–
	FORMAL	arasoimashō	–
IMPERATIVE		arasoe	arasou na

	Affirmative		Affirmative
POTENTIAL	arasoeru	**CAUS. PASSIVE**	arasowaserareru/ arasowasareru
PASSIVE	arasowareru	**HONORIFIC**	oarasoi ni naru/ arasowareru
CAUSATIVE	arasowaseru	**HUMBLE**	(oarasoi suru)

Examples:

1. *Kyonen, sono futatsu no chiimu wa yūshō o arasotta.*
   去年、その二つのチームは優勝を争った。
   Those two teams fought for victory last year.

2. *Suzuki-san wa Sato-san to shōshin o arasotte iru.*
   鈴木さんは佐藤さんと昇進を争っている。
   Mr. Suzuki is competing with Mr. Sato for the promotion.

3. *Sono tochi ga dare no mono ka, hōtei de arasowareta.*
   その土地が誰の物か、法廷で争われた。
   We fought in court over whose land it was.

4. *Arasou no wa suki ja nai.*
   争うのは好きじゃない。
   I do not like fighting.

5. *Ima wa ikkoku o arasou toki desu.*
   今は一刻を争う時です。
   There's no time to lose now.

arau あらう

洗う to wash, inquire into, wash one's hands of an affair: (trans.)

		Affirmative	Negative
PLAIN FORM	PRESENT	arau	arawanai
	PAST	aratta	arawanakatta
MASU FORM	PRESENT	araimasu	araimasen
	PAST	araimashita	araimasen deshita
TE FORM		aratte	arawanakute
CONDITIONAL	PLAIN	araeba/aratta ra	arawanakereba/ arawanakatta ra
	FORMAL	araimashita ra	araimasen deshita ra
VOLITIONAL	PLAIN	araō	–
	FORMAL	araimashō	–
IMPERATIVE		arae	arau na

	Affirmative		Affirmative
POTENTIAL	araeru	**CAUS. PASSIVE**	arawaserareru/ arawasareru
PASSIVE	arawareru	**HONORIFIC**	oarai ni naru/ arawareru
CAUSATIVE	arawaseru	**HUMBLE**	oarai suru

Examples:

1. *Shokuji no mae ni, te o araimashita.*
   食事の前に、手を洗いました。
   I washed my hands before a meal.

2. *Kono sētā wa mizu demo araemasu.*
   このセーターは水でも洗えます。
   You can wash this sweater even with water.

3. *Kanojo wa kodomotachi ni osara o arawasemasu.*
   彼女は子供たちにお皿を洗わせます。
   She makes her children wash up dishes.

4. *Nando arattemo, kono shimi wa ochinai.*
   何度洗っても、このしみは落ちない。
   This stain does not go off even if I wash it many times.

5. *Shizen no naka ni iru to, kokoro ga arawareru yō da.*
   自然の中にいると、心が洗われるようだ。
   It is refreshing when I spend time outdoors.

arawareru あらわれる

現れる to appear; 表れる to become visible, show: (both intrans.)

		Affirmative	*Negative*
PLAIN FORM	PRESENT	arawareru	arawarenai
	PAST	arawareta	arawarenakatta
MASU FORM	PRESENT	arawaremasu	arawaremasen
	PAST	arawaremashita	arawaremasen deshita
TE FORM		arawarete	arawarenakute
CONDITIONAL	PLAIN	arawarereba/ arawareta ra	arawarenakereba/ arawarenakatta ra
	FORMAL	arawaremasnita ra	arawaremasen deshita ra
VOLITIONAL	PLAIN	arawareyō	–
	FORMAL	arawaremashō	–
IMPERATIVE		araware ro	arawareru na

	Affirmative		*Affirmative*
POTENTIAL	arawarerareru	**CAUS. PASSIVE**	arawaresaserareru
PASSIVE	arawarerareru	**HONORIFIC**	oaraware ni naru/ arawarerareru
CAUSATIVE	arawaresaseru	**HUMBLE**	(oaraware suru)

Examples:

1. *Mori kara kuma ga arawareta.*
   森から熊が現れた。
   A bear came out of the woods.

2. *Ichi-jikan matte mo, kare wa arawarenakatta.*
   一時間待っても、彼は現れなかった。
   I waited for an hour, but he didn't appear.

3. *Kare wa iradachi ga koe ni arawareteita.*
   彼は、いら立ちが声に表れていた。
   He had an edge to his voice.

4. *Kanojo wa kimochi ga sugu kao ni arawareru.*
   彼女は気持ちがすぐ顔に表れる。
   She soon shows her feelings through her face.

5. *Yuki ga tokete, jimen ga araware-dashimashita.*
   雪がとけて、地面が現れ出しました。
   Since the snow was melting, the ground began to be exposed.

arawasu あらわす

現す to appear; 表す to show, express; 著す to write: (all trans.)

		Affirmative	*Negative*
PLAIN FORM	PRESENT	arawasu	arawasanai
	PAST	arawashita	arawasanakatta
MASU FORM	PRESENT	arawashimasu	arawashimasen
	PAST	arawashimashita	arawashimasen deshita
TE FORM		arawashite	arawasanakute
CONDITIONAL	PLAIN	arawaseba/ arawashita ra	arawasanakereba/ arawasanakatta ra
	FORMAL	arawashimashita ra	arawashimasen deshita ra
VOLITIONAL	PLAIN	arawasō	–
	FORMAL	arawashimashō	–
IMPERATIVE		arawase	arawasu na

	Affirmative		*Affirmative*
POTENTIAL	arawaseru	**CAUS. PASSIVE**	arawasaserareru
PASSIVE	arawasareru	**HONORIFIC**	oarawashi ni naru/ arawasareru
CAUSATIVE	arawasaseru	**HUMBLE**	oarawashi suru

Examples:

1. *Totsuzen monokage kara otoko ga sugata o arawashita.*
   突然物陰から男が姿を現した。
   Suddenly, a man appeared from hiding.

2. *Kanojo wa kanjō o taido ni arawashimasen.*
   彼女は感情を態度に表しません。
   She shows no feelings in her behavior.

3. *Ano kanban wa nani o arawashite iru no deshō ka.*
   あの看板は何を表しているのでしょうか。
   I wonder what that sign means.

4. *Sono keshiki no utsukushisa wa kotoba de wa arawasenai.*
   その景色の美しさは言葉では表せない。
   I can't express how beautiful the scenery is

5. *Kare wa nakunaru ichi-nen mae ni jiden o arawashimashita.*
   彼は亡くなる一年前に自伝を著しました。
   He wrote his autobiography one year before he died.

aru ある

有る or 在る to be, have: (intrans.)

		Affirmative	*Negative*
PLAIN FORM	PRESENT	aru	nai
	PAST	atta	nakatta
MASU FORM	PRESENT	arimasu	arimasen
	PAST	arimashita	arimasen deshita
TE FORM		atte	nakute
CONDITIONAL	PLAIN	areba/atta ra	nakereba/nakatta ra
	FORMAL	arimashita ra	arimasen desnita ra
VOLITIONAL	PLAIN	(arō)	–
	FORMAL	(arimashō)	–
IMPERATIVE		(are)	(aru na)

	Affirmative		*Affirmative*
POTENTIAL	(areru)	**CAUS. PASSIVE**	(araserareru)
PASSIVE	(arareru)	**HONORIFIC**	gozaru*
CAUSATIVE	(araseru)	**HUMBLE**	(oari suru)

Examples:

1. *Yūbin-kyoku wa eki no soba ni arimasu.*
   郵便局は駅のそばにあります。
   The post office is near the station.

2. *Jikan to okane ga areba, Kyōto e ikitai desu.*
   時間とお金があれば、京都へ行きたいです。
   If I have time and money, I'd like to go to Kyoto.

3. *Tanaka-san kara denwa ga arimashita.*
   田中さんから電話がありました。
   There was a phone call from Mr. Tanaka.

4. *San-ji kara kaigi ga aru node, shitsurei shimasu.*
   3時から会議があるので、失礼します。
   Please excuse me. I must go since I have a meeting at three o'clock.

5. *Yūbe osoku ni jishin ga arimashita.*
   ゆうべ遅くに地震がありました。
   We had an earthquake late last night.

* See *gozaru.*

aruku あるく

歩く to walk: (intrans.)*

		Affirmative	Negative
PLAIN FORM	PRESENT	aruku	arukanai
	PAST	aruita	arukanakatta
MASU FORM	PRESENT	arukimasu	arukimasen
	PAST	arukimashita	arukimasen deshita
TE FORM		aruite	arukanakute
CONDITIONAL	PLAIN	arukeba/aruita ra	arukanakereba/ arukanakatta ra
	FORMAL	arukimashita ra	arukimasen deshita ra
VOLITIONAL	PLAIN	arukō	–
	FORMAL	arukimashō	–
IMPERATIVE		aruke	aruku na

	Affirmative		Affirmative
POTENTIAL	arukeru	**CAUS. PASSIVE**	arukaserareru/ arukasareru
PASSIVE	arukareru	**HONORIFIC**	oaruki ni naru/ arukareru
CAUSATIVE	arukaseru	**HUMBLE**	oaruki suru

Examples:

1. *Ginza no machi o arukimashita.*
   銀座の街を歩きました。
   I walked in the city of Ginza.

2. *San-jup-pun aruite, yatto eki ni tsuita.*
   三十分歩いて、やっと駅に着いた。
   After walking for thirty minutes, we finally arrived at the station.

3. *Chotto arukō ka.*
   ちょっと歩こうか。
   Shall we walk for a while?

4. *Eki kara ie made aruite go-fun gurai desu.*
   駅から家まで歩いて五分ぐらいです。
   It's about a five-minute walk from the station to my house.

5. *Ashi ga itakute, arukemasen.*
   足が痛くて、歩けません。
   Since my leg hurts, I cannot walk.

* As with other verbs indicating movement, *aruku* 歩く may take a direct object, thus giving an idea of "going through a defined area." (See example 1.)

asobu あそぶ

遊ぶ to play, enjoy oneself: (intrans.)

		Affirmative	Negative
PLAIN FORM	PRESENT	asobu	asobanai
	PAST	asonda	asobanakatta
MASU FORM	PRESENT	asobimasu	asobimasen
	PAST	asobimashita	asobimasen deshita
TE FORM		asonde	asobanakute
CONDITIONAL	PLAIN	asobeba/asonda ra	asobanakereba/ asobanakatta ra
	FORMAL	asobimashita ra	asobimasen deshita ra
VOLITIONAL	PLAIN	asobō	–
	FORMAL	asobimashō	–
IMPERATIVE		asobe	asobu na

	Affirmative		Affirmative
POTENTIAL	asoberu	**CAUS. PASSIVE**	asobaserareru/ asobasareru
PASSIVE	asobareru	**HONORIFIC**	oasobi ni naru/ asobareru
CAUSATIVE	asobaseru	**HUMBLE**	oasobi suru

Examples:

1. *Shūmatsu, tomodachi to Roppongi de asonda.*
   週末、友達と六本木で遊んだ。
   We enjoyed ourselves at Roppongi last weekend.

2. *Otōto to gēmu o shite asobu tsumori desu.*
   弟とゲームをして遊ぶつもりです。
   I intend to play some games with my younger brother.

3. *Asonde bakari inai de, benkyō shinasai.*
   遊んでばかりいないで、勉強しなさい。
   Stop playing around and start studying!

4. *Kiken. Kono kawa de asobu na.*
   危険。この川で遊ぶな。
   It's dangerous. Do not play in this river.

5. *Dōzo chikai uchi ni asobi ni kite kudasai.*
   どうぞ近いうちに遊びに来てください。
   Please come visit us soon.

ataru あたる

当たる to hit, shine upon: (intrans.)

		Affirmative	Negative
PLAIN FORM	PRESENT	ataru	ataranai
	PAST	atatta	ataranakatta
MASU FORM	PRESENT	atarimasu	atarimasen
	PAST	atarimashita	atarimasen deshita
TE FORM		atatte	ataranakute
CONDITIONAL	PLAIN	atareba/atatta ra	ataranakereba/ ataranakatta ra
	FORMAL	atarimashita ra	atarimasen desnita ra
VOLITIONAL	PLAIN	atarō	–
	FORMAL	atarimashō	–
IMPERATIVE		atare	nataru na

	Affirmative		Affirmative
POTENTIAL	atareru	**CAUS. PASSIVE**	ataraserareru/ atarasareru
PASSIVE	atarareru	**HONORIFIC**	oatari ni naru/ atarareru
CAUSATIVE	ataraseru	**HUMBLE**	oatari suru

Examples:

1. *Bōru ga mado ni atatte, garasu ga wareta.*
   ボールが窓に当たって、ガラスが割れた。
   The ball hit the window and smashed the glass.

2. *Tenki-yohō ga atatte, gogo kara yuki ga futta.*
   天気予報が当たって、午後から雪が降った。
   It snowed in the afternoon just as the weather forecasted.

3. *Takarakuji de hyaku-man en ga atatta.*
   宝くじで百万円が当たった。
   I won one million yen in the lottery.

4. *Sono eiga wa totemo atatta.*
   その映画はとても当たった。
   The movie was a great hit.

5. *Watashi no heya wa hi ga ataranai.*
   私の部屋は日が当たらない。
   My room gets no sunshine.

ateru あてる

当てる to hit, guess, put; あてる to address to: (both trans.)

		Affirmative	*Negative*
PLAIN FORM	PRESENT	*ateru*	*atenai*
	PAST	*ateta*	*atenakatta*
MASU FORM	PRESENT	*atemasu*	*atemasen*
	PAST	*atemashita*	*atemasen deshita*
TE FORM		*atete*	*atenakute*
CONDITIONAL	PLAIN	*atereba/ateta ra*	*atenakereba/ atenakatta ra*
	FORMAL	*atemashita ra*	*atemasen deshita ra*
VOLITIONAL	PLAIN	*ateyō*	–
	FORMAL	*atemashō*	–
IMPERATIVE		*atero*	*ateru na*

	Affirmative		*Affirmative*
POTENTIAL	*aterareru/atereru*	**CAUS. PASSIVE**	*atesaserareru*
PASSIVE	*aterareru*	**HONORIFIC**	*oate ni naru/ aterareru*
CAUSATIVE	*atesaseru*	**HUMBLE**	*oate suru*

Examples:

1. *Dātsu o mato no chūshin ni ateru no wa muzukashii.*
   ダーツを的の中心に当てるのは難しい。
   It is difficult to hit the center of the target when I play darts.

2. *Kuizu no kotae o atemashita.*
   クイズの答えを当てました。
   In the quiz, I guessed the right answer.

3. *Kono hako no naka wa nani ka atete mite kudasai.*
   この箱の中身は何か当ててみてください。
   Please guess what's in this box.

4. *Hitai ni te o atete mitara, atsukatta.*
   額に手を当ててみたら、熱かった。
   When I put my hand on my forehead, it felt hot.

5. *Kore wa anata ni ateta tegami desu.*
   これはあなたにあてた手紙です。
   This is a letter addressed to you.

atsumaru あつまる

集まる to get together, assemble: (intrans.)

		Affirmative	*Negative*
PLAIN FORM	PRESENT	atsumaru	atsumaranai
	PAST	atsumatta	atsumaranakatta
MASU FORM	PRESENT	atsumarimasu	atsumarimasen
	PAST	atsumarimashita	atsumarimasen deshita
TE FORM		atsumatte	atsumaranakute
CONDITIONAL	PLAIN	atsumareba/ atsumatta ra	atsumaranakereba/ atsumaranakatta ra
	FORMAL	atsumarimashita ra	atsumarimasen deshita ra
VOLITIONAL	PLAIN	atsumarō	–
	FORMAL	atsumarimashō	–
IMPERATIVE		atsumare	atsumaru na

	Affirmative		*Affirmative*
POTENTIAL	atsumareru	**CAUS. PASSIVE**	atsumaraserareru/ atsumarasareru
PASSIVE	atsumarareru	**HONORIFIC**	oatsumari ni naru/ atsumarareru
CAUSATIVE	atsumaraseru	**HUMBLE**	(oatsumari suru)

Examples:

1. *Kitte ga takusan atsumatta.*
切手がたくさん集まった。
A lot of stamps were gathered.

2. *Ashita wa nan-ji ni atsumareba ii desu ka.*
明日は何時に集まればいいですか。
What time should we meet tomorrow?

3. *Jū-ji ni atsumatte kudasai.*
十時に集まってください。
Assemble at ten o'clock, please.

4. *Mata itsuka atsumarimashō.*
またいつか集まりましょう。
Let's get together again sometime.

5. *Konsāto ni san-zen-nin gurai no hito ga atsumarimashita.*
コンサートに三千人ぐらいの人が集まりました。
About three thousand people gathered for the concert.

atsumeru あつめる

集める to collect, gather: (trans.)

		Affirmative	*Negative*
PLAIN FORM	PRESENT	atsumeru	atsumenai
	PAST	atsumeta	atsumenakatta
MASU FORM	PRESENT	atsumemasu	atsumemasen
	PAST	atsumemashita	atsumemasen deshita
TE FORM		atsumete	atsumenakute
CONDITIONAL	PLAIN	atsumereba/ atsumeta ra	atsumenakereba/ atsumenakatta ra
	FORMAL	atsumemashita ra	atsumemasen deshita ra
VOLITIONAL	PLAIN	atsumeyō	–
	FORMAL	atsumemashō	–
IMPERATIVE		atsumero	atsumeru na

	Affirmative		*Affirmative*
POTENTIAL	atsumerareru/ atsumereru	**CAUS. PASSIVE**	atsumesaserareru
PASSIVE	atsumerareru	**HONORIFIC**	oatsume ni naru/ atsumerareru
CAUSATIVE	atsumesaseru	**HUMBLE**	oatsume suru

Examples:

1. *Watashi wa kitte o atsumete imasu.*
   私は切手を集めています。
   I collect stamps.

2. *Seito-tachi wa zen-in kōtei ni atsumerareta.*
   生徒たちは全員校庭に集められた。
   All the students were assembled in the school ground.

3. *Ronbun o kaku tame ni, shiryō o atsumete okimasu.*
   論文を書くために、資料を集めておきます。
   I will gather material in order to write a thesis.

4. *Atsumeta gomi o moyashimashō.*
   集めたごみを燃やしましょう。
   Let's burn the trash we collected.

5. *Kanojo no fuku wa mawari no hito no chūmoku o atsumeta.*
   彼女の服は、周りの人の注目を集めた。
   Her clothes attracted the attention of passers-by.

au あう

会う to meet; 合う to match, fit: (both intrans.)*

		Affirmative	*Negative*
PLAIN FORM	PRESENT	au	awanai
	PAST	atta	awanakatta
MASU FORM	PRESENT	aimasu	aimasen
	PAST	aimashita	aimasen deshita
TE FORM		atte	awanakute
CONDITIONAL	PLAIN	aeba/atta ra	awanakereba/awanakatta ra
	FORMAL	aimashita ra	aimasen deshita ra
VOLITIONAL	PLAIN	aō	–
	FORMAL	aimashō	–
IMPERATIVE		ae	au na

	Affirmative		*Affirmative*
POTENTIAL	aeru	**CAUS. PASSIVE**	awaserareru/awasareru
PASSIVE	awareru	**HONORIFIC**	oai ni naru/awareru
CAUSATIVE	awaseru	**HUMBLE**	oai suru/ome ni kakaru

Examples:

1. *Shigoto no ato de tomodachi to atte, shokuji ni ikimasu.*
   仕事の後で友達と会って、食事に行きます。
   When I finish work, I will meet a friend for dinner.

2. *Ashita san-ji ni eki de aimashō.*
   明日三時に駅で会いましょう。
   Let's meet at the station at three o'clock tomorrow.

3. *Dokoka de oai shimasendeshita ka.*
   どこかでお会いしませんでしたか。
   Haven't we met somewhere before?

4. *Kono kutsu wa saizu ga aimasen. Mō sukoshi chiisai no o kudasai.*
   この靴はサイズが合いません。もう少し小さいのをください。
   This pair of shoes doesn't fit me. Please show me a smaller size.

5. *Kotae ga atte iru ka dō ka, tashikamete kudasai.*
   答えが合っているかどうか、確かめてください。
   Please check if my answer is correct.

* The *au* 合う meaning "to match, fit" generally has no imperative, volitional, potential, or passive forms.

ayamaru あやまる

謝る to apologize; 誤る to make a mistake: (both trans.)*

		Affirmative	Negative
PLAIN FORM	PRESENT	ayamaru	ayamaranai
	PAST	ayamatta	ayamaranakatta
MASU FORM	PRESENT	ayamarimasu	ayamarimasen
	PAST	ayamarimashita	ayamarimasen deshita
TE FORM		ayamatte	ayamaranakute
CONDITIONAL	PLAIN	ayamareba/ayamatta ra	ayamaranakereba/ ayamaranakatta ra
	FORMAL	ayamarimashita ra	ayamarimasen deshita ra
VOLITIONAL	PLAIN	ayamarō	–
	FORMAL	ayamarimashō	–
IMPERATIVE		ayamare	ayamaru na

	Affirmative		Affirmative
POTENTIAL	ayamareru	**CAUS. PASSIVE**	ayamaraserareru/ ayamarasareru
PASSIVE	ayamarareru	**HONORIFIC**	oayamari ni naru/ ayamarareru
CAUSATIVE	ayamaraseru	**HUMBLE**	oayamari suru

Examples:

1. *Okureta koto o kare ni ayamatta hō ga ii.*
   遅れたことを彼に謝ったほうがいい。
   You should apologize to him for being late.

2. *Shōjiki ni ayamattara, kanojo wa yurushite kureta.*
   正直に謝ったら、彼女は許してくれた。
   When I apologized to her truthfully, she forgave me.

3. *Kanojo wa totemo okotte, kare ni ayamaraseta.*
   彼女はとても怒って、彼に謝らせた。
   She was very angry with him and she made him apologize to her.

4. *Handan o ayamatta kamo-shirenai.*
   判断を誤ったかもしれない。
   I might have made a wrong judgment.

5. *Ayamatte, taisetsu na shorui o sutete shimatta.*
   誤って、大切な書類を捨ててしまった。
   I accidentally threw away the important documents.

* The verb 誤る *ayamaru* meaning "to make a mistake" generally has no volitional, potential, passive, humble, causative, or causative passive forms.

azukaru あずかる

預かる to keep, take charge of: (trans.)

		Affirmative	Negative
PLAIN FORM	PRESENT	azukaru	azukaranai
	PAST	azukatta	azukaranakatta
MASU FORM	PRESENT	azukarimasu	azukarimasen
	PAST	azukarimashita	azukarimasen deshita
TE FORM		azukatte	azukaranakute
CONDITIONAL	PLAIN	azukareba/azukatta ra	azukaranakereba/ azukaranakatta ra
	FORMAL	azukarimashita ra	azukarimasen deshita ra
VOLITIONAL	PLAIN	azukarō	–
	FORMAL	azukarimashō	–
IMPERATIVE		azukare	azukaru na

	Affirmative		Affirmative
POTENTIAL	azukareru	**CAUS. PASSIVE**	azukaraserareru/ azukarasareru
PASSIVE	azukarareru	**HONORIFIC**	oazukari ni naru/ azukarareru
CAUSATIVE	azukaraseru	**HUMBLE**	oazukari suru

Examples:

1. *Anata no nimotsu o azukatte imasu.*
   あなたの荷物を預かっています。
   I am keeping the luggage for you.

2. *Kono kaban o azukatte moraemasu ka.*
   このかばんを預かってもらえますか。
   Can you keep this bag for me?

3. *Kōto wa doko de azukatte kuremasu ka.*
   コートはどこで預かってくれますか。
   Where can I leave my coat?

4. *Kochira de oazukari itashimasu.*
   こちらでお預かりいたします。
   We'll keep your coat here.

5. *Tomodachi ga kodomo o azukatte kureta.*
   友達が子供を預かってくれた。
   My friend took care of my child for me.

azukeru あずける

預ける to leave a person or thing under someone's care, deposit: (trans.)

		Affirmative	Negative
PLAIN FORM	PRESENT	azukeru	azukenai
	PAST	azuketa	azukenakatta
MASU FORM	PRESENT	azukemasu	azukemasen
	PAST	azukemashita	azukemasen deshita
TE FORM		azukete	azukenakute
CONDITIONAL	PLAIN	azukereba/azuketa ra	azukenakereba/ azukenakatta ra
	FORMAL	azukemashita ra	azukemasen deshita ra
VOLITIONAL	PLAIN	azukeyō	–
	FORMAL	azukemashō	–
IMPERATIVE		azukero	azukeru na

	Affirmative		Affirmative
POTENTIAL	azukerareru/ azukereru	**CAUS. PASSIVE**	azukesaserareru
PASSIVE	azukerareru	**HONORIFIC**	oazuke ni naru/ azukerareru
CAUSATIVE	azukesaseru	**HUMBLE**	oazuke suru

Examples:

1. *Nimotsu o uketsuke ni azukemashita.*
荷物を受付に預けました。
I left my luggage at the reception desk.

2. *Nimotsu o azukeru tokoro wa doko desu ka.*
荷物を預ける所は、どこですか。
Where can I leave my luggage?

3. *Asoko ni azukeraremasu yo.*
あそこに預けられますよ。
You can leave it over there.

4. *Karera wa kodomo o hoikuen ni azukete hataraite iru.*
彼らは子供を保育園に預けて働いている。
They work, leaving their child in the care of a nursery school.

5. *Suzuki-san wa ginkō ni hyaku-man en o azukete iru.*
鈴木さんは銀行に百万円を預けている。
Mr. Suzuki has one million yen deposited in the bank.

butsukaru ぶつかる

ぶつかる to hit, face (difficulties), fall on (dates): (intrans.)

		Affirmative	Negative
PLAIN FORM	PRESENT	butsukaru	butsukaranai
	PAST	butsukatta	butsukaranakatta
MASU FORM	PRESENT	butsukarimasu	butsukarimasen
	PAST	butsukarimashita	butsukarimasen desnita
TE FORM		butsukatte	butsukaranakute
CONDITIONAL	PLAIN	butsukareba/ butsukatta ra	butsukaranakereba/ butsukaranakatta ra
	FORMAL	butsukarimashita ra	butsukarimasen deshita ra
VOLITIONAL	PLAIN	butsukarō	–
	FORMAL	butsukarimashō	–
IMPERATIVE		butsukare	butsukaru na

	Affirmative		Affirmative
POTENTIAL	butsukareru	**CAUS. PASSIVE**	butsukaraserareru/ butsukarasareru
PASSIVE	butsukarareru	**HONORIFIC**	obutsukari ni naru/ butsukarareru
CAUSATIVE	butsukaraseru	**HUMBLE**	(obutsukari suru)

Examples:

1. *Kata ga doa ni butsukarimashita.*
   肩がドアにぶつかりました。
   My shoulder struck the door.

2. *Kōsaten de kuruma to baiku ga butsukatta.*
   交差点で車とバイクがぶつかった。
   A car and a motorcycle ran into each other at the crossing.

3. *Kono michi wa sukoshi saki de kawa to butsukarimasu.*
   この道は少し先で川とぶつかります。
   This road meets a river a little ahead.

4. *Yamada-san wa yoku jōshi to butsukatte iru.*
   山田さんはよく上司とぶつかっている。
   Mr. Yamada often quarrels with his boss.

5. *Kyonen wa Kurisumasu to Nichiyōbi ga butsukatta.*
   去年はクリスマスと日曜日がぶつかった。
   Christmas fell on a Sunday last year.

butsukeru ぶつける

GROUP 2

ぶつける to hit against, strike, throw: (trans.)

		Affirmative	*Negative*
PLAIN FORM	PRESENT	butsukeru	butsukenai
	PAST	butsuketa	butsukenakatta
MASU FORM	PRESENT	butsukemasu	butsukemasen
	PAST	butsukemashita	butsukemasen deshita
TE FORM		butsukete	butsukenakute
CONDITIONAL	PLAIN	butsukereba/butsuketa ra	butsukenakereba/ butsukenakatta ra
	FORMAL	butsukemashita ra	butsukemasen deshita ra
VOLITIONAL	PLAIN	butsukeyō	–
	FORMAL	butsukemashō	–
IMPERATIVE		butsukero	butsukeru na

	Affirmative		*Affirmative*
POTENTIAL	butsukerareru/ butsukereru	**CAUS. PASSIVE**	butsukesaserareru
PASSIVE	butsukerareru	**HONORIFIC**	obutsuke ni naru/ butsukerareru
CAUSATIVE	butsukesaseru	**HUMBLE**	(obutsuke suru)

Examples:

1. *Ashi o tsukue no kado ni butsukete shimatta.*
   足を机の角にぶつけてしまった。
   I hit my leg against the corner of the desk.

2. *Kanojo wa kuruma o gādorēru ni butsukemashita.*
   彼女は車をガードレールにぶつけました。
   She hit her car against the guardrail.

3. *Koronde, atama o yuka ni butsuke sō ni natta.*
   転んで、頭を床にぶつけそうになった。
   I fell down and almost hit my head on the floor.

4. *Kuruma o chūshajō ni tomete oita ra, dareka ni butsukerareta.*
   車を駐車場に止めておいたら、誰かにぶつけられた。
   When I left my car in the parking lot, it was hit by somebody.

5. *Iraira o hito ni butsukeru no wa yamete kudasai.*
   イライラを人にぶつけるのは、やめてください。
   Please stop venting your frustration on everybody.

chigau ちがう

違う to differ, be wrong: (intrans.)

		Affirmative	Negative
PLAIN FORM	PRESENT	chigau	chigawanai
	PAST	chigatta	chigawanakatta
MASU FORM	PRESENT	chigaimasu	chigaimasen
	PAST	chigaimashita	chigaimasen deshita
TE FORM		chigatte	chigawanakute
CONDITIONAL	PLAIN	chigaeba/chigatta ra	chigawanakereba/ chigawanakatta ra
	FORMAL	chigaimashita ra	chigaimasen deshita ra
VOLITIONAL	PLAIN	chigaō	–
	FORMAL	chigaimashō	–
IMPERATIVE		chigae	chigau na

	Affirmative		Affirmative
POTENTIAL	chigaeru	**CAUS. PASSIVE**	chigawaserareru/ chigawasareru
PASSIVE	chigawareru	**HONORIFIC**	ochigai ni naru/ chigawareru
CAUSATIVE	chigawaseru	**HUMBLE**	(ochigai suru)

Examples:

1. *Ano hito wa Nihon-jin desu ka. / Iie, chigaimasu.*
   あの人は日本人ですか。／いいえ、違います。
   Is that person Japanese? / No, he isn't.

2. *Kono heya to ano heya wa ōkisa ga chigaimasu.*
   この部屋とあの部屋は大きさが違います。
   This room is different from that room in size.

3. *Watashi wa kanojo to iken ga chigau.*
   私は彼女と意見が違う。
   My opinion differs from hers.

4. *Denwa-bangō ga chigaimasu yo.*
   電話番号が違いますよ。
   You have the wrong telephone number.

5. *Shūkan wa kuni ni yotte chigau mono desu.*
   習慣は国によって違うものです。
   Each country has different customs.

chikazukeru ちかづける

近づける to bring a thing close, allow a person to approach: (trans.)

		Affirmative	*Negative*
PLAIN FORM	PRESENT	chikazukeru	chikazukenai
	PAST	chikazuketa	chikazukenakatta
MASU FORM	PRESENT	chikazukemasu	chikazukemasen
	PAST	chikazukemashita	chikazukemasen deshita
TE FORM		chikazukete	chikazukenakute
CONDITIONAL	PLAIN	chikazukereba/ chikazuketa ra	chikazukenakereba/ chikazukenakatta ra
	FORMAL	chikazukemashita ra	chikazukemasen deshita ra
VOLITIONAL	PLAIN	chikazukeyō	–
	FORMAL	chikazukemashō	–
IMPERATIVE		chikazukero	chikazukeru na

	Affirmative		*Affirmative*
POTENTIAL	chikazukerareru/ chikazukereru	**CAUS. PASSIVE**	chikazukesaserareru
PASSIVE	chikazukerareru	**HONORIFIC**	ochikazuke ni naru/ chikazukerareru
CAUSATIVE	chikazukesaseru	**HUMBLE**	ochikazuke suru

Examples:

1. *Isu o tsukue ni chikazukete kudasai.*
   いすを机に近づけてください。
   Please move your chair nearer to the desk.

2. *Suzuki-san wa shigoto-chū hito o chikazukenai.*
   鈴木さんは仕事中、人を近づけない。
   Mr. Suzuki keeps away from people while he is working.

3. *Kare wa kao o mado ni chikazukete, soto o mita.*
   彼は顔を窓に近づけて、外を見た。
   He moved close to the window and looked outside.

4. *Kodomo o sutōbu ni chikazukenaide kudasai.*
   子供をストーブに近づけないでください。
   Please keep children away from the stove.

5. *Warui yūjin o chikazukenai yō ni shinasai.*
   悪い友人を近づけないようにしなさい。
   Keep a fair distance from bad friends.

chikazuku ちかづく

近づく to approach, get near, associate with: (intrans.)

		Affirmative	Negative
PLAIN FORM	PRESENT	chikazuku	chikazukanai
	PAST	chikazuita	chikazukanakatta
MASU FORM	PRESENT	chikazukimasu	chikazukimasen
	PAST	chikazukimashita	chikazukimasen deshita
TE FORM		chikazuite	chikazukanakute
CONDITIONAL	PLAIN	chikazukeba/ chikazuita ra	chikazukanakereba/ chikazukanakatta ra
	FORMAL	chikazukimashita ra	chikazukimasen deshita ra
VOLITIONAL	PLAIN	chikazukō	–
	FORMAL	chikazukimashō	–
IMPERATIVE		chikazuke	chikazuku na

	Affirmative		Affirmative
POTENTIAL	chikazukeru	**CAUS. PASSIVE**	chikazukaserareru/ chikazukasareru
PASSIVE	chikazukareru	**HONORIFIC**	ochikazuki ni naru/ chikazukareru
CAUSATIVE	chikazukaseru	**HUMBLE**	ochikazuki suru

Examples:

1. *Densha wa eki ni chikazuita*
   電車は駅に近づいた。
   The train is nearing the station.

2. *Abunai kara, sono kikai ni chikazuite wa ikenai.*
   危ないから、その機械に近づいてはいけない。
   Because the machine is dangerous, you must not approach it.

3. *Kurisumasu ga chikazuku to, machi wa nigiyaka ni naru.*
   クリスマスが近づくと、街はにぎやかになる。
   When Christmas approaches, the town livens up.

4. *Tenki yohō ni yoruto, taifū ga chikazuite iru sō da.*
   天気予報によると、台風が近づいているそうだ。
   According to the weather forecast, a typhoon seems to be approaching.

5. *Kare wa hidoi kaze o hiite iru kara, chikazukanai hō ga ii.*
   彼はひどい風邪をひいているから、近づかないほうがいい。
   We should stay away from him because he has a bad cold.

daku だく

抱く to hug: (trans.)

		Affirmative	*Negative*
PLAIN FORM	PRESENT	daku	dakanai
	PAST	daita	dakannakatta
MASU FORM	PRESENT	dakimasu	dakimashita
	PAST	dakimasen	dakimasen deshita
TE FORM		daite	dakanakute
CONDITIONAL	PLAIN	dakeba/daita ra	dakanakereba/ dakanakatta ra
	FORMAL	dakimashita ra	dakimasen deshita ra
VOLITIONAL	PLAIN	dakō	–
	FORMAL	dakimashō	–
IMPERATIVE		dake	daku na

	Affirmative		*Affirmative*
POTENTIAL	dakeru	**CAUS. PASSIVE**	dakaserareru/dakasareru
PASSIVE	dakareru	**HONORIFIC**	odaki ni naru/ dakareru
CAUSATIVE	dakaseru	**HUMBLE**	odaki suru

Examples:

1. *Kodomo wa kuma no nuigurumi o daite iru.*
   子供は熊のぬいぐるみを抱いている。
   The child is hugging a stuffed teddy bear.

2. *Kare wa musuko o ryōude ni shikkari daita.*
   彼は息子を両腕にしっかり抱いた。
   He held his son firmly in his arms.

3. *Tomodachi no akachan o dakasete moratta.*
   友達の赤ちゃんを抱かせてもらった。
   My friend let me hold his baby.

4. *Sono otoko no ko wa haha oya ni dakarete, nemutte-shimatta.*
   その男の子は母親に抱かれて、眠ってしまった。
   The boy fell asleep while being embraced by his mother.

5. *Kare wa ōki na yume o daite, kokyō o deta.*
   彼は大きな夢を抱いて、故郷を出た。
   He left his hometown with a big dream.

damasu だます

だます to deceive, cheat: (trans.)

		Affirmative	Negative
PLAIN FORM	PRESENT	damasu	damasanai
	PAST	damashita	damasanakatta
MASU FORM	PRESENT	damashimasu	damashimasen
	PAST	damashimashita	damashimasen deshita
TE FORM		damashite	damasanakute
CONDITIONAL	PLAIN	damaseba/damashita ra	damasanakereba/ damasanakatta ra
	FORMAL	damashimashita ra	damashimasen deshita ra
VOLITIONAL	PLAIN	damasō	–
	FORMAL	damashimashō	–
IMPERATIVE		damase	damasu na

	Affirmative		Affirmative
POTENTIAL	damaseru	**CAUS. PASSIVE**	damasaserareru
PASSIVE	damasareru	**HONORIFIC**	odamashi ni naru/ damasareru
CAUSATIVE	damasaseru	**HUMBLE**	odamashi suru

Examples:

1. *Sono otoko wa takusan no hito o damashita.*
   その男はたくさんの人をだました。
   That man deceived many people.

2. *Karera wa kankō-kyaku o damashite, takai mono o kawaseta.*
   彼らは観光客をだまして、高い物を買わせた。
   They cheated tourists into buying expensive things.

3. *Kare wa uso ga jōzu de, sukkari damasarete shimatta.*
   彼はうそが上手で、すっかりだまされてしまった。
   He was good at lying, and I was completely deceived.

4. *Sonna heta na iiwake de wa, oya wa damasenai deshō.*
   そんな下手な言い訳では、親はだませないでしょう。
   You cannot deceive your parents with such a poor excuse.

5. *Kanojo o damasu tsumori wa nakatta.*
   彼女をだますつもりはなかった。
   I didn't mean to deceive her.

dasu だす

出す to put out, send, pay, submit: (trans.); begin doing: (intrans.)

		Affirmative	*Negative*
PLAIN FORM	PRESENT	dasu	dasanai
	PAST	dashita	dasanakatta
MASU FORM	PRESENT	dashimasu	dashimasen
	PAST	dashimashita	dashimasen deshita
TE FORM		dashite	dasanakute
CONDITIONAL	PLAIN	daseba/dashita ra	dasanakereba/ dasanakatta ra
	FORMAL	dashimashita ra	dashimasen deshita ra
VOLITIONAL	PLAIN	dasō	–
	FORMAL	dashimashō	–
IMPERATIVE		dase	dasu na

	Affirmative		*Affirmative*
POTENTIAL	daseru	**CAUS. PASSIVE**	dasaserareru
PASSIVE	dasareru	**HONORIFIC**	odashi ni naru/ dasareru
CAUSATIVE	dasaseru	**HUMBLE**	odashi suru

Examples:

1. *Kaban kara saifu o dashimashita.*
   かばんから財布を出しました。
   I took the wallet out of the bag.

2. *Gomi wa asa hachi-ji made ni dashite kudasai.*
   ごみは朝八時までに出してください。
   Please take out your garbage by 8:00 a.m.

3. *Kinō haha ni tegami o dashimashita.*
   昨日、母に手紙を出しました。
   I sent the letter to my mother yesterday.

4. *Kono repōto wa nan-nichi made ni dasanakereba narimasen ka.*
   このレポートは何日までに出さなければなりませんか。
   By what date do I have to submit this report?

5. *Kyū ni ame ga furi-dashimashita.*
   急に雨が降り出しました。
   Suddenly it started raining.

dekakeru でかける

出かける to go out, set off (to): (intrans.)

		Affirmative	*Negative*
PLAIN FORM	PRESENT	dekakeru	dekakenai
	PAST	dekaketa	dekakenakatta
MASU FORM	PRESENT	dekakemasu	dekakemasen
	PAST	dekakemashita	dekakemasen deshita
TE FORM		dekakete	dekakenakute
CONDITIONAL	PLAIN	dekakereba/dekaketa ra	dekakenakereba/ dekakenakatta ra
	FORMAL	dekakemashita ra	dekakemasen deshita ra
VOLITIONAL	PLAIN	dekakeyō	–
	FORMAL	dekakemashō	–
IMPERATIVE		dekakero	dekakeru na

	Affirmative		*Affirmative*
POTENTIAL	dekakerareru/ dekakereru	**CAUS. PASSIVE**	dekakesaserareru
PASSIVE	dekakerareru	**HONORIFIC**	odekake ni naru/ dekakerareru
CAUSATIVE	dekakesaseru	**HUMBLE**	odekake suru

Examples:

1. *Dekakemashō.*
   出かけましょう。
   Let's go out.

2. *Katō-san wa kaimono ni dekaketa.*
   加藤さんは買い物に出かけた。
   Mr. Kato went shopping.

3. *Nichiyōbi, doko ni mo dekakemasen deshita.*
   日曜日、どこにも出かけませんでした。
   I din't go anywhere on Sunday.

4. *Gogo, yōji ga atte, dekakenakereba naranai.*
   午後、用事があって、出かけなければならない。
   I have something to do later, so I have to go out in the afternoon.

5. *Sensei wa roku-ji goro odekake ni narimashita.*
   先生は六時ごろお出かけになりました。
   The teacher went out at around six o'clock.

dekiru できる

できる(出来る) to be completed, can, be made of: (intrans.)

		Affirmative	Negative
PLAIN FORM	PRESENT	dekiru	dekinai
	PAST	dekita	dekinakatta
MASU FORM	PRESENT	dekimasu	dekimasen
	PAST	dekimashita	dekimasen deshita
TE FORM		dekite	dekinakute
CONDITIONAL	PLAIN	dekireba/dekita ra	dekinakereba/ dekinakatta ra
	FORMAL	dekimashita ra	dekimasen deshita ra
VOLITIONAL	PLAIN	(dekiyō)	–
	FORMAL	(dekimashō)	–
IMPERATIVE		(dekiro)	(dekiru na)

	Affirmative		Affirmative
POTENTIAL	–	**CAUS. PASSIVE**	(dekisaserareru)
PASSIVE	(dekirareru)	**HONORIFIC**	odeki ni naru/ (dekirareru)
CAUSATIVE	(dekisaseru)	**HUMBLE**	(odeki suru)

Examples:

1. *Shokuji no yōi ga dekita.*
   食事の用意ができた。
   Dinner is ready.

2. *Nihon-go ga dekimasu ka.*
   日本語ができますか。
   Can you speak Japanese?

3. *Kanojo wa piano o hiku koto ga dekimasu.*
   彼女はピアノを弾くことができます。
   She can play the piano.

4. *Mōshikomi-sho wa dekiru dake hayaku dashite kudasai.*
   申込書は、できるだけ早く出して下さい。
   Please submit the application form as soon as possible.

5. *Eki no chikaku ni atarashii sūpā ga dekita sō desu.*
   駅の近くに新しいスーパーができたそうです。
   I hear that a new supermarket opened near the station.

Note: The verb *dekiru* できる is the potential form of the verb *suru* する.

deru でる

出る to come out, leave, attend, be published: (intrans.)*

		Affirmative	*Negative*
PLAIN FORM	PRESENT	deru	denai
	PAST	deta	denakatta
MASU FORM	PRESENT	demasu	demasen
	PAST	demashita	demasen deshita
TE FORM		dete	denakute
CONDITIONAL	PLAIN	dereba/deta ra	denakereba/ denakatta ra
	FORMAL	demashita ra	demasen deshita ra
VOLITIONAL	PLAIN	deyō	–
	FORMAL	demashō	–
IMPERATIVE		dero	deru na

	Affirmative		*Affirmative*
POTENTIAL	derareru/dereru	**CAUS. PASSIVE**	desaserareru
PASSIVE	derareru	**HONORIFIC**	ode ni naru/derareru
CAUSATIVE	desaseru	**HUMBLE**	(ode suru)

Examples:

1. *Mori-san wa mō kaisha o demashita ka.*
   森さんは、もう会社を出ましたか。
   Has Mr. Mori left the office yet?

2. *San-ji ni kaigi ni denakereba naranai node, shitsurei shimasu.*
   三時に会議に出なければならないので、失礼します。
   Excuse me, but I have to attend a meeting at three o'clock.

3. *Shinbun ni jishin no kiji ga dete imasu.*
   新聞に地震の記事が出ています。
   An article on the earthquake appeared in the newspaper.

4. *Kare wa Amerika no daigaku o deta sō desu.*
   彼はアメリカの大学を出たそうです。
   I hear that he graduated from an American university.

5. *Marason taikai ni deru tame ni, mainichi hashitte imasu.*
   マラソン大会に出るために、毎日走っています。
   I run every day in preparation for a marathon meet.

* As with other verbs indicating motion, *deru* 出る may take a direct object, thus giving an idea of "going through a defined area." (See example 1.)

erabu えらぶ

選ぶ to choose, decide on, elect: (trans.)

		Affirmative	*Negative*
PLAIN FORM	PRESENT	erabu	erabanai
	PAST	eranda	erabanakatta
MASU FORM	PRESENT	erabimasu	erabimasen
	PAST	erabimashita	erabimasen deshita
TE FORM		erande	erabanakute
CONDITIONAL	PLAIN	erabeba/eranda ra	erabanakereba/ erabanakatta ra
	FORMAL	erabimashita ra	erabimasen deshita ra
VOLITIONAL	PLAIN	erabō	–
	FORMAL	erabimashō	–
IMPERATIVE		erabe	erabu na

	Affirmative		*Affirmative*
POTENTIAL	eraberu	**CAUS. PASSIVE**	erabaserareru/ erabasareru
PASSIVE	erabareru	**HONORIFIC**	oerabi ni naru/ erabareru
CAUSATIVE	erabaseru	**HUMBLE**	oerabi suru

Examples:

1. *Dōshite sono shigoto o erabimashita ka.*
   どうしてその仕事を選びましたか。
   Why did you choose that job?

2. *Dōzo o-suki na mono o oerabi kudasai.*
   どうぞお好きな物をお選びください。
   Please choose any one you like.

3. *Tanaka-san wa gichō ni erabaremashita.*
   田中さんは議長に選ばれました。
   Mr. Tanaka was elected as a chairperson

4. *Maiasa, imōto wa fuku o erabu no ni jikan ga kakaru.*
   毎朝、妹は服を選ぶのに時間がかかる。
   My younger sister takes time to choose her clothes every morning.

5. *Sensei ni ii jisho o erande itadakimashita.*
   先生にいい辞書を選んでいただきました。
   I had a teacher choose a good dictionary (for me).

fueru ふえる

増える to increase: (intrans.)

		Affirmative	Negative
PLAIN FORM	PRESENT	*fueru*	*fuenai*
	PAST	*fueta*	*fuenakatta*
MASU FORM	PRESENT	*fuemasu*	*fuemasen*
	PAST	*fuemashita*	*fuemasen deshita*
TE FORM		*fuete*	*fuenakute*
CONDITIONAL	PLAIN	*fuereba/fueta ra*	*fuenakereba/ fuenakatta ra*
	FORMAL	*fuemashita ra*	*fuemasen deshita ra*
VOLITIONAL	PLAIN	*fueyō*	–
	FORMAL	*fuemashō*	–
IMPERATIVE		*fuero*	*fueru na*

	Affirmative		Affirmative
POTENTIAL	*fuerareru/fuereru*	**CAUS. PASSIVE**	*fuesaserareru*
PASSIVE	*fuerareru*	**HONORIFIC**	*ofue ni naru/ fuerareru*
CAUSATIVE	*fuesaseru*	**HUMBLE**	*(ofue suru)*

Examples:

1. *Nihon-go no goi ga fueta.*
   日本語の語彙が増えた。
   My Japanese vocabulary has increased.

2. *Taijū ga go kiro fuemashita.*
   体重が5キロ増えました。
   I have gained five kilograms.

3. *Sekai no jinkō wa fue-tsuzukete iru.*
   世界の人口は増え続けている。
   The population of the world keeps on increasing.

4. *Saikin, denki jidōsha no kazu ga fuete iru.*
   最近、電気自動車の数が増えている。
   The number of electric cars has been increasing recently.

5. *Tenshoku shite kara shūnyū ga fueta.*
   転職してから収入が増えた。
   My income increased after I changed jobs.

fuku ふく

ふく to wipe; 吹く to blow, play an instrument:* (both trans.)

		Affirmative	Negative
PLAIN FORM	PRESENT	fuku	fukanai
	PAST	fuita	fukanakatta
MASU FORM	PRESENT	fukimasu	fukimasen
	PAST	fukimashita	fukimasen deshita
TE FORM		fuite	fukanakute
CONDITIONAL	PLAIN	fukeba/fuita ra	fukanakereba/fukanakatta ra
	FORMAL	fukimashita ra	fukimasen deshita ra
VOLITIONAL	PLAIN	fukō	–
	FORMAL	fukimashō	–
IMPERATIVE		fuke	fuku na

	Affirmative		Affirmative
POTENTIAL	fukeru	**CAUS. PASSIVE**	fukaserareru/fukasareru
PASSIVE	fukareru	**HONORIFIC**	ofuki ni naru/fukareru
CAUSATIVE	fukaseru	**HUMBLE**	ofuki suru

Examples:

1. *Kitanai kara, tsukue no ue o fuite kudasai.*
   汚いから、机の上をふいて下さい。
   Because the desk is dirty, please clean it.

2. *Ame de nureta kaminoke o taoru de fuita.*
   雨でぬれた髪の毛をタオルでふいた。
   I dried my rain-soaked hair with a towel.

3. *Soto wa tsuyoi kaze ga fuite iru.*
   外は強い風が吹いている。
   It's blowing hard outside.

4. *Tanaka-san wa furūto ga fukemasu.*
   田中さんはフルートが吹けます。
   Mr. Tanaka can play the flute.

5. *Otōto wa kuchibue o fuku no ga jōzu da.*
   弟は口笛を吹くのが上手だ。
   My younger brother is good at whistling.

* play the flute/clarinet/trumpet → *furūto/kurarinetto/toranpetto o fuku* 吹く
  play the piano/guitar/violin → *piano/gitā/baiorin o hiku* 弾く

fukumeru ふくめる

含める to include, to convince: (trans.)

		Affirmative	Negative
PLAIN FORM	PRESENT	fukumeru	fukumenai
	PAST	fukumeta	fukumenakatta
MASU FORM	PRESENT	fukumemasu	fukumemasen
	PAST	fukumemashita	fukumemasen deshita
TE FORM		fukumete	fukumenakute
CONDITIONAL	PLAIN	fukumereba/fukumeta ra	fukumenakereba/ fukumenakatta ra
	FORMAL	fukumemashita ra	fukumemasen deshita ra
VOLITIONAL	PLAIN	fukumeyō	–
	FORMAL	fukumemashō	–
IMPERATIVE		fukumero	fukumeru na

	Affirmative		Affirmative
POTENTIAL	fukumerareru/ fukumereru	**CAUS. PASSIVE**	fukumesaserareru
PASSIVE	fukumerareru	**HONORIFIC**	ofukume ni naru/ fukumerareru
CAUSATIVE	fukumesaseru	**HUMBLE**	ofukume suru

Examples:

1. *Zeikin o fukumete, san-man go-sen en desu.*
   税金を含めて、三万五千円です。
   The total is 35,000 yen, including tax.

2. *Suzuki-san o fukumeru to, zenbu de jū nin ni narimasu.*
   鈴木さんを含めると、全部で十人になります。
   Including Mr. Suzuki, there are ten people in all.

3. *Ryōshūsho ni kono hon no daikin o fukumenaide kudasai.*
   領収書にこの本の代金を含めないでください。
   Please don't include the price of this book in the receipt.

4. *Heya-dai o fukumezu ni, ichi nichi wa go-sen en gurai deshita.*
   部屋代を含めずに、一日は五千円ぐらいでした。
   Excluding the cost of the room, one day costs about 5,000 yen.

5. *Kanojo wa kande fukumeru yō ni kodomo ni setsumei shita.*
   彼女はかんで含めるように子供に説明した。
   She explained to the child repeatedly in easier terms.

fukumu ふくむ

含む to contain, include, hold something in the mouth: (trans. or intrans.)

		Affirmative	*Negative*
PLAIN FORM	PRESENT	fukumu	fukumanai
	PAST	fukunda	fukumanakatta
MASU FORM	PRESENT	fukumimasu	fukumimasen
	PAST	fukumimashita	fukumimasen deshita
TE FORM		fukunde	fukumanakute
CONDITIONAL	PLAIN	fukumeba/fukunda ra	fukumanakereba/ fukumanakatta ra
	FORMAL	fukumimashita ra	fukumimasen deshita ra
VOLITIONAL	PLAIN	fukumō	–
	FORMAL	fukumimashō	–
IMPERATIVE		fukume	fukumu na

	Affirmative		*Affirmative*
POTENTIAL	(fukumeru)	**CAUS. PASSIVE**	fukumaserareru/ fukumasareru
PASSIVE	fukumareru	**HONORIFIC**	ofukumi ni naru/ fukemareru
CAUSATIVE	fukumaseru	**HUMBLE**	ofukumi suru

Examples:

1. *Kono nedan ni wa shōhi-zei ga fukumarete imasu ka.*
   この値段には消費税が含まれていますか。
   Is the consumption tax included in this price?

2. *Kono ame ni wa satō wa fukumarete imasen.*
   このあめには砂糖は含まれていません。
   There's no sugar in this candy.

3. *Sono jiken wa fukuzatsu na mondai o fukunde iru yō da.*
   その事件は複雑な問題を含んでいるようだ。
   The incident seems to have caused complex problems.

4. *Kusuri o kuchi ni fukunde, mizu de nagashikonda.*
   薬を口に含んで、水で流し込んだ。
   I held medicine in my mouth and then swallowed it.

5. *Jinkō no tenkabutsu o fukumanai shokuhin o kau yō ni shite iru.*
   人工の添加物を含まない食品を買うようにしている。
   I am trying to buy food that does not contain any artificial additives.

fureru ふれる

触れる to touch, mention; (intrans. and trans.)

		Affirmative	Negative
PLAIN FORM	PRESENT	fureru	furenai
	PAST	fureta	furenakatta
MASU FORM	PRESENT	furemasu	furemasen
	PAST	furemashita	furemasen deshita
TE FORM		furete	furenakute
CONDITIONAL	PLAIN	furereba/fureta ra	furenakereba/ furenakatta ra
	FORMAL	furemashita ra	furemasen deshita ra
VOLITIONAL	PLAIN	fureyō	–
	FORMAL	furemashō	–
IMPERATIVE		furero	fureru na

	Affirmative		Affirmative
POTENTIAL	furerareru/furereru	**CAUS. PASSIVE**	furesaserareru
PASSIVE	furerareru	**HONORIFIC**	ofure ni naru/ furerareru
CAUSATIVE	furesaseru	**HUMBLE**	ofure suru

Examples:

1. *Kono botan ni fureru to, doa ga akimasu.*
   このボタンに触れると、ドアが開きます。
   The door opens when you touch this button.

2. *Tenjihin ni te o furenaide kudasai.*
   展示品に手を触れないで下さい。
   Please do not touch articles on display.

3. *Sono wadai ni wa furenai hō ga ii.*
   その話題には触れないほうがいい。
   You should not mention that topic.

4. *Michi de sono kanban ga me ni fureta.*
   道でその看板が目に触れた。
   I was attracted by the sign on the street.

5. *Hō ni fureru yō na kōi wa shita koto ga nai.*
   法に触れるような行為はしたことがない。
   I have never done anything to break the law.

furu ふる

降る to fall: (intrans.); * 振る to wave, to reject, to attach: (trans.)

		Affirmative	*Negative*
PLAIN FORM	PRESENT	furu	furanai
	PAST	futta	furanakatta
MASU FORM	PRESENT	furimasu	furimasen
	PAST	furimashita	furimasen deshita
TE FORM		futte	furanakute
CONDITIONAL	PLAIN	fureba/futta ra	furanakereba/furanakatta ra
	FORMAL	furimashita ra	furimasen deshita ra
VOLITIONAL	PLAIN	furō	–
	FORMAL	furimashō	–
IMPERATIVE		fure	furu na

	Affirmative		*Affirmative*
POTENTIAL	fureru	**CAUS. PASSIVE**	furaserareru/furasareru
PASSIVE	furareru	**HONORIFIC**	ofuri ni naru/furareru
CAUSATIVE	furaseru	**HUMBLE**	ofuri suru

Examples:

1. *Yuki ga futte imasu.*
   雪が降っています。
   It's snowing.

2. *Ame ni furarete bishonure desu.*
   雨に降られて、びしょぬれです。
   I was caught in the rain and got drenched.

3. *Kanojo wa te o futte, sayōnara to itta.*
   彼女は手を振って、さようならと言った。
   She waved her hand and said "good-bye."

4. *Kare wa kanojo ni furarete, ochikonde imasu.*
   彼は彼女に振られて、落ち込んでいます。
   Because he was rejected by her, he is depressed.

5. *Kanji ni kana o futte kuremasen ka.*
   漢字にかなを振ってくれませんか。
   Would you attach *kana* to the Kanji characters?

* In general, the intransitive *furu* 降る meaning "to fall" does not use the volitional, potential, honorific, humble, or causative passive forms.

futoru ふとる

太る to put on weight: (intrans.)

		Affirmative	Negative
PLAIN FORM	PRESENT	futoru	futoranai
	PAST	futotta	futoranakatta
MASU FORM	PRESENT	futorimasu	futorimasen
	PAST	futorimashita	futorimasen deshita
TE FORM		futotte	futoranakute
CONDITIONAL	PLAIN	futoreba/futotta ra	futoranakereba/ futoranakatta ra
	FORMAL	futorimashita ra	futorimasen deshita ra
VOLITIONAL	PLAIN	futorō	–
	FORMAL	futorimashō	–
IMPERATIVE		futore	futoru na

	Affirmative		Affirmative
POTENTIAL	futoreru	**CAUS. PASSIVE**	futoraserareru/ futorasareru
PASSIVE	futorareru	**HONORIFIC**	ofutori ni naru/ futorareru
CAUSATIVE	futoraseru	**HUMBLE**	(ofutori suru)

Examples:

1. *Tabe-sugite, chotto futotte shimaimashita.*
   食べ過ぎて、ちょっと太ってしまいました。
   I overate and have gained a little weight.

2. *Tanaka-san wa futotte imasu.*
   田中さんは太っています。
   Mr. Tanaka is fat.

3. *Kore ijō futoranai yō ni, undo o hajimeta.*
   これ以上太らないように、運動を始めた。
   I started exercising in order not to gain more weight.

4. *Mō sukoshi futotta hō ga ii desu yo.*
   もう少し太ったほうがいいですよ。
   You should put on a little more weight.

5. *Kanojo wa futotta neko o katte iru.*
   彼女は太った猫を飼っている。
   She keeps a fat cat.

fuyasu ふやす

増やす to increase: (trans.)

		Affirmative	Negative
PLAIN FORM	PRESENT	fuyasu	fuyasanai
	PAST	fuyashita	fuyasanakatta
MASU FORM	PRESENT	fuyashimasu	fuyashimasen
	PAST	fuyashimashita	fuyashimasen deshita
TE FORM		fuyashite	fuyasanakute
CONDITIONAL	PLAIN	fuyaseba/fuyashita ra	fuyasanakereba/ fuyasanakatta ra
	FORMAL	fuyashimashita ra	fuyashimasen desnita ra
VOLITIONAL	PLAIN	fuyasō	–
	FORMAL	fuyashimashō	–
IMPERATIVE		fuyase	fuyasu na

	Affirmative		Affirmative
POTENTIAL	fuyaseru	**CAUS. PASSIVE**	fuyasaserareru
PASSIVE	fuyasareru	**HONORIFIC**	ofuyashi ni naru/ fuyasareru
CAUSATIVE	fuyasaseru	**HUMBLE**	ofuyashi suru

Examples:

1. *Motto Nihon-go no goi o fuyashi-tai.*
   もっと日本語の語彙を増やしたい。
   I want to increase my Japanese vocabulary even more.

2. *Gakkō wa Nihon-go no kurasu o mō hitotsu fuyashimashita.*
   学校は日本語のクラスをもう一つ増やしました。
   The school added one more Japanese class.

3. *Kore ijō shigoto o fuyasanaide kudasai.*
   これ以上、仕事を増やさないでください。
   Don't give me any more work, please.

4. *Musuko wa motto kozukai o fuyashite hoshii to itta.*
   息子はもっと小遣いを増やしてほしいと言った。
   My son asked me to increase his allowance.

5. *Benkyō no jikan o fuyashita hō ga ii.*
   勉強の時間を増やしたほうがいい。
   You should increase your study time.

ganbaru がんばる

頑張る to hold out, do one's best: (intrans.)

		Affirmative	*Negative*
PLAIN FORM	PRESENT	ganbaru	ganbaranai
	PAST	ganbatta	ganbaranakatta
MASU FORM	PRESENT	ganbarimasu	ganbarimasen
	PAST	ganbarimashita	ganbarimasen deshita
TE FORM		ganbatte	ganbaranakute
CONDITIONAL	PLAIN	ganbareba/ganbatta ra	ganbaranakereba/ ganbaranakatta ra
	FORMAL	ganbarimashita ra	ganbarimasen deshita ra
VOLITIONAL	PLAIN	ganbarō	–
	FORMAL	ganbarimashō	–
IMPERATIVE		ganbare	ganbaru na

	Affirmative		*Affirmative*
POTENTIAL	ganbareru	**CAUS. PASSIVE**	ganbaraserareru/ ganbarasareru
PASSIVE	ganbarareru	**HONORIFIC**	(oganbari ni naru)/ ganbarareru
CAUSATIVE	ganbaraseru	**HUMBLE**	(oganbari suru)

Examples:

1. *Ganbatte kudasai.*
   頑張ってください。
   Do your best. / Cheer up.

2. *Ganbare!*
   頑張れ。
   Hold out!

3. *Kare wa kazoku no tame ni ganbatte hataraite iru.*
   彼は家族のために頑張って働いている。
   He works hard for his family.

4. *Shigoto wa taihen desu ga, ganbari-tai to omoimasu.*
   仕事は大変ですが、頑張りたいと思います。
   The job is hard, but I'll do my best.

5. *Akiramezu ni, saigo made ganbarō.*
   あきらめずに、最後まで頑張ろう。
   Let's do our best without giving up.

gozaru ござる

ござる to be: * (intrans.)

		Affirmative	*Negative*
PLAIN FORM	PRESENT	*(gozaru)*	*(gozaranai)*
	PAST	*(gozatta)*	*(gozaranakatta)*
MASU FORM	PRESENT	*gozaimasu***	*gozaimasen*
	PAST	*gozaimashita*	*gozaimasen deshita*
TE FORM		*(gozatte)*	*(gozaranakute)*
CONDITIONAL	PLAIN	*(gozareba)/(gozatta ra)*	*(gozaranakereba)/ (gozaranakatta ra)*
	FORMAL	*gozaimashita ra*	*gozaimasen deshita ra*
VOLITIONAL	PLAIN	*(gozarō)*	–
	FORMAL	*gozaimashō*	–
IMPERATIVE		–	

	Affirmative		*Affirmative*
POTENTIAL	–	**CAUS. PASSIVE**	–
PASSIVE	–	**HONORIFIC**	–
CAUSATIVE	–	**HUMBLE**	–

Examples:

1. *Denwa wa doko ni gozaimasu ka.*
   電話はどこにございますか。
   Where is a telephone? [That is, "where can I find a telephone?"]

   Nikai *ni gozaimasu.*
   二階にございます。
   On the second floor.

2. *Shitsurei desu ga, Yamada sensei de wa gozaimasen ka.*
   失礼ですが、山田先生ではございませんか。
   Excuse me, but would you be Professor Yamada?

   Hai, *Yamada de gozaimasu ga, dochira-sama desu ka.*
   はい、山田でございますが、どちら様ですか。
   Yes, I am Yamada. And may I ask who you are?

3. *Arigatō gozaimasu.*
   ありがとうございます。
   Thank you.

* In modern day Japanese, *gozaru* ござる most often is used as the humble equivalent of *aru* and *de aru*, but occasionally it is used as the humble equivalent of *iru, kuru,* and *iku.*

**For euphonic reasons, *gozaimasu* is used rather than *gozarimasu.*

hairu はいる

入る to enter, join, contain, accommodate: (intrans.)

		Affirmative	*Negative*
PLAIN FORM	PRESENT	hairu	hairanai
	PAST	haitta	hairanakatta
MASU FORM	PRESENT	hairimasu	hairimasen
	PAST	hairimashita	hairimasen deshita
TE FORM		haitte	hairanakute
CONDITIONAL	PLAIN	haireba/haitta ra	hairanakereba/ hairanakatta ra
	FORMAL	hairimashita ra	hairimasen desnita ra
VOLITIONAL	PLAIN	hairō	–
	FORMAL	hairimashō	–
IMPERATIVE		haire	hairu na

	Affirmative		*Affirmative*
POTENTIAL	haireru	**CAUS. PASSIVE**	hairaserareru/ hairasareru
PASSIVE	hairareru	**HONORIFIC**	ohairi ni naru/ hairareru
CAUSATIVE	hairaseru	**HUMBLE**	ohairi suru

Examples:

1. *Heya ni haitte mo ii desu ka. / Dōzo ohairi kudasai.*
   部屋に入ってもいいですか。/ どうぞお入りください。
   May I come in the room? / Come in, please.

2. *Kissaten ni haitte, kōhii demo nomimashō.*
   喫茶店に入って、コーヒーでも飲みましょう。
   Let's go to a coffee shop and drink a cup of coffee.

3. *Jikan ga areba, supōtsu kurabu ni hairi-tai.*
   時間があれば、スポーツクラブに入りたい。
   If I have time, I'd like to join a sports club.

4. *Kono hako ni nani ga haitte iru no?*
   この箱に何が入っているの。
   What's in this box?

5. *Kono yakyūjō wa san-man nin haire masu.*
   この野球場は三万人入れます。
   This ballpark can accommodate 30,000 people.

hajimaru はじまる

始まる to begin, start, break out: (intrans.)

		Affirmative	Negative
PLAIN FORM	PRESENT	hajimaru	hajimaranai
	PAST	hajimatta	hajimaranakatta
MASU FORM	PRESENT	hajimarimasu	hajimarimasen
	PAST	hajimarimashita	hajimarimasen deshita
TE FORM		hajimatte	hajimaranakute
CONDITIONAL	PLAIN	hajimareba/hajimatta ra	hajimaranakereba/ hajimaranakatta ra
	FORMAL	hajimarimashita ra	hajimarimasen deshita ra
VOLITIONAL	PLAIN	hajimarō	–
	FORMAL	hajimarimashō	–
IMPERATIVE		hajimare	hajimaru na

	Affirmative		Affirmative
POTENTIAL	hajimareru	**CAUS. PASSIVE**	hajimaraserareru/ hajimarasareru
PASSIVE	hajimarareru	**HONORIFIC**	ohajimari ni naru/ hajimarareru
CAUSATIVE	hajimaraseru	**HUMBLE**	(ohajimari suru)

Examples:

1. *Eiga wa nan-ji ni hajimarimasu ka.*
   映画は何時に始まりますか。
   What time does the movie start?

2. *Kaigi wa mō hajimatte imasu.*
   会議はもう始まっています。
   The meeting has already begun.

3. *Yakyū no shiai wa ima hajimatta tokoro desu.*
   野球の試合は今始まったところです。
   The baseball game has just begun.

4. *Jugyō ga hajimaru mae ni, sensei ni shitsumon shimashita.*
   授業が始まる前に、先生に質問しました。
   I asked my teacher some questions before my class began.

5. *Sunde shimatta koto o kōkai shite mo hajimaranai.*
   済んでしまった事を後悔しても始まらない。
   "It's no use crying over spilt milk."

hajimeru はじめる

GROUP 2

始める to begin, open: (trans.)

		Affirmative	Negative
PLAIN FORM	PRESENT	hajimeru	hajimenai
	PAST	hajimeta	hajimenakatta
MASU FORM	PRESENT	hajimemasu	hajimemasen
	PAST	hajimemashita	hajimemasen deshita
TE FORM		hajimete	hajimenakute
CONDITIONAL	PLAIN	hajimereba/hajimeta ra	hajimenakereba/ hajimenakatta ra
	FORMAL	hajimemashita ra	hajimemasen deshita ra
VOLITIONAL	PLAIN	hajimeyō	–
	FORMAL	hajimemashō	–
IMPERATIVE		hajimero	hajimeru na

	Affirmative		Affirmative
POTENTIAL	hajimerareru/ hajimereru	**CAUS. PASSIVE**	hajimesaserareru
PASSIVE	hajimerareru	**HONORIFIC**	ohajime ni naru/ hajimerareru
CAUSATIVE	hajimesaseru	**HUMBLE**	ohajime suru

Examples:

1. *Benkyō o hajimemashō.*
   勉強を始めましょう。
   Let's start studying.

2. *Jū-ji ni kaigi o hajimemasu.*
   十時に会議を始めます。
   We'll have a meeting at ten o'clock.

3. *Nani kara hajimemashō ka.*
   何から始めましょうか。
   What shall we begin with?

4. *Bōeki no shigoto o hajimeyō to omotte imasu.*
   貿易の仕事を始めようと思っています。
   I intend to begin a trading business.

5. *Hon o yomi-hajimeru to, jikan o wasurete-shimau.*
   本を読み始めると、時間を忘れてしまう。
   I lose track of time when I start reading a book.

hakaru はかる

測る or 量る or 計る to measure; weigh; 図る to attempt, deceive: (both trans.)

		Affirmative	*Negative*
PLAIN FORM	PRESENT	hakaru	hakaranai
	PAST	hakatta	hakaranakatta
MASU FORM	PRESENT	hakarimasu	hakarimasen
	PAST	hakarimashita	hakarimasen deshita
TE FORM		hakatte	hakaranakute
CONDITIONAL	PLAIN	hakareba/hakatta ra	hakaranakereba/ hakaranakatta ra
	FORMAL	hakarimashita ra	hakarimasen deshita ra
VOLITIONAL	PLAIN	hakarō	–
	FORMAL	hakarimashō	–
IMPERATIVE		hakare	hakaru na

	Affirmative		*Affirmative*
POTENTIAL	hakareru	**CAUS. PASSIVE**	hakaraserareru/ hakarasareru
PASSIVE	hakarareru	**HONORIFIC**	ohakari ni naru/ hakarareru
CAUSATIVE	hakaraseru	**HUMBLE**	ohakari suru

Examples:

1. *Taijū o hakarimashita.*
   体重を量りました。
   I weighed myself.

2. *Samuke ga suru kara, netsu o hakatte mita.*
   寒気がするから、熱を測ってみた。
   Because I felt chilly, I checked my temperature.

3. *Kozutsumi no omosa o hakatte itadakemasen ka.*
   小包の重さを量っていただけませんか。
   Would you weigh this parcel?

4. *Nagasa o hakaru.*
   長さを測る。
   I measure the length.

5. *Heiwa-teki na kaiketsu o hakaru beki da.*
   平和的な解決を図るべきだ。
   We should work together for a peaceful solution.

hakobu はこぶ

運ぶ to carry: (trans.)

			Affirmative	*Negative*
PLAIN FORM	PRESENT		hakobu	hakobanai
	PAST		hakonda	hakobanakatta
MASU FORM	PRESENT		hakobimasu	hakobimasen
	PAST		hakobimashita	hakobimasen deshita
TE FORM			hakonde	hakobanakute
CONDITIONAL	PLAIN		hakobeba/hakondara	hakobanakereba/ hakobanakatta ra
	FORMAL		hakobimashita ra	hakobimasen deshita ra
VOLITIONAL	PLAIN		hakobō	–
	FORMAL		hakobimashō	–
IMPERATIVE			hakobe	hakobu na

	Affirmative		*Affirmative*
POTENTIAL	hakoberu	**CAUS. PASSIVE**	hakobaserareru/ hakobasareru
PASSIVE	hakobareru	**HONORIFIC**	ohakobi ni naru/ hakobareru
CAUSATIVE	hakobaseru	**HUMBLE**	ohakobi suru

Examples:

1. *Kono kaban o heya ni hakonde kudasai.*
   このかばんを部屋に運んでください。
   Please carry this bag to the room.

2. *Hikkoshi no nimotsu o hakobu no o tomodachi ni tetsudatte moratta.*
   引っ越しの荷物を運ぶのを友達に手伝ってもらった。
   I had my friend help me move my laggage to my new place.

3. *Kōtsūjiko de kega o shita hito ga kyūkyūsha de byōin e hakobareta.*
   交通事故でけがをした人が救急車で病院へ運ばれた。
   A person hurt in a traffic accident was transported to the hospital by ambulance.

4. *Kono ōkii hako wa hitori de hakobe sō mo nai.*
   この大きい箱は一人で運べそうもない。
   I doubt I could carry this big box alone.

5. *Ane to kaimono ni itte, omoi nimotsu o hakobasareta.*
   姉と買い物に行って、重い荷物を運ばされた。
   I went shopping with my elder sister and was made to carry heavy baggage.

haku はく

履く to put on (footwear); 吐く to vomit, breathe out; 掃く to sweep: (all trans.)

		Affirmative	Negative
PLAIN FORM	PRESENT	haku	haita
	PAST	hakanai	hakanakatta
MASU FORM	PRESENT	hakimasu	hakimasen
	PAST	hakimashita	hakimasen deshita
TE FORM		haite	hakanakute
CONDITIONAL	PLAIN	hakeba/haita ra	hakanakereba/ hakanakatta ra
	FORMAL	hakimashita ra	hakimasen deshita ra
VOLITIONAL	PLAIN	hakō	–
	FORMAL	hakimashō	–
IMPERATIVE		hake	haku na

	Affirmative		Affirmative
POTENTIAL	hakeru	**CAUS. PASSIVE**	hakaserareru/hakasareru
PASSIVE	hakareru	**HONORIFIC**	ohaki ni naru/ hakareru
CAUSATIVE	hakaseru	**HUMBLE**	ohaki suru

Examples:

1. *Kyō kanojo wa atarashii suniikā o haite imasu.*
   今日、彼女は新しいスニーカーを履いています。
   She wears new sneakers today.

2. *Kono kutsu o haite mite mo ii desu ka.*
   この靴を履いてみてもいいですか。
   May I try on these shoes?

3. *Kibun ga warukute, haite shimaimashita.*
   気分が悪くて、吐いてしまいました。
   I felt sick and threw up.

4. *Iki o sutte, yukkuri haite kudasai.*
   息を吸って、ゆっくり吐いてください。
   Please breathe in and out slowly.

5. *Yuka o hōki de haita.*
   床をほうきで掃いた。
   I swept the floor with a broom.

hanasu はなす

話す to speak; 離す to keep away; 放す to set free, let go: (all trans.)

		Affirmative	Negative
PLAIN FORM	PRESENT	hanasu	hanasanai
	PAST	hanashita	hanasanakatta
MASU FORM	PRESENT	hanashimasu	hanashimasen
	PAST	hanashimashita	hanashimasen deshita
TE FORM		hanashite	hanasanakute
CONDITIONAL	PLAIN	hanaseba/hanashita ra	hanasanakereba/ hanasanakatta ra
	FORMAL	hanashimashita ra	hanashimasen deshita ra
VOLITIONAL	PLAIN	hanasō	–
	FORMAL	hanashimashō	–
IMPERATIVE		hanase	hanasu na

	Affirmative		Affirmative
POTENTIAL	hanaseru	**CAUS. PASSIVE**	hanasaserareru
PASSIVE	hanasareru	**HONORIFIC**	ohanashi ni naru/ hanasareru
CAUSATIVE	hanasaseru	**HUMBLE**	ohanashi suru

Examples:

1. *Jon wa Nihon-go ga hanasemasu.*
   ジョンは日本語が話せます。
   John can speak Japanese.

2. *Sumimasen ga, mō sukoshi yukkuri hanashite itadakemasen ka.*
   すみませんが、もう少しゆっくり話していただけませんか。
   Excuse me, but could you please speak a little more slowly?

3. *Yamada-san to wa hanashita koto ga arimasen.*
   山田さんとは話したことがありません。
   I have never spoken to Mr. Yamada.

4. *Gomen nasai. Ima shigoto de te ga hanasemasen.*
   ごめんなさい。今仕事で手が離せません。
   I'm sorry. Right now, I'm too busy to do it. (lit., can't free my hands)

5. *Kono kōen de inu o hanashite wa ikemasen.*
   この公園で犬を放してはいけません。
   You must not let go of your dog in this park.

harau はらう

払う to pay, sweep, wipe, pay attention: (trans.)

		Affirmative	Negative
PLAIN FORM	PRESENT	harau	harawanai
	PAST	haratta	harawanakatta
MASU FORM	PRESENT	haraimasu	haraimasen
	PAST	haraimashita	haraimasen deshita
TE FORM		haratte	harawanakute
CONDITIONAL	PLAIN	haraeba/haratta ra	harawanakereba/ harawanakatta ra
	FORMAL	haraimashita ra	haraimasen deshita ra
VOLITIONAL	PLAIN	haraō	–
	FORMAL	haraimashō	–
IMPERATIVE		harae	harau na

	Affirmative		Affirmative
POTENTIAL	haraeru	CAUS. PASSIVE	harawaserareru/ harawasareru
PASSIVE	harawareru	HONORIFIC	oharai ni naru/ harawareru
CAUSATIVE	harawaseru	HUMBLE	oharai suru

Examples:

1. *Maitsuki, getsumatsu ni yachin o haraimasu.*
   毎月、月末に家賃を払います。
   I pay my rent at the end of every month.

2. *Kādo de haratte mo ii desu ka.*
   カードで払ってもいいですか。
   May I pay with my credit card?

3. *Kono mise no daikin wa watashi ni harawasete kudasai.*
   この店の代金は私に払わせてください。
   Let me pay for what you bought at this store.

4. *Sonna takai okane, totemo watashi ni wa haraenai.*
   そんな高いお金、とても私には払えない。
   There is no way I can pay that much.

5. *Unten suru toki, hokōsha ni chūi o harau yō ni.*
   運転する時、歩行者に注意を払うように。
   When you drive a car, pay attention to the pedestrians.

hareru はれる

晴れる to clear up, be dispelled;* 腫れる to swell: (both intrans.)

		Affirmative	*Negative*
PLAIN FORM	PRESENT	*hareru*	*harenai*
	PAST	*hareta*	*harenakatta*
MASU FORM	PRESENT	*haremasu*	*haremasen*
	PAST	*haremashita*	*haremasen deshita*
TE FORM		*harete*	*harenakute*
CONDITIONAL	PLAIN	*harereba/hareta ra*	*harenakereba/ harenakatta ra*
	FORMAL	*haremashita ra*	*haremasen deshita ra*
VOLITIONAL	PLAIN	*hareyō*	–
	FORMAL	*haremashō*	–
IMPERATIVE		*harero*	*hareru na*

	Affirmative		*Affirmative*
POTENTIAL	*harerareru/harereru*	**CAUS. PASSIVE**	*haresaserareru*
PASSIVE	*harerareru*	**HONORIFIC**	*ohare ni naru/ harerareru*
CAUSATIVE	*haresaseru*	**HUMBLE**	*(ohare suru)*

Examples:

1. *Tabun ashita wa hareru deshō.*
   たぶん明日は晴れるでしょう。
   It will probably be nice weather tomorrow.

2. *Gogo wa hareta-ri kumotta-ri deshita.*
   午後は晴れたり曇ったりでした。
   It was alternately fair and cloudy in the afternoon.

3. *Kiri ga hare-sō desu.*
   霧が晴れそうです。
   The fog seems to be lifting.

4. *Kare wa satsujin no yōgi ga hareta.*
   彼は殺人の容疑が晴れた。
   He was cleared of the murder charge.

5. *Kega o shita ashikubi ga harete iru.*
   けがをした足首が腫れている。
   My injured ankle is swollen.

---

* Besides those forms listed above, the verb *hareru* 晴れる meaning "to clear up" generally has no honorific, causative, or causative passive forms.

haru はる

はる to stick (trans.); 張る to pitch, stretch, extend: (trans. & intrans.)

		Affirmative	*Negative*
PLAIN FORM	PRESENT	haru	haranai
	PAST	hatta	haranakatta
MASU FORM	PRESENT	harimasu	harimasen
	PAST	harimashita	harimasen deshita
TE FORM		hatte	haranakute
CONDITIONAL	PLAIN	hareba/hatta ra	haranakereba/ haranakatta ra
	FORMAL	harimashita ra	harimasen deshita ra
VOLITIONAL	PLAIN	harō	–
	FORMAL	harimashō	–
IMPERATIVE		hare	haru na

	Affirmative		*Affirmative*
POTENTIAL	hareru	**CAUS. PASSIVE**	haraserareru/harasareru
PASSIVE	harareru	**HONORIFIC**	ohari ni naru/ harareru
CAUSATIVE	haraseru	**HUMBLE**	ohari suru

Examples:

1. *Fūtō ni kitte o hatta.*
   封筒に切手をはった。
   I stuck a stamp on the envelope.

2. *Kabe ni posutā ga hatte aru.*
   壁にポスターがはってある。
   A poster has been posted on the wall.

3. *Watashi-tachi wa kawara de tento o hatta.*
   私たちは河原でテントを張った。
   We pitched a tent by the riverside.

4. *Beranda ni rōpu o hatte, sentakumono o hoshita.*
   ベランダにロープを張って、洗濯物を干した。
   I strung a clothesline across the balcony and hung up the laundry.

5. *Kōen no ike ni kōri ga hatte iru.*
   公園の池に氷が張っている。
   The pond in the park is frozen.

hashiru はしる

走る to run: (intrans.)*

		Affirmative	*Negative*
PLAIN FORM	PRESENT	hashiru	hashiranai
	PAST	hashitta	hashiranakatta
MASU FORM	PRESENT	hashirimasu	hashirimasen
	PAST	hashirimashita	hashirimasen deshita
TE FORM		hashitte	hashiranakute
CONDITIONAL	PLAIN	hashireba/hashitta ra	hashiranakereba/ hashiranakatta ra
	FORMAL	hashirimashita ra	hashirimasen deshita ra
VOLITIONAL	PLAIN	hashirō	–
	FORMAL	hashirimashō	–
IMPERATIVE		hashire	hashiru na

	Affirmative		*Affirmative*
POTENTIAL	hashireru	**CAUS. PASSIVE**	hashiraserareru/ hashirasareru
PASSIVE	hashirareru	**HONORIFIC**	ohashiri ni naru/ hashirareru
CAUSATIVE	hashiraseru	**HUMBLE**	(ohashiri suru)

Examples:

1. *Jikan ga nakatta kara, eki made hashirimashita.*
   時間がなかったから、駅まで走りました。
   I was running out of time so I ran to the station.

2. *Rōka o hashiru na.*
   廊下を走るな。
   Don't run in the corridor!

3. *Ashi ga itakute, hashirenai.*
   足が痛くて、走れない。
   My leg hurts so I cannot run.

4. *Gakusei no toki, yoku sensei ni kōtei o hashirasareta.*
   学生の時、よく先生に校庭を走らされた。
   When I was a student, I was often made to run around the school grounds by my teacher.

5. *Eki kara sono kyōgijō made basu ga hashitte imasu.*
   駅からその競技場までバスが走っています。
   A bus runs from the station to the stadium.

---

* As with other verbs indicating movement, *hashiru* 走る may take a direct object, thus giving an idea of "going through a defined area." (See examples 2 and 4.)

hataraku はたらく

働く to work, operate by: (intrans.); commit a crime: (trans.)

		Affirmative	*Negative*
PLAIN FORM	PRESENT	hataraku	hatarakanai
	PAST	hataraita	hatarakanakatta
MASU FORM	PRESENT	hatarakimasu	hatarakimasen
	PAST	hatarakimashita	hatarakimasen deshita
TE FORM		hataraite	hatarakanakute
CONDITIONAL	PLAIN	hatarakeba/hataraita ra	hatarakanakereba/ hatarakanakatta ra
	FORMAL	hatarakimashita ra	hatarakimasen deshita ra
VOLITIONAL	PLAIN	hatarakō	–
	FORMAL	hatarakimashō	–
IMPERATIVE		hatarake	hataraku na

	Affirmative		*Affirmative*
POTENTIAL	hatarakeru	**CAUS. PASSIVE**	hatarakaserareru/ hatarakasareru
PASSIVE	hatarakareru	**HONORIFIC**	ohataraki ni naru/ hatarakareru
CAUSATIVE	hatarakaseru	**HUMBLE**	ohataraki suru

Examples:

1. *Tanaka-san wa ku-ji kara go-ji made hatarakimasu.*
   田中さんは九時から五時まで働きます。
   Mr. Tanaka works from nine to five.

2. *Suzuki-san wa bōeki-gaisha de hataraite imasu.*
   鈴木さんは貿易会社で働いています。
   Mr. Suzuki works at a trading company.

3. *Kare wa hataraki-nagara daigaku o deta.*
   彼は働きながら大学を出た。
   He graduated from a university while working.

4. *Kyō wa dōmo atama ga hatarakanai.*
   今日はどうも頭が働かない。
   Somehow my brain doesn't seem to function today.

5. *Karera wa ginkō gōtō o hataraite, taiho sareta.*
   彼らは銀行強盗を働いて、逮捕された。
   They committed a bank robbery and were arrested.

hayaru はやる

はやる to be in fashion, popular, prevail: (intrans.)

		Affirmative	Negative
PLAIN FORM	PRESENT	hayaru	hayaranai
	PAST	hayatta	hayaranakatta
MASU FORM	PRESENT	hayarimasu	hayarimasen
	PAST	hayarimashita	hayarimasen deshita
TE FORM		hayatte	hayaranakute
CONDITIONAL	PLAIN	hayareba/hayatta ra	hayaranakereba/ hayaranakatta ra
	FORMAL	hayarimashita ra	hayarimasen deshita ra
VOLITIONAL	PLAIN	hayarō	–
	FORMAL	hayarimashō	–
IMPERATIVE		hayare	hayaru na

	Affirmative		Affirmative
POTENTIAL	hayareru	CAUS. PASSIVE	hayaraserareru/ hayarasareru
PASSIVE	hayarareru	HONORIFIC	ohayari ni naru/ hayarareru
CAUSATIVE	hayaraseru	HUMBLE	(ohayari suru)

Examples:

1. *Ima donna fasshon ga hayatte imasu ka.*
   今どんなファッションがはやっていますか。
   What kind of fashion is popular now?

2. *Kuroi fuku ga hayatte imasu.*
   黒い服が、はやっています。
   Black clothes are in fashion.

3. *Sono uta wa ni-jū nen gurai mae ni totemo hayatta.*
   その歌は、二十年ぐらい前にとてもはやった。
   That song was very popular about twenty years ago.

4. *Kotoshi no fuyu wa infuruenza ga hayaru sō da.*
   今年の冬はインフルエンザがはやるそうだ。
   I hear that there will be a breakout of influenza this winter.

5. *Ano resutoran wa totemo hayatte imasu.*
   あのレストランは、とてもはやっています。
   That restaurant is very popular.

herasu へらす

減らす to decrease, reduce: (trans.)

		Affirmative	*Negative*
PLAIN FORM	PRESENT	herasu	herasanai
	PAST	herashita	herasanakatta
MASU FORM	PRESENT	herashimasu	herashimasen
	PAST	herashimashita	herashimasen deshita
TE FORM		herashite	herasanakute
CONDITIONAL	PLAIN	heraseba/herashita ra	herasanakereba/ herasanakatta ra
	FORMAL	herashimashita ra	herashimasen deshita ra
VOLITIONAL	PLAIN	herasō	–
	FORMAL	herashimashō	–
IMPERATIVE		herase	herasu na

	Affirmative		*Affirmative*
POTENTIAL	heraseru	**CAUS. PASSIVE**	herasaserareru
PASSIVE	herasareru	**HONORIFIC**	oherashi ni naru/ herasareru
CAUSATIVE	herasaseru	**HUMBLE**	oherashi suru

Examples:

1. *Shuppi o herasanakereba naranai.*
   出費を減らさなければならない。
   We must cut down our expenses.

2. *Keiei-fushin de kyūryō ga herasaremashita.*
   経営不振で給料が減らされました。
   Because of financial difficulties, salaries were reduced.

3. *Dono kaisha mo keihi o herasu doryoku o shite iru.*
   どの会社も経費を減らす努力をしている。
   All companies are trying to cut down their expenses.

4. *Mō sukoshi taijū o herase to isha ni iwaremashita.*
   もう少し体重を減らせと医者に言われました。
   I was told by the doctor to lose a little more weight.

5. *Kodomotachi wa onaka o herashite kaette kita.*
   子供達は、おなかを減らして帰ってきた。
   My children came home hungry.

heru へる

減る to decrease: (intrans.)

		Affirmative	*Negative*
PLAIN FORM	PRESENT	heru	heranai
	PAST	hetta	heranakatta
MASU FORM	PRESENT	herimasu	herimasen
	PAST	herimashita	herimasen deshita
TE FORM		hette	heranakute
CONDITIONAL	PLAIN	hereba/hetta ra	heranakereba/ heranakatta ra
	FORMAL	herimashita ra	herimasen deshita ra
VOLITIONAL	PLAIN	herō	–
	FORMAL	herimashō	–
IMPERATIVE		here	heru na

	Affirmative		*Affirmative*
POTENTIAL	hereru	**CAUS. PASSIVE**	heraserareru/herasareru
PASSIVE	herareru	**HONORIFIC**	oheri ni naru/ herasareru
CAUSATIVE	heraseru	**HUMBLE**	(oheri suru)

Examples:

1. *Yasei dōbutsu no kazu ga hette iru.*
   野生動物の数が減っている。
   The number of wild animals is decreasing.

2. *Kyonen to kurabete, uriage ga jūgo-pāsento hetta.*
   去年と比べて、売り上げが15パーセント減った。
   Sales decreased by 15% in comparison with last year.

3. *Kanojo wa taijū ga go kiro herimashita.*
   彼女は体重が五キロ減りました。
   She lost five kilos in weight.

4. *Kaimono shi-sugite, choking ga hette shimatta.*
   買い物しすぎて、貯金が減ってしまった。
   I spent too much money on shopping so my savings have gone down a little.

5. *Hara ga hetta.*
   腹が減った。
   I'm hungry.

hiku ひく

引く to pull, draw (a line), catch (a cold), consult (a dictionary);
弾く to play (string instruments): (both trans.)

		Affirmative	*Negative*
PLAIN FORM	PRESENT	hiku	hikanai
	PAST	hiita	hikanakatta
MASU FORM	PRESENT	hikimasu	hikimasen
	PAST	hikimashita	hikimasen deshita
TE FORM		hiite	hikanakute
CONDITIONAL	PLAIN	hikeba/hiita ra	hikanakereba/ hikanakatta ra
	FORMAL	hikimashita ra	hikimasen deshita ra
VOLITIONAL	PLAIN	hikō	–
	FORMAL	hikimashō	–
IMPERATIVE		hike	hiku na

	Affirmative		*Affirmative*
POTENTIAL	hikeru	**CAUS. PASSIVE**	hikaserareru/hikasareru
PASSIVE	hikareru	**HONORIFIC**	ohiki ni naru/ hikareru
CAUSATIVE	hikaseru	**HUMBLE**	ohiki suru

Examples:

1. *Kono doa wa osanaide, hiite kudasai.*
   このドアは押さないで、引いてください。
   Don't push this door, pull it please!

2. *Mise no hito wa sono nedan kara go-pāsento hiite kureta.*
   店の人はその値段から5パーセント引いてくれた。
   The sales clerk discounted 5% from my purchase.

3. *Ima kaze o hiite imasu.*
   今風邪をひいています。
   I have a cold now.

4. *Imi ga wakaranakereba, jisho o hiki-nasai.*
   意味が分からなければ、辞書を引きなさい。
   If you don't know the meaning, look it up in a dictionary.

5. *Piano mo gitā mo sukoshi hikemasu.*
   ピアノもギターも少し弾けます。
   I can play both the piano and the guitar a little.

hirou ひろう

拾う to pick up, find: (trans.)

		Affirmative	Negative
PLAIN FORM	PRESENT	hirou	hirowanai
	PAST	hirotta	hirowanakatta
MASU FORM	PRESENT	hiroimasu	hiroimasen
	PAST	hiroimashita	hiroimasen deshita
TE FORM		hirotte	hirowanakute
CONDITIONAL	PLAIN	hiroeba/hirotta ra	hirowanakereba/ hirowanakatta ra
	FORMAL	hiroimashita ra	hiroimasen deshita ra
VOLITIONAL	PLAIN	hirooo	–
	FORMAL	hiroimashō	–
IMPERATIVE		hiroe	hirou na

	Affirmative		Affirmative
POTENTIAL	hiroeru	**CAUS. PASSIVE**	hirowaserareru/ hirowasareru
PASSIVE	hirowareru	**HONORIFIC**	ohiroi ni naru/ hirowareru
CAUSATIVE	hirowaseru	**HUMBLE**	ohiroi suru

Examples:

1. *Gomi o hirotte kudasai.*
   ごみを拾ってください。
   Please pick up the rubbish.

2. *Otoko no ko wa michi de saifu o hirotta.*
   男の子は道で財布を拾った。
   The boy found a wallet on the street.

3. *Doko ka de takushii o hirotte kaerō.*
   どこかでタクシーを拾って帰ろう。
   Let's get a taxi somewhere and go home.

4. *Tochū de tomodachi o hirotte, kūkō e mukatta.*
   途中で友達を拾って、空港へ向かった。
   On the way to the airport I picked up my friend.

5. *Shitsugyō-chū ni, shachō ni hirowareta.*
   失業中に、社長に拾われた。
   When I was unemployed, I was given work by the company president.

homeru ほめる

褒める to praise, commend: (trans.)

		Affirmative	*Negative*
PLAIN FORM	PRESENT	homeru	homenai
	PAST	hometa	homenakatta
MASU FORM	PRESENT	homemasu	homemasen
	PAST	homemashita	homemasen deshita
TE FORM		homete	homenakute
CONDITIONAL	PLAIN	homereba/hometa ra	homenakereba/ homenakatta ra
	FORMAL	homemashita ra	homemasen deshita ra
VOLITIONAL	PLAIN	homeyō	–
	FORMAL	homemashō	–
IMPERATIVE		homero	homeru na

	Affirmative		*Affirmative*
POTENTIAL	homerareru/ homereru	**CAUS. PASSIVE**	homesaserareru
PASSIVE	homerareru	**HONORIFIC**	ohome ni naru/ homerareru
CAUSATIVE	homesaseru	**HUMBLE**	ohome suru

Examples:

1. *Sensei wa seito-tachi o hometa.*
   先生は生徒達を褒めた。
   The teacher praised the students.

2. *Kare no doryoku o homete age-tai.*
   彼の努力を褒めてあげたい。
   I'd like to commend him for his efforts.

3. *Okāsan ni homerarete, sono ko wa ureshi-sō datta.*
   お母さんに褒められて、その子は嬉しそうだった。
   The child seemed to be happy when he was praised by his mother.

4. *Kanojo wa yoku anata no yasashisa o homete imasu.*
   彼女はよくあなたの優しさを褒めています。
   She often speaks well of your kindness.

5. *Sore wa amari homerareta koto ja nai.*
   それはあまり褒められたことじゃない。
   Not too much can be said for that.

ikiru いきる

生きる to live, become alive: (intrans.)

		Affirmative	*Negative*
PLAIN FORM	PRESENT	*ikiru*	*ikinai*
	PAST	*ikita*	*ikinakatta*
MASU FORM	PRESENT	*ikimasu*	*ikimasen*
	PAST	*ikimashita*	*ikimasen deshita*
TE FORM		*ikite*	*ikinakute*
CONDITIONAL	PLAIN	*ikireba/ikita ra*	*ikinakereba/ikinakatta ra*
	FORMAL	*ikimashita ra*	*ikimasen deshita ra*
VOLITIONAL	PLAIN	*ikiyō*	–
	FORMAL	*ikimashō*	–
IMPERATIVE		*ikiro*	*ikiru na*

	Affirmative		*Affirmative*
POTENTIAL	*ikirareru/ikireru*	**CAUS. PASSIVE**	*ikisaserareru*
PASSIVE	*ikirareru*	**HONORIFIC**	*oiki ni naru/ikirareru*
CAUSATIVE	*ikisaseru*	**HUMBLE**	*(oiki suru)*

Examples:

1. *Sofu wa kyū-jū-ni sai made ikita.*
   祖父は九十二歳まで生きた。
   My grandfather lived to be ninety-two.

2. *Kono sakana wa mada ikite imasu.*
   この魚はまだ生きています。
   This fish is still alive.

3. *Kare wa ikiru tameni isshōkenmei hataraita.*
   彼は生きるために一生懸命働いた。
   He worked hard to survive.

4. *Gōkaku no happyō ga aru made, ikita kokochi ga shinai.*
   合格の発表があるまで、生きた心地がしない。
   I can't settle down until test results are announced.

5. *Uwagi o muji ni shita hō ga, sono shatsu ga ikiru to omoimasu.*
   上着を無地にしたほうが、そのシャツが生きると思います。
   Solid colored jacket would go better with your shirt.

iku いく

行く to go: (intrans.)

		Affirmative	*Negative*
PLAIN FORM	PRESENT	iku	ikanai
	PAST	itta	ikanakatta
MASU FORM	PRESENT	ikimasu	ikimasen
	PAST	ikimashita	ikimasen deshita
TE FORM		itte	ikanakute
CONDITIONAL	PLAIN	ikeba/itta ra	ikanakereba/ ikanakatta ra
	FORMAL	ikimashita ra	ikimasen deshita ra
VOLITIONAL	PLAIN	ikō	–
	FORMAL	ikimashō	–
IMPERATIVE		ike	iku na

	Affirmative		*Affirmative*
POTENTIAL	ikeru	**CAUS. PASSIVE**	ikaserareru/ikasareru
PASSIVE	ikareru	**HONORIFIC**	irassharu/ikareru
CAUSATIVE	ikaseru	**HUMBLE**	mairu

Examples:

1. *Ashita ku-ji ni gakkō e ikimasu.*
   明日九時に学校へ行きます。
   I'm going to school at nine o'clock tomorrow.

2. *Kyōto e itta koto ga arimasu ka.*
   京都へ行ったことがありますか。
   Have you been to Kyoto?

3. *Kono michi o massugu itte kudasai.*
   この道をまっすぐ行ってください。
   Please go straight down this road.

4. *Isogashikute, kaimono ni ikemasen.*
   忙しくて、買い物に行けません。
   I am too busy to go shopping.

5. *Ashita tenki ga yokereba, kōen ni ikimashō.*
   明日天気が良ければ、公園に行きましょう。
   If the weather is fine, let's go to the park tomorrow.

inoru いのる

祈る to pray, hope: (trans.)

		Affirmative	Negative
PLAIN FORM	PRESENT	inoru	inoranai
	PAST	inotta	inoranakatta
MASU FORM	PRESENT	inorimasu	inorimasen
	PAST	inorimashita	inorimasen deshita
TE FORM		inotte	inoranakute
CONDITIONAL	PLAIN	inoreba/inotta ra	inoranakereba/ inoranakatta ra
	FORMAL	inorimashita ra	inorimasen deshita ra
VOLITIONAL	PLAIN	inorō	–
	FORMAL	inorimashō	–
IMPERATIVE		inore	inoru na

	Affirmative		Affirmative
POTENTIAL	inoreru	**CAUS. PASSIVE**	inoraserareru/ inorasareru
PASSIVE	inorareru	**HONORIFIC**	oinori ni naru/ inorareru
CAUSATIVE	inoraseru	**HUMBLE**	oinori suru

Examples:

1. *Maitoshi shōgatsu ni jinja de ichi-nen no shiawase o inorimasu.*
   毎年正月に神社で一年の幸せを祈ります。
   At the beginning of every year, I pray for that year's happiness at a Shinto shrine.

2. *Haha wa kodomo no byōki no kaifuku o inotta.*
   母は子供の病気の回復を祈った。
   The mother prayed for the child's recovery.

3. *Kare no kentō o inotte, kanpai shimashō.*
   彼の健闘を祈って、乾杯しましょう。
   A toast to his luck!

4. *Umaku iku yō ni inotte kudasai.*
   うまくいくように祈ってください。
   I would like you to pray for my good luck.

5. *Minna me o tojite, shisha no meifuku o inotta.*
   みんな目を閉じて、死者の冥福を祈った。
   Everybody closed their eyes and prayed that the dead person's soul may rest in peace.

irassharu いらっしゃる

いらっしゃる to go, come, to be:* (intrans.)

		Affirmative	Negative
PLAIN FORM	PRESENT	*irassharu*	*irassharanai*
	PAST	*irasshatta*	*irassharanakatta*
MASU FORM	PRESENT	*irasshaimasu***	*irasshaimasen*
	PAST	*irasshaimashita*	*irasshaimasen deshita*
TE FORM		*irasshatte*	*irassharanakute*
CONDITIONAL	PLAIN	*irasshareba/irasshatta ra*	*irassharanakereba/ irassharanakatta ra*
	FORMAL	*irasshaimashita ra*	*irasshaimasen deshita ra*
VOLITIONAL	PLAIN	*irassharō*	–
	FORMAL	*irasshaimashō*	–
IMPERATIVE		–	–

	Affirmative		Affirmative
POTENTIAL	*irasshareru*	**CAUS. PASSIVE**	–
PASSIVE	*irassharareru*	**HONORIFIC**	–
CAUSATIVE	–	**HUMBLE**	–

Examples:

1. *Sensei ga irasshatta ra, kore o watashite itadakemasen ka.*
   先生がいらっしゃったら、これを渡していただけませんか。
   When the teacher comes, could you hand this to him?

2. *Shachō wa raishū Rondon e irassharu deshō.*
   社長は来週ロンドンへいらっしゃるでしょう。
   The company president is probably going to London next week.

3. *Yamada-san, irasshaimasu ka. / Hai, watashi desu ga…*
   山田さん、いらっしゃいますか。/ はい、私ですが。
   Is Miss Yamada there? / Yes, speaking…

4. *Suzuki-sensei wa musuko-san ga futari irassharu sō desu.*
   鈴木先生は息子さんが二人いらっしゃるそうです。
   I heard that Professor Suzuki has two sons.

5. *Asu wa otaku ni irasshaimasu ka.*
   明日はお宅にいらっしゃいますか。
   Will you be at home tomorrow?

* *Irassharu* いらっしゃる is the honorific equivalent of *iku, kuru, iru,* and *aru*.

** For euphonic reasons, *irasshaimasu* is used rather than *irassharimasu*.

ireru いれる

入れる to put in, include, pour in: (trans.)

		Affirmative	*Negative*
PLAIN FORM	PRESENT	ireru	irenai
	PAST	ireta	irenakatta
MASU FORM	PRESENT	iremasu	iremasen
	PAST	iremashita	iremasen deshita
TE FORM		irete	irenakute
CONDITIONAL	PLAIN	irereba/ireta ra	irenakereba/ irenakatta ra
	FORMAL	iremashita ra	iremasen deshita ra
VOLITIONAL	PLAIN	ireyō	–
	FORMAL	iremashō	–
IMPERATIVE		irero	ireru na

	Affirmative		*Affirmative*
POTENTIAL	irerareru/irereru	**CAUS. PASSIVE**	iresaserareru
PASSIVE	irerareru	**HONORIFIC**	oire ni naru/irerareru
CAUSATIVE	iresaseru	**HUMBLE**	oire suru

Examples:

1. *Kōhii ni satō ka miruku o iremasu ka.*
   コーヒーに砂糖かミルクを入れますか。
   Will you put sugar or milk in the coffee?

2. *Terebi no suitchi o irete kudasai.*
   テレビのスイッチを入れてください。
   Please turn on the TV.

3. *Kippu wa uwagi no poketto ni irete aru.*
   切符は上着のポケットに入れてある。
   The ticket is in my jacket pocket.

4. *Shain wa watashi o irete, ni-jū-go nin desu.*
   社員は私を入れて、二十五人です。
   There are twenty-five people, including me, on the staff of this company.

5. *Ocha o oire shimashō ka.*
   お茶をお入れしましょうか。
   Shall I make tea for you?

iru いる

居る to be, stay; いる to keep, be doing:* (both intrans.)

		Affirmative	*Negative*
PLAIN FORM	PRESENT	iru	inai
	PAST	ita	inakatta
MASU FORM	PRESENT	imasu	imasen
	PAST	imashita	imasen deshita
TE FORM		ite	inakute
CONDITIONAL	PLAIN	ireba/ita ra	inakereba/inakatta ra
	FORMAL	imashita ra	imasen deshita ra
VOLITIONAL	PLAIN	iyō	–
	FORMAL	imashō	–
IMPERATIVE		iro	iru na

	Affirmative		*Affirmative*
POTENTIAL	irareru/ireru	**CAUS. PASSIVE**	isaserareru
PASSIVE	irareru	**HONORIFIC**	irassharu/irareru
CAUSATIVE	isaseru	**HUMBLE**	oru

Examples:

1. *Asoko ni Mori-san ga imasu.*
   あそこに森さんがいます。
   Mr. Mori is over there.

2. *Tōkyō ni dono gurai iru yotei desu ka.*
   東京にどのぐらいいる予定ですか。
   How long do you plan to stay in Tokyo?

3. *Watashi wa imōto ga hitori imasu.*
   私は妹が一人います。
   I have one younger sister.

4. *Ima nani o shite imasu ka.*
   今何をしていますか。
   What are you doing now?

5. *Ie o deta toki, ame ga futte ita.*
   家を出た時、雨が降っていた。
   It was raining when I left home.

* Used in conjunction with other verbs to form the present and past progressive tenses. (See examples 4 and 5.)

iru いる

要る to need: (intrans.)

		Affirmative	Negative
PLAIN FORM	PRESENT	iru	iranai
	PAST	itta	iranakatta
MASU FORM	PRESENT	irimasu	irimasen
	PAST	irimashita	irimasen deshita
TE FORM		itte	iranakute
CONDITIONAL	PLAIN	ireba/itta ra	iranakereba/iranakatta ra
	FORMAL	irimashita ra	irimasen deshita ra
VOLITIONAL	PLAIN	(irō)	–
	FORMAL	(irimashō)	–
IMPERATIVE		(ire)	(iru na)

	Affirmative		Affirmative
POTENTIAL	(ireru)	**CAUS. PASSIVE**	(iraserareru)
PASSIVE	(irareru)	**HONORIFIC**	oiri ni naru/irareru
CAUSATIVE	(iraseru)	**HUMBLE**	(oiri suru)

Examples:

1. *Atarashii kutsu ga irimasu.*
   新しい靴が要ります。
   I need new shoes.

2. *Shukudai o suru no ni jisho ga iru.*
   宿題をするのに辞書が要る。
   I need a dictionary for my homework.

3. *Hoka ni nani ka iru mono ga arimasu ka. / Iie, mō nani mo irimasen.*
   ほかに何か要る物がありますか。 / いいえ、もう何も要りません。
   Is there anything else you need? / No, I don't need anything else.

4. *Sono hon ga iranakereba, watashi ni kuremasen ka.*
   その本が要らなければ、私にくれませんか。
   If you don't need that book, would you give it to me?

5. *Hikkoshi suru toki, iranai mono o suteta.*
   引っ越しする時、要らない物を捨てた。
   When I moved, I threw away all of my unnecessary things.

isogu いそぐ

急ぐ to hurry: (intrans. and trans.)

		Affirmative	*Negative*
PLAIN FORM	PRESENT	*isogu*	*isoganai*
	PAST	*isoida*	*isoganakatta*
MASU FORM	PRESENT	*isogimasu*	*isogimasen*
	PAST	*isogimashita*	*isogimasen deshita*
TE FORM		*isoide*	*isoganakute*
CONDITIONAL	PLAIN	*isogeba/isoida ra*	*isoganakereba/ isoganakatta ra*
	FORMAL	*isogimashita ra*	*isogimasen deshita ra*
VOLITIONAL	PLAIN	*isogō*	–
	FORMAL	*isogimashō*	–
IMPERATIVE		*isoge*	*isogu na*

	Affirmative		*Affirmative*
POTENTIAL	*isogeru*	**CAUS. PASSIVE**	*isogaserareru/ isogasareru*
PASSIVE	*isogareru*	**HONORIFIC**	*oisogi ni naru/ isogareru*
CAUSATIVE	*isogaseru*	**HUMBLE**	*oisogi suru*

Examples:

1. *Eki e isogō.*
   駅へ急ごう。
   Let's hurry to the station.

2. *Isoganai to, maniawanai.*
   急がないと、間に合わない。
   If we don't hurry, we won't be on time.

3. *Kanojo wa isoide uchi ni kaetta.*
   彼女は急いでうちに帰った。
   She rushed back to her house.

4. *Shigoto o isoida hō ga ii desu.*
   仕事を急いだほうがいいです。
   We should speed up our work.

5. *Sonna ni isogasenaide kudasai.*
   そんなに急がせないでください。
   Please don't rush me.

itasu いたす

致す to do, cause:* (trans.)

		Affirmative	Negative
PLAIN FORM	PRESENT	itasu	itasanai
	PAST	itashita	itasanakatta
MASU FORM	PRESENT	itashimasu	itashimasen
	PAST	itashimashita	itashimasen deshita
TE FORM		itashite	itasanakute
CONDITIONAL	PLAIN	itaseba/itashita ra	itasanakereba/ itasanakatta ra
	FORMAL	itashimashita ra	itashimasen deshita ra
VOLITIONAL	PLAIN	itasō	–
	FORMAL	itashimashō	–
IMPERATIVE		–	

	Affirmative		Affirmative
POTENTIAL	–	**CAUS. PASSIVE**	–
PASSIVE	–	**HONORIFIC**	–
CAUSATIVE	–	**HUMBLE**	–

Examples:

1. *Ikaga itashimashō ka.*
   いかがいたしましょうか。
   What shall I do?

2. *O-tetsudai itashimashō.*
   お手伝いいたしましょう。
   Let me help you.

3. *Nochi hodo mata go-renraku itashimasu.*
   後程またご連絡いたします。
   I will contact you again later.

4. *O-matase itashimashita.*
   お待たせいたしました。
   I am sorry to keep you waiting.

5. *Yoroshiku onegai itashimasu.*
   よろしくお願いいたします。
   Thanking you in advance.

* *Itasu* 致す is the humble equivalent of *suru* する.

iu いう

言う to say, tell: (trans.)

		Affirmative	Negative
PLAIN FORM	PRESENT	*iu*	*iwanai*
	PAST	*itta*	*iwanakatta*
MASU FORM	PRESENT	*iimasu*	*iimasen*
	PAST	*iimashita*	*iimasen deshita*
TE FORM		*itte*	*iwanakute*
CONDITIONAL	PLAIN	*ieba/itta ra*	*iwanakereba/ iwanakatta ra*
	FORMAL	*iimashita ra*	*iimasen deshita ra*
VOLITIONAL	PLAIN	*iō*	–
	FORMAL	*iimashō*	–
IMPERATIVE		*ie*	*iu na*

	Affirmative		Affirmative
POTENTIAL	*ieru*	**CAUS. PASSIVE**	*iwaserareru/iwasareru*
PASSIVE	*iwareru*	**HONORIFIC**	*ossharu/iwareru*
CAUSATIVE	*iwaseru*	**HUMBLE**	*mōsu*

Examples:

1. *Suzuki-san wa yoku jōdan o iimasu.*
   鈴木さんはよく冗談を言います。
   Mr. Suzuki often tells jokes.

2. *Sumimasen ga, mō ichido itte kudasai.*
   すみませんが、もう一度言ってください。
   Excuse me, but please say it again.

3. *"Cherry blossom" wa Nihongo de nan to iimasu ka. / "Sakura" to iimasu.*
   "Cherry blossom"は日本語で何と言いますか。/ "桜"と言います。
   How would you say "Cherry blossom" in Japanese? / We say "Sakura."

4. *Watashi wa Satō to mōshimasu. Dōzo yoroshiku.*
   私は佐藤と申します。どうぞよろしく。
   My name is Sato. It is nice to meet you.

5. *Sensei wa nan to osshaimashita ka.*
   先生は何とおっしゃいましたか。
   What did the teacher say?

   Ashita *tesuto ga aru to osshaimashita.*
   明日テストがあるとおっしゃいました。
   He said that there is an exam tomorrow.

iwau いわう

祝う to congratulate, celebrate: (trans.)

		Affirmative	Negative
PLAIN FORM	PRESENT	iwau	iwawanai
	PAST	iwatta	iwawanakatta
MASU FORM	PRESENT	iwaimasu	iwaimasen
	PAST	iwaimashita	iwaimasen deshita
TE FORM		iwatte	iwawanakute
CONDITIONAL	PLAIN	iwaeba/iwatta ra	iwawanakereba/ iwawanakatta ra
	FORMAL	iwaimashita ra	iwaimasen deshita ra
VOLITIONAL	PLAIN	iwaō	–
	FORMAL	iwaimashō	–
IMPERATIVE		iwae	iwau na

	Affirmative		Affirmative
POTENTIAL	iwaeru	**CAUS. PASSIVE**	iwawaserareru/ iwawasareru
PASSIVE	iwawareru	**HONORIFIC**	oiwai ni naru/ iwawareru
CAUSATIVE	iwawaseru	**HUMBLE**	oiwai suru

Examples:

1. *Watashi-tachi wa tomodachi no tanjōbi o iwaimashita.*
   私達は友達の誕生日を祝いました。
   We celebrated a friend's birthday.

2. *Go-kekkon o oiwai mōshi-agemasu.*
   ご結婚をお祝い申し上げます。
   I congratulate you on your wedding.

3. *Chiimu no yūshō o iwatte, kanpai shimashō.*
   チームの優勝を祝って、乾杯しましょう。
   Let's toast to our team's victory.

4. *Minna ga watashi no byōki no kaifuku o iwatte kuremashita.*
   みんなが私の病気の回復を祝ってくれました。
   Everybody congratulated me on my recovery from illness.

5. *Kare no yūshō o iwau tame ni, tomodachi ga minna atsumarimashita.*
   彼の優勝を祝うために、友達がみんな集まりました。
   All his friends gathered to congratulate him for winning.

kaeru かえる

帰る to go home; 返る to return: (both intrans.)

		Affirmative	Negative
PLAIN FORM	PRESENT	kaeru	kaeranai
	PAST	kaetta	kaeranakatta
MASU FORM	PRESENT	kaerimasu	kaerimasen
	PAST	kaerimashita	kaerimasen deshita
TE FORM		kaette	kaeranakute
CONDITIONAL	PLAIN	kaereba/kaetta ra	kaeranakereba/ kaeranakatta ra
	FORMAL	kaerimashita ra	kaerimasen deshita ra
VOLITIONAL	PLAIN	kaerō	–
	FORMAL	kaerimashō	–
IMPERATIVE		kaere	kaeru na

	Affirmative		Affirmative
POTENTIAL	kaereru	**CAUS. PASSIVE**	kaeraserareru/ kaerasareru
PASSIVE	kaerareru	**HONORIFIC**	okaeri ni naru/ kaerareru
CAUSATIVE	kaeraseru	**HUMBLE**	(okaeri suru)

Examples:

1. *Kinō go-ji ni uchi ni kaerimashita.*
   昨日五時にうちに帰りました。
   I went home at five o'clock yesterday.

2. *Suzuki-san wa raigetsu Amerika kara kaette kimasu.*
   鈴木さんは来月アメリカから帰って来ます。
   Mr. Suzuki will come back from the U.S. next month.

3. *Shachō wa mō otaku e okaeri ni narimashita.*
   社長はもうお宅へお帰りになりました。
   The president has already gone home.

4. *Kibun ga warui node, kaette mo ii desu ka.*
   気分が悪いので、帰ってもいいですか。
   I feel sick. May I go home?

5. *Densha ni wasureta kaban ga kaette kimashita.*
   電車に忘れたかばんが返って来ました。
   The bag which I left in the train was returned to me.

kaeru かえる

変える or 換える or 替える or 代える to change: (trans.)

		Affirmative	Negative
PLAIN FORM	PRESENT	kaeru	kaenai
	PAST	kaeta	kaenakatta
MASU FORM	PRESENT	kaemasu	kaemasen
	PAST	kaemashita	kaemasen deshita
TE FORM		kaete	kaenakute
CONDITIONAL	PLAIN	kaereba/kaeta ra	kaenakereba/ kaenakatta ra
	FORMAL	kaemashita ra	kaemasen deshita ra
VOLITIONAL	PLAIN	kaeyō	–
	FORMAL	kaemashō	–
IMPERATIVE		kaero	kaeru na

	Affirmative		Affirmative
POTENTIAL	kaerareru/kaereru	**CAUS. PASSIVE**	kaesaserareru
PASSIVE	kaerareru	**HONORIFIC**	okae ni naru/ kaerareru
CAUSATIVE	kaesaseru	**HUMBLE**	okae suru

Examples:

1. *Ryokō no ikisaki o Kyōto kara Kanazawa ni kaemashita.*
   旅行の行き先を京都から金沢に変えました。
   I changed my trip from Kyoto to Kanazawa.

2. *Kamigata o kaeyō to omotte imasu.*
   髪型を変えようと思っています。
   I think I'll change my hairstyle.

3. *Sen-en satsu o hyaku-en dama ni kaete moratta.*
   千円札を百円玉に換えてもらった。
   I had a 1,000-yen note changed into 100-yen coins.

4. *Sumimasen ga, seki o kaete itadakemasen ka.*
   すみませんが、席を換えていただけませんか。
   Excuse me, but would you please change my seat to another one?

5. *Umaku ikanakatta ra, yarikata o kaete miyō.*
   うまくいかなかったら、やり方を変えてみよう。
   If it doesn't work out, let's do it another way.

kaesu かえす

返す to return, restore: (trans.)

		Affirmative	*Negative*
PLAIN FORM	PRESENT	kaesu	kaesanai
	PAST	kaeshita	kaesanakatta
MASU FORM	PRESENT	kaeshimasu	kaeshimasen
	PAST	kaeshimashita	kaeshimasen deshita
TE FORM		kaeshite	kaesanakute
CONDITIONAL	PLAIN	kaeseba/kaeshita ra	kaesanakereba/ kaesanakatta ra
	FORMAL	kaeshimashita ra	kaeshimasen deshita ra
VOLITIONAL	PLAIN	kaesō	–
	FORMAL	kaeshimashō	–
IMPERATIVE		kaese	kaesu na

	Affirmative		*Affirmative*
POTENTIAL	kaeseru	**CAUS. PASSIVE**	kaesaserareru
PASSIVE	kaesareru	**HONORIFIC**	okaeshi ni naru/ kaesareru
CAUSATIVE	kaesaseru	**HUMBLE**	okaeshi suru

Examples:

1. *Ashita kasa o kaeshimasu.*
   明日傘を返します。
   I'll return the umbrella tomorrow.

2. *CD wa itsu okaeshi sureba ii desu ka.*
   CDはいつお返しすればいいですか。
   When should I return the CD?

   Raishū kaeshite kudasai.
   来週返してください。
   Please return it next week.

3. *Yonda hon wa moto no tokoro ni kaeshite kudasai.*
   読んだ本は元の所に返してください。
   Please return the books to their original places.

4. *Tomodachi ni karita okane o kaesanakereba naranai.*
   友達に借りたお金を返さなければならない。
   I have to return the money I borrowed from my friend.

kakaru かかる

懸かる or 掛かる to take, hang; 係る to depend on; かかる to be taken ill: (all intrans.)

		Affirmative	Negative
PLAIN FORM	PRESENT	kakaru	kakaranai
	PAST	kakatta	kakaranakatta
MASU FORM	PRESENT	kakarimasu	kakarimasen
	PAST	kakarimashita	kakarimasen deshita
TE FORM		kakatte	kakaranakute
CONDITIONAL	PLAIN	kakareba/kakatta ra	kakaranakereba/ kakaranakatta ra
	FORMAL	kakarimashita ra	kakarimasen deshita ra
VOLITIONAL	PLAIN	kakarō	–
	FORMAL	kakarimashō	–
IMPERATIVE		kakare	kakaru na

	Affirmative		Affirmative
POTENTIAL	kakareru	**CAUS. PASSIVE**	kakaraserareru/ kakarasareru
PASSIVE	kakarareru	**HONORIFIC**	okakari ni naru/ kakarareru
CAUSATIVE	kakaraseru	**HUMBLE**	(okakari suru)

Examples:

1. *Uchi kara gakkō made sanju-ppun gurai kakarimasu.*
   うちから学校まで三十分ぐらいかかります。
   It takes around 30 minutes from my house to the school.

2. *Kono jitensha o shūri suru no ni ikura gurai kakarimasu ka.*
   この自転車を修理するのにいくらぐらいかかりますか。
   How much does it cost to repair this bicycle?

3. *Kabe ni kirei na e ga kakatte iru.*
   壁にきれいな絵がかかっている。
   A beautiful picture hangs on the wall.

4. *Kaigi-shitsu ni kagi ga kakatte ite, hairemasen.*
   会議室に鍵がかかっていて、入れません。
   The meeting room is locked so I cannot enter.

5. *Kanojo wa infuruenza ni kakatte, kaisha o yasunde iru.*
   彼女はインフルエンザにかかって、会社を休んでいる。
   Because she suffers from influenza, she is absent from her office.

kakeru かける

掛ける to hang, telephone, lock, spend, sit; かける to bet: (both trans.)

		Affirmative	*Negative*
PLAIN FORM	PRESENT	kakeru	kakenai
	PAST	kaketa	kakenakatta
MASU FORM	PRESENT	kakemasu	kakemasen
	PAST	kakemashita	kakemasen deshita
TE FORM		kakete	kakenakute
CONDITIONAL	PLAIN	kakereba/kaketa ra	kakenakereba/ kakenakatta ra
	FORMAL	kakemashita ra	kakemasen deshita ra
VOLITIONAL	PLAIN	kakeyō	–
	FORMAL	kakemashō	–
IMPERATIVE		kakero	kakeru na

	Affirmative		*Affirmative*
POTENTIAL	kakerareru/kakereru	**CAUS. PASSIVE**	kakesaserareru
PASSIVE	kakerareru	**HONORIFIC**	okake ni naru/kakerareru
CAUSATIVE	kakesaseru	**HUMBLE**	okake suru

Examples:

1. *Kōto o hangā ni kakemashita.*
   コートをハンガーに掛けました。
   I hung my coat on the hanger.

2. *Tanaka-san ni denwa o kakemashita.*
   田中さんに電話を掛けました。
   I telephoned Mr. Tanaka.

3. *Doa ni kagi o kakeru no o wasurenaide kudasai.*
   ドアに鍵を掛けるのを忘れないでください。
   Don't forget to lock the door.

4. *Dōzo kochira no isu ni okake kudasai.*
   どうぞこちらのいすにお掛けください。
   Please sit on this chair.

5. *Kare wa sono uma ni ichi-man en o kaketa.*
   彼はその馬に一万円をかけた。
   He bet 10,000 yen on that horse.

kaku かく

書く to write; かく to draw, paint: (both trans.)

		Affirmative	Negative
PLAIN FORM	PRESENT	*kaku*	*kakanai*
	PAST	*kaita*	*kakanakatta*
MASU FORM	PRESENT	*kakimasu*	*kakimasen*
	PAST	*kakimashita*	*kakimasen deshita*
TE FORM		*kaite*	*kakanakute*
CONDITIONAL	PLAIN	*kakeba/kaita ra*	*kakanakereba/ kakanakatta ra*
	FORMAL	*kakimashita ra*	*kakimasen deshita ra*
VOLITIONAL	PLAIN	*kakō*	–
	FORMAL	*kakimashō*	–
IMPERATIVE		*kake*	*kaku na*

	Affirmative		*Affirmative*
POTENTIAL	*kakeru*	**CAUS. PASSIVE**	*kakaserareru/kakasareru*
PASSIVE	*kakareru*	**HONORIFIC**	*okaki ni naru/kakareru*
CAUSATIVE	*kakaseru*	**HUMBLE**	*okaki suru*

Examples:

1. *Igirisu-jin no tomodachi ni tegami o kakimashita.*
   イギリス人の友達に手紙を書きました。
   I wrote a letter to my English friend.

2. *Kanji ga ikutsu gurai kakemasu ka.*
   漢字がいくつぐらい書けますか。
   How many characters can you write?

3. *Ano kanban ni nan to kaite arimasu ka.*
   あの看板に何と書いてありますか。
   What is written on that sign?

4. *Kare wa Shinjuku no chizu o kaite kureta.*
   彼は新宿の地図をかいてくれた。
   He drew a map of Shinjuku for me.

5. *Kanojo no shumi wa e o kaku koto desu.*
   彼女の趣味は絵をかくことです。
   Her hobby is drawing.

kakureru かくれる

隠れる to hide, conceal: (intrans.)

		Affirmative	*Negative*
PLAIN FORM	PRESENT	kakureru	kakurenai
	PAST	kakureta	kakurenakatta
MASU FORM	PRESENT	kakuremasu	kakuremasen
	PAST	kakuremashita	kakuremasen deshita
TE FORM		kakurete	kakurenakute
CONDITIONAL	PLAIN	kakurereba/kakureta ra	kakurenakereba/ kakurenakatta ra
	FORMAL	kakuremashita ra	kakuremasen deshita ra
VOLITIONAL	PLAIN	kakureyō	–
	FORMAL	kakuremashō	–
IMPERATIVE		kakurero	kakureru na

	Affirmative		*Affirmative*
POTENTIAL	kakurerareru/ kakurereru	**CAUS. PASSIVE**	kakuresaserareru
PASSIVE	kakurerareru	**HONORIFIC**	okakure ni naru/ kakurerareru
CAUSATIVE	kakuresaseru	**HUMBLE**	(okakure suru)

Examples:

1. *Kare wa kokage ni kakureta.*
   彼は木陰に隠れた。
   He hid in the shade of a tree.

2. *Fuji-san wa kumo ni kakurete shimatte, mienakatta.*
   富士山は雲に隠れてしまって、見えなかった。
   Mt. Fuji was covered by clouds so we couldn't see it.

3. *Kodomo-tachi no kakureta sainō o hiki-dashi-tai.*
   子供達の隠れた才能を引き出したい。
   I'd like to draw out the children's latent talents.

4. *Sono gakusei wa kyōshi ni kakurete kanningu o shita.*
   その学生は教師に隠れてカンニングをした。
   That student cheated on the exam without attracting the teacher's attention.

5. *Chōsa ga susumu to, kakurete ita mondai ga akiraka ni natta.*
   調査が進むと、隠れていた問題が明らかになった。
   The problem became clearer as the investigation advanced.

kakusu かくす

隠す to hide, cover: (trans.)

		Affirmative	Negative
PLAIN FORM	PRESENT	kakusu	kakusanai
	PAST	kakushita	kakusanakatta
MASU FORM	PRESENT	kakushimasu	kakushimasen
	PAST	kakushimashita	kakushimasen deshita
TE FORM		kakushite	kakusanakute
CONDITIONAL	PLAIN	kakuseba/kakushita ra	kakusanakereba/ kakusanakatta ra
	FORMAL	kakushimashita ra	kakushimasen deshita ra
VOLITIONAL	PLAIN	kakusō	–
	FORMAL	kakushimashō	–
IMPERATIVE		kakuse	kakusu na

	Affirmative		Affirmative
POTENTIAL	kakuseru	**CAUS. PASSIVE**	kakusaserareru
PASSIVE	kakusareru	**HONORIFIC**	okakushi ni naru/ kakusareru
CAUSATIVE	kakusaseru	**HUMBLE**	okakushi suru

Examples:

1. *Kare wa dare ni mo mitsukerarenai yōni, okane o kakushita.*
   彼は誰にも見つけられないように、お金を隠した。
   He hid money so that nobody could find it.

2. *Kanojo wa hazukashisa no amari, ryōte de kao o kakushite shimatta.*
   彼女は恥ずかしさのあまり、両手で顔を隠してしまった。
   She covered her face with her hands out of embarrassment.

3. *Kodomo-tachi wa natsuyasumi ga hajimaru yorokobi o kakusenai yō datta.*
   子供達は夏休みが始まる喜びを隠せないようだった。
   Children were unable to hide their joy since summer vacation started.

4. *Karera wa jijitsu o kakusō to shita.*
   彼らは事実を隠そうとした。
   They tried to conceal the truth.

5. *Kakusanaide hontō no koto o itte hoshii.*
   隠さないで、本当の事を言って欲しい。
   I'd like you to tell me the truth without hiding anything.

kamau かまう

構う to mind, care: (trans.)

		Affirmative	Negative
PLAIN FORM	PRESENT	kamau	kamawanai
	PAST	kamatta	kamawanakatta
MASU FORM	PRESENT	kamaimasu	kamaimasen
	PAST	kamaimashita	kamaimasen deshita
TE FORM		kamatte	kamawanakute
CONDITIONAL	PLAIN	kamaeba/kamatta ra	kamawanakereba/ kamawanakatta ra
	FORMAL	kamaimashita ra	kamaimasen deshita ra
VOLITIONAL	PLAIN	kamaō	–
	FORMAL	kamaimashō	–
IMPERATIVE		kamae	kamau na

	Affirmative		Affirmative
POTENTIAL	kamaeru	**CAUS. PASSIVE**	kamawaserareru/ kamawasareru
PASSIVE	kamawareru	**HONORIFIC**	okamai ni naru/ kamawareru
CAUSATIVE	kamawaseru	**HUMBLE**	okamai suru

Examples:

1. *Koko ni nimotsu o oite mo kamaimasen ka.*
   ここに荷物を置いても構いませんか。
   May I put my baggage here?

2. *Kōhii to kōcha to dochira ga yoroshii desu ka. / Dochira demo kamaimasen.*
   コーヒーと紅茶とどちらがよろしいですか。/ どちらでも構いません。
   Which do you prefer, coffee or tea? / Either is fine.

3. *Mō kaeranakereba... / Sō desu ka. O-kamai mo shimasen de.*
   もう帰らなければ。/そうですか。お構いもしませんで。
   I must leave now. / Is that so? I hope you'd enjoyed your visit.

4. *Watashi ni kamawanaide, saki ni kaette kudasai.*
   私に構わないで、先に帰ってください。
   Please go home without worrying about me.

5. *Kanojo wa amari minari ni kamawanai.*
   彼女はあまり身なりに構わない。
   She doesn't care much about her appearance.

kangaeru かんがえる

考える to think of, consider: (trans.)

		Affirmative	*Negative*
PLAIN FORM	PRESENT	kangaeru	kangaenai
	PAST	kangaeta	kangaenakatta
MASU FORM	PRESENT	kangaemasu	kangaemasen
	PAST	kangaemashita	kangaemasen deshita
TE FORM		kangaete	kangaenakute
CONDITIONAL	PLAIN	kangaereba/kangaeta ra	kangaenakereba/ kangaenakatta ra
	FORMAL	kangaemashita ra	kangaemasen deshita ra
VOLITIONAL	PLAIN	kangaeyō	–
	FORMAL	kangaemashō	–
IMPERATIVE		kangaero	kangaeru na

	Affirmative		*Affirmative*
POTENTIAL	kangaerareru/ kangaereru	**CAUS. PASSIVE**	kangaesaserareru
PASSIVE	kangaerareru	**HONORIFIC**	okangae ni naru/ kangaerareru
CAUSATIVE	kangaesaseru	**HUMBLE**	(okangae suru)

Examples:

1. *Mō ichido kangaete mimasu.*
   もう一度考えてみます。
   I'll try to re-consider.

2. *Kono mondai ni tsuite, dō okangae ni narimasu ka.*
   この問題について、どうお考えになりますか。
   What do you think about this problem?

3. *Kare ga uso o tsuita to wa kangaerarenai.*
   彼がうそをついたとは考えられない。
   It's unthinkable that he told a lie.

4. *Jon wa Nihon de hataraku koto o kangaete iru.*
   ジョンは日本で働く事を考えている。
   John is thinking of working in Japan.

5. *Sono ken wa mō sukoshi kangaesasete kuremasen ka.*
   その件はもう少し考えさせてくれませんか。
   Please let me think over that matter a little more.

kanjiru かんじる

感じる to feel: (intrans. and trans.)

		Affirmative	Negative
PLAIN FORM	PRESENT	kanjiru	kanjinai
	PAST	kanjita	kanjinakatta
MASU FORM	PRESENT	kanjimasu	kanjimasen
	PAST	kanjimashita	kanjimasen deshita
TE FORM		kanjite	kanjinakute
CONDITIONAL	PLAIN	kanjireba/kanjita ra	kanjinakereba/ kanjinakatta ra
	FORMAL	kanjimashita ra	kanjimasen deshita ra
VOLITIONAL	PLAIN	kanjiyō	–
	FORMAL	kanjimashō	–
IMPERATIVE		kanjiro	kanjiru na

	Affirmative		Affirmative
POTENTIAL	kanjirareru/kanjireru	**CAUS. PASSIVE**	kanjisaserareru
PASSIVE	kanjirareru	**HONORIFIC**	okanji ni naru/ kanjirareru
CAUSATIVE	kanjisaseru	**HUMBLE**	(okanji suru)

Examples:

1. *Kyō no shiken wa itsumo yori muzukashiku kanjita.*
   今日の試験はいつもより難しく感じた。
   Today's exam seems more difficult than usual.

2. *Kare wa kata ni hageshii itami o kanjimashita.*
   彼は肩に激しい痛みを感じました。
   He felt a sharp pain in his shoulder.

3. *Kare no taido ni wa seii ga kanjirarenai.*
   彼の態度には誠意が感じられない。
   I feel no good faith from his behavior.

4. *Dareka ga chikazuite kuru no o kanjite, ushiro o furikaetta.*
   誰かが近づいてくるのを感じて、後ろを振り返った。
   I looked back as I felt somebody approaching me.

5. *Sono senshu no purē wa toshi o kanjisasenai, subarashii mono datta.*
   その選手のプレーは年を感じさせない、素晴らしいものだった。
   It was a splendid play considering the athlete's age.

kariru かりる

借りる to borrow, rent: (trans.)

		Affirmative	*Negative*
PLAIN FORM	PRESENT	kariru	karinai
	PAST	karita	karinakatta
MASU FORM	PRESENT	karimasu	karimasen
	PAST	karimashita	karimasen deshita
TE FORM		karite	karinakute
CONDITIONAL	PLAIN	karireba/karita ra	karinakereba/ karinakatta ra
	FORMAL	karimashita ra	karimasen deshita ra
VOLITIONAL	PLAIN	kariyō	–
	FORMAL	karimashō	–
IMPERATIVE		kariro	kariru na

	Affirmative		*Affirmative*
POTENTIAL	karirareru/karireru	**CAUS. PASSIVE**	karisaserareru
PASSIVE	karirareru	**HONORIFIC**	okari ni naru/ karirareru
CAUSATIVE	karisaseru	**HUMBLE**	okari suru

Examples:

1. *Tomodachi kara okane o karimashita.*
   友達からお金を借りました。
   I borrowed money from my friend.

2. *Kono toshokan de wa ichido ni ju-ssatsu no hon ga kariraremasu.*
   この図書館では一度に十冊の本が借りられます。
   Ten books can be borrowed at one time from this library.

3. *Denwa o okari shite mo ii desu ka.*
   電話をお借りしてもいいですか。
   May I use the phone?

4. *Kare wa Tōkyō de apāto o karite iru.*
   彼は東京でアパートを借りている。
   He rents an apartment in Tokyo.

5. *Neko no te mo kari-tai kurai isogashii.*
   猫の手も借りたいくらい忙しい。
   I wish I had three hands. (*lit.*, I'd like to borrow even a cat's paw.)

kasu かす

貸す to lend, give a hand: (trans.)

		Affirmative	*Negative*
PLAIN FORM	PRESENT	kasu	kasanai
	PAST	kashita	kasanakatta
MASU FORM	PRESENT	kashimasu	kashimasen
	PAST	kashimashita	kashimasen deshita
TE FORM		kashite	kasanakute
CONDITIONAL	PLAIN	kaseba/kashita ra	kasanakereba/ kasanakatta ra
	FORMAL	kashimashita ra	kashimasen deshita ra
VOLITIONAL	PLAIN	kasō	–
	FORMAL	kashimashō	–
IMPERATIVE		kase	kasu na

	Affirmative		*Affirmative*
POTENTIAL	kaseru	**CAUS. PASSIVE**	kasaserareru
PASSIVE	kasareru	**HONORIFIC**	okashi ni naru/ kasareru
CAUSATIVE	kasaseru	**HUMBLE**	okashi suru

Examples:

1. *Tomodachi ni okane o kashimashita.*
   友達にお金を貸しました。
   I lent some money to a friend.

2. *Enpitsu o kashite itadakemasen ka.*
   鉛筆を貸していただけませんか。
   Would you kindly lend me a pencil?

3. *Chotto te o kashite kudasai.*
   ちょっと手を貸してください。
   Could you please give me a hand?

4. *Kanojo wa tomodachi no chūkoku ni mimi o kasanakatta.*
   彼女は友達の忠告に耳を貸さなかった。
   She didn't pay attention to her friend's advice. (*lit.*, lend an ear)

5. *Yoroshikatta ra, kono jisho o okashi shimashō ka.*
   よろしかったら、この辞書をお貸ししましょうか。
   If you like, I'll lend you this dictionary.

katazukeru かたづける

片付ける to put in order, tidy up, finish: (trans.)

		Affirmative	Negative
PLAIN FORM	PRESENT	katazukeru	katazukenai
	PAST	katazuketa	katazukenakatta
MASU FORM	PRESENT	katazukemasu	katazukemasen
	PAST	katazukemashita	katazukemasen deshita
TE FORM		katazukete	katazukenakute
CONDITIONAL	PLAIN	katazukereba/ katazuketa ra	katazukenakereba/ katazukenakatta ra
	FORMAL	katazukemashitara	katazukemasen deshita ra
VOLITIONAL	PLAIN	katazukeyō	–
	FORMAL	katazukemashō	–
IMPERATIVE		katazukero	katazukeru na

	Affirmative		Affirmative
POTENTIAL	katazukerareru/ katazukereru	**CAUS. PASSIVE**	katazukesaserareru
PASSIVE	katazukerareru	**HONORIFIC**	okatazuke ni naru/ katazukerareru
CAUSATIVE	katazukesaseru	**HUMBLE**	okatazuke suru

Examples:

1. *Tsukue no ue o katazukemasu.*
   机の上を片付けます。
   I'll tidy up the top of the desk.

2. *Koppu ya sara o katazukete kuremasen ka.*
   コップや皿を片付けてくれませんか。
   Will you please clear away the cups and plates?

3. *Kono mondai o dekiru dake hayaku katazuke-tai.*
   この問題をできるだけ早く片付けたい。
   We want to settle this problem as soon as possible.

4. *Go-ji made ni shigoto o katazukenakereba narimasen.*
   五時までに仕事を片付けなければなりません。
   I have to finish my work by five o'clock.

5. *Amari ni mo kitanakatta kara, otōto ni heya o katazukesaseta.*
   あまりにも汚かったから、弟に部屋を片付けさせた。
   The room was so messy that I let my younger brother tidy up.

katsu かつ

勝つ to win: (intrans.)

		Affirmative	*Negative*
PLAIN FORM	PRESENT	katsu	katanai
	PAST	katta	katanakatta
MASU FORM	PRESENT	kachimasu	kachimasen
	PAST	kachimashita	kachimasen deshita
TE FORM		katte	katanakute
CONDITIONAL	PLAIN	kateba/katta ra	katanakereba/ katanakatta ra
	FORMAL	kachimashita ra	kachimasen deshita ra
VOLITIONAL	PLAIN	katō	–
	FORMAL	kachimashō	–
IMPERATIVE		kate	katsu na

	Affirmative		*Affirmative*
POTENTIAL	kateru	**CAUS. PASSIVE**	kataserareru/katasareru
PASSIVE	katareru	**HONORIFIC**	okachi ni naru/katareru
CAUSATIVE	kataseru	**HUMBLE**	(okachi suru)

Examples:

1. *Kare wa tenisu no shiai ni katta.*
   彼はテニスの試合に勝った。
   He won his tennis match.

2. *Yon tai san de karera no chiimu ga kachimashita.*
   四対三で彼らのチームが勝ちました。
   Their team won by a score of four to three.

3. *Ima, dotchi ga katte imasu ka.*
   今、どっちが勝っていますか。
   Which side is now winning?

4. *Dōshitemo chesu de chichi ni katenai.*
   どうしてもチェスで父に勝てない。
   I can never beat my father at chess.

5. *Kono shiai ni kate. Zettai ni makeru na.*
   この試合に勝て。絶対に負けるな。
   Win this game. Never lose.

kau かう

買う to buy, incur, appreciate; 飼う to keep animals: (both trans.)

			Affirmative	Negative
PLAIN FORM	PRESENT		kau	kawanai
	PAST		katta	kawanakatta
MASU FORM	PRESENT		kaimasu	kaimasen
	PAST		kaimashita	kaimasen deshita
TE FORM			katte	kawanakute
CONDITIONAL	PLAIN		kaeba/katta ra	kawanakereba/ kawanakatta ra
	FORMAL		kaimashita ra	kaimasen deshita ra
VOLITIONAL	PLAIN		kaō	–
	FORMAL		kaimashō	–
IMPERATIVE			kae	kau na

	Affirmative		Affirmative
POTENTIAL	kaeru	**CAUS. PASSIVE**	kawaserareru/ kawasareru
PASSIVE	kawareru	**HONORIFIC**	okai ni naru/kawareru
CAUSATIVE	kawaseru	**HUMBLE**	okai suru

Examples:

1. *Akihabara de pasokon o kaimashita.*
   秋葉原でパソコンを買いました。
   I bought a PC in Akihabara.

2. *Shinkansen no kippu wa doko de kaemasu ka.*
   新幹線の切符はどこで買えますか。
   Where can I buy a ticket for the Shinkansen?

3. *Atarashii kuruma o kaō to omotte imasu.*
   新しい車を買おうと思っています。
   I intend to buy a new car.

4. *Nihongo no jisho o kawanakereba narimasen.*
   日本語の辞書を買わなければなりません。
   I have to buy a Japanese dictionary.

5. *Kanojo wa neko o ippiki katte imasu.*
   彼女は猫を一匹飼っています。
   She has a cat.

kawakasu かわかす

乾かす to dry: (trans.)

		Affirmative	Negative
PLAIN FORM	PRESENT	kawakasu	kawakasanai
	PAST	kawakashita	kawakasanakatta
MASU FORM	PRESENT	kawakashimasu	kawakashimasen
	PAST	kawakashimashita	kawakashimasen deshita
TE FORM		kawakashite	kawakasanakute
CONDITIONAL	PLAIN	kawakaseba/ kawakashita ra	kawakasanakereba/ kawakasanakatta ra
	FORMAL	kawakashimashita ra	kawakashimasen deshita ra
VOLITIONAL	PLAIN	kawakasō	–
	FORMAL	kawakashimashō	–
IMPERATIVE		kawakase	kawakasu na

	Affirmative		Affirmative
POTENTIAL	kawakaseru	**CAUS. PASSIVE**	kawakasaserareru
PASSIVE	kawakasareru	**HONORIFIC**	okawakashi ni naru/ kawakasareru
CAUSATIVE	kawakasaseru	**HUMBLE**	okawakashi suru

Examples:

1. *Nureta shatsu o kawakashimashita.*
   ぬれたシャツを乾かしました。
   I dried my wet shirt.

2. *Itsumo doraiyā de kami o kawakashimasu.*
   いつもドライヤーで髪を乾かします。
   I always dry my hair with a blow-dryer.

3. *Koko de kutsu o kawakashite mo ii desu.*
   ここで靴を乾かしてもいいです。
   You can dry your shoes here.

4. *Shatsu o hangā ni kakete kawakasanai to, shiwa ni narimasu.*
   シャツをハンガーに掛けて乾かさないと、しわになります。
   If you don't hang a shirt to dry, it will wrinkle.

5. *Tenki no ii hi ni futon o hi ni atete kawakashimasu.*
   天気のいい日に布団を日に当てて乾かします。
   I air my futon in the sun on a fine day.

kawaku かわく

乾く to get dry; 渇く to get dry, be thirsty: (both intrans.)

		Affirmative	Negative
PLAIN FORM	PRESENT	kawaku	kawakanai
	PAST	kawaita	kawakanakatta
MASU FORM	PRESENT	kawakimasu	kawakimasen
	PAST	kawakimashita	kawakimasen deshita
TE FORM		kawaite	kawakanakute
CONDITIONAL	PLAIN	kawakeba/kawaita ra	kawakanakereba/ kawakanakatta ra
	FORMAL	kawakimashita ra	kawakimasen deshita ra
VOLITIONAL	PLAIN	kawakō	–
	FORMAL	kawakimashō	–
IMPERATIVE		kawake	kawaku na

	Affirmative		Affirmative
POTENTIAL	kawakeru	**CAUS. PASSIVE**	kawakaserareru/ kawakasareru
PASSIVE	kawakareru	**HONORIFIC**	okawaki ni naru/ kawakareru
CAUSATIVE	kawakaseru	**HUMBLE**	(okawaki suru)

Examples:

1. *Sentaku-mono wa kawakimashita ka. / Iie, mada kawaite imasen.*
   洗濯物は乾きましたか。／いいえ、まだ乾いていません
   Has the laundry dried? / No, it hasn't yet.

2. *Sono shatsu wa sugu kawaku deshō.*
   そのシャツはすぐ乾くでしょう。
   That shirt will dry soon.

3. *Kūki ga kawaite iru.*
   空気が乾いている。
   The air is dry.

4. *Penki ga kawaite inai kara, sono kabe ni sawaranaide kudasai.*
   ペンキが乾いていないから、その壁に触らないでください。
   Please don't touch the wall. The paint has not dried yet.

5. *Nodo ga kawaita.*
   のどが渇いた。
   I'm thirsty. (*lit.*, My throat is dry.)

kawaru かわる

変わる or 換わる or 替わる or 代わる to change, be different, alternate, exchange, replace: (all intrans.)

		Affirmative	*Negative*
PLAIN FORM	PRESENT	kawaru	kawaranai
	PAST	kawatta	kawaranakatta
MASU FORM	PRESENT	kawarimasu	kawarimasen
	PAST	kawarimashita	kawarimasen deshita
TE FORM		kawatte	kawaranakute
CONDITIONAL	PLAIN	kawareba/kawatta ra	kawaranakereba/ kawaranakatta ra
	FORMAL	kawarimashita ra	kawarimasen deshita ra
VOLITIONAL	PLAIN	kawarō	–
	FORMAL	kawarimashō	–
IMPERATIVE		kaware	kawaru na

	Affirmative		*Affirmative*
POTENTIAL	kawareru	**CAUS. PASSIVE**	kawaraserareru/ kawarasareru
PASSIVE	kawarareru	**HONORIFIC**	okawari ni naru/ kawarareru
CAUSATIVE	kawaraseru	**HUMBLE**	okawari suru

Examples:

1. *Kyōshitsu ga ni-kai kara yon-kai ni kawarimashita.*
   教室が二階から四階に変わりました。
   The classroom changed to the 4th floor from the 2nd floor.

2. *Denwa bangō ga kawatta koto o tomodachi ni shiraseta.*
   電話番号が変わったことを友達に知らせた。
   I let my friends know that my phone number has changed.

3. *Seki o kawatte kuremasen ka.*
   席を替わってくれませんか。
   Would you please change seats?

4. *Tsugō ga warukatta node, baito o hoka no hito ni kawatte moratta.*
   都合が悪かったので、バイトをほかの人に代わってもらった。
   Because I had other matters to attend to, I asked a co-worker to take over my shift.

5. *Ano hito wa chotto kawatte iru.*
   あの人はちょっと変わっている。
   That person is a little strange.

kazoeru かぞえる

数える to count:(trans.)

		Affirmative	Negative
PLAIN FORM	PRESENT	kazoeru	kazoenai
	PAST	kazoeta	kazoenakatta
MASU FORM	PRESENT	kazoemasu	kazoemasen
	PAST	kazoemashita	kazoemasen deshita
TE FORM		kazoete	kazoenakute
CONDITIONAL	PLAIN	kazoereba/kazoeta ra	kazoenakereba/ kazoenakatta ra
	FORMAL	kazoemashita ra	kazoemasen deshita ra
VOLITIONAL	PLAIN	kazoeyō	–
	FORMAL	kazoemashō	–
IMPERATIVE		kazoero	kazoeru na

	Affirmative		Affirmative
POTENTIAL	kazoerareru/ kazoereru	**CAUS. PASSIVE**	kazoesaserareru
PASSIVE	kazoerareru	**HONORIFIC**	okazoe ni naru/ kazoerareru
CAUSATIVE	kazoesaseru	**HUMBLE**	okazoe suru

Examples:

1. *Saifu ni ikura haitte iru ka, okane o kazoemashita.*
   財布にいくら入っているか、お金を数えました。
   I counted the money in my wallet.

2. *Reizōko ni nan-bon biiru ga aru ka, kazoete kudasai.*
   冷蔵庫に何本ビールがあるか、数えてください。
   Please count how many bottles of beer there are in the refrigerator.

3. *Kazoe-kirenai hodo ōzei hito ga imashita.*
   数えきれないほど大勢人がいました。
   There were too many people to be counted.

4. *Kore wa kare no daihyōsaku no hitotsu ni kazoerarete iru.*
   これは彼の代表作の一つに数えられている。
   This is counted as one of his masterpieces.

5. *Nihongo wa mono ni yotte kazoe-kata ga chigaimasu.*
   日本語はものによって数え方が違います。
   There are different ways to count different things in Japanese.

kesu けす

消す to extinguish, turn off, erase, disappear: (trans.)

		Affirmative	Negative
PLAIN FORM	PRESENT	kesu	kesanai
	PAST	keshita	kesanakatta
MASU FORM	PRESENT	keshimasu	keshimasen
	PAST	keshimashita	keshimasen deshita
TE FORM		keshite	kesanakute
CONDITIONAL	PLAIN	keseba/keshita ra	kesanakereba/ kesanakatta ra
	FORMAL	keshimashita ra	keshimasen deshita ra
VOLITIONAL	PLAIN	kesō	–
	FORMAL	keshimashō	–
IMPERATIVE		kese	kesu na

	Affirmative		Affirmative
POTENTIAL	keseru	CAUS. PASSIVE	kesaserareru
PASSIVE	kesareru	HONORIFIC	okeshi ni naru/kesareru
CAUSATIVE	kesaseru	HUMBLE	okeshi suru

Examples:

1. *Heya o deru toki, denki o keshite kudasai.*
   部屋を出る時、電気を消してください。
   When you leave the room, please turn off the lights.

2. *Tabako no hi o kesu no o wasurenaide kudasai.*
   たばこの火を消すのを忘れないでください。
   Please don't forget to extinguish your cigarette.

3. *Kore wa keshigomu de kesemasen.*
   これは消しゴムで消せません。
   This cannot be erased by an eraser.

4. *Terebi o keshite mo ii desu ka.*
   テレビを消してもいいですか。
   May I turn off the TV?

5. *Haha ni gēmu no dēta o kesarete shimatta.*
   母にゲームのデータを消されてしまった。
   My mother deleted my game data. (*lit.*, My game data was deleted by my mother.)

kieru きえる

消える to go out, disappear, vanish: (intrans.)

		Affirmative	Negative
PLAIN FORM	PRESENT	kieru	kienai
	PAST	kieta	kienakatta
MASU FORM	PRESENT	kiemasu	kiemasen
	PAST	kiemashita	kiemasen deshita
TE FORM		kiete	kienakute
CONDITIONAL	PLAIN	kiereba/kieta ra	kienakereba/ kienakatta ra
	FORMAL	kiemashita ra	kiemasen deshita ra
VOLITIONAL	PLAIN	kieyō	–
	FORMAL	kiemashō	–
IMPERATIVE		kiero	kieru na

	Affirmative		Affirmative
POTENTIAL	kierareru/kiereru	**CAUS. PASSIVE**	kiesaserareru
PASSIVE	kierareru	**HONORIFIC**	okie ni naru/kierareru
CAUSATIVE	kiesaseru	**HUMBLE**	(okie suru)

Examples:

1. *Kono raito wa jidōteki ni kieru.*
   このライトは自動的に消える。
   This light turns off automatically.

2. *Ie no mae ni tomete oita jitensha ga kieta.*
   家の前に止めておいた自転車が消えた。
   The bicycle I parked in front of my house disappeared.

3. *Rōsoku no higa kiesō desu.*
   ろうそくの火が消えそうです。
   The flame of the candle looks like it is going out.

4. *Pasokon no koshō de, dēta ga kiete-shimatta.*
   パソコンの故障で、データが消えてしまった。
   My computer data was lost due to an error.

5. *Kusuri o nonde mo, ha no itami wa kienakatta.*
   薬を飲んでも、歯の痛みは消えなかった。
   Even after taking painkillers, my toothache didn't go away.

kikoeru きこえる

聞こえる to hear, sound, can be heard: (intrans.)

		Affirmative	*Negative*
PLAIN FORM	PRESENT	kikoeru	kikoenai
	PAST	kikoeta	kikoenakatta
MASU FORM	PRESENT	kikoemasu	kikoemasen
	PAST	kikoemashita	kikoemasen deshita
TE FORM		kikoete	kikoenakute
CONDITIONAL	PLAIN	kikoereba/kikoeta ra	kikoenakereba/ kikoenakatta ra
	FORMAL	kikoemashita ra	kikoemasen deshita ra
VOLITIONAL	PLAIN	kikoeyō	–
	FORMAL	kikoemashō	–
IMPERATIVE		kikoero	kikoeru na

	Affirmative		*Affirmative*
POTENTIAL	–	**CAUS. PASSIVE**	(kikoesaserareru)
PASSIVE	(kikoerareru)	**HONORIFIC**	(okikoe ni naru)/ (kikoerareru)
CAUSATIVE	(kikoesaseru)	**HUMBLE**	(okikoe suru)

Examples:

1. *Moshi moshi, kikoemasu ka.*
   もしもし、聞こえますか。
   Hello, can you hear me?

2. *Kuruma no oto ga kikoemasu.*
   車の音が聞こえます。
   I can hear the sound of a car.

3. *Kodomo-tachi ga asonde iru no ga kikoeta.*
   子供達が遊んでいるのが聞こえた。
   I heard the children playing.

4. *Hen ni kikoeru kamo-shirenai keredo, hontō no hanashi desu.*
   変に聞こえるかもしれないけれど、本当の話です。
   It may sound strange, but it's true.

5. *Yoku kikoenai node, motto ōkii koe de hanashite kudasai.*
   よく聞こえないので、もっと大きい声で話してください。
   Please speak louder as I cannot hear you.

kiku きく

聞く or 聴く to hear, listen, ask: (trans.); 効く or 利く to be effective: (intrans.)*

		Affirmative	*Negative*
PLAIN FORM	PRESENT	kiku	kikanai
	PAST	kiita	kikanakatta
MASU FORM	PRESENT	kikimasu	kikimasen
	PAST	kikimashita	kikimasen deshita
TE FORM		kiite	kikanakute
CONDITIONAL	PLAIN	kikeba/kiita ra	kikanakereba/ kikanakatta ra
	FORMAL	kikimashita ra	kikimasen deshita ra
VOLITIONAL	PLAIN	kikō	–
	FORMAL	kikimashō	–
IMPERATIVE		kike	kiku na

	Affirmative		*Affirmative*
POTENTIAL	kikeru	**CAUS. PASSIVE**	kikaserareru/kikasareru
PASSIVE	kikareru	**HONORIFIC**	okiki ni naru/kikareru
CAUSATIVE	kikaseru	**HUMBLE**	okiki suru

Examples:

1. *Heya de rajio o kikimashita.*
   部屋でラジオを聞きました。
   I listened to the radio in the room.

2. *Wakaranakatta ra, sensei ni kiite kudasai.*
   分からなかったら、先生に聞いてください。
   If you don't understand, please ask your teacher.

3. *Omawari-san ni michi o kiite mimashō.*
   おまわりさんに道を聞いてみましょう。
   Let's try to ask a police officer for direction.

4. *Ongaku o kiki-nagara, kōhii o nomimashita.*
   音楽を聴きながら、コーヒーを飲みました。
   I drank a cup of coffee while listening to music.

5. *Kono kusuri wa kaze ni kiku.*
   この薬は風邪に効く。
   This medicine works well on colds.

* The intransitive *kiku* 効く or 利く meaning "to be effective" generally has no imperative, volitional, potential, or passive forms.

kimaru きまる

決まる to be decided, fixed, certain: (intrans.)

		Affirmative	*Negative*
PLAIN FORM	PRESENT	kimaru	kimaranai
	PAST	kimatta	kimaranakatta
MASU FORM	PRESENT	kimarimasu	kimarimasen
	PAST	kimarimashita	kimarimasen deshita
TE FORM		kimatte	kimaranakute
CONDITIONAL	PLAIN	kimareba/kimatta ra	kimaranakereba/ kimaranakatta ra
	FORMAL	kimarimashita ra	kimarimasen deshita ra
VOLITIONAL	PLAIN	kimarō	–
	FORMAL	kimarimashō	–
IMPERATIVE		kimare	kimaru na

	Affirmative		*Affirmative*
POTENTIAL	kimareru	**CAUS. PASSIVE**	kimaraserareru/ kimarasareru
PASSIVE	kimarareru	**HONORIFIC**	okimari ni naru/ kimarareru
CAUSATIVE	kimaraseru	**HUMBLE**	(okimari suru)

Examples:

1. *Ryokō no nittei ga kimarimashita.*
   旅行の日程が決まりました。
   The travel itinerary has been set.

2. *Kobayashi-san wa Osaka ni tenkin suru koto ga kimatta.*
   小林さんは大阪に転勤することが決まった。
   It was decided that Mr. Kobayashi would be transferred to the Osaka office.

3. *Natsuyasumi ni doko e iku ka, mada kimatte inai.*
   夏休みにどこへ行くか、まだ決まっていない。
   We have not yet decided where to go for summer vacation.

4. *Kare wa kuru ni kimatte iru yo.*
   彼は来るに決まっているよ。
   He is certain to come.

5. *Kare wa shigoto ga owaru to, kimatte kono nomiya ni yoru.*
   彼は仕事が終わると、決まってこの飲み屋に寄る。
   He always drops into this bar after he finishes his work.

kimeru きめる

決める to decide, fix, choose: (trans.)

		Affirmative	Negative
PLAIN FORM	PRESENT	kimeru	kimenai
	PAST	kimeta	kimenakatta
MASU FORM	PRESENT	kimemasu	kimemasen
	PAST	kimemashita	kimemasen deshita
TE FORM		kimete	kimenakute
CONDITIONAL	PLAIN	kimereba/kimeta ra	kimenakereba/ kimenakatta ra
	FORMAL	kimemashita ra	kimemasen deshita ra
VOLITIONAL	PLAIN	kimeyō	–
	FORMAL	kimemashō	–
IMPERATIVE		kimero	kimeru na

	Affirmative		Affirmative
POTENTIAL	kimerareru/kimereru	**CAUS. PASSIVE**	kimesaserareru
PASSIVE	kimerareru	**HONORIFIC**	okime ni naru/kimerareru
CAUSATIVE	kimesaseru	**HUMBLE**	okime suru

Examples:

1. *Machiawase no basho to jikan o kimemashō.*
   待ち合わせの場所と時間を決めましょう。
   Let's decide where and when to meet.

2. *Dono daigaku ni iku ka kimenakereba narimasen.*
   どの大学に行くか決めなければなりません。
   I have to choose which university to enter.

3. *Doko ni hikkosu ka mada kimete imasen.*
   どこに引っ越すかまだ決めていません。
   We haven't yet decided where to move to.

4. *Kanojo wa rainen Igirisu e ryūgaku suru koto ni kimete iru.*
   彼女は来年イギリスへ留学することに決めている。
   She has decided to study in England next year.

5. *Kimerareta kisoku o mamotte kudasai.*
   決められた規則を守ってください。
   Observe the rules, please.

kireru きれる

切れる to cut off, expire, be sharp, get mad: (intrans.)

		Affirmative	*Negative*
PLAIN FORM	PRESENT	*kireru*	*kirenai*
	PAST	*kireta*	*kirenakatta*
MASU FORM	PRESENT	*kiremasu*	*kiremasen*
	PAST	*kiremashita*	*kiremasen deshita*
TE FORM		*kirete*	*kirenakute*
CONDITIONAL	PLAIN	*kirereba/kireta ra*	*kirenakereba/ kirenakatta ra*
	FORMAL	*kiremashita ra*	*kiremasen deshita ra*
VOLITIONAL	PLAIN	*kireyō*	–
	FORMAL	*kiremashō*	–
IMPERATIVE		*kirero*	*kireru na*

	Affirmative		*Affirmative*
POTENTIAL	*kirerareru/kirereru*	**CAUS. PASSIVE**	*kiresaserareru*
PASSIVE	*kirerareru*	**HONORIFIC**	*okire ni naru/kirerareru*
CAUSATIVE	*kiresaseru*	**HUMBLE**	*(okire suru)*

Examples:

1. *Himo ga kirete shimatta.*
   ひもが切れてしまった。
   The strings were cut.

2. *Hanashi-chū ni denwa ga kireta.*
   話し中に電話が切れた。
   I was cut off while talking on the phone.

3. *Pasupōto no kigen ga mō sugu kiremasu.*
   パスポートの期限がもうすぐ切れます。
   My passport will expire soon.

4. *Kono naifu wa yoku kireru.*
   このナイフはよく切れる。
   This knife cuts well.

5. *Tomodachi ni baka ni sarete, kare wa kirete shimatta.*
   友達にバカにされて、彼はキレてしまった。
   He got mad after he was fooled by a friend.

kiru きる

切る to cut, (attached to a verb) to do completely: (trans.)

		Affirmative	*Negative*
PLAIN FORM	PRESENT	kiru	kiranai
	PAST	kitta	kiranakatta
MASU FORM	PRESENT	kirimasu	kirimasen
	PAST	kirimashita	kirimasen deshita
TE FORM		kitte	kiranakute
CONDITIONAL	PLAIN	kireba/kitta ra	kiranakereba/ kiranakatta ra
	FORMAL	kirimashita ra	kirimasen deshita ra
VOLITIONAL	PLAIN	kirō	–
	FORMAL	kirimashō	–
IMPERATIVE		kire	kiru na

	Affirmative		*Affirmative*
POTENTIAL	kireru	**CAUS. PASSIVE**	kiraserareru/kirasareru
PASSIVE	kirareru	**HONORIFIC**	okiri ni naru/kirareru
CAUSATIVE	kiraseru	**HUMBLE**	okiri suru

Examples:

1. *Hasami de himo o kirimashita.*
   はさみでひもを切りました。
   I cut the string with scissors.

2. *Naifu de yubi o kitte shimaimashita.*
   ナイフで指を切ってしまいました。
   I cut my finger with a knife.

3. *Pasokon o tukai-owattara, dengen o kitte kudasai.*
   パソコンを使い終わったら、電源を切ってください。
   Please turn off the PC after you finish using it.

4. *Kare to wa mō te o kirimashita.*
   彼とはもう手を切りました。
   I have nothing to do with him any more.

5. *Minna tsukare-kitte imasu.*
   みんな疲れ切っています。
   Everybody is completely worn out.

kiru きる

着る to wear, put on, take the blame for: (trans.)

		Affirmative	Negative
PLAIN FORM	PRESENT	kiru	kinai
	PAST	kita	kinakatta
MASU FORM	PRESENT	kimasu	kimasen
	PAST	kimashita	kimasen deshita
TE FORM		kite	kinakute
CONDITIONAL	PLAIN	kireba/kita ra	kinakereba/kinakatta ra
	FORMAL	kimashita ra	kimasen deshita ra
VOLITIONAL	PLAIN	kiyō	–
	FORMAL	kimashō	–
IMPERATIVE		kiro	kiru na

	Affirmative		Affirmative
POTENTIAL	kirareru/kireru	**CAUS. PASSIVE**	kisaserareru
PASSIVE	kirareru	**HONORIFIC**	omeshi ni naru/kirareru
CAUSATIVE	kisaseru	**HUMBLE**	(omeshi suru)

Examples:

1. *Kōto o kimashita.*
   コートを着ました。
   I put on a coat.

2. *Kanojo wa itsumo oshare na fuku o kite iru.*
   彼女はいつもおしゃれな服を着ている。
   She always wears fashionable clothes.

3. *Kono jaketto o kite mite mo ii desu ka. / Dōzo omeshi ni natte mite kudasai.*
   このジャケットを着てみてもいいですか。/どうぞお召しになってみてください。
   May I try on this jacket? / Please, by all means.

4. *Futotta node, kono waishatsu wa mō kirarenaku natta.*
   太ったので、このワイシャツはもう着られなくなった。
   Because I gained weight, I can no longer wear this shirt.

5. *Kare wa mujitsu no tsumi o kiserareta.*
   彼は無実の罪を着せられた。
   He was punished for a crime he did not commit.

Note: *megane o kakeru* → to wear a pair of glasses
   bōshi o kaburu → to put on a hat/cap
   shatsu/burausu o kiru → to put on a shirt/blouse
   zubon/sukāto o haku → to put on pants/a skirt
   tebukuro o suru → to put on gloves

koeru こえる

越える or 超える to go over, pass, surpass;* 肥える to be fertile, fat:
(both intrans.)

		Affirmative	Negative
PLAIN FORM	PRESENT	koeru	koenai
	PAST	koeta	koenakatta
MASU FORM	PRESENT	koemasu	koemasen
	PAST	koemashita	koemasen deshita
TE FORM		koete	koenakute
CONDITIONAL	PLAIN	koereba/koeta ra	koenakereba/ koenakatta ra
	FORMAL	koemashita ra	koemasen deshita ra
VOLITIONAL	PLAIN	koeyō	–
	FORMAL	koemashō	–
IMPERATIVE		koero	koeru na

	Affirmative		Affirmative
POTENTIAL	koerareru/koereru	**CAUS. PASSIVE**	koesaserareru
PASSIVE	koerareru	**HONORIFIC**	okoe ni naru/koerareru
CAUSATIVE	koesaseru	**HUMBLE**	(okoe suru)

Examples:

1. *Kono yama o koereba, umi ga mieru deshō.*
   この山を越えれば、海が見えるでしょう。
   We can see the ocean after climbing this mountain.

2. *Ōbosha wa sen nin o koemashita.*
   応募者は千人を超えました。
   There were over one thousand applicants.

3. *Kare wa mō hachiju-ssai o koete iru darō.*
   彼はもう八十歳を超えているだろう。
   I guess that he is already over 80 years old.

4. *Bōru wa fensu o koete, tōku e tonde itta.*
   ボールはフェンスを越えて、遠くへ飛んで行った。
   The ball flew far over the fence.

5. *Kono atari no tochi wa koete iru.*
   この辺りの土地は肥えている。
   The earth around here is fertile.

* *Koeru* 越える or 超える is technically classified as an intransitive verb, but is nearly always used as a transitive verb.

komaru こまる

困る to be in trouble, be in a fix, be at a loss: (intrans.)

		Affirmative	*Negative*
PLAIN FORM	PRESENT	komaru	komaranai
	PAST	komatta	komaranakatta
MASU FORM	PRESENT	komarimasu	komarimasen
	PAST	komarimashita	komarimasen deshita
TE FORM		komatte	komaranakute
CONDITIONAL	PLAIN	komareba/komatta ra	komaranakereba/ komaranakatta ra
	FORMAL	komarimashita ra	komarimasen deshita ra
VOLITIONAL	PLAIN	komarō	–
	FORMAL	komarimashō	–
IMPERATIVE		komare	komaru na

	Affirmative		*Affirmative*
POTENTIAL	komareru	**CAUS. PASSIVE**	komaraserareru/ komarasareru
PASSIVE	komarareru	**HONORIFIC**	okomari ni naru/ komarareru
CAUSATIVE	komaraseru	**HUMBLE**	(okomari suru)

Examples:

1. *Taiya ga panku shite, komatte imasu.*
   タイヤがパンクして、困っています。
   I'm in a fix because I have a flat tire.

2. *Kare wa keizaiteki ni komatte iru.*
   彼は経済的に困っている。
   He has financial difficulties.

3. *Komatta nā. Michi ni mayotte shimatta...*
   困ったなあ。道に迷ってしまった。
   What shall I do? I have lost my way.

4. *Dō kotaeta ra ii ka wakaranakute, komarimashita.*
   どう答えたらいいか分からなくて、困りました。
   I was at a loss for an answer.

5. *Sono ko wa kotae-nikui shitsumon o shite, oya o komaraseta.*
   その子は答えにくい質問をして、親を困らせた。
   That little girl troubled her parents with a difficult-to-answer question.

komu こむ

込む to be crowded, (attached to a verb) to come in, put in: (intrans.)

		Affirmative	*Negative*
PLAIN FORM	PRESENT	*komu*	*komanai*
	PAST	*konda*	*komanakatta*
MASU FORM	PRESENT	*komimasu*	*komimasen*
	PAST	*komimashita*	*komimasen deshita*
TE FORM		*konde*	*komanakute*
CONDITIONAL	PLAIN	*komeba/konda ra*	*komanakereba/ komanakatta ra*
	FORMAL	*komimashita ra*	*komimasen deshita ra*
VOLITIONAL	PLAIN	*komō*	–
	FORMAL	*komimashō*	–
IMPERATIVE		*kome*	*komu na*

	Affirmative		*Affirmative*
POTENTIAL	*komeru*	**CAUS. PASSIVE**	*komaserareru/ komasareru*
PASSIVE	*komareru*	**HONORIFIC**	*okomi ni naru/komareru*
CAUSATIVE	*komaseru*	**HUMBLE**	*(okomi suru)*

Examples:

1. *Tōkyō no densha wa itsumo konde imasu ne.*
   東京の電車はいつも込んでいますね。
   Trains are always crowded in Tokyo, aren't they?

2. *Sono bijutsukan wa amari konde inakatta.*
   その美術館はあまり込んでいなかった。
   The art museum was not so crowded.

3. *Yūgata no rasshu de michi ga komanai uchini kaerimashō.*
   夕方のラッシュで道が込まないうちに帰りましょう。
   Let's go home before the evening rush and the street become crowded.

4. *Kono ran ni namae o kaki-konde kudasai.*
   この欄に名前を書き込んでください。
   Please fill in your name in this blank.

5. *Kare wa pūro ni tobi-konde, oyogi-hajimeta.*
   彼はプールに飛び込んで、泳ぎ始めた。
   He jumped into the pool and started swimming.

korosu ころす

殺す to kill, murder: (trans.)

		Affirmative	*Negative*
PLAIN FORM	PRESENT	korosu	korosanai
	PAST	koroshita	korosanakatta
MASU FORM	PRESENT	koroshimasu	koroshimasen
	PAST	koroshimashita	koroshimasen deshita
TE FORM		koroshite	korosanakute
CONDITIONAL	PLAIN	koroseba/koroshita ra	korosanakereba/ korosanakatta ra
	FORMAL	koroshimashita ra	koroshimasen deshita ra
VOLITIONAL	PLAIN	korosō	–
	FORMAL	koroshimashō	–
IMPERATIVE		korose	korosu na

	Affirmative		*Affirmative*
POTENTIAL	koroseru	**CAUS. PASSIVE**	korosaserareru
PASSIVE	korosareru	**HONORIFIC**	okoroshi ni naru/ korosareru
CAUSATIVE	korosaseru	**HUMBLE**	okoroshi suru

Examples:

1. *Hannin wa naifu de kare o koroshita.*
   犯人はナイフで彼を殺した。
   The criminal killed kim with a knife.

2. *Niwa no mushi o korosu tame ni, kusuri o katte kita.*
   庭の虫を殺すために、薬を買ってきた。
   I bought insecticide to kill the insects in the garden.

3. *Dansei ga heya de korosarete iru no ga hakken sareta.*
   男性が部屋で殺されているのが発見された。
   The man was found murdered in the room.

4. *Kanojo wa mushi ippiki korosenai hodo yasashii hito da.*
   彼女は虫一匹殺せないほど優しい人だ。
   She is so gentle that she couldn't hurt a fly.

5. *Yakusoku o yabutta ra, kanojo ni korosare sō da.*
   約束を破ったら、彼女に殺されそうだ。
   She might kill me if I break the promise.

kosu こす

越す or 超す to cross, go over, go through: (intrans.)*

		Affirmative	*Negative*
PLAIN FORM	PRESENT	kosu	kosanai
	PAST	koshita	kosanakatta
MASU FORM	PRESENT	koshimasu	koshimasen
	PAST	koshimashita	koshimasen deshita
TE FORM		koshite	kosanakute
CONDITIONAL	PLAIN	koseba/koshita ra	kosanakereba/ kosanakatta ra
	FORMAL	koshimashita ra	koshimasen deshita ra
VOLITIONAL	PLAIN	kosō	–
	FORMAL	koshimashō	–
IMPERATIVE		kose	kosu na

	Affirmative		*Affirmative*
POTENTIAL	koseru	**CAUS. PASSIVE**	kosaserareru
PASSIVE	kosareru	**HONORIFIC**	okoshi ni naru/kosareru
CAUSATIVE	kosaseru	**HUMBLE**	(okoshi suru)

Examples:

1. *Sanman-nin o kosu hitobito ga kyūjō ni atsumatta.*
   三万人を超す人々が球場に集まった。
   More than 30,000 people gathered at the ball park.

2. *Tonari no ie ni wakai kazoku ga koshite kita.*
   隣の家に若い家族が越してきた。
   A young family moved into a neighboring house.

3. *Kibishii fuyu o kosanakereba narimasen.*
   厳しい冬を越さなければなりません。
   We have to make it through the severe winter.

4. *Kion wa yon-jū do o koshimashita.*
   気温は四十度を超しました。
   The temperature went up to over forty degrees.

5. *Tanaka-sama, furonto made okoshi kudasai.*
   田中様、フロントまでお越しください。
   Mr. Tanaka, would you please come to the front desk?

* *Kosu* 越す or 超す is technically classified as an intransitive verb, but is nearly always used as a transitive verb.

kotaeru こたえる

答える to answer, respond; こたえる have an effect on: (both intrans.)

		Affirmative	*Negative*
PLAIN FORM	PRESENT	kotaeru	kotaenai
	PAST	kotaeta	kotaenakatta
MASU FORM	PRESENT	kotaemasu	kotaemasen
	PAST	kotaemashita	kotaemasen deshita
TE FORM		kotaete	kotaenakute
CONDITIONAL	PLAIN	kotaereba/kotaeta ra	kotaenakereba/ kotaenakatta ra
	FORMAL	kotaemashita ra	kotaemasen deshita ra
VOLITIONAL	PLAIN	kotaeyō	–
	FORMAL	kotaemashō	–
IMPERATIVE		kotaero	kotaeru na

	Affirmative		*Affirmative*
POTENTIAL	kotaerareru/ kotaereru	**CAUS. PASSIVE**	kotaesaserareru
PASSIVE	kotaerareru	**HONORIFIC**	okotae ni naru/ kotaerareru
CAUSATIVE	kotaesaseru	**HUMBLE**	okotae suru

Examples:

1. *Nihon-go de kotaete kudasai.*
   日本語で答えてください。
   Please answer in Japanese.

2. *Ano shitsumon ni kotaerarenakatta.*
   あの質問に答えられなかった。
   I couldn't answer that question.

3. *Doa o nokku shita ga, dare mo kotaenakatta.*
   ドアをノックしたが、誰も答えなかった。
   I knocked on the door, but no one answered.

4. *Shiken wa mondai o yoku yonde kara, kotae nasai.*
   試験は問題をよく読んでから答えなさい。
   Read the exam questions carefully and then answer.

5. *Sono chiimu wa fan no kitai ni kotaete yūshō shita.*
   そのチームはファンの期待にこたえて優勝した。
   Just as the fans expected, the team won the championship.

kotowaru ことわる

断る to refuse, decline, ask permission, warn: (trans.)

		Affirmative	Negative
PLAIN FORM	PRESENT	kotowaru	kotowaranai
	PAST	kotowatta	kotowaranakatta
MASU FORM	PRESENT	kotowarimasu	kotowarimasen
	PAST	kotowarimashita	kotowarimasen deshita
TE FORM		kotowatte	kotowaranakute
CONDITIONAL	PLAIN	kotowareba/kotowatta ra	kotowaranakereba/ kotowaranakatta ra
	FORMAL	kotowarimashita ra	kotowarimasen deshita ra
VOLITIONAL	PLAIN	kotowarō	–
	FORMAL	kotowarimashō	–
IMPERATIVE		kotoware	kotowaru na

	Affirmative		Affirmative
POTENTIAL	kotowareru	**CAUS. PASSIVE**	kotowaraserareru/ kotowarasareru
PASSIVE	kotowarareru	**HONORIFIC**	okotowari ni naru/ kotowarareru
CAUSATIVE	kotowaraseru	**HUMBLE**	okotowari suru

Examples:

1. *Tsugō ga warukute, tomodachi no sasoi o kotowatta.*
   都合が悪くて、友達の誘いを断った。
   I declined my friend's invitation as I had other business to attend to.

2. *Kanojo ni dēto o kotowararemashita.*
   彼女にデートを断られました。
   She refused to go on a date with me.

3. *Zannen desu ga, sono shigoto wa okotowari shimasu.*
   残念ですが、その仕事はお断りします。
   Unfortunately I decline that job.

4. *Kanojo no tanomi de wa kotowarenai.*
   彼女の頼みでは断れない。
   I cannot refuse her request.

5. *Yameru toki wa ikka-getsu mae ni kotowatte kudasai.*
   辞める時は一か月前に断ってください。
   Please inform a month in advance if you want to quit.

kowareru こわれる

壊れる to be broken, be damaged, be out of order: (intrans.)

		Affirmative	Negative
PLAIN FORM	PRESENT	kowareru	kowarenai
	PAST	kowareta	kowarenakatta
MASU FORM	PRESENT	kowaremasu	kowaremasen
	PAST	kowaremashita	kowaremasen deshita
TE FORM		kowarete	kowarenakute
CONDITIONAL	PLAIN	kowarereba/kowareta ra	kowarenakereba/ kowarenakatta ra
	FORMAL	kowaremashita ra	kowaremasen deshita ra
VOLITIONAL	PLAIN	kowareyō	–
	FORMAL	kowaremashō	–
IMPERATIVE		kowarero	kowareru na

	Affirmative		Affirmative
POTENTIAL	(kowarerareru)	**CAUS. PASSIVE**	(kowaresaserareru)
PASSIVE	(kowarerareru)	**HONORIFIC**	(okoware ni naru)/ (kowarerareru)
CAUSATIVE	(kowaresaseru)	**HUMBLE**	(okoware suru)

Examples:

1. *Tokei ga kowaremashita.*
   時計が壊れました。
   The watch is broken.

2. *Kono terebi wa kowarete imasu.*
   このテレビは壊れています。
   This TV is broken.

3. *Kowareta denwa-ki o shūri site moratta.*
   壊れた電話機を修理してもらった。
   I had him repair my broken telephone.

4. *Kono kikai wa koware-yasui node, ki o tsukete hakonde kudasai.*
   この機械は壊れやすいので、気を付けて運んでください。
   Please carry this machine carefully since it is easily broken.

5. *Sono isu wa koware sō desu.*
   そのいすは壊れそうです。
   That chair looks like it might break.

kowasu こわす

壊す to break, destroy, injure: (trans.)

		Affirmative	Negative
PLAIN FORM	PRESENT	kowasu	kowasanai
	PAST	kowashita	kowasanakatta
MASU FORM	PRESENT	kowashimasu	kowashimasen
	PAST	kowashimashita	kowashimasen deshita
TE FORM		kowashite	kowasanakute
CONDITIONAL	PLAIN	kowaseba/kowashita ra	kowasanakereba/ kowasanakatta ra
	FORMAL	kowashimashita ra	kowashimasen deshita ra
VOLITIONAL	PLAIN	kowasō	–
	FORMAL	kowashimashō	–
IMPERATIVE		kowase	kowasu na

	Affirmative		Affirmative
POTENTIAL	kowaseru	**CAUS. PASSIVE**	kowasaserareru
PASSIVE	kowasareru	**HONORIFIC**	okowashi ni naru/ kowasareru
CAUSATIVE	kowasaseru	**HUMBLE**	okowashi suru

Examples:

1. *Kono isu o kowashita no wa dare desu ka.*
   このいすを壊したのは誰ですか。
   Who broke this chair?

2. *Keitai denwa o ofuro ni otoshite, kowashite shimatta.*
   携帯電話をお風呂に落として、壊してしまった。
   My cell-phone was damaged after I dropped it into the bath.

3. *Otōto ni pasokon o kowasaremashita.*
   弟にパソコンを壊されました。
   My younger brother broke the computer.

4. *Hataraki-sugite, karada o kowashite shimaimashita.*
   働きすぎて、体を壊してしまいました。
   I ruined my health by working too much.

5. *Tabe-sugite, onaka o kowasanai yōni shite kudasai.*
   食べすぎて、おなかを壊さないようにしてください。
   Please refrain from eating too much in order not to hurt your stomach.

kumoru くもる

曇る to become cloudy, be gloomy: (intrans.)

		Affirmative	*Negative*
PLAIN FORM	PRESENT	*kumoru*	*kumoranai*
	PAST	*kumotta*	*kumoranakatta*
MASU FORM	PRESENT	*kumorimasu*	*kumorimasen*
	PAST	*kumorimashita*	*kumorimasen deshita*
TE FORM		*kumotte*	*kumoranakute*
CONDITIONAL	PLAIN	*kumoreba/kumotta ra*	*kumoranakereba/ kumoranakatta ra*
	FORMAL	*kumorimashita ra*	*kumorimasen deshita ra*
VOLITIONAL	PLAIN	*(kumorō)*	–
	FORMAL	*(kumorimashō)*	–
IMPERATIVE		*(kumore)*	*(kumoru na)*

	Affirmative		*Affirmative*
POTENTIAL	*(kumoreru)*	**CAUS. PASSIVE**	*kumoraserareru*
PASSIVE	*(komorareru)*	**HONORIFIC**	*okumori ni naru/ kumorareru*
CAUSATIVE	*kumoraseru*	**HUMBLE**	*(okumori suru)*

Examples:

1. *Kinō wa ichinichi-jū kumotte imashita.*
   昨日は一日中曇っていました。
   It was cloudy all day yesterday.

2. *Tenki yohō ni yoruto, asu wa gogo kara kumoru sō da.*
   天気予報によると、明日は午後から曇るそうだ。
   According to the weather forecast, it will become cloudy from tomorrow afternoon.

3. *Sono chihō wa, fuyu wa kumotta hi ga ōi.*
   その地方は、冬は曇った日が多い。
   That area has many cloudy days in winter.

4. *Rāmen o tabetara, megane ga kumotte shimaimashita.*
   ラーメンを食べたら、眼鏡が曇ってしまいました。
   When I ate Chinese noodle, my glasses fogged up.

5. *Kare no kao wa fuan de kumotte ita.*
   彼の顔は、不安で曇っていた。
   His face was clouded with anxiety.

kuraberu くらべる

比べる to compare (trans.)

		Affirmative	Negative
PLAIN FORM	PRESENT	kuraberu	kurabenai
	PAST	kurabeta	kurabenakatta
MASU FORM	PRESENT	kurabemasu	kurabemasen
	PAST	kurabemashita	kurabemasen deshita
TE FORM		kurabete	kurabenakute
CONDITIONAL	PLAIN	kurabereba/kurabeta ra	kurabenakereba/ kurabenakatta ra
	FORMAL	kurabemashita ra	kurabemasen deshita ra
VOLITIONAL	PLAIN	kurabeyō	–
	FORMAL	kurabemashō	–
IMPERATIVE		kurabero	kuraberu na

	Affirmative		Affirmative
POTENTIAL	kuraberareru/ kurabereru	**CAUS. PASSIVE**	kurabesaserareru
PASSIVE	kuraberareru	**HONORIFIC**	okurabe ni naru/ kuraberareru
CAUSATIVE	kurabesaseru	**HUMBLE**	okurabe suru

Examples:

1. *Tōkyō to Nyū Yōku o kuraberu to, dotchi ga samui desu ka.*
   東京とニューヨークを比べると、どっちが寒いですか。
   Which city is colder, Tokyo or New York?

2. *Dare ga ichiban se ga takai ka kurabete mimashō.*
   誰が一番背が高いか比べてみましょう。
   Let's see who is the tallest.

3. *Kotoshi wa kyonen ni kurabete yuki ga ōi desu.*
   今年は去年に比べて雪が多いです。
   There has been more snow this year than last year.

4. *Zenkai to kurabereba, konkai no tesuto wa kantan da.*
   前回と比べれば、今回のテストは簡単だ。
   The exam is easier this time than last time.

5. *Fuji-san no utsukushisa wa hoka no yama to kuraberarenai.*
   富士山の美しさは、ほかの山と比べられない。
   The beauty of Mt. Fuji cannot be compared with other mountains'.

kureru くれる

くれる to give: (trans.); 暮れる to end, get dark: (intrans.)*

		Affirmative	*Negative*
PLAIN FORM	PRESENT	*kureru*	*kurenai*
	PAST	*kureta*	*kurenakatta*
MASU FORM	PRESENT	*kuremasu*	*kuremasen*
	PAST	*kuremashita*	*kuremasen deshita*
TE FORM		*kurete*	*kurenakute*
CONDITIONAL	PLAIN	*kurereba/kureta ra*	*kurenakereba/ kurenakatta ra*
	FORMAL	*kuremashita ra*	*kuremasen deshita ra*
VOLITIONAL	PLAIN	*kureyō*	–
	FORMAL	*kuremashō*	–
IMPERATIVE		*kurero*	*kureru na*

	Affirmative		*Affirmative*
POTENTIAL	*(kurerareru)*	**CAUS. PASSIVE**	*(kuresaserareru)*
PASSIVE	*(kurerareru)*	**HONORIFIC**	*kudasaru*
CAUSATIVE	*(kuresaseru)*	**HUMBLE**	*(okure suru)*

Examples:

1. *Haha wa watashi ni purezento o kuremashita.*
   母は私にプレゼントをくれました。
   My mother gave me a present.

2. *Sensei wa watashi ni hon o katte kuremashita.*
   先生は私に本を買ってくれました。
   My teacher bought me a book.

3. *Kono mondai ga wakaranai'n desu ga, oshiete kuremasen ka.*
   この問題が分からないんですが、教えてくれませんか。
   I don't understand this question, so will you explain it to me?

4. *Chotto atsui'n da kedo, mado o akete kurenai?*
   ちょっと暑いんだけど、窓を開けてくれない。
   It is a little hot in here so can you open the window?

5. *Chichi wa watashi ni kuruma o kashite kurenakatta.*
   父は私に車を貸してくれなかった。
   My father didn't lend me his car.

6. *Hi ga kureru mae ni kaerō.*
   日が暮れる前に帰ろう。
   Let's go home before it gets dark.

142

* Besides the forms shown above, the intransitive verb *kureru* 暮れる meaning "to get dark, to end" generally does not use the imperative, volitional, or honorific forms.

kuru くる

来る to come, arrive: (intrans.)

		Affirmative	Negative
PLAIN FORM	PRESENT	kuru	konai
	PAST	kita	konakatta
MASU FORM	PRESENT	kimasu	kimasen
	PAST	kimashita	kimasen deshita
TE FORM		kite	konakute
CONDITIONAL	PLAIN	kureba/kita ra	konakereba/konakatta ra
	FORMAL	kimashita ra	kimasen deshita ra
VOLITIONAL	PLAIN	koyō	–
	FORMAL	kimashō	–
IMPERATIVE		koi	kuru na

	Affirmative		Affirmative
POTENTIAL	korareru	**CAUS. PASSIVE**	kosaserareru
PASSIVE	korareru	**HONORIFIC**	irassharu/oide ni naru/korareru
CAUSATIVE	kosaseru	**HUMBLE**	mairu

Examples:

1. *Ashita nan-ji ni kimasu ka.*
   明日何時に来ますか。
   What time will you come tomorrow?

2. *Basu wa mada kite imasen.*
   バスはまだ来ていません。
   The bus has not arrived yet.

3. *Nihon e nihongo no benkyō o shi ni kimashita.*
   日本へ日本語の勉強をしに来ました。
   I came to Japan to study Japanese.

4. *Doyōbi ni pātii ga aru'n desu ga, koraremasu ka.*
   土曜日にパーティーがあるんですが、来られますか。
   We are having a party on Saturday, so are you able to come?

5. *Sensei wa gakusei ni jisho o motte kosasemashita.*
   先生は学生に辞書を持って来させました。
   The teacher let his students bring their dictionary.

kuwaeru くわえる

加える to add, increase; くわえる to hold in mouth: (both trans.)

		Affirmative	*Negative*
PLAIN FORM	PRESENT	kuwaeru	kuwaenai
	PAST	kuwaeta	kuwaenakatta
MASU FORM	PRESENT	kuwaemasu	kuwaemasen
	PAST	kuwaemashita	kuwaemasen deshita
TE FORM		kuwaete	kuwaenakute
CONDITIONAL	PLAIN	kuwaereba/kuwaeta ra	kuwaenakaereba/ kuwaenakatta ra
	FORMAL	kuwaemashita ra	kuwaemasen deshita ra
VOLITIONAL	PLAIN	kuwaeyō	–
	FORMAL	kuwaemashō	–
IMPERATIVE		kuwaero	kuwaeru na

	Affirmative		*Affirmative*
POTENTIAL	kuwaerareru/ kuwaereru	**CAUS. PASSIVE**	kuwaesaserareru
PASSIVE	kuwaerareru	**HONORIFIC**	okuwae ni naru/ kuwaerareru
CAUSATIVE	kuwaesaseru	**HUMBLE**	(okuwae suru)

Examples:

1. *Sono nabe ni sukoshi mizu o kuwaete kudasai.*
   その鍋に少し水を加えてください。
   Please add some more water to the pot.

2. *Kono ryōri wa mō sukoshi shio o kuwaeta hō ga ii to omou.*
   この料理は、もう少し塩を加えたほうがいいと思う。
   I think you should add a little more salt to this dish.

3. *Kare o nakama ni kuwaeta ra dō desu ka.*
   彼を仲間に加えたらどうですか。
   Why don't we let him join us?

4. *Kaimono no gōkei kingaku ni shōhizei o kuwaeru to, ikura ni narimasu ka.*
   買い物の合計金額に消費税を加えると、いくらになりますか。
   How much will it be if the consumption tax is added to the total price of my purchase?

5. *Neko ga sakana o kuwaete, nigete itta.*
   猫が魚をくわえて、逃げて行った。
   The cat ran away with the fish in its mouth.

machigaeru まちがえる

GROUP 2

間違える to make a mistake: (trans.)

		Affirmative	*Negative*
PLAIN FORM	PRESENT	machigaeru	machigaenai
	PAST	machigaeta	machigaenakatta
MASU FORM	PRESENT	machigaemasu	machigaemasen
	PAST	machigaemashita	machigaemasen deshita
TE FORM		machigaete	machigaenakute
CONDITIONAL	PLAIN	machigaereba/ machigaeta ra	machigaenakereba/ machigaenakatta ra
	FORMAL	machigaemashita ra	machigaemasen deshita ra
VOLITIONAL	PLAIN	machigaeyō	–
	FORMAL	machigaemashō	–
IMPERATIVE		machigaero	machigaeru na

	Affirmative		*Affirmative*
POTENTIAL	machigaerareru/ machigaereru	**CAUS. PASSIVE**	machigaesaserareru
PASSIVE	machigaerareru	**HONORIFIC**	omachigae ni naru/ machigaerareru
CAUSATIVE	machigaesaseru	**HUMBLE**	(omachigae suru)

Examples:

1. *Michi o machigaemashita.*
   道を間違えました。
   I took the wrong road.

2. *Gomennasai. Denwa bangō o machigaete shimaimashita.*
   ごめんなさい。電話番号を間違えてしまいました。
   I'm sorry. I have got the wrong phone number.

3. *Machigaete, tonari no heya ni haitte shimatta.*
   間違えて、隣の部屋に入ってしまった。
   By mistake, I entered the room next door.

4. *Kasa o machigaenai yōni, namae o kaite oita.*
   傘を間違えないように、名前を書いておいた。
   I wrote my name on the umbrella in order not to mistake it for another.

5. *Watashi wa yoku ani to machigaeraremasu.*
   私はよく兄と間違えられます。
   I am often mistaken for my older brother.

machigau まちがう

間違う to make a mistake: (intrans.)*

		Affirmative	*Negative*
PLAIN FORM	PRESENT	machigau	machigawanai
	PAST	machigatta	machigawanakatta
MASU FORM	PRESENT	machigaimasu	machigaimasen
	PAST	machigaimashita	machigaimasen deshita
TE FORM		machigatte	machigawanakute
CONDITIONAL	PLAIN	machigaeba/ machigatta ra	machigawanakereba/ machigawanakatta ra
	FORMAL	machigaimashita ra	machigaimasen deshita ra
VOLITIONAL	PLAIN	machigaō	–
	FORMAL	machigaimashō	–
IMPERATIVE		machigae	machigau na

	Affirmative		*Affirmative*
POTENTIAL	(machigaeru)	**CAUS. PASSIVE**	machigawaserareru/ machigawasareru
PASSIVE	machigawareru	**HONORIFIC**	omachigai ni naru/ machigawareru
CAUSATIVE	machigawaseru	**HUMBLE**	(omachigai suru)

Examples:

1. *Kono tegami wa jūsho ga machigatte iru.*
   この手紙は住所が間違っている。
   The address on this letter is wrong.

2. *Shiken no kotae o futatsu machigatta.*
   試験の答えを二つ間違った。
   I made two mistakes on the exam.

3. *Machigatte, kono hon o motte kite shimatta.*
   間違って、この本を持って来てしまった。
   I brought this book by mistake.

4. *Machigatta densha ni notte shimatta.*
   間違った電車に乗ってしまった。
   I have gotten on the wrong train.

5. *Machigatte mo kare ni itte wa ikemasen.*
   間違っても彼に言ってはいけません。
   Whatever you do, don't mention it to him.

* Also used as a transitive verb. (See example 2)

magaru まがる

曲がる to bend, curve, turn: (intrans.)

		Affirmative	Negative
PLAIN FORM	PRESENT	magaru	magaranai
	PAST	magatta	magaranakatta
MASU FORM	PRESENT	magarimasu	magarimasen
	PAST	magarimashita	magarimasen deshita
TE FORM		magatte	magaranakute
CONDITIONAL	PLAIN	magareba/magatta ra	magaranakereba/ magaranakatta ra
	FORMAL	magarimashita ra	magarimasen deshita ra
VOLITIONAL	PLAIN	magarō	–
	FORMAL	magarimashō	–
IMPERATIVE		magare	magaru na

	Affirmative		Affirmative
POTENTIAL	magareru	**CAUS. PASSIVE**	magaraserareru/ magarasareru
PASSIVE	magarareru	**HONORIFIC**	omagari ni naru/ magarareru
CAUSATIVE	magaraseru	**HUMBLE**	(omagari suru)

Examples:

1. *Tsugi no kōsaten o migi ni magatte kudasai.*
   次の交差点を右に曲がってください。
   Please turn right at the next intersection.

2. *Nekutai ga magatte imasu yo.*
   ネクタイが曲がっていますよ。
   Your tie is crooked.

3. *Kono jōgi wa sukoshi magatte iru yō desu.*
   この定規は少し曲がっているようです。
   This ruler looks slightly askew.

4. *Hidari e magaru to, kōen ga arimasu yo.*
   左へ曲がると、公園がありますよ。
   When you turn left, you'll find the park.

5. *Kare wa magatta koto ga kirai da.*
   彼は曲がったことが嫌いだ。
   He dislikes dishonesty.

mageru まげる

曲げる to bend, curve, twist: (trans.)

		Affirmative	*Negative*
PLAIN FORM	PRESENT	mageru	magenai
	PAST	mageta	magenakatta
MASU FORM	PRESENT	magemasu	magemasen
	PAST	magemashita	magemasen deshita
TE FORM		magete	magenakute
CONDITIONAL	PLAIN	magereba/mageta ra	magenakereba/ magenakatta ra
	FORMAL	magemashita ra	magemasen deshita ra
VOLITIONAL	PLAIN	mageyō	–
	FORMAL	magemashō	–
IMPERATIVE		magero	mageru na

	Affirmative		*Affirmative*
POTENTIAL	magerareru/ magereru	**CAUS. PASSIVE**	magesaserareru
PASSIVE	magerareru	**HONORIFIC**	omage ni naru/ magerareru
CAUSATIVE	magesaseru	**HUMBLE**	omage suru

Examples:

1. *Harigane o magete, kago o tsukutta.*
   針金を曲げて、籠を作った。
   I made a basket by bending wires.

2. *Kega o shita node, ashi ga magerarenaku natta.*
   けがをしたので、足が曲げられなくなった。
   I hurt myself and couldn't bend my leg.

3. *Kasa no hone o magete shimatta.*
   傘の骨を曲げてしまった。
   I accidentally bent the ribs of my umbrella.

4. *Kono shorui wa ori-magenaide hokan shite kudasai.*
   この書類は折り曲げないで保管してください。
   Please keep this document in a safe place without folding it.

5. *Dōshite mo kare wa iken o mageyō to shinai.*
   どうしても彼は意見を曲げようとしない。
   He won't change his opinion for anything.

makaseru まかせる

任せる to entrust to, leave to: (trans.)

		Affirmative	*Negative*
PLAIN FORM	PRESENT	makaseru	makasenai
	PAST	makaseta	makasenakatta
MASU FORM	PRESENT	makasemasu	makasemasen
	PAST	makasemashita	makasemasen deshita
TE FORM		makasete	makasenakute
CONDITIONAL	PLAIN	makasereba/makaseta ra	makasenakereba/ makasenakatta ra
	FORMAL	makasemashita ra	makasemasen deshita ra
VOLITIONAL	PLAIN	makaseyō	–
	FORMAL	makasemashō	–
IMPERATIVE		makasero	makaseru na

	Affirmative		*Affirmative*
POTENTIAL	makaserareru/ makasereru	**CAUS. PASSIVE**	makasesaserareru
PASSIVE	makaserareru	**HONORIFIC**	omakase ni naru/ makaserareru
CAUSATIVE	makasesaseru	**HUMBLE**	omakase suru

Examples:

1. *Kono shigoto wa watashi ni makasete kudasai.*
   この仕事は私に任せてください。
   Please leave this job to me.

2. *Ryokō no aida, inu no sewa o imōto ni makaseta.*
   旅行の間、犬の世話を妹に任せた。
   I let my younger sister take care of my dog while I was traveling.

3. *Kare wa mada keiken ga nai kara, kono shigoto wa makaserarenai.*
   彼はまだ経験がないから、この仕事は任せられない。
   I cannot leave this job to him because he has little experience.

4. *Dōyatte soko e iku ka, anata ni omakase shimasu.*
   どうやってそこへ行くか、あなたにお任せします。
   It is up to you how we will get there.

5. *Sono ken wa Yamada-san ni makaserarete iru.*
   その件は山田さんに任せられている。
   This matter has been left to Mr. Yamada.

makeru まける

負ける to be defeated, to lose: (intrans.); まける give a price reduction: (trans.)

		Affirmative	Negative
PLAIN FORM	PRESENT	makeru	makenai
	PAST	maketa	makenakatta
MASU FORM	PRESENT	makemasu	makemasen
	PAST	makemashita	makemasen deshita
TE FORM		makete	makenakute
CONDITIONAL	PLAIN	makereba/maketa ra	makenakereba/ makenakatta ra
	FORMAL	makemashita ra	makemasen deshita ra
VOLITIONAL	PLAIN	makeyō	–
	FORMAL	makemashō	–
IMPERATIVE		makero	makeru na

	Affirmative		Affirmative
POTENTIAL	makerareru/makereru	**CAUS. PASSIVE**	makesaserareru
PASSIVE	makerareru	**HONORIFIC**	omake ni naru/ makerareru
CAUSATIVE	makesaseru	**HUMBLE**	omake suru

Examples:

1. *Tenisu no shiai de kare ni makete shimatta.*
   テニスの試合で彼に負けてしまった。
   I lost the tennis match to him.

2. *Sono chiimu wa yon tai san de aite chiimu ni makemashita.*
   そのチームは四対三で相手チームに負けました。
   That team lost by 4 to 3 to the other team.

3. *Tsugi no shiai ni wa makenai yō ni ganbarō.*
   次の試合には負けないように頑張ろう。
   Let's stick in there and win the next game.

4. *Kanojo wa yūwaku ni makete, sono yubiwa o katte shimatta.*
   彼女は誘惑に負けて、その指輪を買ってしまった。
   She yielded to temptation and bought the ring.

5. *Nedan o makete itadakemasen ka.*
   値段をまけていただけませんか。
   Could you make it cheaper?

maku まく

巻く to bind, roll up; まく to sprinkle, seed: (both trans.)

		Affirmative	Negative
PLAIN FORM	PRESENT	maku	makanai
	PAST	maita	makanakatta
MASU FORM	PRESENT	makimasu	makimasen
	PAST	makimashita	makimasen deshita
TE FORM		maite	makanakute
CONDITIONAL	PLAIN	makeba/maita ra	makanakereba/ makanakatta ra
	FORMAL	makimashita ra	makimasen deshita ra
VOLITIONAL	PLAIN	makō	–
	FORMAL	makimashō	–
IMPERATIVE		make	maku na

	Affirmative		Affirmative
POTENTIAL	makeru	**CAUS. PASSIVE**	makaserareru/ makasareru
PASSIVE	makareru	**HONORIFIC**	omaki ni naru/makareru
CAUSATIVE	makaseru	**HUMBLE**	omaki suru

Examples:

1. *Ashi ni kega o shita node, hōtai o maita.*
   足にけがをしたので、包帯を巻いた。
   I bandaged my leg because I injured it.

2. *Kanojo wa sukāfu o kubi ni maite iru.*
   彼女はスカーフを首に巻いている。
   She has a scarf wrapped around her neck.

3. *Kare no sainō ni wa shita o maita.*
   彼の才能には舌を巻いた。
   I was astounded by his talent. (*lit.*, my tongue was bound)

4. *Niwa ni hana no tane o maita.*
   庭に花の種をまいた。
   I sowed flower seeds in the garden.

5. *Shibafu ni mizu o maite kudasai.*
   芝生に水をまいてください。
   Please water the lawn.

mamoru まもる

守る to protect, keep, defend: (trans.)

		Affirmative	*Negative*
PLAIN FORM	PRESENT	mamoru	mamoranai
	PAST	mamotta	mamoranakatta
MASU FORM	PRESENT	mamorimasu	mamorimasen
	PAST	mamorimashita	mamorimasen deshita
TE FORM		mamotte	mamoranakute
CONDITIONAL	PLAIN	mamoreba/mamotta ra	mamoranakereba/ mamoranakatta ra
	FORMAL	mamorimashita ra	mamorimasen deshita ra
VOLITIONAL	PLAIN	mamorō	–
	FORMAL	mamorimashō	–
IMPERATIVE		mamore	mamoru na

	Affirmative		*Affirmative*
POTENTIAL	mamoreru	**CAUS. PASSIVE**	mamoraserareru/ mamorasareru
PASSIVE	mamorareru	**HONORIFIC**	omamori ni naru/ mamorareru
CAUSATIVE	mamoraseru	**HUMBLE**	omamori suru

Examples:

1. *Karera wa kuni o mamoru tame ni tatakatta.*
   彼らは国を守るために戦った。
   They fought to defend their country.

2. *Kare wa itsumo yakusoku o mamorimasu.*
   彼はいつも約束を守ります。
   He always keeps his promises.

3. *Yamada-san wa itsumo jikan o mamoranakute, komarimasu.*
   山田さんはいつも時間を守らなくて、困ります。
   It annoys me that Mr. Yamada isn't always punctual.

4. *Repōto teishutsu no shimekiri wa zettai ni mamotte kudasai.*
   レポート提出の締め切りは絶対に守ってください。
   Please be sure to meet your deadline for submitting the reports.

5. *Kaihatsu kara shizen o mamorō.*
   開発から自然を守ろう。
   Let's protect nature from being (commercially) developed.

maniau まにあう

間に合う to be in time, be enough, be able to do without: (intrans.)

		Affirmative	Negative
PLAIN FORM	PRESENT	maniau	maniawanai
	PAST	maniatta	maniawanakatta
MASU FORM	PRESENT	maniaimasu	maniaimasen
	PAST	maniaimashita	maniaimasen deshita
TE FORM		maniatte	maniawanakute
CONDITIONAL	PLAIN	maniaeba/maniatta ra	maniawanakereba/ maniawanakatta ra
	FORMAL	maniaimashita ra	maniaimasen deshita ra
VOLITIONAL	PLAIN	maniaō	–
	FORMAL	maniaimashō	–
IMPERATIVE		maniae	maniau na

	Affirmative		Affirmative
POTENTIAL	maniaeru	**CAUS. PASSIVE**	maniawaserareru/ maniawasareru
PASSIVE	maniawareru	**HONORIFIC**	omaniai ni naru/ maniawareru
CAUSATIVE	maniawaseru	**HUMBLE**	(omaniai suru)

Examples:

1. *Shūden ni maniawanakatta.*
   終電に間に合わなかった。
   I missed the last train.

2. *Roku-ji no hikōki ni maniau yō ni isogimashō.*
   六時の飛行機に間に合うように急ぎましょう。
   Let's hurry so we can make it for the six o'clock plane.

3. *Ichi-jikan me no jugyō ni maniai-sō mo nai.*
   一時間目の授業に間に合いそうもない。
   I don't seem to be on time for the first class.

4. *Yakusoku no jikan ni maniawanakereba, kanojo wa okoru darō.*
   約束の時間に間に合わなければ、彼女は怒るだろう。
   If I am not on time for the appointment, she will be angry with me.

5. *Ato go-sen en areba jūbun maniaimasu.*
   あと五千円あれば、十分間に合います。
   If I have five thousand yen more, it'll be more than enough.

matsu まつ

待つ to wait: (trans.)

		Affirmative	Negative
PLAIN FORM	PRESENT	matsu	matanai
	PAST	matta	matanakatta
MASU FORM	PRESENT	machimasu	machimasen
	PAST	machimashita	machimasen deshita
TE FORM		matte	matanakute
CONDITIONAL	PLAIN	mateba/matta ra	matanakereba/ matanakatta ra
	FORMAL	machimashita ra	machimasen deshita ra
VOLITIONAL	PLAIN	matō	–
	FORMAL	machimashō	–
IMPERATIVE		mate	matsu na

	Affirmative		Affirmative
POTENTIAL	materu	**CAUS. PASSIVE**	mataserareru/matasareru
PASSIVE	matareru	**HONORIFIC**	omachi ni naru/matareru
CAUSATIVE	mataseru	**HUMBLE**	omachi suru

Examples:

1. *Chotto matte kudasai.*
   ちょっと待ってください。
   Please wait a moment.

2. *Getsuyōbi no go-ji ni omachi shite orimasu.*
   月曜日の五時にお待ちしております。
   I look forward to seeing you at five o'clock on Monday.

3. *Mō kore ijō matemasen.*
   もうこれ以上待てません。
   I cannot wait any longer.

4. *Tomodachi kara henji ga kuru no o matte imasu.*
   友達から返事が来るのを待っています。
   I am waiting for my friend's reply.

5. *Kanojo ni ichi-jikan mo matasaremashita.*
   彼女に一時間も待たされました。
   She made me wait for one hour.

mawaru まわる

回る to turn around: (intrans.);* go around: (trans.)

		Affirmative	Negative
PLAIN FORM	PRESENT	mawaru	mawaranai
	PAST	mawatta	mawaranakatta
MASU FORM	PRESENT	mawarimasu	mawarimasen
	PAST	mawarimashita	mawarimasen deshita
TE FORM		mawatte	mawaranakute
CONDITIONAL	PLAIN	mawareba/mawatta ra	mawaranakereba/ mawaranakatta ra
	FORMAL	mawarimashita ra	mawarimasen deshita ra
VOLITIONAL	PLAIN	mawarō	–
	FORMAL	mawarimashō	–
IMPERATIVE		maware	mawaru na

	Affirmative		Affirmative
POTENTIAL	mawareru	**CAUS. PASSIVE**	mawaraserareru/ mawarasareru
PASSIVE	mawarareru	**HONORIFIC**	omawari ni naru/ mawarareru
CAUSATIVE	mawaraseru	**HUMBLE**	(omawari suru)

Examples:

1. *Senpūki ga mawatte ite, suzushii.*
   扇風機が回っていて、涼しい。
   It is cool as the electric fan is on.

2. *Kyōto no otera o mite mawaru ni wa basu ga benri desu.*
   京都のお寺を見て回るにはバスが便利です。
   It is convenient for you to go round Kyoto by bus to see the temples.

3. *Utau junban ga mawatte kita.*
   歌う順番が回ってきた。
   My turn to sing came.

4. *Kodomo-tachi ga kōen o hashiri-mawatte imasu.*
   子供達が公園を走り回っています。
   Children are running around the park.

5. *Isogashikute, me ga mawari sō da.*
   忙しくて、目が回りそうだ。
   I am so busy that I feel dizzy.

* The intransitive verb *mawaru* 回る meaning "to turn around" generally does not use the potential, passive, causative passive, honorific, or humble forms.

mawasu まわす

回す to turn, pass round, send on: (trans.)

		Affirmative	*Negative*
PLAIN FORM	PRESENT	mawasu	mawasanai
	PAST	mawashita	mawasanakatta
MASU FORM	PRESENT	mawashimasu	mawashimasen
	PAST	mawashimashita	mawashimasen deshita
TE FORM		mawashite	mawasanakute
CONDITIONAL	PLAIN	mawaseba/mawashita ra	mawasanakereba/ mawasanakatta ra
	FORMAL	mawashimashita ra	mawashimasen deshita ra
VOLITIONAL	PLAIN	mawasō	–
	FORMAL	mawashimashō	–
IMPERATIVE		mawase	mawasu na

	Affirmative		*Affirmative*
POTENTIAL	mawaseru	**CAUS. PASSIVE**	mawasaserareru
PASSIVE	mawasareru	**HONORIFIC**	omawashi ni naru/ mawasareru
CAUSATIVE	mawasaseru	**HUMBLE**	omawashi suru

Examples:

1. *Sono bin no futa wa mawashite akemasu.*
   その瓶の蓋は回して開けます。
   Open the bottle by twisting the cap.

2. *Kono tsumami o migi ni mawaseba, oyu ga demasu.*
   このつまみを右に回せば、お湯が出ます。
   If you turn this knob to the right, hot water comes out.

3. *Satō o mawashite kuremasen ka.*
   砂糖を回してくれませんか。
   Could you pass me the sugar?

4. *Kare wa betsu no ka ni mawasareta.*
   彼は別の課に回された。
   He was transferred to another section.

5. *Sono zasshi o yomi-owattara, watashi ni mawashite kudasai.*
   その雑誌を読み終わったら、私に回してください。
   After you finish reading that magazine, please pass it to me.

mayou まよう

迷う to be lost, be in doubt, be captivated: (intrans.)

		Affirmative	*Negative*
PLAIN FORM	PRESENT	mayou	mayowanai
	PAST	mayotta	mayowanakatta
MASU FORM	PRESENT	mayoimasu	mayoimasen
	PAST	mayoimashita	mayoimasen deshita
TE FORM		mayotte	mayowanakute
CONDITIONAL	PLAIN	mayoeba/mayotta ra	mayowanakereba/ mayowanakatta ra
	FORMAL	mayoimashita ra	mayoimasen deshita ra
VOLITIONAL	PLAIN	mayoō	–
	FORMAL	mayoimashō	–
IMPERATIVE		mayoe	mayou na

	Affirmative		*Affirmative*
POTENTIAL	mayoeru	**CAUS. PASSIVE**	mayowaserareru/ mayowasareru
PASSIVE	mayowareru	**HONORIFIC**	omayoi ni naru/ mayowareru
CAUSATIVE	mayowaseru	**HUMBLE**	(omayoi suru)

Examples:

1. *Yokohama de michi ni mayotte shimatta.*
   横浜で道に迷ってしまった。
   I lost my way in Yokohama.

2. *Dotchi no kutsu o kaō ka mayotte imasu.*
   どっちの靴を買おうか迷っています。
   I'm not sure which shoes to buy.

3. *Tochū de michi ni mayowanai yō ni, chizu o motte ikō.*
   途中で道に迷わないように、地図を持って行こう。
   Let's take the map with us so we don't get lost on the way.

4. *Sono eki no mawari wa michi ga fukuzatu de, mayoi-yasui.*
   その駅の周りは道が複雑で、迷いやすい。
   Because the streets around the station are complicated, it is easy to get lost.

5. *Sonna kotoba ni mayowasarete wa ikenai.*
   そんな言葉に迷わされてはいけない。
   You should not be misled by such words.

medatsu めだつ

目立つ to be outstanding, be remarkable: (intrans.)

		Affirmative	Negative
PLAIN FORM	PRESENT	medatsu	medatanai
	PAST	medatta	medatanakatta
MASU FORM	PRESENT	medachimasu	medachimasen
	PAST	medachimashita	medachimasen deshita
TE FORM		medatte	medatanakute
CONDITIONAL	PLAIN	medateba/medatta ra	medatanakereba/medatanakatta ra
	FORMAL	medachimashita ra	medachimasen deshita ra
VOLITIONAL	PLAIN	medatō	–
	FORMAL	medachimashō	–
IMPERATIVE		medate	medatsu na

	Affirmative		Affirmative
POTENTIAL	(medateru)	**CAUS. PASSIVE**	medataserareru/medatasareru
PASSIVE	(medatareru)	**HONORIFIC**	(omedachi ni naru)/(medatareru)
CAUSATIVE	medataseru	**HUMBLE**	(omedachi suru)

Examples:

1. *Kare wa se ga takai node medachimasu.*
   彼は背が高いので、目立ちます。
   Because he is tall, he sticks out.

2. *Sono fuku wa medachi-sugimasu.*
   その服は目立ちすぎます。
   Those clothes are too eye-catching.

3. *Memo o medatsu basho ni oite okō.*
   メモを目立つ場所に置いておこう。
   Let's put the memo where it will be easily seen.

4. *Kanojo wa Nihon-go ga medatte jōzu ni natta.*
   彼女は日本語が目立って上手になった。
   She made remarkable progress in her Japanese.

5. *Kyō wa medatta nyūsu wa nai.*
   今日は目立ったニュースはない。
   No news catches the eye today.

mieru みえる

見える to be seen, be able to see, to appear, come: (intrans.)

		Affirmative	Negative
PLAIN FORM	PRESENT	mieru	mienai
	PAST	mieta	mienakatta
MASU FORM	PRESENT	miemasu	miemasen
	PAST	miemashita	miemasen deshita
TE FORM		miete	mienakute
CONDITIONAL	PLAIN	miereba/mieta ra	mienakereba/ mienakatta ra
	FORMAL	miemashita ra	miemasen deshita ra
VOLITIONAL	PLAIN	mieyō	–
	FORMAL	miemashō	–
IMPERATIVE		miero	mieru na

	Affirmative		*Affirmative*
POTENTIAL	(mierareru)	**CAUS. PASSIVE**	(miesaserareru)
PASSIVE	(mierareru)	**HONORIFIC**	omie ni naru/mierareru
CAUSATIVE	(miesaseru)	**HUMBLE**	(omie suru)

Examples:

1. *Kyō wa tenki ga ii kara, yama ga yoku mieru.*
   今日は天気がいいから、山がよく見える。
   The weather today is so nice that you can see the mountain well.

2. *Koko kara wa nani mo miemasen.*
   ここからは何も見えません。
   Nothing is visible from here.

3. *Kare wa tsukarete iru yō ni mieta.*
   彼は疲れているように見えた。
   He looked tired.

4. *Yamada-san wa wakaku miemasu ne.*
   山田さんは若く見えますね。
   Mr. Yamada looks young, doesn't he?

5. *Sensei wa mamonaku omie ni narimasu.*
   先生は間もなくお見えになります。
   The teacher will arrive before long.

migaku みがく

磨く to polish, brush, improve, cultivate: (trans.)

		Affirmative	Negative
PLAIN FORM	PRESENT	migaku	migakanai
	PAST	migaita	migakanakatta
MASU FORM	PRESENT	migakimasu	migakimasen
	PAST	migakimashita	migakimasen deshita
TE FORM		migaite	migakanakute
CONDITIONAL	PLAIN	migakeba/migaita ra	migakanakereba/ migakanakatta ra
	FORMAL	migakimashita ra	migakimasen deshita ra
VOLITIONAL	PLAIN	migakō	–
	FORMAL	migakimashō	–
IMPERATIVE		migake	migaku na

	Affirmative		Affirmative
POTENTIAL	migakeru	**CAUS. PASSIVE**	migakaserareru/ migakasareru
PASSIVE	migakareru	**HONORIFIC**	omigaki ni naru/ migakareru
CAUSATIVE	migakaseru	**HUMBLE**	omigaki suru

Examples:

1. *Shokuji no ato de ha o migakimasu.*
   食事の後で歯を磨きます。
   I brush my teeth after every meal.

2. *Dekakeru mae ni kutsu o migakimashita.*
   出かける前に靴を磨きました。
   Before going out, I shined my shoes.

3. *Kare wa megane no renzu o migaite moratta.*
   彼は眼鏡のレンズを磨いてもらった。
   He had the lenses of his glasses polished.

4. *Kanojo no kuruma wa itsumo pikapika ni migaite aru.*
   彼女の車はいつもぴかぴかに磨いてある。
   Her car is always polished to a dazzling shine.

5. *Jūdō no ude o migaku tame ni, Nihon ni kimashita.*
   柔道の腕を磨くために、日本に来ました。
   I came to Japan to improve my judo skills.

miru みる

見る to see, look at, watch; みる to try : (both trans.)

		Affirmative	*Negative*
PLAIN FORM	PRESENT	miru	minai
	PAST	mita	minakatta
MASU FORM	PRESENT	mimasu	mimasen
	PAST	mimashita	mimasen deshita
TE FORM		mite	minakute
CONDITIONAL	PLAIN	mireba/mita ra	minakereba/minakatta ra
	FORMAL	mimashita ra	mimasen deshita ra
VOLITIONAL	PLAIN	miyō	–
	FORMAL	mimashō	–
IMPERATIVE		miro	miru na

	Affirmative		*Affirmative*
POTENTIAL	mirareru/mireru	**CAUS. PASSIVE**	misaserareru
PASSIVE	mirareru	**HONORIFIC**	goran ni naru/mirareru
CAUSATIVE	misaseru	**HUMBLE**	haiken suru

Examples:

1. *Yamada-san wa ano heya de terebi o mite imasu.*
   山田さんはあの部屋でテレビを見ています。
   Mr. Yamada is watching TV in that room.

2. *Eiga demo mi ni ikimasen ka.*
   映画でも見に行きませんか。
   Shall we go to see a movie?

3. *Ano shiai o goran ni narimashita ka.*
   あの試合をご覧になりましたか。
   I was wondering if you watched the game.

4. *Pasupōto o haiken shimasu.*
   パスポートを拝見します。
   May I see your passport?

5. *Dekiru ka dō ka wakarimasen ga, yatte mimasu.*
   できるかどうか分かりませんが、やってみます。
   I don't know whether I can do it or not, but I will try.

miseru みせる

見せる to show, display: (trans.)

		Affirmative	Negative
PLAIN FORM	PRESENT	miseru	misenai
	PAST	miseta	misenakatta
MASU FORM	PRESENT	misemasu	misemasen
	PAST	misemashita	misemasen deshita
TE FORM		misete	misenakute
CONDITIONAL	PLAIN	misereba/miseta ra	misenakereba/ misenakatta ra
	FORMAL	misemashita ra	misemasen deshita ra
VOLITIONAL	PLAIN	miseyō	–
	FORMAL	misemashō	–
IMPERATIVE		misero	miseru na

	Affirmative		Affirmative
POTENTIAL	miserareru/misereru	CAUS. PASSIVE	misesaserareru
PASSIVE	miserareru	HONORIFIC	omise ni naru/miserareru
CAUSATIVE	misesaseru	HUMBLE	omise suru

Examples:

1. *Chotto sono hon o misete kudasai.*
   ちょっとその本を見せてください。
   Please show me that book.

2. *Tanaka-san ni kazoku no shashin o misete moratta.*
   田中さんに家族の写真を見せてもらった。
   I had Mr. Tanaka show me pictures of his family.

3. *Keiki wa kaifuku no kizashi o misete iru.*
   景気は回復の兆しを見せている。
   The economy shows signs of recovering.

4. *Konna zankoku na eiga wa kodomo ni miserarenai.*
   こんな残酷な映画は子供に見せられない。
   Such a horrible movie cannot be shown to children.

5. *Kanarazu yatte misemasu.*
   必ずやってみせます。
   I'll show you I can do it.

mitomeru みとめる

認める to permit, admit, recognize: (trans.)

		Affirmative	Negative
PLAIN FORM	PRESENT	mitomeru	mitomenai
	PAST	mitometa	mitomenakatta
MASU FORM	PRESENT	mitomemasu	mitomemasen
	PAST	mitomemashita	mitomemasen deshita
TE FORM		mitomete	mitomenakute
CONDITIONAL	PLAIN	mitomereba/ mitometa ra	mitomenakereba/ mitomenakatta ra
	FORMAL	mitomemashita ra	mitomemasen deshita ra
VOLITIONAL	PLAIN	mitomeyō	–
	FORMAL	mitomemashō	–
IMPERATIVE		mitomero	mitomeru na

	Affirmative		Affirmative
POTENTIAL	mitomerareru/ mitomereru	**CAUS. PASSIVE**	mitomesaserareru
PASSIVE	mitomerareru	**HONORIFIC**	omitome ni naru/ mitomerareru
CAUSATIVE	mitomesaseru	**HUMBLE**	omitome suru

Examples:

1. *Chichi wa Nihon e no ryūgaku o mitomete kureta.*
父は日本への留学を認めてくれた。
My father allowed me to go to Japan to study.

2. *Yatto Nihon no daigaku no nyūgaku o mitomeraremashita.*
やっと日本の大学の入学を認められました。
At last, I was accepted into a Japanese university.

3. *Kare wa shippai o mitomete, ayamatta.*
彼は失敗を認めて、謝った。
He apologized after admitting his mistake.

4. *Suzuki-san wa jibun ga machigaeta koto o mitomeyō to shinai.*
鈴木さんは自分が間違えたことを認めようとしない。
Mr. Suzuki doesn't want to admit that he made a mistake.

5. *Kanojo wa doryoku to jisseki ga mitomerarete, shōshin shita.*
彼女は努力と実績が認められて、昇進した。
She was promoted after her efforts and competence were recognized.

mitsukaru

見つかる to be found, be discovered: (intrans.)

		Affirmative	Negative
PLAIN FORM	PRESENT	mitsukaru	mitsukaranai
	PAST	mitsukatta	mitsukaranakatta
MASU FORM	PRESENT	mitsukarimasu	mitsukarimasen
	PAST	mitsukarimashita	mitsukarimasen deshita
TE FORM		mitsukatte	mitsukaranakute
CONDITIONAL	PLAIN	mitsukareba/ mitsukatta ra	mitsukaranakereba/ mitsukaranakatta ra
	FORMAL	mitsukarimashita ra	mitsukarimasen deshita ra
VOLITIONAL	PLAIN	mitsukarō	–
	FORMAL	mitsukarimashō	–
IMPERATIVE		mitsukare	mitsukaru na

	Affirmative		Affirmative
POTENTIAL	mitsukareru	**CAUS. PASSIVE**	mitsukaraserareru/ mitsukarasareru
PASSIVE	mitsukarareru	**HONORIFIC**	omitsukari ni naru/ mitsukarareru
CAUSATIVE	mitsukaraseru	**HUMBLE**	(omitsukari suru)

Examples:

1. *Apāto ga mitsukatta? / Un, ii no ga mitsukatta yo.*
アパートが見つかった。/ うん、いいのが見つかったよ。
Did you find an apartment? / Yes, I found a good one.

2. *Sagashite ita hon ga yatto mitsukarimashita.*
捜していた本がやっと見つかりました。
At last I found the book that I was looking for.

3. *Atarashii shigoto ga mada mitsukaranai.*
新しい仕事がまだ見つからない。
I have not yet found a new job.

4. *Heya no kagi ga mitsukaranakute, komarimashita.*
部屋の鍵が見つからなくて、困りました。
I was in trouble because I couldn't find the room key.

5. *Sono gakusei wa sensei ni mitsukaranai yōni, kossori kyōshitsu ni haitta.*
その学生は先生に見つからないように、こっそり教室に入った。
The student entered the classroom secretly so as not to be caught by
a teacher.

mitsukeru みつける

見つける to find, discover, look for: (trans.)

			Affirmative	Negative
PLAIN FORM	PRESENT		mitsukeru	mitsukenai
	PAST		mitsuketa	mitsukenakatta
MASU FORM	PRESENT		mitsukemasu	mitsukemasen
	PAST		mitsukemashita	mitsukemasen deshita
TE FORM			mitsukete	mitsukenakute
CONDITIONAL	PLAIN		mitsukereba/ mitsuketa ra	mitsukenakereba/ mitsukenakatta ra
	FORMAL		mitsukemashita ra	mitsukemasen deshita ra
VOLITIONAL	PLAIN		mitsukeyō	–
	FORMAL		mitsukemashō	–
IMPERATIVE			mitsukero	mitsukeru na

	Affirmative		Affirmative
POTENTIAL	mitsukerareru/ mitsukereru	**CAUS. PASSIVE**	mitsukesaserareru
PASSIVE	mitsukerareru	**HONORIFIC**	omitsuke ni naru/ mitsukerareru
CAUSATIVE	mitsukesaseru	**HUMBLE**	omitsuke suru

Examples:

1. *Omoshiroi hon o mitsuketa node shōkai shimasu.*
   面白い本を見つけたので、紹介します。
   I'd like to tell you about an interesting book I found.

2. *Michi ni saifu ga ochite iru no o mitsukemashita.*
   道に財布が落ちているのを見つけました。
   I found a wallet on the road.

3. *Tanaka-san o mitsuketa ra, watashi ni denwa suru yōni itte kudasai.*
   田中さんを見つけたら、私に電話するように言ってください。
   When you find Mr. Tanaka, please ask him to call me.

4. *Nihon de shigoto o mitsuke-tai to omotte imasu.*
   日本で仕事を見つけたいと思っています。
   I'd like to find a job in Japan

5. *Repōto o kaku no ni chōdo ii shiryō ga mitsukerarenakatta.*
   レポートを書くのに丁度いい資料が見つけられなかった。
   I couldn't find suitable materials to write the report.

mōkaru もうかる

もうかる to make a profit, be lucky: (intrans.)

		Affirmative	Negative
PLAIN FORM	PRESENT	mōkaru	mōkaranai
	PAST	mōkatta	mōkaranakatta
MASU FORM	PRESENT	mōkarimasu	mōkarimasen
	PAST	mōkarimashita	mōkarimasen deshita
TE FORM		mōkatte	mōkaranakute
CONDITIONAL	PLAIN	mōkareba/mōkatta ra	mōkaranakereba/ mōkaranakatta ra
	FORMAL	mōkarimashita ra	mōkarimasen deshita ra
VOLITIONAL	PLAIN	mōkarō	–
	FORMAL	mōkarimashō	–
IMPERATIVE		mōkare	mōkaru na

	Affirmative		Affirmative
POTENTIAL	mōkareru	**CAUS. PASSIVE**	mōkaraserareru/ mōkarasareru
PASSIVE	mōkarareru	**HONORIFIC**	omōkari ni naru/ mōkarareru
CAUSATIVE	mōkaraseru	**HUMBLE**	(omōkari suru)

Examples:

1. *Kare no kaisha wa totemo mōkatte iru rashii.*
   彼の会社はとてももうかっているらしい。
   His company seems to be making handsome profits

2. *Kajino de ikura mōkarimashita ka. / jū-man en mōkarimashita.*
   カジノでいくらもうかりましたか。 / 十万円もうかりました。
   How much did you win at the casino? / I won hundred thousand yen.

3. *Sono shōbai wa kitai shita hodo mōkaranakatta.*
   その商売は期待したほどもうからなかった。
   That business didn't do as well as expected.

4. *Mōkattara, gochisō shite kudasai ne.*
   もうかったら、ごちそうしてくださいね。
   Please treat me if you make a lot of money.

5. *Kare ga kaisha made kuruma ni nosete kureta node mōkatta.*
   彼が会社まで車に乗せてくれたので、もうかった。
   I was lucky because he gave me a lift to the company.

mōkeru もうける

もうける to make a profit, to have a child; 設ける to set up: (both trans.)

		Affirmative	Negative
PLAIN FORM	PRESENT	mōkeru	mōkenai
	PAST	mōketa	mōkenakatta
MASU FORM	PRESENT	mōkemasu	mōkemasen
	PAST	mōkemashita	mōkemasen deshita
TE FORM		mōkete	mōkenakute
CONDITIONAL	PLAIN	mōkereba/mōketa ra	mōkenakereba/ mōkenakatta ra
	FORMAL	mōkemashita ra	mōkemasen deshita ra
VOLITIONAL	PLAIN	mōkeyō	–
	FORMAL	mōkemashō	–
IMPERATIVE		mōkero	mōkeru na

	Affirmative		Affirmative
POTENTIAL	mōkerareru/ mōkereru	**CAUS. PASSIVE**	mōkesaserareru
PASSIVE	mōkerareru	**HONORIFIC**	omōke ni naru/ mōkerareru
CAUSATIVE	mōkesaseru	**HUMBLE**	(omōke suru)

Examples:

1. *Kare wa tōshi de okane o mōkemashita.*
   彼は投資でお金をもうけました。
   He profited well on his investment.

2. *Keiba de ikura mōkemashita ka. / San-man en gurai mōkemashita.*
   競馬でいくらもうけましたか。/ 三万円ぐらいもうけました。
   How much did you make on horse racing? / I made about thirty thousand yen.

3. *Sonna kantan ni mōkerareru shigoto wa nai darō.*
   そんな簡単にもうけられる仕事はないだろう。
   There is no job that can make you so much money so easily.

4. *Kare wa eki mae no biru ni jimusho o mōketa.*
   彼は駅前のビルに事務所を設けた。
   He set up his office in front of the station.

5. *Yakusho no ikkai ni sōdan madoguchi ga mōkerarete iru.*
   役所の一階に相談窓口が設けられている。
   The consulting desk is located on the first floor of the government office.

morasu もらす

漏らす to let leak out, escape: (trans.)

		Affirmative	Negative
PLAIN FORM	PRESENT	morasu	morasanai
	PAST	morashita	morasanakatta
MASU FORM	PRESENT	morashimasu	morashimasen
	PAST	morashimashita	morashimasen deshita
TE FORM		morashite	morasanakute
CONDITIONAL	PLAIN	moraseba/morashita ra	morasanakereba/ morasanakatta ra
	FORMAL	morashimashita ra	morashimasen deshita ra
VOLITIONAL	PLAIN	morasō	–
	FORMAL	morashimashō	–
IMPERATIVE		morase	morasu na

	Affirmative		Affirmative
POTENTIAL	moraseru	**CAUS. PASSIVE**	morasaserareru
PASSIVE	morasareru	**HONORIFIC**	omorashi ni naru/ morasareru
CAUSATIVE	morasaseru	**HUMBLE**	(omorashi suru)

Examples:

1. *Himitsu o morasanaide kudasai.*
   秘密を漏らさないでください。
   Please don't reveal our secret.

2. *Kono kāten wa hikari o soto ni morasanai.*
   このカーテンは光を外に漏らさない。
   This curtain does not let the light out.

3. *Dareka ga kaisha no jōhō o soto ni morashite iru.*
   誰かが会社の情報を外に漏らしている。
   Somebody is leaking company information to the outside.

4. *Kanojo wa omowazu tameiki o morashita.*
   彼女は思わずため息を漏らした。
   She sighed unintentionally.

5. *Kare no setsumei o kiki-morashite shimatta.*
   彼の説明を聞き漏らしてしまった。
   I did not catch his explanation.

morau もらう

もらう to get, receive, to marry: (trans.)

		Affirmative	Negative
PLAIN FORM	PRESENT	morau	morawanai
	PAST	moratta	morawanakatta
MASU FORM	PRESENT	moraimasu	moraimasen
	PAST	moraimashita	moraimasen deshita
TE FORM		moratte	morawanakute
CONDITIONAL	PLAIN	moraeba/moratta ra	morawanakereba/ morawanakatta ra
	FORMAL	moraimashita ra	moraimasen deshita ra
VOLITIONAL	PLAIN	moraō	–
	FORMAL	moraimashō	–
IMPERATIVE		morae	morau na

	Affirmative		Affirmative
POTENTIAL	moraeru	**CAUS. PASSIVE**	morawaserareru/ morawasareru
PASSIVE	morawareru	**HONORIFIC**	omorai ni naru/ morawareru
CAUSATIVE	morawaseru	**HUMBLE**	itadaku

Examples:

1. *Tomodachi kara tanjōbi no purezento o moraimashita.*
   友達から誕生日のプレゼントをもらいました。
   I received a birthday present from a friend.

2. *Kore wa sensei kara itadaita jisho desu.*
   これは先生から頂いた辞書です。
   This is a dictionary that I got from my teacher.

3. *Tomodachi ni kūkō made kuruma de okutte moratta.*
   友達に空港まで車で送ってもらった。
   My friend kindly took me to the airport by car.

4. *Sumimasen ga, mō sukoshi shizuka ni shite moraemasen ka.*
   すみませんが、もう少し静かにしてもらえませんか。
   Excuse me, but can you be more quiet please?

5. *Michi ga wakaranai'n desu ga, oshiete itadakemasen ka.*
   道がわからないんですが、教えていただけませんか。
   Excuse me, but I am lost. Could you please show me the way?

moreru もれる

漏れる to leak out, escape: (intrans.)

		Affirmative	*Negative*
PLAIN FORM	PRESENT	moreru	morenai
	PAST	moreta	morenakatta
MASU FORM	PRESENT	moremasu	moremasen
	PAST	moremashita	moremasen deshita
TE FORM		morete	morenakute
CONDITIONAL	PLAIN	morereba/moreta ra	morenakereba/ morenakatta ra
	FORMAL	moremashita ra	moremasen deshita ra
VOLITIONAL	PLAIN	moreyō	–
	FORMAL	moremashō	–
IMPERATIVE		morero	moreru na

	Affirmative		*Affirmative*
POTENTIAL	morerareru/ morereru	**CAUS. PASSIVE**	moresaserareru
PASSIVE	morerareru	**HONORIFIC**	omore ni naru/ morerareru
CAUSATIVE	moresaseru	**HUMBLE**	(omore suru)

Examples:

1. *Hōsu kara mizu ga morete iru.*
   ホースから水が漏れている。
   Water leaks from the hose.

2. *Hen na nioi ga shimasu ga, gasu ga morete imasen ka.*
   変なにおいがしますが、ガスが漏れていませんか。
   It smells strange. Could it be gas leaking?

3. *Kāten no sukima kara akari ga morete imasu.*
   カーテンのすき間から明かりが漏れています。
   Light is shining through the opening between the curtains.

4. *Meibo kara kare no namae ga morete ita.*
   名簿から彼の名前が漏れていた。
   His name has been omitted from the list.

5. *Himitsu wa kare no kuchi kara moreta rashii.*
   秘密は彼の口から漏れたらしい。
   It seems like the secrets were leaked out from his mouth.

motomeru もとめる

求める to demand, ask, seek, buy: (trans.)

		Affirmative	Negative
PLAIN FORM	PRESENT	motomeru	motomenai
	PAST	motometa	motomenakatta
MASU FORM	PRESENT	motomemasu	motomemasen
	PAST	motomemashita	motomemasen deshita
TE FORM		motomete	motomenakute
CONDITIONAL	PLAIN	motomereba/ motometa ra	motomenakereba/ motomenakatta ra
	FORMAL	motomemashita ra	motomemasen deshita ra
VOLITIONAL	PLAIN	motomeyō	–
	FORMAL	motomemashō	–
IMPERATIVE		motomero	motomeru na

	Affirmative		Affirmative
POTENTIAL	motomerareru/ motomereru	CAUS. PASSIVE	motomesaserareru
PASSIVE	motomerareru	HONORIFIC	omotome ni naru/ motomerareru
CAUSATIVE	motomesaseru	HUMBLE	omotome suru

Examples:

1. *Shachō ni menkai o motomemashita.*
   社長に面会を求めました。
   They requested an interview with the president.

2. *Koe o agete, tasuke o motometa.*
   声を上げて、助けを求めた。
   He shouted for help.

3. *Sono kaisha wa ichi-nen ijō keiken no aru hito o motomete iru.*
   その会社は一年以上経験のある人を求めている。
   The company is looking for a person with over a year's experience.

4. *Sono kaban wa doko de omotome ni narimashita ka.*
   そのかばんは、どこでお求めになりましたか。
   Where did you buy the bag?

5. *Nyūjōken wa iriguchi no madoguchi de omotome kudasai.*
   入場券は入口の窓口でお求めください。
   Please buy the admission ticket at the entrance window.

motsu もつ

持つ to have, hold, own: (trans.)

		Affirmative	Negative
PLAIN FORM	PRESENT	motsu	motanai
	PAST	motta	motanakatta
MASU FORM	PRESENT	mochimasu	mochimasen
	PAST	mochimashita	mochimasen deshita
TE FORM		motte	motanakute
CONDITIONAL	PLAIN	moteba/motta ra	motanakereba/ motanakatta ra
	FORMAL	mochimashita ra	mochimasen deshita ra
VOLITIONAL	PLAIN	motō	–
	FORMAL	mochimashō	–
IMPERATIVE		mote	motsu na

	Affirmative		Affirmative
POTENTIAL	moteru	**CAUS. PASSIVE**	motaserareru/motasareru
PASSIVE	motareru	**HONORIFIC**	omochi ni naru/motareru
CAUSATIVE	motaseru	**HUMBLE**	omochi suru

Examples:

1. *Sumimasen ga, nimotsu o motte kuremasen ka.*
   すみませんが、荷物を持ってくれませんか。
   Excuse me, but could you please hold the baggage?

2. *Watashi wa ima okane o motte imasen.*
   私は今お金を持っていません。
   I don't have any money now.

3. *Sono kaban o omochi shimashō ka.*
   そのかばんをお持ちしましょうか。
   Shall I carry the bag for you?

4. *Haha ni omoi kaimono bukuro o motasareta.*
   母に重い買い物袋を持たされた。
   My mother made me carry her heavy shopping bag.

5. *Mori-san wa ōki na mise o motte imasu.*
   森さんは大きな店を持っています。
   Mr. Mori runs a big shop.

mukeru むける

向ける to turn toward, point at: (trans.)

		Affirmative	*Negative*
PLAIN FORM	PRESENT	mukeru	mukenai
	PAST	muketa	mukenakatta
MASU FORM	PRESENT	mukemasu	mukemasen
	PAST	mukemashita	mukemasen deshita
TE FORM		mukete	mukenakute
CONDITIONAL	PLAIN	mukereba/muketa ra	mukenakereba/ mukenakatta ra
	FORMAL	mukemashita ra	mukemasen deshita ra
VOLITIONAL	PLAIN	mukeyō	–
	FORMAL	mukemashō	–
IMPERATIVE		mukero	mukeru na

	Affirmative		*Affirmative*
POTENTIAL	mukerareru/ mukereru	**CAUS. PASSIVE**	mukesaserareru
PASSIVE	mukerareru	**HONORIFIC**	omuke ni naru/ mukerareru
CAUSATIVE	mukesaseru	**HUMBLE**	omuke suru

Examples:

1. *Kare wa kyū ni kao o kochira ni muketa.*
   彼は急に顔をこちらに向けた。
   He suddenly turned his face toward us.

2. *Kanojo wa okotte, watashi ni se o muketa.*
   彼女は怒って、私に背を向けた。
   She turned her back on me in anger.

3. *Kare wa Nihon ni mukete, shuppatsu shita.*
   彼は日本に向けて、出発した。
   He set off for Japan.

4. *Marason taikai ni mukete, mainichi hashitte imasu.*
   マラソン大会に向けて、毎日走っています。
   I am running every day for the marathon meet.

5. *Kishadan no shitsumon wa subete sono seijika ni mukerareta.*
   記者団の質問は、すべてその政治家に向けられた。
   Every question from the press corps was directed to that politician.

muku

向く to look toward, to suit: (intrans.);* むく to peel, to strip off: (trans.)

		Affirmative	*Negative*
PLAIN FORM	PRESENT	*muku*	*mukanai*
	PAST	*muita*	*mukanakatta*
MASU FORM	PRESENT	*mukimasu*	*mukimasen*
	PAST	*mukimashita*	*mukimasen deshita*
TE FORM		*muite*	*mukanakute*
CONDITIONAL	PLAIN	*mukeba/muita ra*	*mukanakereba/ mukanakatta ra*
	FORMAL	*mukimashita ra*	*mukimasen deshita ra*
VOLITIONAL	PLAIN	*mukō*	–
	FORMAL	*mukimashō*	–
IMPERATIVE		*muke*	*muku na*

	Affirmative		*Affirmative*
POTENTIAL	*mukeru*	**CAUS. PASSIVE**	*mukaserareru/ mukasareru*
PASSIVE	*mukareru*	**HONORIFIC**	*omuki ni naru/ mukareru*
CAUSATIVE	*mukaseru*	**HUMBLE**	*omuki suru*

Examples:

1. *Shashin o torimasu kara, kochira o muite kudasai.*
   写真を撮りますから、こちらを向いてください。
   Please look this way. I'm going to take a photo.

2. *Kono heya wa minami ni muite iru.*
   この部屋は南に向いている。
   This room faces south.

3. *Kanojo wa kyōshi ni muite iru to omoimasu.*
   彼女は教師に向いていると思います。
   I think that she is suitable as a teacher.

4. *Kono fuku wa wakai hito ni mukimasen.*
   この服は若い人に向きません。
   These clothes are not suitable for young people.

5. *Jagaimo no kawa o muite kudasai.*
   じゃがいもの皮をむいてください。
   Please peel the potato.

* The verb *muku* 向く meaning "to look toward, to suit" generally does not use either potential or passive forms.

musubu むすぶ

結ぶ to tie, contract, connect, link: (trans.)

		Affirmative	Negative
PLAIN FORM	PRESENT	musubu	musubanai
	PAST	musunda	musubanakatta
MASU FORM	PRESENT	musubimasu	musubimasen
	PAST	musubimashita	musubimasen deshita
TE FORM		musunde	musubanakute
CONDITIONAL	PLAIN	musubeba/musunda ra	musubanakereba/ musubanakatta ra
	FORMAL	musubimashita ra	musubimasen deshita ra
VOLITIONAL	PLAIN	musubō	–
	FORMAL	musubimashō	–
IMPERATIVE		musube	musubu na

	Affirmative		Affirmative
POTENTIAL	musuberu	**CAUS. PASSIVE**	musubaserareru/ musubasareru
PASSIVE	musubareru	**HONORIFIC**	omusubi ni naru/ musubareru
CAUSATIVE	musubaseru	**HUMBLE**	omusubi suru

Examples:

1. *Kimono no obi o musubu no wa muzukashii.*
   着物の帯を結ぶのは難しい。
   Tying up the Obi (belt) of the kimono is difficult.

2. *Kono basu wa futatsu no toshi o musunde iru.*
   このバスは二つの都市を結んでいる。
   This bus connects two cities.

3. *Kanojo wa kaminoke o musunde, poniitēru ni shita.*
   彼女は髪の毛を結んで、ポニーテールにした。
   She tied her hair into a ponytail.

4. *Nihon no kaisha to keiyaku o musubu koto ga dekita.*
   日本の会社と契約を結ぶことができた。
   We were able to make a contract with a Japanese company.

5. *Futari wa jū nen-kan kōsai shite, yatto musubaremashita.*
   二人は十年間交際して、やっと結ばれました。
   The two finally married after seeing each other for ten years.

nageru

投げる to throw, pitch: (trans.)

		Affirmative	Negative
PLAIN FORM	PRESENT	nageru	nagenai
	PAST	nageta	nagenakatta
MASU FORM	PRESENT	nagemasu	nagemasen
	PAST	nagemashita	nagemasen deshita
TE FORM		nagete	nagenakute
CONDITIONAL	PLAIN	nagereba/nageta ra	nagenakereba/ nagenakatta ra
	FORMAL	nagemashita ra	nagemasen deshita ra
VOLITIONAL	PLAIN	nageyō	–
	FORMAL	nagemashō	–
IMPERATIVE		nagero	nageru na

	Affirmative		Affirmative
POTENTIAL	nagerareru/nagereru	**CAUS. PASSIVE**	nagesaserareru
PASSIVE	nagerareru	**HONORIFIC**	onage ni naru/nagerareru
CAUSATIVE	nagesaseru	**HUMBLE**	onage suru

Examples:

1. *Kodomo-tachi ga bōru o nagete asonde imasu.*
   子供達がボールを投げて遊んでいます。
   The children are playing catch-ball.

2. *Soko ni aru kagi o kocchi ni nagete kudasai.*
   そこにある鍵をこっちに投げてください。
   Will you please throw me that key.

3. *Sono picchā wa hayai tama o nageru.*
   そのピッチャーは速い球を投げる。
   That pitcher can throw a fast ball.

4. *Kare wa kata o kowashite shimatte, bōru ga nagerarenai.*
   彼は肩を壊してしまって、ボールが投げられない。
   He cannot throw a ball since he got a shoulder injury.

5. *Tochū de nagenaide, saigo made ganbarō.*
   途中で投げないで、最後まで頑張ろう。
   Let's do our best till the end without giving up.

naku なく

鳴く to cry (for birds, insects), to bark, roar, mew, etc.; 泣く to cry (for persons): (both intrans.)

			Affirmative	Negative
PLAIN FORM		PRESENT	naku	nakanai
		PAST	naita	nakanakatta
MASU FORM		PRESENT	nakimasu	nakimasen
		PAST	nakimashita	nakimasen deshita
TE FORM			naite	nakanakute
CONDITIONAL		PLAIN	nakeba/naita ra	nakanakereba/ nakanakatta ra
		FORMAL	nakimashita ra	nakimasen deshita ra
VOLITIONAL		PLAIN	nakō	–
		FORMAL	nakimashō	–
IMPERATIVE			nake	naku na

	Affirmative		Affirmative
POTENTIAL	nakeru	**CAUS. PASSIVE**	nakaserareru/nakasareru
PASSIVE	nakareru	**HONORIFIC**	onaki ni naru/nakareru
CAUSATIVE	nakaseru	**HUMBLE**	onaki suru

Examples:

1. *Tori ga naite imasu.*
   鳥が鳴いています。
   The bird is singing.

2. *Akachan ga naite iru koe ga kikoeru.*
   赤ちゃんが泣いている声が聞こえる。
   I hear a baby crying.

3. *Shiken ni ukari, ureshikute naita.*
   試験に受かり、うれしくて泣いた。
   I cried for joy because I passed the examination.

4. *Kanojo o nakasete shimatta.*
   彼女を泣かせてしまった。
   I made her cry.

5. *Kyonen no natsu, nōka wa mizu busoku ni nakasareta.*
   去年の夏、農家は水不足に泣かされた。
   The farmer was severely shocked by the shortage of water last year.

nakunaru なくなる

無くなる to be missing, to run out; 亡くなる to die, pass away:
(both intrans.)

		Affirmative	Negative
PLAIN FORM	PRESENT	nakunaru	nakunaranai
	PAST	nakunatta	nakunaranakatta
MASU FORM	PRESENT	nakunarimasu	nakunarimasen
	PAST	nakunarimashita	nakunarimasen deshita
TE FORM		nakunatte	nakunaranakute
CONDITIONAL	PLAIN	nakunareba/ nakunatta ra	nakunaranakereba/ nakunaranakatta ra
	FORMAL	nakunarimashita ra	nakunarimasen deshita ra
VOLITIONAL	PLAIN	nakunarō	–
	FORMAL	nakunarimashō	–
IMPERATIVE		nakunare	nakunaru na

	Affirmative		Affirmative
POTENTIAL	nakunareru	**CAUS. PASSIVE**	nakunaraserareru/ nakunarasareru
PASSIVE	nakunarareru	**HONORIFIC**	onakunari ni naru/ nakunarareru
CAUSATIVE	nakunaraseru	**HUMBLE**	(onakunari suru)

Examples:

1. *Hon ga nakunatte shimatta.*
   本がなくなってしまった。
   The book is lost.

2. *Kabu ni wa kyōmi ga nakunarimashita.*
   株には興味がなくなりました。
   I have lost interest in stocks.

3. *Gyūnyū ga nakunari sō da kara, katte kite kudasai.*
   牛乳がなくなりそうだから、買って来てください。
   We are almost out of milk, so I would like you to buy some.

4. *Sofu ga nakunatte, go-nen ni narimasu.*
   祖父が亡くなって、五年になります。
   It has been five years since my grandfather died.

5. *Yamada-san wa kyonen onakunari ni narimashita.*
   山田さんは去年お亡くなりになりました。
   Mr. Yamada died last year.

nakusu なくす

無くす to lose (things); 亡くす to lose (person):* (both trans.)

		Affirmative	Negative
PLAIN FORM	PRESENT	nakusu	nakusanai
	PAST	nakushita	nakusanakatta
MASU FORM	PRESENT	nakushimasu	nakushimasen
	PAST	nakushimashita	nakushimasen deshita
TE FORM		nakushite	nakusanakute
CONDITIONAL	PLAIN	nakuseba/nakushita ra	nakusanakereba/ nakusanakatta ra
	FORMAL	nakushimashita ra	nakushimasen deshita ra
VOLITIONAL	PLAIN	nakusō	–
	FORMAL	nakushimashō	–
IMPERATIVE		nakuse	nakusu na

	Affirmative		Affirmative
POTENTIAL	nakuseru	**CAUS. PASSIVE**	nakusaserareru
PASSIVE	nakusareru	**HONORIFIC**	onakushi ni naru/ nakusareru
CAUSATIVE	nakusaseru	**HUMBLE**	(onakushi suru)

Examples:

1. *Dokoka de saifu o nakushite shimatta.*
   どこかで財布を無くしてしまった。
   I lost my wallet somewhere.

2. *Kono shorui wa zettai ni nakusanai de kudasai.*
   この書類は絶対に無くさないでください。
   You must never lose these documents please.

3. *Shiken ni ochite, jishin o nakushite shimatta.*
   試験に落ちて、自信を無くしてしまった。
   Because I failed the exam, I lost my confidence.

4. *Imōto ni daiji na hon o nakusareta.*
   妹に大事な本を無くされた。
   Unfortunately my younger sister lost my important book.

5. *Kanojo wa jiko de ryōshin o nakushita.*
   彼女は事故で両親を亡くした。
   She lost her parents in an accident.

* *Nakusu* 亡くす meaning "to lose (person)" generally does not use the imperative or volitional forms.

naoru なおる

直る to be corrected, be repaired;* 治る to recover, get well: (both intrans.)

		Affirmative	*Negative*
PLAIN FORM	PRESENT	naoru	naoranai
	PAST	naotta	naoranakatta
MASU FORM	PRESENT	naorimasu	naorimasen
	PAST	naorimashita	naoimasen deshita
TE FORM		naotte	naoranakute
CONDITIONAL	PLAIN	naoreba/naotta ra	naoranakereba/ naoranakatta ra
	FORMAL	naorimashita ra	naorimasen deshita ra
VOLITIONAL	PLAIN	naorō	–
	FORMAL	naorimashō	–
IMPERATIVE		naore	naoru na

	Affirmative		*Affirmative*
POTENTIAL	(naoreru)	**CAUS. PASSIVE**	naoraserareru/ naorasareru
PASSIVE	(naorareru)	**HONORIFIC**	onaori ni naru/naorareru
CAUSATIVE	naoraseru	**HUMBLE**	(onaori suru)

Examples:

1. *Tokei ga naorimashita.*
   時計が直りました。
   The watch was fixed.

2. *Kono pasokon wa mō naoranai to iwaremashita.*
   このパソコンはもう直らないと言われました。
   I was told that this PC could never be repaired.

3. *Mō kaze wa naorimashita ka. / Ee, sukkari yoku narimashita.*
   もう風邪は治りましたか。 / ええ、すっかりよくなりました。
   Have you gotten rid of your cold? / Yes, I have completely recovered.

4. *Byōki ga naoru yō ni, yukkuri yasunde kudasai.*
   病気が治るように、ゆっくり休んでください。
   Please rest well, so that you will get better.

5. *Ashi no kega wa mada kanzen ni naotte inai.*
   足のけがは、まだ完全に治っていない。
   My foot injury has not completely healed.

* The intransitive verb *naoru* 直る meaning "to be corrected, repaired" generally does not use any honorific, causative, or causative passive forms.

naosu なおす

直す to correct, fix, change; 治す to cure: (both trans.)

		Affirmative	Negative
PLAIN FORM	PRESENT	naosu	naosanai
	PAST	naoshita	naosanakatta
MASU FORM	PRESENT	naoshimasu	naoshimasen
	PAST	naoshimashita	naoshimasen deshita
TE FORM		naoshite	naosanakute
CONDITIONAL	PLAIN	naoseba/naoshita ra	naosanakereba/ naosanakatta ra
	FORMAL	naoshimashita ra	naoshimasen deshita ra
VOLITIONAL	PLAIN	naosō	–
	FORMAL	naoshimashō	–
IMPERATIVE		naose	naosu na

	Affirmative		Affirmative
POTENTIAL	naoseru	**CAUS. PASSIVE**	naosaserareru
PASSIVE	naosareru	**HONORIFIC**	onaoshi ni naru/naosareru
CAUSATIVE	naosaseru	**HUMBLE**	onaoshi suru

Examples:

1. *Nihongo de tegami o kaita'n desu ga, machigai o naoshite moraemasen ka.*
   日本語で手紙を書いたんですが、間違いを直してもらえま
   せんか。
   I wrote a letter in Japanese, but could you please correct my mistakes?

2. *Kuruma o naoshite moraimashita.*
   車を直してもらいました。
   I had my car fixed.

3. *Kowareta jitensha o naosu no ni ichiman-en mo kakatta.*
   壊れた自転車を直すのに一万円もかかった。
   It cost me 10,000 yen to repair my broken bicycle.

4. *Go-man en o doru ni naosu to, ikura desu ka.*
   五万円をドルに直すと、いくらですか。
   How much is 50,000 yen in dollars?

5. *Kinjo no haisha de mushiba o naoshite moratta.*
   近所の歯医者で虫歯を治してもらった。
   I had my cavities fixed by the dentist near my house.

naraberu ならべる

並べる to line up, arrange, display: (trans.)

		Affirmative	Negative
PLAIN FORM	PRESENT	naraberu	narabenai
	PAST	narabeta	narabenakatta
MASU FORM	PRESENT	narabemasu	narabemasen
	PAST	narabemashita	narabemasen deshita
TE FORM		narabete	narabenakute
CONDITIONAL	PLAIN	narabereba/narabeta ra	narabenakereba/narabenakatta ra
	FORMAL	narabemashita ra	narabemasen deshita ra
VOLITIONAL	PLAIN	narabeyō	–
	FORMAL	narabemashō	–
IMPERATIVE		narabero	naraberu na

	Affirmative		Affirmative
POTENTIAL	naraberareru/narabereru	**CAUS. PASSIVE**	narabesaserareru
PASSIVE	naraberareru	**HONORIFIC**	onarabe ni naru/nareberareru
CAUSATIVE	narabesaseru	**HUMBLE**	onarabe suru

Examples:

1. *Shokki o tēburu ni narabete kudasai.*
   食器をテーブルに並べてください。
   Please arrange the tableware on the table.

2. *Isu o ni-retsu ni narabemashita.*
   いすを二列に並べました
   We lined up the chairs in two rows.

3. *Fairu wa bangō no junban ni narebete oite kudasai.*
   ファイルは番号の順番に並べておいてください。
   Please display the files in order of serial numbers.

4. *Shinamono wa shōkēsu ni narabete arimasu.*
   品物はショーケースに並べてあります。
   The goods are on display in the showcase.

5. *Hon wa gojū-on jun ni naraberarete iru.*
   本は五十音順に並べられている。
   The books are placed in the order of the Japanese syllabary.

narabu ならぶ

並ぶ to stand in a line, to equal: (intrans.)

		Affirmative	Negative
PLAIN FORM	PRESENT	narabu	narabanai
	PAST	naranda	narabanakatta
MASU FORM	PRESENT	narabimasu	narabimasen
	PAST	narabimashita	narabimasen deshita
TE FORM		narande	narabanakute
CONDITIONAL	PLAIN	narabeba/naranda ra	narabanakereba/ narabanakatta ra
	FORMAL	narabimashita ra	narabimasen deshita ra
VOLITIONAL	PLAIN	narabō	–
	FORMAL	narabimashō	–
IMPERATIVE		narabe	narabu na

	Affirmative		Affirmative
POTENTIAL	naraberu	**CAUS. PASSIVE**	narabaserareru/ narabasareru
PASSIVE	narabareru	**HONORIFIC**	onarabi ni naru/ narabareru
CAUSATIVE	narabaseru	**HUMBLE**	onarabi suru

Examples:

1. *Ichi-retsu ni narande kudasai.*
   一列に並んでください。
   Please stand in a line.

2. *Eigakan no mae ni takusan no hito ga narande imasu.*
   映画館の前にたくさんの人が並んでいます。
   Many people are lined up in front of the movie theater.

3. *Sensei wa gakusei o kōtei ni narabaseta.*
   先生は学生を校庭に並ばせた。
   The teacher made his students stand in line on the school ground.

4. *Sono tōri ni wa iroirona mise ga narande iru.*
   その通りには、いろいろな店が並んでいる。
   There is a variety of shops along the street.

5. *Tenisu de wa kare ni narabu mono wa inai.*
   テニスでは彼に並ぶ者はいない。
   No one equals him in tennis.

narau ならう

習う to learn: (trans.)

		Affirmative	*Negative*
PLAIN FORM	PRESENT	narau	narawanai
	PAST	naratta	narawanakatta
MASU FORM	PRESENT	naraimasu	naraimasen
	PAST	naraimashita	naraimasen deshita
TE FORM		naratte	narawanakute
CONDITIONAL	PLAIN	naraeba/naratta ra	narawanakereba/ narawanakatta ra
	FORMAL	naraimashita ra	naraimasen deshita ra
VOLITIONAL	PLAIN	naraō	–
	FORMAL	naraimashō	–
IMPERATIVE		narae	narau na

	Affirmative		*Affirmative*
POTENTIAL	naraeru	**CAUS. PASSIVE**	narawaserareru/ narawasareru
PASSIVE	narawareru	**HONORIFIC**	onarai ni naru/ narawareru
CAUSATIVE	narawaseru	**HUMBLE**	onarai suru

Examples:

1. *Nihon-jin no tomodachi kara Nihon-go o naraimashita.*
   日本人の友達から日本語を習いました。
   I learned Japanese from my Japanese friend.

2. *Ikebana o naraō to omotte imasu.*
   生け花を習おうと思っています。
   I intend to learn Ikebana (Japanese flower arrangement).

3. *Yamada-san wa gitā o naraita-gatte iru.*
   山田さんはギターを習いたがっている。
   Mr. Yamada wants to learn how to play the guitar.

4. *Kanojo wa musume ni eigo o narawaseta.*
   彼女は娘に英語を習わせた。
   She made her daughter learn English.

5. *Kodomo no toki, piano o narawasaremashita.*
   子供の時、ピアノを習わされました。
   When I was a child, I was made to learn the piano.

nareru なれる

慣れる to get used to, become skilled at: (intrans.)

		Affirmative	Negative
PLAIN FORM	PRESENT	nareru	narenai
	PAST	nareta	narenakatta
MASU FORM	PRESENT	naremasu	naremasen
	PAST	naremashita	naremasen deshita
TE FORM		narete	narenakute
CONDITIONAL	PLAIN	narereba/nareta ra	narenakereba/ narenakatta ra
	FORMAL	naremashita ra	naremasen deshita ra
VOLITIONAL	PLAIN	nareyō	–
	FORMAL	naremashō	–
IMPERATIVE		narero	nareru na

	Affirmative		Affirmative
POTENTIAL	(narerareru)	**CAUS. PASSIVE**	naresaserareru
PASSIVE	(narerareru)	**HONORIFIC**	onare ni naru/narerareru
CAUSATIVE	naresaseru	**HUMBLE**	(onare suru)

Examples:

1. *Nihon no seikatsu ni naremashita ka. / Ee, sukkari naremashita.*
   日本の生活に慣れましたか。/ ええ、すっかり慣れました。
   Have you gotten used to living in Japan? / Yes, I've gotten completely used to it.

2. *Ōzei no hito no mae de hanasu koto ni narete imasen.*
   大勢の人の前で話すことに慣れていません。
   I am not used to speaking in front of large groups of people.

3. *Kodomo wa atarashii kankyō ni nareru no ga hayai.*
   子供は新しい環境に慣れるのが早い。
   Children are fast to adopt to a new environments.

4. *Kanojo wa nareta tetsuki de fude o tsukatta.*
   彼女は慣れた手つきで筆を使った。
   She used her brush with a practiced hand.

5. *Pikunikku wa haki-nareta kutsu de kite kudasai.*
   ピクニックは、はき慣れた靴で来てください。
   Please come to the picnic wearing your most comfortable shoes.

naru なる

なる or 成る to become; 鳴る to ring, sound:* (both intrans.)

		Affirmative	Negative
PLAIN FORM	PRESENT	naru	naranai
	PAST	natta	naranakatta
MASU FORM	PRESENT	narimasu	narimasen
	PAST	narimashita	narimasen deshita
TE FORM		natte	naranakute
CONDITIONAL	PLAIN	nareba/natta ra	naranakereba/ naranakatta ra
	FORMAL	narimashita ra	narimasen deshita ra
VOLITIONAL	PLAIN	narō	–
	FORMAL	narimashō	–
IMPERATIVE		nare	naru na

	Affirmative		Affirmative
POTENTIAL	nareru	**CAUS. PASSIVE**	naraserareru/narasareru
PASSIVE	narareru	**HONORIFIC**	onari ni naru/narareru
CAUSATIVE	naraseru	**HUMBLE**	(onari suru)

Examples:

1. *Isshōkenmei renshū shite, tenisu ga jōzu ni narimashita.*
   一生懸命練習して、テニスが上手になりました。
   I became good at tennis after practicing very hard.

2. *Hiragana ga zenbu yomeru yō ni natta.*
   ひらがなが全部読めるようになった。
   I became able to read all Hiragana.

3. *Sono ko wa ōkiku natta ra, isha ni naritai sō da.*
   その子は大きくなったら、医者になりたいそうだ。
   I hear that the child wants to be a doctor when he grows up.

4. *Roku-ji ni mezamashi-dokei ga natta.*
   六時に目覚まし時計が鳴った。
   The alarm rang at 6 o'clock.

5. *Denwa ga natte imasu.*
   電話が鳴っています。
   The telephone is ringing.

* The verb *naru* 鳴る meaning "to ring, sound" generally does not use the imperative, volitional, potential, honorific, humble, or passive forms.

nasaru なさる

なさる to do:* (trans.)

		Affirmative	Negative
PLAIN FORM	PRESENT	nasaru	nasaranai
	PAST	nasatta	nasaranakatta
MASU FORM	PRESENT	nasaimasu**	nasaimasen
	PAST	nasaimashita	nasaimasen deshita
TE FORM		nasatte	nasaranakute
CONDITIONAL	PLAIN	nasareba/nasatta ra	nasaranakereba/ nasaranakatta ra
	FORMAL	nasaimashita ra	nasaimasen deshita ra
VOLITIONAL	PLAIN	nasarō	–
	FORMAL	nasaimashō	–
IMPERATIVE		(nasare)	(nasaru na)

	Affirmative		Affirmative
POTENTIAL	nasareru	**CAUS. PASSIVE**	(nasaraserareru)
PASSIVE	nasarareru	**HONORIFIC**	–
CAUSATIVE	(nasaraseru)	**HUMBLE**	–

Examples:

1. *Ichinichi ni nan-jikan Nihon-go o benkyō nasaimasu ka.*
   一日に何時間日本語を勉強なさいますか。
   How many hours a day do you study Japanese?

2. *Suzuki kyōju wa tenisu o nasaru to omoimasu ka.*
   鈴木教授はテニスをなさると思いますか。
   Do you think Professor Suzuki plays tennis?

3. *Oshigoto wa nani o nasatte imasu ka. / Kyōshi o shite orimasu.*
   お仕事は何をなさっていますか。/ 教師をしております。
   I was wondering what kind of work you do. / I work as a teacher.

4. *Nomimono wa nani ni nasaimasu ka. / Kōhii ni shimasu.*
   飲み物は何になさいますか。/ コーヒーにします。
   What would you like to drink? / I'll have a coffee.

5. *Dō nasatta'n desu ka. / Atama ga itai'n desu.*
   どうなさったんですか。/ 頭が痛いんです。
   Could you tell me what is wrong? / My head hurts.

* *Nasaru* なさる is the honorific equivalent of *suru*.

** For euphonic reasons, *nasaimasu* is used rather than *nasarimasu*.

nemuru ねむる

眠る to sleep, fall asleep: (intrans.)

		Affirmative	Negative
PLAIN FORM	PRESENT	nemuru	nemuranai
	PAST	nemutta	nemuranakatta
MASU FORM	PRESENT	nemurimasu	nemurimasen
	PAST	nemurimashita	nemurimasen deshita
TE FORM		nemutte	nemuranakute
CONDITIONAL	PLAIN	nemureba/nemutta ra	nemuranakereba/ nemuranakatta ra
	FORMAL	nemurimashita ra	nemurimasen deshita ra
VOLITIONAL	PLAIN	nemurō	–
	FORMAL	nemurimashō	–
IMPERATIVE		nemure	nemuru na

	Affirmative		Affirmative
POTENTIAL	nemureru	CAUS. PASSIVE	nemuraserareru/ nemurasareru
PASSIVE	nemurareru	HONORIFIC	onemuri ni naru/ nemurareru
CAUSATIVE	nemuraseru	HUMBLE	(onemuri suru)

Examples:

1. *Yūbe wa yoku nemuremashita ka. / Watashi wa gussuri nemuremashita.*
   ゆうべはよく眠れましたか。/ 私はぐっすり眠れました。
   Were you able to sleep well last night? / I slept soundly.

2. *Tesuto no benkyō o shinakereba naranakatta noni, nemutte shimatta.*
   テストの勉強をしなければならなかったのに、眠ってしまった。
   Even though I had to study for the coming exam, I fell asleep.

3. *Akachan ga nemutte iru node, shizuka ni shite kudasai.*
   赤ちゃんが眠っているので、静かにしてください。
   A baby is sleeping, so please be quiet.

4. *Jugyōchū, omowazu nemuri-sō ni natta.*
   授業中、思わず眠りそうになった。
   I almost fell asleep during class.

5. *Watashi wa hachi-jikan ijō nemuranai to, chōshi ga warui.*
   私は八時間以上眠らないと、調子が悪い。
   If I don't sleep for at least 8 hours, I feel bad.

neru ねる

寝る to go to bed, lie down: (intrans.)

		Affirmative	*Negative*
PLAIN FORM	PRESENT	neru	nenai
	PAST	neta	nenakatta
MASU FORM	PRESENT	nemasu	nemasen
	PAST	nemashita	nemasen deshita
TE FORM		nete	nenakute
CONDITIONAL	PLAIN	nereba/neta ra	nenakereba/nenakatta ra
	FORMAL	nemashita ra	nemasen deshita ra
VOLITIONAL	PLAIN	neyō	–
	FORMAL	nemashō	–
IMPERATIVE		nero	neru na

	Affirmative		*Affirmative*
POTENTIAL	nerareru/nereru	**CAUS. PASSIVE**	nesaserareru
PASSIVE	nerareru	**HONORIFIC**	oyasumi ni naru/nerareru
CAUSATIVE	nesaseru	**HUMBLE**	oyasumi suru

Examples:

1. *Itsumo nan-ji goro nemasu ka.*
   いつも何時ごろ寝ますか。
   What time do you usually go to bed?

2. *Kare wa ne-nagara hon o yonde iru.*
   彼は寝ながら本を読んでいる。
   He is reading a book while lying down.

3. *Yūbe neru mae ni shukudai o shimashita.*
   ゆうべ寝る前に宿題をしました。
   I did my homework before going to bed last night.

4. *Sorosoro neru jikan desu ne. Oyasuminasai.*
   そろそろ寝る時間ですね。お休みなさい。
   It is about time to go to bed. Good night.

5. *Kanojo wa isshūkan mo kaze de nete iru.*
   彼女は一週間も風邪で寝ている。
   She has been lying in bed for one week because of a cold.

nigeru にげる

逃げる to run away, escape: (intrans.)

		Affirmative	Negative
PLAIN FORM	PRESENT	nigeru	nigenai
	PAST	nigeta	nigenakatta
MASU FORM	PRESENT	nigemasu	nigemasen
	PAST	nigemashita	nigemasen deshita
TE FORM		nigete	nigenakute
CONDITIONAL	PLAIN	nigereba/nigeta ra	nigenakereba/ nigenakatta ra
	FORMAL	nigemashita ra	nigemasen deshita ra
VOLITIONAL	PLAIN	nigeyō	–
	FORMAL	nigemashō	–
IMPERATIVE		nigero	nigeru na

	Affirmative		Affirmative
POTENTIAL	nigerareru/nigereru	**CAUS. PASSIVE**	nigesaserareru
PASSIVE	nigerareru	**HONORIFIC**	onige ni naru/nigerareru
CAUSATIVE	nigesaseru	**HUMBLE**	(onige suru)

Examples:

1. *Tori ga kago kara nigemashita.*
   鳥が籠から逃げました。
   The bird escaped from its cage.

2. *Dorobō wa kuruma de nigeta rashii.*
   泥棒は車で逃げたらしい。
   It seems that the thief escaped by car.

3. *Keikan wa nigeta hannin o otte itta.*
   警官は逃げた犯人を追って行った。
   The police officer chased after the escaped criminal.

4. *Kaji no ba-ai wa, hijōguchi kara nigete kudasai.*
   火事の場合は、非常口から逃げてください。
   In case of fire, please use the emergency exit.

5. *Kare wa shitsumon kara umaku nigeta.*
   彼は質問からうまく逃げた。
   He deftly evaded the question.

niru にる

煮る to boil: (trans.); 似る to look like, resemble: (intrans.)

			Affirmative	Negative
PLAIN FORM		PRESENT	niru	ninai
		PAST	nita	ninakatta
MASU FORM		PRESENT	nimasu	nimasen
		PAST	nimashita	nimasen deshita
TE FORM			nite	ninakute
CONDITIONAL		PLAIN	nireba/nita ra	ninakereba/ninakatta ra
		FORMAL	nimashita ra	nimasen deshita ra
VOLITIONAL		PLAIN	niyō	–
		FORMAL	nimashō	–
IMPERATIVE			niro	niru na

	Affirmative		Affirmative
POTENTIAL	nirareru/nireru	**CAUS. PASSIVE**	nisaserareru/nisasareru
PASSIVE	nirareru	**HONORIFIC**	(oni ni naru)/(nirareru)
CAUSATIVE	nisaseru	**HUMBLE**	(oni suru)

Examples:

1. *Kono sakana wa nama de taberaremasu ka. / Iie, nite tabete kudasai.*
   この魚は生で食べられますか。/ いいえ、煮て食べてください。
   Can I eat this fish raw? / No, please eat it after you have boiled it.

2. *Kono yasai wa mō sukoshi nita hō ga ii.*
   この野菜はもう少し煮たほうがいい。
   You should boil this vegetable a little more.

3. *Anata wa otōsan ni nite imasu ne.*
   あなたはお父さんに似ていますね。
   You look like your father, don't you?

4. *Ano kyōdai wa kao wa nite iru ga, seikaku wa zenzen nite inai.*
   あの兄弟は顔は似ているが、性格は全然似ていない。
   The brothers' faces look alike, but their personalities are totally different.

5. *Katachi no nita kanji ga aru node, ki o tsukete kudasai.*
   形の似た漢字があるので、気をつけてください。
   Because there are some similarly-shaped kanji, please be careful.

nobasu のばす

伸ばす to lengthen, stretch, spread out; 延ばす to postpone, extend: (both trans.)

		Affirmative	Negative
PLAIN FORM	PRESENT	nobasu	nobasanai
	PAST	nobashita	nobasanakatta
MASU FORM	PRESENT	nobashimasu	nobashimasen
	PAST	nobashimashita	nobashimasen deshita
TE FORM		nobashite	nobasanakute
CONDITIONAL	PLAIN	nobaseba/nobashita ra	nobasanakereba/ nobasanakatta ra
	FORMAL	nobashimashita ra	nobashimasen deshita ra
VOLITIONAL	PLAIN	nobasō	–
	FORMAL	nobashimashō	–
IMPERATIVE		nobase	nobasu na

	Affirmative		Affirmative
POTENTIAL	nobaseru	**CAUS. PASSIVE**	nobasaserareru
PASSIVE	nobasareru	**HONORIFIC**	onobashi ni naru/ nobasareru
CAUSATIVE	nobasaseru	**HUMBLE**	onobashi suru

Examples:

1. *Kanojo wa kami o nagaku nobashite imasu.*
   彼女は髪を長く伸ばしています。
   She is letting her hair grow long.

2. *Te o nobashite, hondana no ue no jisho o totta.*
   手を伸ばして、本棚の上の辞書を取った。
   I reached out my hand and took the dictionary from the bookshelf.

3. *Sono kaisha wa ima gyōseki o nobashite iru.*
   その会社は今、業績を伸ばしている。
   That company is growing their business these days.

4. *Nihon taizai o isshūkan nobashimashita.*
   日本滞在を一週間延ばしました。
   I extended my stay in Japan for one more week.

5. *Repōto no teishutsu kigen o raishū ni nobashite moratta.*
   レポートの提出期限を来週に延ばしてもらった。
   The deadline for my report was luckily extended.

nobiru のびる

伸びる to grow, improve; 延びる to be extended, postpone: (both intrans.)

		Affirmative	Negative
PLAIN FORM	PRESENT	nobiru	nobinai
	PAST	nobita	nobinakatta
MASU FORM	PRESENT	nobimasu	nobimasen
	PAST	nobimashita	nobimasen deshita
TE FORM		nobite	nobinakute
CONDITIONAL	PLAIN	nobireba/nobita ra	nobinakereba/ nobinakatta ra
	FORMAL	nobimashita ra	nobimasen deshita ra
VOLITIONAL	PLAIN	nobiyō	–
	FORMAL	nobimashō	–
IMPERATIVE		nobiro	nobiru na

	Affirmative		Affirmative
POTENTIAL	nobirareru/nobireru	**CAUS. PASSIVE**	nobisaserareru
PASSIVE	nobirareru	**HONORIFIC**	onobi ni naru/nobirareru
CAUSATIVE	nobisaseru	**HUMBLE**	onobi suru

Examples:

1. *Hantoshi de se ga go-senchi mo nobimashita.*
   半年で背が五センチも伸びました。
   I grew five centimeters in the last six months.

2. *Kami ga nobi-sugita node, biyōin ni iki-tai.*
   髪が伸びすぎたので、美容院に行きたい。
   Because my hair grew too long, I want to go to the beauty parlor.

3. *Saikin, kare wa Nihongo o hanasu chikara ga nobimashita.*
   最近、彼は日本語を話す力が伸びました。
   He has improved his speaking skill in Japanese recently.

4. *Konogoro hi ga nobite kimashita ne.*
   この頃、日が延びてきましたね。
   The days are getting longer, aren't they?

5. *Taifū no tame ni shuppatsu ga mikka nobita.*
   台風のために出発が三日延びた。
   My departure has been postponed by three days because of a typhoon.

noboru のぼる

上る to go up; 登る to climb (steps, mountains); 昇る to rise: (all intrans.)*

		Affirmative	Negative
PLAIN FORM	PRESENT	noboru	noboranai
	PAST	nobotta	noboranakatta
MASU FORM	PRESENT	noborimasu	noborimasen
	PAST	noborimashita	noborimasen deshita
TE FORM		nobotte	noboranakute
CONDITIONAL	PLAIN	noboreba/nobotta ra	noboranakereba/ noboranakatta ra
	FORMAL	noborimashita ra	noborimasen deshita ra
VOLITIONAL	PLAIN	noborō	–
	FORMAL	noborimashō	–
IMPERATIVE		nobore	noboru na

	Affirmative		Affirmative
POTENTIAL	noboreru	**CAUS. PASSIVE**	noboraserareru/ noborasareru
PASSIVE	noborareru	**HONORIFIC**	onobori ni naru/ noborareru
CAUSATIVE	noboraseru	**HUMBLE**	onobori suru

Examples:

1. *Tōkyō tawā ni nobottara,tōku no yama ga miemasu.*
   東京タワーに上ったら、遠くの山が見えます。
   If you climb Tokyo Tower, you can see the far-off mountains.

2. *Jitensha de sakamichi o noboru no wa taihen da.*
   自転車で坂道を上るのは大変だ。
   It is very hard to go up the slope by bicycle.

3. *Fuji-san ni nobotta koto ga arimasu ka. / Iie. Demo, itsuka nobotte mitai desu.*
   富士山に登ったことがありますか。/ いいえ。でも、いつか登ってみたいです。
   Have you ever climbed Mount Fuji? / No, but I would like to do it someday.

4. *Kodomo ga ki ni nobotte asonde iru.*
   子供が木に登って遊んでいる。
   A child climbed the tree and is now playing there.

5. *Hi ga noboru mae ni, jinja e inori ni dekaketa.*
   日が昇る前に、神社へ祈りに出かけた。
   Before the sun rose, I went to the Shinto shrine to pray.

* The intransitive *noboru* 昇る meaning "to rise" generally does not use the potential, passive, honorific, humble, causative, or causative passive forms.

Note: The verb *noboru* 上る and 登る can be sometimes used as a transitive verb—as in

nokoru のこる

残る to remain, be left: (intrans.)

		Affirmative	*Negative*
PLAIN FORM	PRESENT	nokoru	nokoranai
	PAST	nokotta	nokoranakatta
MASU FORM	PRESENT	nokorimasu	nokorimasen
	PAST	nokorimashita	nokorimasen deshita
TE FORM		nokotte	nokoranakute
CONDITIONAL	PLAIN	nokoreba/nokotta ra	nokoranakereba/ nokoranakatta ra
	FORMAL	nokorimashita ra	nokorimasen deshita ra
VOLITIONAL	PLAIN	nokorō	–
	FORMAL	nokorimashō	–
IMPERATIVE		nokore	nokoru na

	Affirmative		*Affirmative*
POTENTIAL	nokoreru	**CAUS. PASSIVE**	nokoraserareru/ nokorasareru
PASSIVE	nokorareru	**HONORIFIC**	onokori ni naru/ nokorareru
CAUSATIVE	nokoraseru	**HUMBLE**	onokori suru

Examples:

1. *Hōkago nokotte, benkyō shita.*
   放課後残って、勉強した。
   I stayed behind after school to study.

2. *Mada shigoto ga nokotte iru kara, kaeremasen.*
   まだ仕事が残っているから、帰れません。
   I cannot go home now beause I have unfinished work to do.

3. *Ryōri ga nokotta ra, reizōko ni irete oite kudasai.*
   料理が残ったら、冷蔵庫に入れておいてください。
   If there are any leftovers, please put them in the refrigerator.

4. *Kare wa Nihon ni nokotte, benkyō o tsuzukeru sō desu.*
   彼は日本に残って、勉強を続けるそうです。
   I hear that he will remain in Japan and continue his studies.

5. *Zenzen okane ga nokotte inai.*
   全然お金が残っていない。
   There is no money remaining at all.

nokosu のこす

残す to save, leave behind :(trans.)

		Affirmative	Negative
PLAIN FORM	PRESENT	nokosu	nokosanai
	PAST	nokoshita	nokosanakatta
MASU FORM	PRESENT	nokoshimasu	nokoshimasen
	PAST	nokoshimashita	nokoshimasen deshita
TE FORM		nokoshite	nokosanakute
CONDITIONAL	PLAIN	nokoseba/nokoshita ra	nokosanakereba/ nokosanakatta ra
	FORMAL	nokoshimashita ra	nokoshimasen deshita ra
VOLITIONAL	PLAIN	nokosō	–
	FORMAL	nokoshimashō	–
IMPERATIVE		nokose	nokosu na

	Affirmative		Affirmative
POTENTIAL	nokoseru	**CAUS. PASSIVE**	nokosaserareru
PASSIVE	nokosareru	**HONORIFIC**	onokoshi ni naru/ nokosareru
CAUSATIVE	nokosaseru	**HUMBLE**	onokoshi suru

Examples:

1. *Nokosanaide zenbu tabete kudasai.*
   残さないで全部食べてください。
   Please eat up the remainder.

2. *Shukudai o wasureta node, sensei ni nokosaremashita.*
   宿題を忘れたので、先生に残されました。
   The teacher made me stay back because I forgot my homework.

3. *Utsukushii shizen o shison ni nokosanakereba naranai.*
   美しい自然を子孫に残さなければならない。
   We must preserve nature's beauty for our descendants.

4. *Kono kēki wa nokoshite oite, ashita tabeyō.*
   このケーキは残しておいて、明日食べよう。
   Let's save this cake so we can eat it tomorrow.

5. *Suzuki-san wa kazoku o Tōkyō ni nokoshite, Ōsaka ni tenkin shita.*
   鈴木さんは家族を東京に残して、大阪に転勤した。
   Mr. Suzuki left his family behind in Tokyo and transferred to Osaka.

nomu のむ

飲む to drink, hold one's breath: (trans.)

		Affirmative	Negative
PLAIN FORM	PRESENT	nomu	nomanai
	PAST	nonda	nomanakatta
MASU FORM	PRESENT	nomimasu	nomimasen
	PAST	nomimashita	nomimasen deshita
TE FORM		nonde	nomanakute
CONDITIONAL	PLAIN	nomeba/nonda ra	nomanakereba/ nomanakatta ra
	FORMAL	nomimashita ra	nomimasen deshita ra
VOLITIONAL	PLAIN	nomō	–
	FORMAL	nomimashō	–
IMPERATIVE		nome	nomu na

	Affirmative		Affirmative
POTENTIAL	nomeru	**CAUS. PASSIVE**	nomaserareru/ nomasareru
PASSIVE	nomareru	**HONORIFIC**	meshiagaru/onomi ni naru/nomareru
CAUSATIVE	nomaseru	**HUMBLE**	itadaku

Examples:

1. *Kōhii o nomimashō.*
   コーヒーを飲みましょう。
   Let's drink some coffee.

2. *Ocha o nomi-nagara hanashi-atta.*
   お茶を飲みながら話し合った。
   They talked while drinking tea.

3. *Shokuji no ato de, kusuri o nomanakereba naranai.*
   食事の後で、薬を飲まなければならない。
   I have to take medicine after every meal.

4. *Nihon de hatachi miman no hito wa osake ga nomemasen.*
   日本で二十歳未満の人はお酒が飲めません。
   People under 20 years old are not allowed to drink liquor in Japan.

5. *Nani ka onomi ni narimasen ka. / Jā, ocha o itadakimasu.*
   何かお飲みになりませんか。/ じゃあ、お茶をいただきます
   Would you like to drink something? / Well, I would like a cup of tea.

noru のる

乗る to ride, to participate, be fooled; 載る to be printed, be reported:
(both intrans.)

		Affirmative	*Negative*
PLAIN FORM	PRESENT	noru	noranai
	PAST	notta	noranakatta
MASU FORM	PRESENT	norimasu	norimasen
	PAST	norimashita	norimasen deshita
TE FORM		notte	noranakute
CONDITIONAL	PLAIN	noreba/notta ra	noranakereba/ noranakatta ra
	FORMAL	norimashita ra	norimasen deshita ra
VOLITIONAL	PLAIN	norō	–
	FORMAL	norimashō	–
IMPERATIVE		nore	noru na

	Affirmative		*Affirmative*
POTENTIAL	noreru	**CAUS. PASSIVE**	noraserareru/ norasareru
PASSIVE	norareru	**HONORIFIC**	onori ni naru/ norareru
CAUSATIVE	noraseru	**HUMBLE**	onori suru

Examples:

1. *Jitensha ni notte, toshokan e itta.*
   自転車に乗って、図書館へ行った。
   I rode a bicycle to the library.

2. *Shinkansen ni notta koto ga arimasu ka.*
   新幹線に乗ったことがありますか。
   Have you ever ridden on the Shinkansen?

3. *Ku-ji sanjuppun hatsu no hikōki ni noranakereba naranai.*
   九時三十分発の飛行機に乗らなければならない。
   I have to board the airplane that departs at 9:30.

4. *Jisho wa ano tana no ue ni notte imasu.*
   辞書はあの棚の上に載っています。
   The dictionary is on that shelf.

5. *Kono resutoran wa sengetsu no zasshi ni notte ita.*
   このレストランは先月の雑誌に載っていた。
   This restaurant appeared in last month's magazine.

nozoku のぞく

除く to leave out, omit (trans.); のぞく to look in; peep in: (trans. and intrans.)

		Affirmative	Negative
PLAIN FORM	PRESENT	nozoku	nozokanai
	PAST	nozoita	nozokanakatta
MASU FORM	PRESENT	nozokimasu	nozokimasen
	PAST	nozokimashita	nozokimasen deshita
TE FORM		nozoite	nozokanakute
CONDITIONAL	PLAIN	nozokeba/nozoita ra	nozokanakereba/ nozokanakatta ra
	FORMAL	nozokimashita ra	nozokimasen deshita ra
VOLITIONAL	PLAIN	nozokō	–
	FORMAL	nozokimashō	–
IMPERATIVE		nozoke	nozoku na

	Affirmative		Affirmative
POTENTIAL	nozokeru	**CAUS. PASSIVE**	nozokaserareru/ nozokasareru
PASSIVE	nozokareru	**HONORIFIC**	onozoki ni naru/ nozokareru
CAUSATIVE	nozokaseru	**HUMBLE**	(onozoki suru)

Examples:

1. *Kaigi ni wa Yamada-san o nozoite zen-in shusseki shita.*
   会議には山田さんを除いて全員出席した。
   All the menbers except Mr. Yamada attended the meeting.

2. *Sono kissaten wa nichiyōbi o nozoite, jū-ji kara roku-ji made aite iru.*
   その喫茶店は日曜日を除いて、十時から六時まで開いている。
   That coffee shop is open from 10:00 to 6:00 except Sunday.

3. *Saisho no go-pēji wa nozoite mo ii desu.*
   最初の五ページは除いてもいいです。
   You may omit the first five pages.

4. *Ano mise o nozoite miyō yo.*
   あの店をのぞいてみようよ。
   Let's take a look in the shop.

5. *Hen na oto ga shita kara, doa no sukima kara heya no naka o nozoita.*
   変な音がしたから、ドアの隙間から部屋の中をのぞいた。
   Because I heard a strange sound, I peeped into the room from the gap of the door.

nugu ぬぐ

脱ぐ take off clothes: (trans.)

		Affirmative	Negative
PLAIN FORM	PRESENT	nugu	nuganai
	PAST	nuida	nuganakatta
MASU FORM	PRESENT	nugimasu	nugimasen
	PAST	nugimashita	nugimasen deshita
TE FORM		nuide	nuganakute
CONDITIONAL	PLAIN	nugeba/nuida ra	nuganakereba/ nuganakatta ra
	FORMAL	nugimashita ra	nugimasen deshita ra
VOLITIONAL	PLAIN	nugō	–
	FORMAL	nugimashō	–
IMPERATIVE		nuge	nugu na

	Affirmative		Affirmative
POTENTIAL	nugeru	**CAUS. PASSIVE**	nugaserareru/nugasareru
PASSIVE	nugareru	**HONORIFIC**	onugi ni naru/nugareru
CAUSATIVE	nugaseru	**HUMBLE**	onugi suru

Examples:

1. *Yōfuku o nuide, yukata o kita.*
   洋服を脱いで、浴衣を着た。
   I undressed and put on a cotton kimono.

2. *Nihon de wa kutsu o nuide, heya ni agarimasu.*
   日本では靴を脱いで、部屋に上がります。
   In Japan, you take off your shoes before entering a room.

3. *Nureta fuku o hayaku nuida hō ga ii desu yo.*
   ぬれた服を早く脱いだほうがいいですよ。
   You should take off your wet clothes immediately.

4. *Koko de kōto o nuide mo ii desu ka. / Hai, dōzo nuide kudasai.*
   ここでコートを脱いでもいいですか。/ はい、どうぞ脱いで
   ください。
   May I take off my coat here? / Yes, please do.

5. *Isha wa musuko no shatsu o nugasete shinsatsu shita.*
   医者は息子のシャツを脱がせて診察した。
   The doctor had my son take off his shirt and then examined him.

nureru ぬれる

ぬれる to get wet, be moist: (intrans.)

		Affirmative	Negative
PLAIN FORM	PRESENT	nureru	nurenai
	PAST	nureta	nurenakatta
MASU FORM	PRESENT	nuremasu	nuremasen
	PAST	nuremashita	nuremasen deshita
TE FORM		nurete	nurenakute
CONDITIONAL	PLAIN	nurereba/nureta ra	nurenakereba/ nurenakatta ra
	FORMAL	nuremashita ra	nuremasen deshita ra
VOLITIONAL	PLAIN	nureyō	–
	FORMAL	nuremashō	–
IMPERATIVE		nurero	nureru na

	Affirmative		Affirmative
POTENTIAL	(nurerareru)	**CAUS. PASSIVE**	(nuresaserareru)
PASSIVE	(nurerareru)	**HONORIFIC**	onure ni naru/nurerareru
CAUSATIVE	(nuresaseru)	**HUMBLE**	(onure suru)

Examples:

1. *Ame de fuku ga nureta.*
   雨で服がぬれた。
   My clothes got wet in the rain.

2. *Sono shatsu wa aratta bakari de, mada nurete imasu.*
   そのシャツは洗ったばかりで、まだぬれています。
   I have just washed the shirt so it is still wet.

3. *Shorui ga nurenai yō ni, kaban ni shimatta.*
   書類がぬれないように、かばんにしまった。
   I put the documents in my bag so that they wouldn't get wet.

4. *Nureta kasa o soko ni okanaide kudasai.*
   ぬれた傘をそこに置かないでください。
   Please do not put your wet umbrella there.

5. *Yūbe kami no ke ga nureta mama nete shimatta.*
   ゆうべ髪の毛がぬれたまま寝てしまった。
   Last night I fell asleep while my hair was wet.

nuru ぬる

塗る to paint, spread, put on (make-up): (trans.)

		Affirmative	Negative
PLAIN FORM	PRESENT	nuru	nuranai
	PAST	nutta	nuranakatta
MASU FORM	PRESENT	nurimasu	nurimasen
	PAST	nurimashita	nurimasen deshita
TE FORM		nutte	nuranakute
CONDITIONAL	PLAIN	nureba/nutta ra	nuranakereba/ nuranakatta ra
	FORMAL	nurimashita ra	nurimasen deshita ra
VOLITIONAL	PLAIN	nurō	–
	FORMAL	nurimashō	–
IMPERATIVE		nure	nuru na

	Affirmative		Affirmative
POTENTIAL	nureru	**CAUS. PASSIVE**	nuraserareru/nurasareru
PASSIVE	nurareru	**HONORIFIC**	onuri ni naru/nurareru
CAUSATIVE	nuraseru	**HUMBLE**	onuri suru

Examples:

1. *Ie no kabe ni penki o nutte moratta.*
   家の壁にペンキを塗ってもらった。
   I had the walls of my house painted.

2. *Pan ni batā o nutte kudasai.*
   パンにバターを塗ってください。
   Please spread butter on the bread.

3. *Ka ni sasareta tokoro ni kusuri o nutta.*
   蚊に刺されたところに薬を塗った。
   I applied medicine to the spot where I was bitten by a mosquito.

4. *Umi ni iku nara, hiyake-dome o nutta hō ga ii.*
   海に行くなら、日焼け止めを塗ったほうがいい。
   You should put on sunscreen if you go to the sea.

5. *Kanojo wa makka na kuchibeni o nutte iru.*
   彼女は真っ赤な口紅を塗っている。
   She is putting on bright red lipstick.

nusumu ぬすむ

盗む steal, do stealthily: (trans.)

		Affirmative	Negative
PLAIN FORM	PRESENT	nusumu	nusumanai
	PAST	nusunda	nusumanakatta
MASU FORM	PRESENT	nusumimasu	nusumimasen
	PAST	nusumimashita	nusumimasen deshita
TE FORM		nusunde	nusumanakute
CONDITIONAL	PLAIN	nusumeba/nusunda ra	nusumanakereba/ nusumanakatta ra
	FORMAL	nusumimashita ra	nusumimasen deshita ra
VOLITIONAL	PLAIN	nusumō	–
	FORMAL	nusumimashō	–
IMPERATIVE		nusume	nusumu na

	Affirmative		Affirmative
POTENTIAL	nusumeru	**CAUS. PASSIVE**	nusumaserareru/ nusumasareru
PASSIVE	nusumareru	**HONORIFIC**	onusumi ni naru/ nusumarerun
CAUSATIVE	nusumaseru	**HUMBLE**	(onusumi suru)

Examples:

1. *Eigakan de saifu o nusumareta.*
   映画館で財布を盗まれた。
   My wallet was stolen in the movie theater.

2. *Ginkō ni dorobō ga nusumi ni hairimashita.*
   銀行に泥棒が盗みに入りました。
   A thief broke into the bank.

3. *Jitensha ga nusumarenai yō ni, kagi o kakete oita.*
   自転車が盗まれないように、鍵をかけておいた。
   I locked my bicycle so that it would not be stolen.

4. *Oya no me o nusunde sake o nonda.*
   親の目を盗んで酒を飲んだ。
   I drank sake behind the parents' back.

5. *Karera wa hitome o nusunde atta.*
   彼らは人目を盗んで会った。
   They met secretly.

oboeru おぼえる

覚える to remember, memorize, learn: (trans.)

		Affirmative	Negative
PLAIN FORM	PRESENT	oboeru	oboenai
	PAST	oboeta	oboenakatta
MASU FORM	PRESENT	oboemasu	oboemasen
	PAST	oboemashita	oboemasen deshita
TE FORM		oboete	oboenakute
CONDITIONAL	PLAIN	oboereba/oboeta ra	oboenakereba/ oboenakatta ra
	FORMAL	oboemashita ra	oboemasen deshita ra
VOLITIONAL	PLAIN	oboeyō	–
	FORMAL	oboemashō	–
IMPERATIVE		oboero	oboeru na

	Affirmative		Affirmative
POTENTIAL	oboerareru/oboereru	**CAUS. PASSIVE**	oboesaserareru
PASSIVE	oboerareru	**HONORIFIC**	ōboe ni naru/oboerareru
CAUSATIVE	oboesaseru	**HUMBLE**	(ōboe suru)

Examples:

1. *Kanji no kaki-kata o oboeru no wa muzukashii desu.*
   漢字の書き方を覚えるのは難しいです。
   It is difficult to memorize how to write kanji.

2. *Senshū itta mise no namae o oboete imasu ka.*
   先週行った店の名前を覚えていますか。
   Do you remember the name of the restaurant where we went last week?

3. *Kare wa mō shigoto o oboeta yō da.*
   彼はもう仕事を覚えたようだ。
   He seemed to have already mastered his job.

4. *Haha wa keitai-denwa no tsukai-kata ga nakanaka oboerarenai.*
   母は携帯電話の使い方がなかなか覚えられない。
   My mother cannot learn how to use the cell-phone easily.

5. *Ashita no kaigi wa ni-ji han kara desu. Oboete oite kudasai.*
   明日の会議は二時半からです。覚えておいてください。
   Tomorrow's meeting will be from half past two. Please remember it.

ochiru おちる

落ちる to fall, come off: (intrans.)

		Affirmative	Negative
PLAIN FORM	PRESENT	ochiru	ochinai
	PAST	ochita	ochinakatta
MASU FORM	PRESENT	ochimasu	ochimasen
	PAST	ochimashita	ochimasen deshita
TE FORM		ochite	ochinakute
CONDITIONAL	PLAIN	ochireba/ochita ra	ochinakereba/ ochinakatta ra
	FORMAL	ochimashita ra	ochimasen deshita ra
VOLITIONAL	PLAIN	ochiyō	–
	FORMAL	ochimashō	–
IMPERATIVE		ochiro	ochiru na

	Affirmative		Affirmative
POTENTIAL	ochirareru/ochireru	**CAUS. PASSIVE**	ochisaserareru
PASSIVE	ochirareru	**HONORIFIC**	ōchi ni naru/ochirareru
CAUSATIVE	ochisaseru	**HUMBLE**	(ōchi suru)

Examples:

1. *Kaidan kara ochite, ashi ni kega o shimasita.*
   階段から落ちて、足にけがをしました。
   I fell downstairs and injured my leg.

2. *Hyaku-en dama ga yuka ni ochite iru.*
   百円玉が床に落ちている。
   A 100-yen coin has fallen onto the floor.

3. *Shimi ga nakanaka ochinai.*
   しみがなかなか落ちない。
   The stain cannot be easily removed.

4. *Tana kara nimotsu ga ochi-sō desu.*
   棚から荷物が落ちそうです。
   The baggage looks like it will fall from the shelf.

5. *Shiken ni ochite, gakkari shita.*
   試験に落ちて、がっかりした。
   I'm disappointed because I failed the examination.

odoroku おどろく

驚く to be surprised, amazed, shocked: (intrans.)

		Affirmative	*Negative*
PLAIN FORM	PRESENT	odoroku	odorokanai
	PAST	odoroita	odorokanakatta
MASU FORM	PRESENT	odorokimasu	odorokimasen
	PAST	odorokimashita	odorokimasen deshita
TE FORM		odoroite	odorokanakute
CONDITIONAL	PLAIN	odorokeba/odoroita ra	odorokanakereba/ odorokanakatta ra
	FORMAL	odorokimashita ra	odorokimasen deshita ra
VOLITIONAL	PLAIN	odorokō	–
	FORMAL	odorokimashō	–
IMPERATIVE		odoroke	odoroku na

	Affirmative		*Affirmative*
POTENTIAL	odorokeru	**CAUS. PASSIVE**	odorokaserareru/ odorokasareru
PASSIVE	odorokareru	**HONORIFIC**	ōdoroki ni naru/ odorokareru
CAUSATIVE	odorokaseru	**HUMBLE**	(ōdoroki suru)

Examples:

1. *Sono nyūsu o kiite, odorokimashita.*
   そのニュースを聞いて、驚きました。
   I was surprised to hear that news.

2. *Ā, odoroita!*
   ああ、驚いた。
   What a surprise!

3. *Kare no shitsurei na taido ni wa odorokasareta.*
   彼の失礼な態度には驚かされた。
   I was surprised at his rude behavior.

4. *Kanojo wa odoroku hodo uta ga umai.*
   彼女は驚くほど歌がうまい。
   She is amazingly good at singing.

5. *Odoroita koto ni, Tanaka-san wa kaisha o yamete shimatta.*
   驚いたことに、田中さんは会社を辞めてしまった。
   To my surprise, Mr. Tanaka has left the company.

odoru おどる

踊る to dance; 躍る to jump up, be excited: (both intrans.)

		Affirmative	Negative
PLAIN FORM	PRESENT	odoru	odoranai
	PAST	odotta	odoranakatta
MASU FORM	PRESENT	odorimasu	odorimasen
	PAST	odorimashita	odorimasen deshita
TE FORM		odotte	odoranakute
CONDITIONAL	PLAIN	odoreba/odotta ra	odoranakereba/ odoranakatta ra
	FORMAL	odorimashita ra	odorimasen deshita ra
VOLITIONAL	PLAIN	odorō	–
	FORMAL	odorimashō	–
IMPERATIVE		odore	odoru na

	Affirmative		Affirmative
POTENTIAL	odoreru	**CAUS. PASSIVE**	odoraserareru/ odorasareru
PASSIVE	odorareru	**HONORIFIC**	ōdori ni naru/odorareru
CAUSATIVE	odoraseru	**HUMBLE**	ōdori suru

Examples:

1. *Issho ni odorō.*
一緒に踊ろう。
Let's dance!

2. *Shūmatsu, odori ni ikimasen ka.*
週末、踊りに行きませんか。
Shall we go to dance on the weekend?

3. *Tango o odotta koto ga arimasen.*
タンゴを踊ったことがありません。
I have never danced the Tango.

4. *Ashikubi o itemete ite, odoremasen.*
足首を痛めていて、踊れません。
I hurt my ankle so I cannot dance.

5. *Yorokobi de mune ga odotta.*
喜びで胸が躍った。
My heart leaped with joy.

okiru おきる

起きる to wake up, get up, to occur:* (intrans.)

		Affirmative	*Negative*
PLAIN FORM	PRESENT	*okiru*	*okinai*
	PAST	*okita*	*okinakatta*
MASU FORM	PRESENT	*okimasu*	*okimasen*
	PAST	*okimashita*	*okimasen deshita*
TE FORM		*okite*	*okinakute*
CONDITIONAL	PLAIN	*okireba/okita ra*	*okinakereba/ okinakatta ra*
	FORMAL	*okimashita ra*	*okimasen deshita ra*
VOLITIONAL	PLAIN	*okiyō*	–
	FORMAL	*okimashō*	–
IMPERATIVE		*okiro*	*okiru na*

	Affirmative		*Affirmative*
POTENTIAL	*okirareru/okireru*	**CAUS. PASSIVE**	*okisaserareru*
PASSIVE	*okirareru*	**HONORIFIC**	*ōki ni naru/okirareru*
CAUSATIVE	*okisaseru*	**HUMBLE**	*(ōki suru)*

Examples:

1. *Kesa nan-ji ni okimashita ka. / Asa roku-ji ni okimashita.*
   今朝何時に起きましたか。／朝六時に起きました。
   What time did you get up this morning? / I got up at six o'clock.

2. *Yamada-san wa asa hayaku okirarenai.*
   山田さんは朝早く起きられない。
   Mr. Yamada can't get up early in the morning.

3. *Yūbe osoku made okite ita kara, kyō wa totemo nemui.*
   ゆうべ遅くまで起きていたから、今日はとても眠い。
   Because I have been awake till late last night, I am very sleepy today.

4. *Okiro. Itsu made nete iru'n da.*
   起きろ。いつまで寝ているんだ。
   Wake up! How long are you going to sleep?

5. *Sono kōsaten de kōtsūjiko ga okimashita.*
   その交差点で交通事故が起きました。
   A traffic accident occurred at that crossing.

---

* The verb *okiru* 起きる meaning "to occur" generally does not use the volitional and honorific forms.

okoru おこる

怒る to get angry; 起こる to occur: (both intrans.)

		Affirmative	*Negative*
PLAIN FORM	PRESENT	okoru	okoranai
	PAST	okotta	okoranakatta
MASU FORM	PRESENT	okorimasu	okorimasen
	PAST	okorimashita	okorimasen deshita
TE FORM		okotte	okoranakute
CONDITIONAL	PLAIN	okoreba/okotta ra	okoranakereba/ okoranakatta ra
	FORMAL	okorimashita ra	okorimasen deshita ra
VOLITIONAL	PLAIN	okorō	–
	FORMAL	okorimashō	–
IMPERATIVE		okore	okoru na

	Affirmative		*Affirmative*
POTENTIAL	okoreru	**CAUS. PASSIVE**	okoraserareru/ okorasareru
PASSIVE	okorareru	**HONORIFIC**	ōkori ni naru/okorareru
CAUSATIVE	okoraseru	**HUMBLE**	(ōkori suru)

Examples:

1. *Kanojo wa kankan ni okotte iru.*
   彼女はかんかんに怒っている。
   She is furious.

2. *Jugyō ni okurete, sensei ni okorareta.*
   授業に遅れて、先生に怒られた。
   Because I came to class late, I was scolded by my teacher.

3. *Yakusoku o wasurete, kanojo o okorasete shimatta.*
   約束を忘れて、彼女を怒らせてしまった。
   I have forgotten the promise I made to her so I made her angry.

4. *Satsujin jiken ga okotta sō da.*
   殺人事件が起こったそうだ。
   I heard that there was a murder case.

5. *Kūki ga kawaite iru kara, yama kaji ga okori-yasui.*
   空気が乾いているから、山火事が起こりやすい。
   Because the air is dry, a forest fire can easily happen.

okosu おこす

起こす to wake up, make happen, pick (a person) up; 興す to start :
(both trans.)

		Affirmative	*Negative*
PLAIN FORM	PRESENT	okosu	okosanai
	PAST	okoshita	okosanakatta
MASU FORM	PRESENT	okoshimasu	okoshimasen
	PAST	okoshimashita	okoshimasen deshita
TE FORM		okoshite	okosanakute
CONDITIONAL	PLAIN	okoseba/okoshita ra	okosanakereba/ okosanakatta ra
	FORMAL	okoshimashita ra	okoshimasen deshita ra
VOLITIONAL	PLAIN	okosō	–
	FORMAL	okoshimashō	–
IMPERATIVE		okose	okosu na

	Affirmative		*Affirmative*
POTENTIAL	okoseru	**CAUS. PASSIVE**	okosaserareru
PASSIVE	okosareru	**HONORIFIC**	ōkoshi ni naru/okosareru
CAUSATIVE	okosaseru	**HUMBLE**	ōkoshi suru

Examples:

1. *Asu no asa shichi-ji ni okoshite kudasai.*
   明日の朝七時に起こしてください。
   Please wake me at seven o'clock tomorrow morning.

2. *Haha ni go-ji ni okosareta.*
   母に五時に起こされた。
   My mother woke me at five o'clock.

3. *Jiko o okosanai yō ni chūi shite kudasai.*
   事故を起こさないように注意してください。
   Please be careful not to cause any accidents.

4. *Koronda kodomo o okoshite ageta.*
   転んだ子供を起こしてあげた。
   I helped a child who had fallen get back on his feet.

5. *Kare wa jigyō o okoshita.*
   彼は事業を興した。
   He launched a new business.

oku おく

置く to put, keep, leave: (trans.)

		Affirmative	Negative
PLAIN FORM	PRESENT	oku	okanai
	PAST	oita	okanakatta
MASU FORM	PRESENT	okimasu	okimasen
	PAST	okimashita	okimasen deshita
TE FORM		oite	okanakute
CONDITIONAL	PLAIN	okeba/oita ra	okanakereba/ okanakatta ra
	FORMAL	okimashita ra	okimasen deshita ra
VOLITIONAL	PLAIN	okō	–
	FORMAL	okimashō	–
IMPERATIVE		oke	oku na

	Affirmative		Affirmative
POTENTIAL	okeru	**CAUS. PASSIVE**	okaserareru/okasareru
PASSIVE	okareru	**HONORIFIC**	ōki ni naru/okareru
CAUSATIVE	okaseru	**HUMBLE**	ōki suru

Examples:

1. *Tsukue no ue ni hon ga oite aru.*
   机の上に本が置いてある。
   There are books placed on the desk.

2. *Koko ni nimotsu o oite mo ii desu ka.*
   ここに荷物を置いてもいいですか。
   May I leave my baggage here?

3. *Atarashii sofa ga hoshii keredomo, oku basho ga nai.*
   新しいソファーが欲しいけれども、置く場所がない。
   Even though I want a new sofa, there is no place to put it.

4. *Yogoreta sara wa soko ni oite oite kudasai.*
   汚れた皿はそこに置いておいてください。
   Please leave the dirty plates there.

5. *Sono kaisha no honsha wa Tōkyō ni okarete iru.*
   その会社の本社は東京に置かれている。
   That company's head office is located in Tokyo.

okureru おくれる

遅れる to be late for, be delayed; 後れる to be far behind: (both intrans.)

		Affirmative	*Negative*
PLAIN FORM	PRESENT	okureru	okurenai
	PAST	okureta	okurenakatta
MASU FORM	PRESENT	okuremasu	okuremasen
	PAST	okuremashita	okuremasen deshita
TE FORM		okurete	okurenakute
CONDITIONAL	PLAIN	okurereba/okureta ra	okurenakereba/ okurenakatta ra
	FORMAL	okuremashita ra	okuremasen deshita ra
VOLITIONAL	PLAIN	okureyō	–
	FORMAL	okuremashō	–
IMPERATIVE		okurero	okureru na

	Affirmative		*Affirmative*
POTENTIAL	okurerareru/ okurereru	**CAUS. PASSIVE**	okuresaserareru
PASSIVE	okurerareru	**HONORIFIC**	ōkure ni naru/ okurerareru
CAUSATIVE	okuresaseru	**HUMBLE**	(ōkure suru)

Examples:

1. *Kiri no tame, hikōki no shuppatsu ga ni-jikan okureta.*
   霧のため、飛行機の出発が二時間遅れた。
   The departure of the plane was delayed by two hours because of fog.

2. *Densha no jiko no sei de, kaisha ni okureta.*
   電車の事故のせいで、会社に遅れた。
   I was late for work because of the train accident.

3. *Gakkō ni okurenai yō ni isoida.*
   学校に遅れないように急いだ。
   I hurried so as not to be late for school.

4. *Okurete shimatte, mōshiwake arimasen.*
   遅れてしまって、申し訳ありません。
   I am sorry for being late.

5. *Kono tokei wa go-fun gurai okurete iru.*
   この時計は五分ぐらい後れている。
   This watch is about 5 minutes slow.

okuru おくる

送る to send, see off; 贈る to present, give (both trans.)

		Affirmative	*Negative*
PLAIN FORM	PRESENT	okuru	okuranai
	PAST	okutta	okuranakatta
MASU FORM	PRESENT	okurimasu	okurimasen
	PAST	okurimashita	okurimasen deshita
TE FORM		okutte	okuranakute
CONDITIONAL	PLAIN	okureba/okutta ra	okuranakereba/ okuranakatta ra
	FORMAL	okurimashita ra	okurimasen deshita ra
VOLITIONAL	PLAIN	okurō	–
	FORMAL	okurimashō	–
IMPERATIVE		okure	okuru na

	Affirmative		*Affirmative*
POTENTIAL	okureru	**CAUS. PASSIVE**	okuraserareru/ okurasareru
PASSIVE	okurareru	**HONORIFIC**	ōkuri ni naru/okurareru
CAUSATIVE	okuraseru	**HUMBLE**	ōkuri suru

Examples:

1. *Tomodachi ni tegami o okurimashita.*
   友達に手紙を送りました。
   I sent a letter to my friend.

2. *Eki made ōkuri shimashō.*
   駅までお送りしましょう。
   I'll go to the station to see you off.

3. *Haha kara kozutsumi ga okurarete kita.*
   母から小包が送られてきた。
   A package has been sent by my mother.

4. *Shinamono ga todoita ra, daikin wa isshū-kan inai ni ōkuri kudasai.*
   品物が届いたら、代金は一週間以内にお送りください。
   When you receive the purchase, please send the money to us within one week.

5. *Daigaku no nyūgaku iwai ni, chichi kara mannenhitsu o okurareta.*
   大学の入学祝いに、父から万年筆を贈られた。
   A fountain pen was given by my father as a celebration gift of my entrance to university.

omou おもう

思う to think: (trans.)

		Affirmative	*Negative*
PLAIN FORM	PRESENT	omou	omowanai
	PAST	omotta	omowanakatta
MASU FORM	PRESENT	omoimasu	omoimasen
	PAST	omoimashita	omoimasen deshita
TE FORM		omotte	omowanakute
CONDITIONAL	PLAIN	omoeba/omotta ra	omowanakereba/ omowanakatta ra
	FORMAL	omoimashita ra	omoimasen deshita ra
VOLITIONAL	PLAIN	omoō	–
	FORMAL	omoimashō	–
IMPERATIVE		omoe	omou na

	Affirmative		*Affirmative*
POTENTIAL	omoeru	**CAUS. PASSIVE**	omowaserareru/ omowasareru
PASSIVE	omowareru	**HONORIFIC**	ōmoi ni naru/omowareru
CAUSATIVE	omowaseru	**HUMBLE**	zonjiru

Examples:

1. *Kyō kanojo wa konai to omoimsu.*
   今日彼女は来ないと思います。
   I don't think that she will come today.

2. *Nihon o dō omoimasu ka. / Omoshiroi kuni da to omoimasu.*
   日本をどう思いますか。/ 面白い国だと思います。
   What do you think of Japan? / I think Japan is an interesting country.

3. *Raigetsu Kyōto e ikō to omotte imasu.*
   来月京都へ行こうと思っています。
   I intend to go to Kyoto next month.

4. *Kare ga shiken ni ochiru to wa omowanakatta.*
   彼が試験に落ちるとは思わなかった。
   I didn't think that he would fail the exam.

5. *Sono eiga wa omotte ita yori omoshirokatta.*
   その映画は思っていたより面白かった。
   That film was more interesting than I thought.

oreru おれる

折れる to be broken, to give in, to turn, be folded: (intrans.)*

		Affirmative	*Negative*
PLAIN FORM	PRESENT	oreru	orenai
	PAST	oreta	orenakatta
MASU FORM	PRESENT	oremasu	oremasen
	PAST	oremashita	oremasen deshita
TE FORM		orete	orenakute
CONDITIONAL	PLAIN	orereba/oreta ra	orenakereba/ orenakatta ra
	FORMAL	oremashita ra	oremasen deshita ra
VOLITIONAL	PLAIN	oreyō	–
	FORMAL	oremashō	–
IMPERATIVE		orero	oreru na

	Affirmative		*Affirmative*
POTENTIAL	orerareru/orereru	**CAUS. PASSIVE**	oresaserareru
PASSIVE	orerareru	**HONORIFIC**	ōre ni naru/orerareru
CAUSATIVE	oresaseru	**HUMBLE**	(ōre suru)

Examples:

1. *Kyōfū de ki no eda ga oreta.*
   強風で木の枝が折れた。
   The branch of the tree was broken by the strong wind.

2. *Zasshi no hyōshi ga orete iru.*
   雑誌の表紙が折れている。
   The magazine cover is folded.

3. *Sono kado o migi ni oreru to, yūbinkyoku ga arimasu.*
   その角を右に折れると、郵便局があります。
   If you turn right at that corner, there is a post office.

4. *Sukii de koronde, ashi no hone ga orete shimatta.*
   スキーで転んで、足の骨が折れてしまった。
   I broke my leg as I fell while skiing.

5. *Nando mo hanashi-atte, kekkyoku watashi no hō ga oremashita.*
   何度も話し合って、結局私のほうが折れました。
   After we discussed it many times, I compromised in the end.

* As with other verbs indicating movement, *oreru* 折れる, when meaning "to turn,"
may take a direct object, thus giving an idea of "going through a defined area." (See
example 3.)

oriru おりる

降りる to get off, fall; 下りる to come down, to be issued: (both intrans.)

		Affirmative	Negative
PLAIN FORM	PRESENT	oriru	orinai
	PAST	orita	orinakatta
MASU FORM	PRESENT	orimasu	orimasen
	PAST	orimashita	orimasen deshita
TE FORM		orite	orinakute
CONDITIONAL	PLAIN	orireba/orita ra	orinakereba/ orinakatta ra
	FORMAL	orimashita ra	orimasen deshita ra
VOLITIONAL	PLAIN	oriyō	–
	FORMAL	orimashō	–
IMPERATIVE		oriro	oriru na

	Affirmative		Affirmative
POTENTIAL	orirareru/orireru	**CAUS. PASSIVE**	orisaserareru
PASSIVE	orirareru	**HONORIFIC**	ōri ni naru/orirareru
CAUSATIVE	orisaseru	**HUMBLE**	ōri suru

Examples:

1. *Shinagawa-eki de shinkansen o orita.*
   品川駅で新幹線を降りた。
   I got off the Shinkansen at Shinagawa Station.

2. *Sono kaidan o orireba, chikatetsu no eki ga arimasu.*
   その階段を下りれば、地下鉄の駅があります。
   When you go down those stairs, you will find the subway station.

3. *Ano erebētā de ikkai ni oriyō.*
   あのエレベーターで一階に下りよう。
   Let's go down to the first floor by that lift.

4. *Kuraku naranai uchi ni, yama o orinakereba naranai*
   暗くならないうちに、山を下りなければならない。
   We have to descend the mountain before it becomes dark.

5. *Yatto biza ga orita.*
   やっとビザが下りた。
   My visa has been issued at last.

oru おる

折る to fold, break, bend: (trans.)

		Affirmative	*Negative*
PLAIN FORM	PRESENT	oru	oranai
	PAST	otta	oranakatta
MASU FORM	PRESENT	orimasu	orimasen
	PAST	orimashita	orimasen deshita
TE FORM		otte	oranakute
CONDITIONAL	PLAIN	oreba/otta ra	oranakereba/ oranakatta ra
	FORMAL	orimashita ra	orimasen deshita ra
VOLITIONAL	PLAIN	orō	–
	FORMAL	orimashō	–
IMPERATIVE		ore	oru na

	Affirmative		*Affirmative*
POTENTIAL	oreru	**CAUS. PASSIVE**	oraserareru/orasareru
PASSIVE	orareru	**HONORIFIC**	ōri ni naru/orareru
CAUSATIVE	oraseru	**HUMBLE**	ōri suru

Examples:

1. *Sakura no eda o oranaide kudasai.*
   桜の枝を折らないでください。
   Don't break the branches of the cherry tree.

2. *Tegami o mittsu ni otte, fūtō ni ireta.*
   手紙を三つに折って、封筒に入れた。
   I folded the letter into three sections and put it in the envelope.

3. *Kanojo wa origami de tsuru o otte kureta.*
   彼女は折り紙で鶴を折ってくれた。
   She made an origami crane for me out of colored paper.

4. *Kare wa jūdō no renshū de ude o otte shimatta.*
   彼は柔道の練習で腕を折ってしまった。
   He has broken his arm during Judo practice.

5. *Hanashi no koshi o oranaide kudasai.*
   話の腰を折らないでください。
   Please don't interrupt us while we're talking.

osaeru おさえる

押さえる to hold, catch; 抑える to suppress, control; おさえる to reserve: (all trans.)

		Affirmative	Negative
PLAIN FORM	PRESENT	osaeru	osaenai
	PAST	osaeta	osaenakatta
MASU FORM	PRESENT	osaemasu	osaemasen
	PAST	osaemashita	osaemasen deshita
TE FORM		osaete	osaenakute
CONDITIONAL	PLAIN	osaereba/osaeta ra	osaenakereba/ osaenakatta ra
	FORMAL	osaemashita ra	osaemasen deshita ra
VOLITIONAL	PLAIN	osaeyō	–
	FORMAL	osaemashō	–
IMPERATIVE		osaero	osaeru na

	Affirmative		Affirmative
POTENTIAL	osaerareru/osaereru	**CAUS. PASSIVE**	osaesaserareru
PASSIVE	osaerareru	**HONORIFIC**	ōsae ni naru/osaerareru
CAUSATIVE	osaesaseru	**HUMBLE**	ōsae suru

Examples:

1. *Bōshi ga kaze de tobanai yō ni, ryōte de osaeta.*
   帽子が風で飛ばないように、両手で押さえた。
   I held onto my hat with both hands so that it wouldn't fly off my head by the wind.

2. *Ōkina oto ga shite, omowazu mimi o osaeta.*
   大きな音がして、思わず耳を押さえた。
   A big sound caused me to cover my ears.

3. *Kanojo wa jibun no kanjō o osaerarenai.*
   彼女は自分の感情を抑えられない。
   She can't restrain her emotions.

4. *Sono myūjikaru no ii seki o osaete arimasu.*
   そのミュージカルのいい席をおさえてあります。
   I have reserved some good seats for the musical.

5. *Kare wa koe o osaete hanashita.*
   彼は声を抑えて話した。
   He spoke in a low voice.

oshieru おしえる

教える to teach, tell, show: (trans.)

		Affirmative	Negative
PLAIN FORM	PRESENT	oshieru	oshienai
	PAST	oshieta	oshienakatta
MASU FORM	PRESENT	oshiemasu	oshiemasen
	PAST	oshiemashita	oshiemasen deshita
TE FORM		oshiete	oshienakute
CONDITIONAL	PLAIN	oshiereba/oshieta ra	oshienakereba/ oshienakatta ra
	FORMAL	oshiemashita ra	oshiemasen deshita ra
VOLITIONAL	PLAIN	oshieyō	–
	FORMAL	oshiemashō	–
IMPERATIVE		oshiero	oshieru na

	Affirmative		Affirmative
POTENTIAL	oshierareru/oshiereru	**CAUS. PASSIVE**	oshiesaserareru
PASSIVE	oshierareru	**HONORIFIC**	ōshie ni naru/oshierareru
CAUSATIVE	oshiesaseru	**HUMBLE**	ōshie suru

Examples:

1. *Kanojo ni Nihon-go o oshiete imasu.*
   彼女に日本語を教えています。
   I am teaching her Japanese.

2. *Kono kanji no yomi-kata o oshiete kudasai.*
   この漢字の読み方を教えてください。
   Please teach me how to read this kanji.

3. *Tomodachi ga oishii resutoran o oshiete kureta.*
   友達がおいしいレストランを教えてくれた。
   My friend told me about a good restaurant.

4. *Eki e ikitai'n desu ga, michi o oshiete itadakemasen ka.*
   駅へ行きたいんですが、道を教えていただけませんか。
   Could you please show me the way to the station?

5. *Haha ni oshiete moratta tōri ni kēki o yaite mita.*
   母に教えてもらった通りにケーキを焼いてみた。
   I tried baking a cake according to my mother's instruction.

osu おす

押す to push, press, stamp: (trans.)

		Affirmative	Negative
PLAIN FORM	PRESENT	osu	osanai
	PAST	oshita	osanakatta
MASU FORM	PRESENT	oshimasu	oshimasen
	PAST	oshimashita	oshimasen deshita
TE FORM		oshite	osanakute
CONDITIONAL	PLAIN	oseba/oshita ra	osanakereba/ osanakatta ra
	FORMAL	oshimashita ra	oshimasen deshita ra
VOLITIONAL	PLAIN	osō	–
	FORMAL	oshimashō	–
IMPERATIVE		ose	osu na

	Affirmative		Affirmative
POTENTIAL	oseru	**CAUS. PASSIVE**	osaserareru
PASSIVE	osareru	**HONORIFIC**	ōshi ni naru/osareru
CAUSATIVE	osaseru	**HUMBLE**	ōshi suru

Examples:

1. *Kono botan o oseba, doa ga akimasu.*
   このボタンを押せば、ドアが開きます。
   When you push this button, the door will open.

2. *Ushiro kara osanaide kudasai.*
   後ろから押さないでください。
   Don't push from behind.

3. *Dareka ni senaka o osaremashita.*
   誰かに背中を押されました。
   My back was pushed by somebody.

4. *Koko ni hanko o oshite kudasai.*
   ここにはんこを押してください。
   Please stamp your seal here.

5. *Kare wa shūi no hantai o oshite, ryūgaku shita.*
   彼は周囲の反対を押して、留学した。
   He studied abroad in spite of the opposition from his acquaintances.

otosu おとす

落とす to drop, remove, lose: (trans.)

		Affirmative	Negative
PLAIN FORM	PRESENT	otosu	otosanai
	PAST	otoshita	otosanakatta
MASU FORM	PRESENT	otoshimasu	otoshimasen
	PAST	otoshimashita	otoshimasen deshita
TE FORM		otoshite	otosanakute
CONDITIONAL	PLAIN	otoseba/otoshita ra	otosanakereba/ otosanakatta ra
	FORMAL	otoshimashita ra	otoshimasen deshita ra
VOLITIONAL	PLAIN	otosō	–
	FORMAL	otoshimashō	–
IMPERATIVE		otose	otosu na

	Affirmative		Affirmative
POTENTIAL	otoseru	**CAUS. PASSIVE**	otosaserareru
PASSIVE	otosareru	**HONORIFIC**	ōtoshi ni naru/otosareru
CAUSATIVE	otosaseru	**HUMBLE**	ōtoshi suru

Examples:

1. *Sumimasen, hankachi o otoshimashita yo.*
   すみません、ハンカチを落としましたよ。
   Excuse me, but you dropped your handkerchief.

2. *Dokoka de heya no kagi o otoshite shimatta.*
   どこかで部屋の鍵を落としてしまった。
   I have lost my room key somewhere.

3. *Mō sukoshi supiido o otoshita hō ga ii.*
   もう少しスピードを落としたほうがいい。
   You should reduce your speed a little more.

4. *Shatsu ni tsuita shimi ga otosenai.*
   シャツに付いたしみが落とせない。
   I cannot remove the stain on the shirt.

5. *Yuka ni tabako no hai o otosanai yō ni shite kudasai.*
   床にたばこの灰を落とさないようにしてください。
   Please do not drop your cigarette ash on the floor.

ou おう

追う to run after, drive out; 負う to bear: (both trans.)

		Affirmative	*Negative*
PLAIN FORM	PRESENT	ou	owanai
	PAST	otta	owanakatta
MASU FORM	PRESENT	oimasu	oimasen
	PAST	oimashita	oimasen deshita
TE FORM		otte	owanakute
CONDITIONAL	PLAIN	oeba/otta ra	owanakereba/ owanakatta ra
	FORMAL	oimashita ra	oimasen deshita ra
VOLITIONAL	PLAIN	oō	–
	FORMAL	oimashō	–
IMPERATIVE		oe	ou na

	Affirmative		*Affirmative*
POTENTIAL	oeru	**CAUS. PASSIVE**	owaserareru/owasareru
PASSIVE	owareru	**HONORIFIC**	ōi ni naru/owareru
CAUSATIVE	owaseru	**HUMBLE**	ōi suru

Examples:

1. *Kanojo wa saki ni deta imōto o otte, eki made hashitta.*
   彼女は先に出た妹を追って、駅まで走った。
   She ran after her younger sister to the station.

2. *Kare wa keisatsu ni owarete iru.*
   彼は警察に追われている。
   He is being pursued by the police.

3. *Mainichi shigoto ni owarete iru.*
   毎日仕事に追われている。
   I am bombarded with work every day.

4. *Kare wa sono kaji de ryōte ni yakedo o otta.*
   彼はその火事で両手にやけどを負った。
   He suffered burns on both of his hands caused by the fire.

5. *Chiimu ga yūshō dekinakatta sekinin o otte, kantoku ga jinin shita.*
   チームが優勝できなかった責任を負って、監督が辞任した。
   Taking responsibility for his team's inability to win the championship, the manager resigned.

owaru おわる

終わる to be finished, be over: (intrans.)

		Affirmative	*Negative*
PLAIN FORM	PRESENT	owaru	owaranai
	PAST	owatta	owaranakatta
MASU FORM	PRESENT	owarimasu	owarimasen
	PAST	owarimashita	owarimasen deshita
TE FORM		owatte	owaranakute
CONDITIONAL	PLAIN	owareba/owatta ra	owaranakereba/ owaranakatta ra
	FORMAL	owarimashita ra	owarimasen deshita ra
VOLITIONAL	PLAIN	owarō	–
	FORMAL	owarimashō	–
IMPERATIVE		oware	owaru na

	Affirmative		*Affirmative*
POTENTIAL	owareru	**CAUS. PASSIVE**	owaraserareru/ owarasareru
PASSIVE	owarareru	**HONORIFIC**	ōwari ni naru/owarareru
CAUSATIVE	owaraseru	**HUMBLE**	(ōwari suru)

Examples:

1. *Jugyō ga ato juppun de owaru.*
   授業があと十分で終わる。
   Classes will end in ten minutes.

2. *Go-ji ni shigoto o owarasete, uchi ni kaetta.*
   五時に仕事を終わらせて、うちに帰った。
   I finished work at 5 o'clock and then went home.

3. *Sono eiga ga owaru no wa nanji desu ka.*
   その映画が終わるのは何時ですか。
   What time does the film end?

4. *Sono hon o yomi-owatta ra, watashi ni kashite kudasai.*
   その本を読み終わったら、私に貸してください。
   After you have finished reading that book, please lend it to me.

5. *Kotae o kaki-owatta ra, dashite kudasai.*
   答えを書き終わったら、出してください。
   Please hand in your answers once you've finished writing.

oyogu およぐ

泳ぐ to swim: (intrans.)

		Affirmative	Negative
PLAIN FORM	PRESENT	oyogu	oyoganai
	PAST	oyoida	oyoganakatta
MASU FORM	PRESENT	oyogimasu	oyogimasen
	PAST	oyogimashita	oyogimasen deshita
TE FORM		oyoide	oyoganakute
CONDITIONAL	PLAIN	oyogeba/oyoida ra	oyoganakereba/oyoganakatta ra
	FORMAL	oyogimashita ra	oyogimasen deshita ra
VOLITIONAL	PLAIN	oyogō	–
	FORMAL	oyogimashō	–
IMPERATIVE		oyoge	oyogu na

	Affirmative		Affirmative
POTENTIAL	oyogeru	**CAUS. PASSIVE**	oyogaserareru/oyogasareru
PASSIVE	oyogareru	**HONORIFIC**	ōyogi ni naru/oyogareru
CAUSATIVE	oyogaseru	**HUMBLE**	(ōyogi suru)

Examples:

1. *Isshūkan ni ni,san-kai, pūru de oyoide imasu.*
   一週間に二、三回、プールで泳いでいます。
   I swim in a pool two or three times a week.

2. *Dore gurai oyogemasu ka. / Zenzen oyogenai'n desu.*
   どれぐらい泳げますか。 / 全然泳げないんです。
   How far can you swim? / I can't swim at all.

3. *Natsu ni natta ra, umi e oyogi ni ikō.*
   夏になったら、海へ泳ぎに行こう。
   When it becomes summer, let's go swimming in the ocean.

4. *Kono kawa de oyogu no wa kiken da.*
   この川で泳ぐのは危険だ。
   It is dangerous to swim in this river.

5. *Sensei wa kodomo-tachi o pūru de oyogaseta.*
   先生は子供達をプールで泳がせた。
   The teacher let his children swim in the pool.

sagaru さがる

下がる fall, drop, hang: (intrans.)

		Affirmative	Negative
PLAIN FORM	PRESENT	sagaru	sagaranai
	PAST	sagatta	sagaranakatta
MASU FORM	PRESENT	sagarimasu	sagarimasen
	PAST	sagarimashita	sagarimasen deshita
TE FORM		sagatte	sagaranakute
CONDITIONAL	PLAIN	sagareba/sagatta ra	sagaranakereba/ sagaranakatta ra
	FORMAL	sagarimashita ra	sagarimasen deshita ra
VOLITIONAL	PLAIN	sagarō	–
	FORMAL	sagarimashō	–
IMPERATIVE		sagare	sagaru na

	Affirmative		Affirmative
POTENTIAL	sagareru	**CAUS. PASSIVE**	sagaraserareru/ sagarasareru
PASSIVE	sagarareru	**HONORIFIC**	osagari ni naru/ sagarareru
CAUSATIVE	sagaraseru	**HUMBLE**	osagari suru

Examples:

1. *Asu wa kion ga sagaru darō.*
   明日は気温が下がるだろう。
   The temperature probably will drop tomorrow.

2. *Kusuri o nonde, netsu ga sagatta.*
   薬を飲んで、熱が下がった。
   After I took the medicine, my temperature went down.

3. *En no sōba wa agatta ri sagatta ri shite imasu.*
   円の相場は上がったり下がったりしています。
   The Japanese yen's exchange rate goes up and down.

4. *Densha ga kuru node, sukoshi ushiro ni sagatte kudasai.*
   電車が来るので、少し後ろに下がってください。
   There is a train coming, so please step back a little.

5. *Gakkō no seiseki ga sagatte shimatta.*
   学校の成績が下がってしまった。
   My school grade has gone down.

sagasu さがす

捜す or 探す to look for, investigate: (trans.)

		Affirmative	Negative
PLAIN FORM	PRESENT	sagasu	sagasanai
	PAST	sagashita	sagasanakatta
MASU FORM	PRESENT	sagashimasu	sagashimasen
	PAST	sagashimashita	sagashimasen deshita
TE FORM		sagashite	sagasanakute
CONDITIONAL	PLAIN	sagaseba/sagashita ra	sagasanakereba/ sagasanakatta ra
	FORMAL	sagashimashita ra	sagashimasen deshita ra
VOLITIONAL	PLAIN	sagasō	–
	FORMAL	sagashimashō	–
IMPERATIVE		sagase	sagasu na

	Affirmative		Affirmative
POTENTIAL	sagaseru	**CAUS. PASSIVE**	sagasaserareru
PASSIVE	sagasareru	**HONORIFIC**	osagashi ni naru/ sagasareru
CAUSATIVE	sagasaseru	**HUMBLE**	osagashi suru

Examples:

1. *Nani o sagashite iru no?*
   何を捜しているの。
   What are you looking for?

2. *Apāto o sagasu no ni kurō shimashita.*
   アパートを探すのに苦労しました。
   I had trouble finding the apartment.

3. *Heya-jū sagashita keredomo, kagi wa mitsukaranakatta.*
   部屋中捜したけれども、鍵は見つからなかった。
   Although I searched the whole room, I could not find my key.

4. *Atarashii baito o sagasanakereba narimasen.*
   新しいバイトを探さなければなりません。
   I have to look for a new part-time job.

5. *Kagi o sono hen ni otoshita'n da kedo, issho ni sagashite kurenai.*
   鍵をその辺に落としたんだけど、一緒に捜してくれない。
   I lost my key somewhere around, so will you help me find it?

sageru さげる

下げる to lower, hang, pull back: (trans.)

		Affirmative	Negative
PLAIN FORM	PRESENT	sageru	sagenai
	PAST	sageta	sagenakatta
MASU FORM	PRESENT	sagemasu	sagemasen
	PAST	sagemashita	sagemasen deshita
TE FORM		sagete	sagenakute
CONDITIONAL	PLAIN	sagereba/sageta ra	sagenakereba/ sagenakatta ra
	FORMAL	sagemashita ra	sagemasen deshita ra
VOLITIONAL	PLAIN	sageyō	–
	FORMAL	sagemashō	–
IMPERATIVE		sagero	sageru na

	Affirmative		Affirmative
POTENTIAL	sagerareru/sagereru	**CAUS. PASSIVE**	sagesaserareru
PASSIVE	sagerareru	**HONORIFIC**	osage ni naru/sagerareru
CAUSATIVE	sagesaseru	**HUMBLE**	osage suru

Examples:

1. *Mabushii node, buraindo o sagete mo ii desu ka.*
   まぶしいので、ブラインドを下げてもいいですか。
   It is too bright, so may I lower the window shade?

2. *Sukoshi terebi no oto o sagete moraemasen ka.*
   少しテレビの音を下げてもらえませんか。
   Could you please lower the TV volume?

3. *Chotto atsui kara, eakon no ondo o sageyō.*
   ちょっと暑いから、エアコンの温度を下げよう。
   Because it is a bit hot, let's lower the temperature of the air-conditioner.

4. *Shokuji ga owatta ra, shokki o daidokoro ni sagete kudasai.*
   食事が終わったら、食器を台所に下げてください。
   When you have finished eating, please bring the tableware back to the kitchen.

5. *Sēru chū wa shōhin no nedan o san-wari sagete utte iru.*
   セール中は商品の値段を三割下げて売っている。
   They are selling their products at a 30% discount.

sakeru さける

裂ける to tear, split: (intrans.);* 避ける to avoid, keep away from: (trans.)

		Affirmative	*Negative*
PLAIN FORM	PRESENT	sakeru	sakenai
	PAST	saketa	sakenakatta
MASU FORM	PRESENT	sakemasu	sakemasen
	PAST	sakemashita	sakemasen deshita
TE FORM		sakete	sakenakute
CONDITIONAL	PLAIN	sakereba/saketa ra	sakenakereba/ sakenakatta ra
	FORMAL	sakemashita ra	sakemasen deshita ra
VOLITIONAL	PLAIN	sakeyō	–
	FORMAL	sakemashō	–
IMPERATIVE		sakero	sakeru na

	Affirmative		*Affirmative*
POTENTIAL	sakerareru/sakereru	**CAUS. PASSIVE**	sakesaserareru
PASSIVE	sakerareru	**HONORIFIC**	osake ni naru/sakerareru
CAUSATIVE	sakesaseru	**HUMBLE**	(osake suru)

Examples:

1. *Tsumekomi-sugite, fukuro ga sakete shimatta.*
   詰め込み過ぎて、袋が裂けてしまった。
   I stuffed too much in the bag, and it tore.

2. *Sore wa kuchi ga sakete mo ienai.*
   それは口が裂けても言えない。
   Nothing will make me reveal it.

3. *Rasshu o sakeru tame ni, asa hayaku ie o deta.*
   ラッシュを避けるために、朝早く家を出た。
   I left my house early in the morning to avoid the rush hour.

4. *Kare wa watashi o sakete iru yō da.*
   彼は私を避けているようだ。
   He is trying to avoid me.

5. *Sutoraiki totsunyū wa sakerarenai darō.*
   ストライキ突入は避けられないだろう。
   We probably can't avoid a strike confrontation.

* The intransitive verb *sakeru* 裂ける meaning "to tear, split" generally does not use the potential, passive, honorific, humble, causative, or causative passive forms.

saku さく

咲く bloom: (intrans.);* 裂く to tear ; 割く to make (time), to cut: (both trans.)

		Affirmative	Negative
PLAIN FORM	PRESENT	saku	sakanai
	PAST	saita	sakanakatta
MASU FORM	PRESENT	sakimasu	sakimasen
	PAST	sakimashita	sakimasen deshita
TE FORM		saite	sakanakute
CONDITIONAL	PLAIN	sakeba/saita ra	sakanakereba/ sakanakatta ra
	FORMAL	sakimashita ra	sakimasen deshita ra
VOLITIONAL	PLAIN	sakō	–
	FORMAL	sakimashō	–
IMPERATIVE		sake	saku na

	Affirmative		Affirmative
POTENTIAL	sakeru	**CAUS. PASSIVE**	sakaserareru/sakasareru
PASSIVE	sakareru	**HONORIFIC**	osaki ni naru/sakareru
CAUSATIVE	sakaseru	**HUMBLE**	osaki suru

Examples:

1. *Sakura no hana ga saite imasu.*
   桜の花が咲いています。
   The cherry blossoms have begun to blossom.

2. *Kono hana wa mō sugu saki-sō da.*
   この花はもうすぐ咲きそうだ。
   This flower looks ready to bloom.

3. *Ume no hana wa ni-gatsu goro sakimasu.*
   梅の花は二月ごろ咲きます。
   The flower of the plum blooms around February.

4. *Shorui o komakaku saite suteta.*
   書類を細かく裂いて捨てた。
   I tore the documents into small pieces and threw them away.

5. *O-jikan o jup-pun hodo saite itadakemasen ka.*
   お時間を十分ほど割いていただけませんか。
   Could you please spare me ten minutes?

* The intransitive verb *saku* 咲く meaning "to bloom" does not generally use the volitional, potential, passive, honorific, humble, causative, or causative passive forms.

sasaeru ささえる

支える to support, keep: (trans.)

		Affirmative	Negative
PLAIN FORM	PRESENT	sasaeru	sasaenai
	PAST	sasaeta	sasaenakatta
MASU FORM	PRESENT	sasaemasu	sasaemasen
	PAST	sasaemashita	sasaemasen deshita
TE FORM		sasaete	sasaenakute
CONDITIONAL	PLAIN	sasaereba/sasaeta ra	sasaenakereba/ sasaenakatta ra
	FORMAL	sasaemashita ra	sasaemasen deshita ra
VOLITIONAL	PLAIN	sasaeyō	–
	FORMAL	sasaemashō	–
IMPERATIVE		sasaero	sasaeru na

	Affirmative		Affirmative
POTENTIAL	sasaerareru/ sasaereru	**CAUS. PASSIVE**	sasaesaserareru
PASSIVE	sasaerareru	**HONORIFIC**	osasae ni naru/ sasaerareru
CAUSATIVE	sasaesaseru	**HUMBLE**	osasae suru

Examples:

1. *Kare wa tsue de karada o sasaete iru.*
   彼はつえで体を支えている。
   He is supporting himself with a stick.

2. *Kare wa dai-kazoku o sasaete ikanakereba narimasen.*
   彼は大家族を支えていかなければなりません。
   He has to support a large family.

3. *Taore-sō na hondana ga bō de sasaete aru.*
   倒れそうな本棚が棒で支えてある。
   The bookshelf that looks as if it is about to fall over is being supported by a pole.

4. *Ochikonde ita toki, tomodachi ga sasaete kureta.*
   落ち込んでいたとき、友達が支えてくれた。
   When I was depressed, my friend supported me.

5. *Sono jizen katsudō wa kifukin de sasaerarete iru.*
   その慈善活動は寄付金で支えられている。
   That charity movement has been supported by donations.

sasou さそう

誘う to invite, ask, tempt: (trans.)

		Affirmative	Negative
PLAIN FORM	PRESENT	sasou	sasowanai
	PAST	sasotta	sasowanakatta
MASU FORM	PRESENT	sasoimasu	sasoimasen
	PAST	sasoimashita	sasoimasen deshita
TE FORM		sasotte	sasowanakute
CONDITIONAL	PLAIN	sasoeba/sasotta ra	sasowanakereba/ sasowanakatta ra
	FORMAL	sasoimashita ra	sasoimasen deshita ra
VOLITIONAL	PLAIN	sasoō	–
	FORMAL	sasoimashō	–
IMPERATIVE		sasoe	sasou na

	Affirmative		Affirmative
POTENTIAL	sasoeru	**CAUS. PASSIVE**	sasowaserareru/ sasowasareru
PASSIVE	sasowareru	**HONORIFIC**	osasoi ni naru/ sasowareru
CAUSATIVE	sasowaseru	**HUMBLE**	osasoi suru

Examples:

1. *Tomodachi o sasotte, kaimono ni itta.*
   友達を誘って、買い物に行った。
   I invited my friend to go shopping with me.

2. *Kanojo o dēto ni sasoō to omotte imasu.*
   彼女をデートに誘おうと思っています。
   I intend to ask her out on a date.

3. *Yamada-san ni shokuji ni sasowaremashita.*
   山田さんに食事に誘われました。
   I was invited for a meal by Mr. Yamada.

4. *Pātii ni sasotte kurete, arigatō.*
   パーティーに誘ってくれて、ありがとう。
   Thank you for inviting me to the party.

5. *Omoshiroi tenrankai ga atta ra, zehi sasotte kudasai.*
   面白い展覧会があったら、是非誘ってください。
   If you can find an interesting exhibition, please invite me.

sasu さす

刺す to pierce, sting; 指す to point to, call on; 差す to insert, put up: (all trans.)

		Affirmative	Negative
PLAIN FORM	PRESENT	sasu	sasanai
	PAST	sashita	sasanakatta
MASU FORM	PRESENT	sashimasu	sashimasen
	PAST	sashimashita	sashimasen deshita
TE FORM		sashite	sasanakute
CONDITIONAL	PLAIN	saseba/sashita ra	sasanakereba/ sasanakatta ra
	FORMAL	sashimashita ra	sashimasen deshita ra
VOLITIONAL	PLAIN	sasō	–
	FORMAL	sashimashō	–
IMPERATIVE		sase	sasu na

	Affirmative		Affirmative
POTENTIAL	saseru	**CAUS. PASSIVE**	sasaserareru
PASSIVE	sasareru	**HONORIFIC**	osashi ni naru/sasareru
CAUSATIVE	sasaseru	**HUMBLE**	osashi suru

Examples:

1. *Hari de yubi o sashite shimatta.*
   針で指を刺してしまった。
   I have pricked my finger with a needle.

2. *Mushi ni ashi o sasareta.*
   虫に足を刺された。
   I was bitten on the leg by an insect.

3. *Yajirushi no sasu hōkō ni susunde kudasai.*
   矢印の指す方向に進んでください。
   Please move ahead in the direction indicated by the arrow.

4. *Hito o yubi de sasu no wa shitsurei desu.*
   人を指で指すのは失礼です。
   It is rude to point.

5. *Ame ga furi-dashita kara, kasa o sashita ho ga ii.*
   雨が降り出したから、傘をさしたほうがいい。
   You should open your umbrella since it started raining.

sawagu さわぐ

騒ぐ to be noisy: (intrans.)

		Affirmative	Negative
PLAIN FORM	PRESENT	sawagu	sawaganai
	PAST	sawaida	sawaganakatta
MASU FORM	PRESENT	sawagimasu	sawagimasen
	PAST	sawagimashita	sawagimasen deshita
TE FORM		sawaide	sawaganakute
CONDITIONAL	PLAIN	sawageba/sawaida ra	sawaganakereba/sawaganakatta ra
	FORMAL	sawagimashita ra	sawagimasen deshita ra
VOLITIONAL	PLAIN	sawagō	–
	FORMAL	sawagimashō	–
IMPERATIVE		sawage	sawagu na

	Affirmative		Affirmative
POTENTIAL	sawageru	**CAUS. PASSIVE**	sawagaserareru/sawagasareru
PASSIVE	sawagareru	**HONORIFIC**	osawagi ni naru/sawagareru
CAUSATIVE	sawagaseru	**HUMBLE**	osawagi suru

Examples:

1. *Kyōshitsu de sawaganaide kudasai.*
   教室で騒がないでください。
   Don't make a ruckus in the classroom.

2. *O-sake o nonde, sawaide iru hito wa dare desu ka.*
   お酒を飲んで、騒いでいる人は誰ですか。
   Who is that drunk making a nuisance of himself?

3. *Sono jiken wa seken o sawagaseta.*
   その事件は世間を騒がせた。
   That incident disturbed people.

4. *Watashi ga sawaida ra, dorobō wa nigete itta.*
   私が騒いだら、泥棒は逃げて行った。
   When I made lots of noise, the thief ran away.

5. *Sawagu na, ochitsuke yo.*
   騒ぐな、落ちつけよ。
   Keep calm, and don't get excited.

shibaru しばる

縛る to tie, bind: (trans.)

		Affirmative	Negative
PLAIN FORM	PRESENT	shibaru	shibaranai
	PAST	shibatta	shibaranakatta
MASU FORM	PRESENT	shibarimasu	shibarimasen
	PAST	shibarimashita	shibarimasen deshita
TE FORM		shibatte	shibaranakute
CONDITIONAL	PLAIN	shibareba/shibatta ra	shibaranakereba/ shibaranakatta ra
	FORMAL	shibarimashita ra	shibarimasen deshita ra
VOLITIONAL	PLAIN	shibarō	–
	FORMAL	shibarimashō	–
IMPERATIVE		shibare	shibaru na

	Affirmative		Affirmative
POTENTIAL	shibareru	**CAUS. PASSIVE**	shibaraserareru/ shibarasareru
PASSIVE	shibarareru	**HONORIFIC**	oshibari ni naru/ shibarareru
CAUSATIVE	shibaraseru	**HUMBLE**	oshibari suru

Examples:

1. *Furui zasshi o himo de shibatte, heya no sumi ni oita.*
   古い雑誌をひもで縛って、部屋の隅に置いた。
   I tied up the old magazines with string and put them in the corner of the room.

2. *Kaminoke o ushiro de hitotsu ni shibatta.*
   髪の毛を後ろで一つに縛った。
   I gathered my hair into a single bunch and tied it behind my head.

3. *Inu no himo o kui ni shibatte oita.*
   犬のひもを杭に縛っておいた。
   I tied the dog to a post.

4. *Kare wa ichinichi-jū shigoto ni shibararete ita.*
   彼は一日中仕事に縛られていた。
   He was tied up with work all day.

5. *Jikan ni shibararete ite, jiyū ni ugokenai.*
   時間に縛られていて、自由に動けない。
   I am too busy so I don't have any free time.

shikaru しかる

叱る scold: (trans.)

		Affirmative	Negative
PLAIN FORM	PRESENT	shikaru	shikaranai
	PAST	shikatta	shikaranakatta
MASU FORM	PRESENT	shikarimasu	shikarimasen
	PAST	shikarimashita	shikarimasen deshita
TE FORM		shikatte	shikaranakute
CONDITIONAL	PLAIN	shikareba/shikatta ra	shikaranakereba/ shikaranakatta ra
	FORMAL	shikarimashita ra	shikarimasen deshita ra
VOLITIONAL	PLAIN	shikarō	–
	FORMAL	shikarimashō	–
IMPERATIVE		shikare	shikaru na

	Affirmative		Affirmative
POTENTIAL	shikareru	**CAUS. PASSIVE**	shikaraserareru/ shikarasareru
PASSIVE	shikarareru	**HONORIFIC**	oshikari ni naru/ shikarareru
CAUSATIVE	shikaraseru	**HUMBLE**	oshikari suru

Examples:

1. *Chikoku shite, sensei ni shikarareta.*
   遅刻して、先生に叱られた。
   I was scolded by my teacher for being late.

2. *Otōsan wa kibishiku musuko o shikarimashita.*
   お父さんは厳しく息子を叱りました。
   The father severely scolded his son.

3. *Haha ni shikararenai yō ni, heya o katazuketa.*
   母に叱られないように、部屋を片付けた。
   I cleared up my room so I would not be scolded by my mother.

4. *Ikura shikatte mo, musume wa iu koto o kikanai.*
   いくら叱っても、娘は言う事を聞かない。
   No matter how many times I scold my daughter, she never listens to me.

5. *Sonna ni gami gami shikaranaide kudasai.*
   そんなにがみがみ叱らないでください。
   Please do not scold me so harshly.

shiku しく

敷く to spread, lay, promulgate (a law): (trans.)

		Affirmative	*Negative*
PLAIN FORM	PRESENT	shiku	shikanai
	PAST	shiita	shikanakatta
MASU FORM	PRESENT	shikimasu	shikimasen
	PAST	shikimashita	shikimasen deshita
TE FORM		shiite	shikanakute
CONDITIONAL	PLAIN	shikeba/shiita ra	shikanakereba/shikanakatta ra
	FORMAL	shikimashita ra	shikimasen deshita ra
VOLITIONAL	PLAIN	shikō	–
	FORMAL	shikimashō	–
IMPERATIVE		shike	shiku na

	Affirmative		*Affirmative*
POTENTIAL	shikeru	**CAUS. PASSIVE**	shikaserareru/shikasareru
PASSIVE	shikareru	**HONORIFIC**	oshiki ni naru/shikareru
CAUSATIVE	shikaseru	**HUMBLE**	oshiki suru

Examples:

1. *Ryokan de wa tatami ni futon o shiite nemasu.*
   旅館では畳に布団を敷いて寝ます。
   We spread the futon on the *tatami* mat in the *ryokan* (Japanese inn) and go to bed.

2. *Yuka ni akai jūtan o shiki-tai.*
   床に赤いじゅうたんを敷きたい。
   I want to lay a red carpet on the floor.

3. *Beddo ni atarashii shiitsu ga shiite aru.*
   ベッドに新しいシーツが敷いてある。
   A new sheet is spread over the bed.

4. *Kare wa nyōbō no shiri ni shikarete iru.*
   彼は女房の尻に敷かれている。
   He is under his wife's thumb. (*lit.*, flattened by wife's buttocks)

5. *Kūkō kara kono machi made tetsudō o shiku keikaku ga aru.*
   空港からこの町まで鉄道を敷く計画がある。
   There is a plan to extend the railroad from the airport to this town.

shimaru しまる

閉まる be closed, shut; 締まる be tight, firm, be thrifty: (both intrans.)

		Affirmative	Negative
PLAIN FORM	PRESENT	shimaru	shimaranai
	PAST	shimatta	shimaranakatta
MASU FORM	PRESENT	shimarimasu	shimarimasen
	PAST	shimarimashita	shimarimasen deshita
TE FORM		shimatte	shimaranakute
CONDITIONAL	PLAIN	shimareba/shimatta ra	shimaranakereba/ shimaranakatta ra
	FORMAL	shimarimashita ra	shimarimasen deshita ra
VOLITIONAL	PLAIN	shimarō	–
	FORMAL	shimarimashō	–
IMPERATIVE		shimare	shimaru na

	Affirmative		Affirmative
POTENTIAL	shimareru	**CAUS. PASSIVE**	shimaraserareru/ shimarasareru
PASSIVE	shimarareru	**HONORIFIC**	oshimari ni naru/ shimarareru
CAUSATIVE	shimaraseru	**HUMBLE**	(oshimari suru)

Examples:

1. *Doa wa jidōteki ni shimarimasu.*
   ドアは自動的に閉まります。
   The door shuts automatically.

2. *Toshokan wa roku-ji ni shimaru.*
   図書館は六時に閉まる。
   The library closes at six o'clock.

3. *Mado ga zenbu shimatte iru ka, tashikamete kudasai.*
   窓が全部閉まっているか、確かめてください。
   Please make sure that all the windows are closed.

4. *Kono neji wa kanzen ni shimatte inai.*
   このねじは完全に締まっていない。
   This screw has not been completely tightened.

5. *Kutsu-himo ga kataku shimatte ite, hodokenai.*
   靴ひもが固く締まっていて、ほどけない。
   The shoestring is tied so tightly that I can't undo it.

shimau しまう

しまう to put away, put back, finish, end up doing: (intrans. and trans.)

		Affirmative	*Negative*
PLAIN FORM	PRESENT	shimau	shimawanai
	PAST	shimatta	shimawanakatta
MASU FORM	PRESENT	shimaimasu	shimaimasen
	PAST	shimaimashita	shimaimasen deshita
TE FORM		shimatte	shimawanakute
CONDITIONAL	PLAIN	shimaeba/shimatta ra	shimawanakereba/ shimawanakatta ra
	FORMAL	shimaimashita ra	shimaimasen deshita ra
VOLITIONAL	PLAIN	shimaō	–
	FORMAL	shimaimashō	–
IMPERATIVE		shimae	shimau na

	Affirmative		*Affirmative*
POTENTIAL	shimaeru	**CAUS. PASSIVE**	shimawaserareru/ shimawasareru
PASSIVE	shimawareru	**HONORIFIC**	oshimai ni naru/ shimawareru
CAUSATIVE	shimawaseru	**HUMBLE**	oshimai suru

Examples:

1. *Kore o tsukue no hikidashi ni shimatte kudasai.*
   これを机の引き出しにしまってください。
   Please put this away in the desk drawer.

2. *Kichōhin wa kinko ni shimatte arimasu.*
   貴重品は金庫にしまってあります。
   The valuables are kept in the safe.

3. *Kyō-jū ni shukudai o yatte shimaimasu.*
   今日中に宿題をやってしまいます。
   I will finish my homework today.

4. *Kono shōsetsu wa mō zenbu yonde shimatta.*
   この小説はもう全部読んでしまった。
   I have already finished reading this novel.

5. *Denwa bangō o machigaete shimaimashita.*
   電話番号を間違えてしまいました。
   I have got a wrong number.

shimeru しめる

閉める or 締める to shut, close, tie, fasten; 占める to take, hold, occupy: (all trans.)

		Affirmative	*Negative*
PLAIN FORM	PRESENT	shimeru	shimenai
	PAST	shimeta	shimenakatta
MASU FORM	PRESENT	shimemasu	shimemasen
	PAST	shimemashita	shimemasen deshita
TE FORM		shimete	shimenakute
CONDITIONAL	PLAIN	shimereba/shimeta ra	shimenakereba/ shimenakatta ra
	FORMAL	shimemashita ra	shimemasen deshita ra
VOLITIONAL	PLAIN	shimeyō	–
	FORMAL	shimemashō	–
IMPERATIVE		shimero	shimeru na

	Affirmative		*Affirmative*
POTENTIAL	shimerareru/ shimereru	**CAUS. PASSIVE**	shimesaserareru
PASSIVE	shimerareru	**HONORIFIC**	oshime ni naru/ shimerareru
CAUSATIVE	shimesaseru	**HUMBLE**	oshime suru

Examples:

1. *Doa o shimete kudasai.*
   ドアを閉めてください。
   Please close the door.

2. *Mado o shimeru no o wasureta.*
   窓を閉めるのを忘れた。
   I forgot to close the window.

3. *Kuruma ni notta ra, shiito-beruto o shimenakereba naranai.*
   車に乗ったら、シートベルトを締めなければならない。
   When you get into a car, you must fasten your seat belt.

4. *Kare wa kaisha de jūyō na chii o shimete iru.*
   彼は会社で重要な地位を占めている。
   He has an important position in the firm.

5. *Denki seihin wa yushutsu no roku-wari o shimete iru.*
   電気製品は輸出の六割を占めている。
   Electrical appliances hold a sixty-percent share of our exports.

shimesu しめす

示す to show, indicate, point out: (trans.)

		Affirmative	Negative
PLAIN FORM	PRESENT	shimesu	shimesanai
	PAST	shimeshita	shimesanakatta
MASU FORM	PRESENT	shimeshimasu	shimeshimasen
	PAST	shimeshimashita	shimeshimasen deshita
TE FORM		shimeshite	shimesanakute
CONDITIONAL	PLAIN	shimeseba/shimeshita ra	shimesanakereba/ shimesanakatta ra
	FORMAL	shimeshimashita ra	shimeshimasen deshita ra
VOLITIONAL	PLAIN	shimesō	–
	FORMAL	shimeshimashō	–
IMPERATIVE		shimese	shimesu na

	Affirmative		Affirmative
POTENTIAL	shimeseru	CAUS. PASSIVE	shimesaserareru
PASSIVE	shimesareru	HONORIFIC	oshimeshi ni naru/ shimesareru
CAUSATIVE	shimesaseru	HUMBLE	oshimeshi suru

Examples:

1. *Ondokei wa reika jū-do o shimeshita.*
   温度計は零下十度を示した。
   The thermometer indicated ten degrees below zero.

2. *Kanojo wa watashi no jijō ni rikai o shimeshite kureta.*
   彼女は私の事情に理解を示してくれた。
   She showed understanding for my situation.

3. *Kare wa watashi no itta koto ni kyōmi o shimesanakatta.*
   彼は私の言った事に興味を示さなかった。
   He showed no interest in what I said.

4. *Kono chizu de toshi wa akai ten de shimesarete iru.*
   この地図で都市は赤い点で示されている。
   The cities are indicated by the red dots on this map.

5. *Shijō wa keiki ga kaifuku suru chōkō o shimeshite iru.*
   市場は景気が回復する兆候を示している。
   The market shows signs of economic recovery.

shinjiru しんじる

信じる to believe, be confident of: (trans.)

		Affirmative	*Negative*
PLAIN FORM	PRESENT	shinjiru	shinjinai
	PAST	shinjita	shinjinakatta
MASU FORM	PRESENT	shinjimasu	shinjimasen
	PAST	shinjimashita	shinjimasen deshita
TE FORM		shinjite	shinjinakute
CONDITIONAL	PLAIN	shinjireba/shinjita ra	shinjinakereba/ shinjinakatta ra
	FORMAL	shinjimashita ra	shinjimasen deshita ra
VOLITIONAL	PLAIN	shinjiyō	–
	FORMAL	shinjimashō	–
IMPERATIVE		shinjiro	shinjiru na

	Affirmative		*Affirmative*
POTENTIAL	shinjirareru/ shinjireru	**CAUS. PASSIVE**	shinjisaserareru
PASSIVE	shinjirareru	**HONORIFIC**	oshinji ni naru/ shinjirareru
CAUSATIVE	shinjisaseru	**HUMBLE**	oshinji suru

Examples:

1. *Watashi wa kanojo no seikō o shinjite imasu.*
   私は彼女の成功を信じています。
   I am sure she will succeed.

2. *Kare no iu koto wa shinjiraremasen.*
   彼の言う事は信じられません。
   I can't believe what he says.

3. *Sonna baka na hanashi wa dare mo shinjinai darō.*
   そんな馬鹿な話は誰も信じないだろう。
   I don't think that anybody will believe such a stupid story.

4. *Yamano ue kara no keshiki wa shinjirarenai gurai subarashikatta.*
   山の上からの景色は信じられないぐらい素晴らしかった。
   The view from the mountain top was unbelievably splendid.

5. *Shinjiyō ga shinji-mai ga, sore wa hontō no hanashi da.*
   信じようが信じまいが、それは本当の話だ。
   Believe it or not, that is the true story.

shinu しぬ

死ぬ to die, pass away: (intrans.)

		Affirmative	Negative
PLAIN FORM	PRESENT	shinu	shinanai
	PAST	shinda	shinanakatta
MASU FORM	PRESENT	shinimasu	shinimasen
	PAST	shinimashita	shinimasen deshita
TE FORM		shinde	shinanakute
CONDITIONAL	PLAIN	shineba/shinda ra	shinanakereba/ shinanakatta ra
	FORMAL	shinimashita ra	shinimasen deshita ra
VOLITIONAL	PLAIN	shinō	–
	FORMAL	shinimashō	–
IMPERATIVE		shine	shinu na

	Affirmative		Affirmative
POTENTIAL	shineru	**CAUS. PASSIVE**	shinaserareru/ shinasareru
PASSIVE	shinareru	**HONORIFIC**	onakunari ni naru/ nakunarareru
CAUSATIVE	shinaseru	**HUMBLE**	–

Examples:

1. *Sono hikōki jiko de ōku no jyōkyaku ga shinda.*
   その飛行機事故で多くの乗客が死んだ。
   Many passengers died in the plane accident.

2. *Chichi ga shinde kara go-nen ni naru.*
   父が死んでから五年になる。
   It has been five years since my father died.

3. *Kare ni ayamaru gurai nara, shinda hō ga mashi da.*
   彼に謝るぐらいなら、死んだほうがましだ。
   I would rather die than apologize to him.

4. *Sono kōgi wa shinu hodo tsumaranakatta.*
   その講義は死ぬほどつまらなかった。
   That lecture was boring me to death.

5. *Okashikute shini-sō deshita.*
   おかしくて死にそうでした。
   I nearly died of laughter.

shiraberu しらべる

GROUP 2

調べる investigate, study, search, check up: (trans.)

		Affirmative	Negative
PLAIN FORM	PRESENT	shiraberu	shirabenai
	PAST	shirabeta	shirabenakatta
MASU FORM	PRESENT	shirabemasu	shirabemasen
	PAST	shirabemashita	shirabemasen deshita
TE FORM		shirabete	shirabenakute
CONDITIONAL	PLAIN	shirabereba/shirabeta ra	shirabenakereba/ shirabenakatta ra
	FORMAL	shirabemashita ra	shirabemasen deshita ra
VOLITIONAL	PLAIN	shirabeyō	–
	FORMAL	shirabemashō	–
IMPERATIVE		shirabero	shiraberu na

	Affirmative		Affirmative
POTENTIAL	shiraberareru/ shirabereru	**CAUS. PASSIVE**	shirabesaserareru
PASSIVE	shiraberareru	**HONORIFIC**	oshirabe ni naru/ shiraberareru
CAUSATIVE	shirabesaseru	**HUMBLE**	oshirabe suru

Examples:

1. *Wakaranai kotoba wa jisho de shirabete kudasai.*
   分からない言葉は辞書で調べてください。
   Please look up the dictionary any words that you don't know.

2. *Repōto o dasu mae ni, bunshō ni machigai ga nai ka dō ka shirabeta.*
   レポートを出す前に、文章に間違いがないかどうか調べた。
   I checked my report to see if there are any mistakes in the sentences before submitting it.

3. *Intānetto de Nihon-ryōri no resutoran o shirabete mita.*
   インターネットで日本料理のレストランを調べてみた。
   I tried searching the Internet for Japanese restaurants.

4. *Keisatsu wa sono jiko no gen-in o shirabete iru tokoro da.*
   警察はその事故の原因を調べているところだ。
   The police are now investigating the cause of the accident.

5. *Kūkō no zeikan de sūtsukēsu o kuwashiku shiraberareta.*
   空港の税関でスーツケースを詳しく調べられた。
   My suitcase was searched by the customs officer at the airport.

shiraseru しらせる

知らせる inform, notify, tell (trans.)

		Affirmative	Negative
PLAIN FORM	PRESENT	shiraseru	shirasenai
	PAST	shiraseta	shirasenakatta
MASU FORM	PRESENT	shirasemasu	shirasemasen
	PAST	shirasemashita	shirasemasen deshita
TE FORM		shirasete	shirasenakute
CONDITIONAL	PLAIN	shirasereba/shiraseta ra	shirasenakereba/shirasenakatta ra
	FORMAL	shirasemashita ra	shirasemasen deshita ra
VOLITIONAL	PLAIN	shiraseyō	–
	FORMAL	shirasemashō	–
IMPERATIVE		shirasero	shiraseru na

	Affirmative		Affirmative
POTENTIAL	shiraserareru/shirasereru	**CAUS. PASSIVE**	shirasesaserareru
PASSIVE	shiraserareru	**HONORIFIC**	oshirase ni naru/shiraserareru
CAUSATIVE	shirasesaseru	**HUMBLE**	oshirase suru

Examples:

1. *Denwa bangō ga kawatta node, tomodachi ni shiraseta.*
   電話番号が変わったので、友達に知らせた。
   Because my phone number has been changed, I let my friend know.

2. *Shiken no gōkaku o shiraseru tegami ga todoita.*
   試験の合格を知らせる手紙が届いた。
   I received a letter informing me that I passed the exam.

3. *Asu no kaigi no jikan ga kimattara, shirasete kudasai.*
   明日の会議の時間が決まったら、知らせてください。
   Once the time for tomorrow's meeting is decided, please let me know.

4. *Shokuji no junbi ga dekimashita ra, oshirase shimasu.*
   食事の準備ができましたら、お知らせします。
   Once the meal is ready, we will let you know.

5. *Kara wa shigoto o kaeta to ato kara shiraserareta.*
   彼は仕事を変えたと後から知らせられた。
   I was informed later that he changed his job.

shiru しる

知る to know, become aware of, become familiar with: (trans.)

		Affirmative	*Negative*
PLAIN FORM	PRESENT	shiru	shiranai
	PAST	shitta	shiranakatta
MASU FORM	PRESENT	shirimasu	shirimasen
	PAST	shirimashita	shirimasen deshita
TE FORM		shitte	shiranakute
CONDITIONAL	PLAIN	shireba/shitta ra	shiranakereba/ shiranakatta ra
	FORMAL	shirimashita ra	shirimasen deshita ra
VOLITIONAL	PLAIN	shirō	–
	FORMAL	shirimashō	–
IMPERATIVE		shire	shiru na

	Affirmative		*Affirmative*
POTENTIAL	shireru	**CAUS. PASSIVE**	shiraserareru/shirasareru
PASSIVE	shirareru	**HONORIFIC**	gozonji da/oshiri ni naru
CAUSATIVE	shiraseru	**HUMBLE**	zonjiru/zonjiageru/ shōchi suru

Examples:

1. *Anata wa kare no namae o shitte imasu ka. / Iie, shirimasen.*
   あなたは彼の名前を知っていますか。/ いいえ、知りません。
   Do you know his name? / No, I don't.

2. *Shachō ga nyūin nasatta koto o gozonji desu ka.*
   社長が入院なさったことをご存知ですか。
   Sir, I was wondering if you knew that the president has been hospitalized.

   Iie, *zonjimasen deshita.*
   いいえ、存じませんでした。
   No, I didn't know that.

3. *Tenpura no tsukuri-kata o shitte ita ra, oshiete kudasai.*
   天ぷらの作り方を知っていたら、教えてください。
   If you know how to make tenpura, please teach me.

4. *Yamada-san ga Chūgoku-go ga hanaseru to wa shiranakatta.*
   山田さんが中国語が話せるとは知らなかった。
   I didn't know that Mr. Yamada could speak Chinese.

5. *Kare wa kenchikuka to shite, sekaijū ni shirarete iru.*
   彼は建築家として、世界中に知られている。
   He is well-known all over the world as an architect.

shitagau したがう

従う to follow, obey, go along with: (intrans.)

		Affirmative	Negative
PLAIN FORM	PRESENT	shitagau	shitagawanai
	PAST	shitagatta	shitagawanakatta
MASU FORM	PRESENT	shitagaimasu	shitagaimasen
	PAST	shitagaimashita	shitagaimasen deshita
TE FORM		shitagatte	shitagawanakute
CONDITIONAL	PLAIN	shitagaeba/shitagatta ra	shitagawanakereba/ shitagawanakatta ra
	FORMAL	shitagaimashita ra	shitagaimasen deshita ra
VOLITIONAL	PLAIN	shitagaō	–
	FORMAL	shitagaimashō	–
IMPERATIVE		shitagae	shitagau na

	Affirmative		Affirmative
POTENTIAL	shitagaeru	**CAUS. PASSIVE**	shitagawaserareru/ shitagawasareru
PASSIVE	shitagawareru	**HONORIFIC**	oshitagai ni naru/ shitagawareru
CAUSATIVE	shitagawaseru	**HUMBLE**	oshitagai suru

Examples:

1. *Kisoku ni wa shitagawanakereba narimasen.*
   規則には従わなければなりません。
   One must abide by the rules.

2. *Isha no chūkoku ni shitagatte, osake o yameta.*
   医者の忠告に従って、お酒をやめた。
   I quit drinking according to my doctor's advice.

3. *Hijō no bāi wa, kakariin no shiji ni shitagatte kudasai.*
   非常の場合は、係員の指示に従ってください。
   In case of emergency, please follow the instruction of the person in charge.

4. *Kare wa jōshi no meirei ni shitagawanakute, kubi ni natta.*
   彼は上司の命令に従わなくて、首になった。
   He was fired because he didn't obey orders from his boss.

5. *Ryōshin no iu koto ni shitagatta hō ga ii yo.*
   両親の言う事に従ったほうがいいよ。
   You had better listen to what your parents say.

shizumu しずむ

沈む to sink, feel depressed (intrans.)

		Affirmative	Negative
PLAIN FORM	PRESENT	shizumu	shizumanai
	PAST	shizunda	shizumanakatta
MASU FORM	PRESENT	shizumimasu	shizumimasen
	PAST	shizumimashita	shizumimasen deshita
TE FORM		shizunde	shizumanakute
CONDITIONAL	PLAIN	shizumeba/shizunda ra	shizumanakereba/ shizumanakatta ra
	FORMAL	shizumimashita ra	shizumimasen deshita ra
VOLITIONAL	PLAIN	shizumō	–
	FORMAL	shizumimashō	–
IMPERATIVE		shizume	shizumu na

	Affirmative		Affirmative
POTENTIAL	shizumeru	**CAUS. PASSIVE**	shizumaserareru/ shizumasareru
PASSIVE	shizumareru	**HONORIFIC**	oshizumi ni naru/ shizumareru
CAUSATIVE	shizumaseru	**HUMBLE**	oshizumi suru

Examples:

1. *Kaigan de umi ni shizumu yūhi o mita.*
   海岸で海に沈む夕日を見た。
   I watched the sun set into the sea at the shore.

2. *Taiyō ga shizunda ra, kyū ni samuku natta.*
   太陽が沈んだら、急に寒くなった。
   Once the sun set, it suddenly became cold.

3. *Fune ga iwa ni butsukatte, shizunde shimatta.*
   船が岩にぶつかって、沈んでしまった。
   The ship hit the rock and sank.

4. *Kanojo wa kanashimi ni shizunde imasu.*
   彼女は悲しみに沈んでいます。
   She is deep in sorrow.

5. *Kodai no fune ga kaitei ni shizunde iru.*
   古代の船が海底に沈んでいる。
   An ancient ship lays sunken on the bottom of the sea.

sodateru そだてる

育てる to bring up, raise, rear: (trans.)

		Affirmative	*Negative*
PLAIN FORM	PRESENT	*sodateru*	*sodatenai*
	PAST	*sodateta*	*sodatenakatta*
MASU FORM	PRESENT	*sodatemasu*	*sodatemasen*
	PAST	*sodatemashita*	*sodatemasen deshita*
TE FORM		*sodatete*	*sodatenakute*
CONDITIONAL	PLAIN	*sodatereba/sodateta ra*	*sodatenakereba/ sodatenakatta ra*
	FORMAL	*sodatemashita ra*	*sodatemasen deshita ra*
VOLITIONAL	PLAIN	*sodateyō*	–
	FORMAL	*sodatemashō*	–
IMPERATIVE		*sodatero*	*sodateru na*

	Affirmative		*Affirmative*
POTENTIAL	*sodaterareru/ sodatereru*	**CAUS. PASSIVE**	*sodatesaserareru*
PASSIVE	*sodaterareru*	**HONORIFIC**	*osodate ni naru/ sodaterareru*
CAUSATIVE	*sodatesaseru*	**HUMBLE**	*osodate suru*

Examples:

1. *Kanojo wa hitori de san-nin no kodomo o sodateta.*
   彼女は一人で三人の子供を育てた。
   She brought up three children by herself.

2. *Haha wa hana o sodateru no ga shumi desu.*
   母は花を育てるのが趣味です。
   My mother's hobby is growing flowers.

3. *Tanaka-san wa ryōshin ni kibishiku sodaterareta sō da.*
   田中さんは両親に厳しく育てられたそうだ。
   I hear that Mr. Tanaka was raised strictly by his parents.

4. *Kare wa shinnyūshain o sodateru shigoto o shite iru.*
   彼は新入社員を育てる仕事をしている。
   His job is to groom new employees.

5. *Sono kōchi wa ōku no yūshū na senshu o sodatete kita.*
   そのコーチは多くの優秀な選手を育ててきた。
   That coach has brought up many excellent players.

sodatsu そだつ

育つ to grow up, be brought up, be raised: (intrans.)

		Affirmative	*Negative*
PLAIN FORM	PRESENT	sodatsu	sodatanai
	PAST	sodatta	sodatanakatta
MASU FORM	PRESENT	sodachimasu	sodachimasen
	PAST	sodachimashita	sodachimasen deshita
TE FORM		sodatte	sodatanakute
CONDITIONAL	PLAIN	sodateba/sodatta ra	sodatanakereba/ sodatanakatta ra
	FORMAL	sodachimashita ra	sodachimasen deshita ra
VOLITIONAL	PLAIN	sodatō	–
	FORMAL	sodachimashō	–
IMPERATIVE		sodate	sodatsu na

	Affirmative		*Affirmative*
POTENTIAL	sodateru	**CAUS. PASSIVE**	sodataserareru/ sodatasareru
PASSIVE	sodatareru	**HONORIFIC**	osodachi ni naru/ sodatareru
CAUSATIVE	sodataseru	**HUMBLE**	osodachi suru

Examples:

1. *Watashi wa Tōkyō de umarete, Yokohama de sodachimashita.*
   私は東京で生まれて、横浜で育ちました。
   I was born in Tokyo and brought up in Yokohama.

2. *Kare wa umare sodatta machi o dete, tokai de hataraite iru.*
   彼は生まれ育った町を出て、都会で働いている。
   He had left his hometown and is now working in the big city.

3. *Kotoshi wa tenki ga yokute, yasai ga yoku sodatta.*
   今年は天気が良くて、野菜が良く育った。
   Vegetables grew well since the weather this year has been fine.

4. *Samui kikō de wa painappuru wa sodachimasen.*
   寒い気候ではパイナップルは育ちません。
   Pineapples can't be grown in cold climates.

5. *Sono kaisha wa sū-nen de dai kigyō e to sodatta.*
   その会社は数年で大企業へと育った。
   That firm grew to be a major corporation in a few years.

sū すう

吸う to take a breath, inhale, suck, absorb: (trans.)

		Affirmative	Negative
PLAIN FORM	PRESENT	sū	suwanai
	PAST	sutta	suwanakatta
MASU FORM	PRESENT	suimasu	suimasen
	PAST	suimashita	suimasen deshita
TE FORM		sutte	suwanakute
CONDITIONAL	PLAIN	sueba/sutta ra	suwanakereba/ suwanakatta ra
	FORMAL	suimashita ra	suimasen deshita ra
VOLITIONAL	PLAIN	suō	–
	FORMAL	suimashō	–
IMPERATIVE		sue	sū na

	Affirmative		Affirmative
POTENTIAL	sueru	**CAUS. PASSIVE**	suwaserareru/suwasareru
PASSIVE	suwareru	**HONORIFIC**	osui ni naru/suwareru
CAUSATIVE	suwaseru	**HUMBLE**	(osui suru)

Examples:

1. *Koko de tabako o sutte mo ii desu ka.*
   ここでたばこを吸ってもいいですか。
   May I smoke here?

   Iie, *suwanaide kudasai.*
   いいえ、吸わないでください。
   No, please don't.

2. *Tabako o osui ni narimasu ka. / Iie, suimasen.*
   たばこをお吸いになりますか。／いいえ、吸いません。
   Do you smoke, Sir? / No, I don't.

3. *Fukaku iki o sutte, yukkuri haite kudasai.*
   深く息を吸って、ゆっくり吐いてください。
   Please breathe in deeply and then exhale slowly.

4. *Shinsen na kūki ga sui-tai.*
   新鮮な空気が吸いたい。
   I want to breathe in fresh air.

5. *Momen no shitagi wa ase o yoku suimasu.*
   木綿の下着は汗をよく吸います。
   The cotton underwear absorbs sweat well.

sugiru すぎる

過ぎる to pass, exceed; (attached to a verb, adjective, or adverb) to be too: (intrans.)*

		Affirmative	*Negative*
PLAIN FORM	PRESENT	sugiru	suginai
	PAST	sugita	suginakatta
MASU FORM	PRESENT	sugimasu	sugimasen
	PAST	sugimashita	sugimasen deshita
TE FORM		sugite	suginakute
CONDITIONAL	PLAIN	sugireba/sugita ra	suginakereba/suginakatta ra
	FORMAL	sugimashita ra	sugimasen deshita ra
VOLITIONAL	PLAIN	sugiyō	–
	FORMAL	sugimashō	–
IMPERATIVE		sugiro	sugiru na

	Affirmative		*Affirmative*
POTENTIAL	sugirareru/sugireru	**CAUS. PASSIVE**	sugisaserareru
PASSIVE	sugirareru	**HONORIFIC**	osugi ni naru/sugirareru
CAUSATIVE	sugisaseru	**HUMBLE**	(osugi suru)

Examples:

1. *Densha wa sukoshi mae ni Shinagawa-eki o sugita.*
   電車は少し前に品川駅を過ぎた。
   The train passed Shinagawa Station just a while ago.

2. *Yakusoku no jikan o sugite mo, kare wa konakatta.*
   約束の時間を過ぎても、彼は来なかった。
   He did not show up at the promised time.

3. *Kare wa yonjussai o sugite iru.*
   彼は四十歳を過ぎている。
   He is over forty years old.

4. *Kono hon wa watashi ni wa muzukashi-sugiru.*
   この本は私には難しすぎる。
   This book is too difficult for me.

5. *Yūbe osake o nomi-sugite, kyō wa futsuka-yoi desu.*
   ゆうべお酒を飲み過ぎて、今日は二日酔いです。
   I drank too much sake last night, so I am having a hangover today.

* *Sugiru* 過ぎる is classified as an intransitive verb, but is also used as a transitive verb. (See examples 1, 2 and 3)

sugosu すごす

過ごす to pass time, spend time, get through: (trans.)

		Affirmative	Negative
PLAIN FORM	PRESENT	sugosu	sugosanai
	PAST	sugoshita	sugosanakatta
MASU FORM	PRESENT	sugoshimasu	sugoshimasen
	PAST	sugoshimashita	sugoshimasen deshita
TE FORM		sugoshite	sugosanakute
CONDITIONAL	PLAIN	sugoseba/sugoshita ra	sugosanakereba/ sugosanakatta ra
	FORMAL	sugoshimashita ra	sugoshimasen deshita ra
VOLITIONAL	PLAIN	sugosō	–
	FORMAL	sugoshimashō	–
IMPERATIVE		sugose	sugosu na

	Affirmative		Affirmative
POTENTIAL	sugoseru	**CAUS. PASSIVE**	sugosaserareru
PASSIVE	sugosareru	**HONORIFIC**	osugoshi ni naru/ sugosareru
CAUSATIVE	sugosaseru	**HUMBLE**	osugoshi suru

Examples:

1. *Tōkyō de ikka-getsu sugoshimashita.*
   東京で一か月過ごしました。
   I spent a month in Tokyo.

2. *Natsuyasumi o minami no shima de sugoseta ra ii noni.*
   夏休みを南の島で過ごせたらいいのに。
   I wish I could spend my summer vacation on a southern island.

3. *Yoi shūmatsu o osugoshi kudasai.*
   よい週末をお過ごしください。
   Please have a good weekend.

4. *Oshōgatsu yasumi wa dō sugosaremashita ka.*
   お正月休みは、どう過ごされましたか。
   How did you spend the New Year?

5. *Jikan o muda ni sugosu na.*
   時間を無駄に過ごすな。
   Don't waste your time.

suku すく

好く to like: (trans.); すく to become empty*, to be not crowded*; (both intrans.)

		Affirmative	Negative
PLAIN FORM	PRESENT	suku	sukanai
	PAST	suita	sukanakatta
MASU FORM	PRESENT	sukimasu	sukimasen
	PAST	sukimashita	sukimasen deshita
TE FORM		suite	sukanakute
CONDITIONAL	PLAIN	sukeba/suita ra	sukanakereba/ sukanakatta ra
	FORMAL	sukimashita ra	sukimasen deshita ra
VOLITIONAL	PLAIN	sukō	–
	FORMAL	sukimashō	–
IMPERATIVE		suke	suku na

	Affirmative		Affirmative
POTENTIAL	sukeru	**CAUS. PASSIVE**	sukaserareru/sukasareru
PASSIVE	sukareru	**HONORIFIC**	osuki ni naru/sukareru
CAUSATIVE	sukaseru	**HUMBLE**	(osuki suru)

Examples:

1. *Kare wa minna ni sukarete iru.*
   彼はみんなに好かれている。
   He is liked by everybody.

2. *Densha wa konde imashita ka, suite imashita ka.*
   電車はこんでいましたか、すいていましたか。
   Was the train crowded or was it empty?

3. *Michi ga suite ita ra, hayaku tsuku deshō.*
   道がすいていたら、早く着くでしょう。
   If the road is not congested, you should be able to arrive early.

4. *Onaka ga suita.*
   おなかがすいた。
   I am hungry.

5. *Te ga suite ita ra, chotto tetsudatte kudasai.*
   手がすいていたら、ちょっと手伝ってください。
   If you have nothing to do, please help me a little.

* The intransitive verb *suku* すく meaning "to become empty" and "to be not crowded" does not generally use volitional, potential, passive, honorific, humble, causative, or causative passive forms.

sumu すむ GROUP 1

住む to live; 済む to end, be over;* 澄む to become clear:* (all intrans.)

		Affirmative	Negative
PLAIN FORM	PRESENT	sumu	sumanai
	PAST	sunda	sumanakatta
MASU FORM	PRESENT	sumimasu	sumimasen
	PAST	sumimashita	sumimasen deshita
TE FORM		sunde	sumanakute
CONDITIONAL	PLAIN	sumeba/sunda ra	sumanakereba/ sumanakatta ra
	FORMAL	sumimashita ra	sumimasen deshita ra
VOLITIONAL	PLAIN	sumō	–
	FORMAL	sumimashō	–
IMPERATIVE		sume	sumu na

	Affirmative		Affirmative
POTENTIAL	sumeru	**CAUS. PASSIVE**	sumaserareru/ sumasareru
PASSIVE	sumareru	**HONORIFIC**	osumi ni naru/sumareru
CAUSATIVE	sumaseru	**HUMBLE**	(osumi suru)

Examples:

1. *Anata wa doko ni sunde imasu ka. / Hirō ni sunde imasu.*
   あなたはどこに住んでいますか。 / 広尾に住んでいます。
   Where do you live? / I live in Hirō.

2. *Kono machi wa totemo sumi-yasui desu.*
   この町はとても住みやすいです。
   This town is very livable.

3. *Ryokō no tehai wa mō sumimashita ka.*
   旅行の手配は、もう済みましたか。
   Have you finalized the arrangements for your trip?

4. *Shigoto ga sunda ra, kōhii demo nomi ni ikimashō.*
   仕事が済んだら、コーヒーでも飲みに行きましょう。
   Let's go have some coffee after work.

5. *Jiko ni atta ga, saiwai kega o shinai de sunda.*
   事故にあったが、幸いけがをしないで済んだ。
   Even though I was in an accident, I was fortunate I was not hurt.

* The verbs *sumu* meaning "to end, be over" 済む and "to become clear" 澄む generally do not use the imperative, volitional, potential, passive, humble, or honorific forms.

suru する

する to do, make, to have a value, cost: (trans. and intrans.)

		Affirmative	Negative
PLAIN FORM	PRESENT	suru	shinai
	PAST	shita	shinakatta
MASU FORM	PRESENT	shimasu	shimasen
	PAST	shimashita	shimasen deshita
TE FORM		shite	shinakute
CONDITIONAL	PLAIN	sureba/shita ra	shinakereba/shinakatta ra
	FORMAL	shimashita ra	shimasen deshita ra
VOLITIONAL	PLAIN	shiyō	–
	FORMAL	shimashō	–
IMPERATIVE		shiro	suru na

	Affirmative		Affirmative
POTENTIAL	dekiru	**CAUS. PASSIVE**	saserareru
PASSIVE	sareru	**HONORIFIC**	nasaru/sareru
CAUSATIVE	saseru	**HUMBLE**	itasu

Examples:

1. *Nichiyōbi ni nani o shimasu ka. / Suru koto ga ippai arimasu.*
   日曜日に何をしますか。／することがいっぱいあります。
   What are you going to do on Sunday? / I have many things to do.

2. *Otōsan wa nani o shite imasu ka. / Sensei o shite imasu.*
   お父さんは何をしていますか。／先生をしています。
   What does your father do? / He is a teacher.

3. *Zubon no suso o mō sukoshi mijikaku shite kudasai.*
   ズボンのすそをもう少し短くしてください。
   Please shorten the cuffs of my pants a little more.

4. *Sono tokei wa ikura shimashita ka.*
   その時計はいくらしましたか。
   How much did that watch cost?

5. *Nomimono wa nani ni shimasu ka. / Kōcha ni shimasu.*
   飲み物は何にしますか。／紅茶にします。
   What would you like to drink? / I will have a cup of tea.

susumeru すすめる

進める to advance, promote; 勧める or 薦める to suggest, to recommend: (all trans.)

		Affirmative	Negative
PLAIN FORM	PRESENT	susumeru	susumenai
	PAST	susumeta	susumenakatta
MASU FORM	PRESENT	susumemasu	susumemasen
	PAST	susumemashita	susumemasen deshita
TE FORM		susumete	susumenakute
CONDITIONAL	PLAIN	susumereba/susumeta ra	susumenakereba/ susumenakatta ra
	FORMAL	susumemashita ra	susumemasen deshita ra
VOLITIONAL	PLAIN	susumeyō	–
	FORMAL	susumemashō	–
IMPERATIVE		susumero	susumeru na

	Affirmative		Affirmative
POTENTIAL	susumerareru/ susumereru	**CAUS. PASSIVE**	susumesaserareru
PASSIVE	susumerareru	**HONORIFIC**	osusume ni naru/ susumerareru
CAUSATIVE	susumesaseru	**HUMBLE**	osusume suru

Examples:

1. *Kono keikaku o susumete kudasai.*
   この計画を進めてください。
   Please go ahead with this plan.

2. *Kōji wa junchō ni susumerarete iru.*
   工事は順調に進められている。
   The construction is progressing smoothly.

3. *Chichi wa watashi ni gaikoku ryūgaku o susumeta.*
   父は私に外国留学を勧めた。
   My father encouraged me to study abroad.

4. *Onsen ni iki-tai nara, Hakone o osusume shimasu.*
   温泉に行きたいなら、箱根をお勧めします。
   If you want to go to a hot spring, I recommend Hakone.

5. *Sensei ni kono jisho o susumerareta.*
   先生にこの辞書を薦められた。
   I was recommended this dictionary by my teacher.

susumu すすむ

進む to advance, progress, go forward: (intrans.)*

		Affirmative	Negative
PLAIN FORM	PRESENT	susumu	susumanai
	PAST	susunda	susumanakatta
MASU FORM	PRESENT	susumimasu	susumimasen
	PAST	susumimashita	susumimasen deshita
TE FORM		susunde	susumanakute
CONDITIONAL	PLAIN	susumeba/susunda ra	susumanakereba/ susumanakatta ra
	FORMAL	susumimashita ra	susumimasen deshita ra
VOLITIONAL	PLAIN	susumō	–
	FORMAL	susumimashō	–
IMPERATIVE		susume	susumu na

	Affirmative		Affirmative
POTENTIAL	susumeru	**CAUS. PASSIVE**	susumaserareru/ susumasareru
PASSIVE	susumareru	**HONORIFIC**	osusumi ni naru/ susumareru
CAUSATIVE	susumaseru	**HUMBLE**	(osusumi suru)

Examples:

1. *Watashitachi wa hayashi no naka o go-kiro susunda.*
   私たちは、林の中を五キロ進んだ。
   We moved forward five kilometers through the woods.

2. *Kono kuni no kagaku gijutsu wa taihen susunde imasu.*
   この国の科学技術は大変進んでいます。
   Scientific technology is very advanced in this country.

3. *Minna no iken ga wakarete, kaigi ga susumanakatta.*
   みんなの意見が分かれて、会議が進まなかった。
   The meeting did not progress since everyone's opinion was divided.

4. *Kare wa susunde shigoto o tetsudatte kureta.*
   彼は進んで仕事を手伝ってくれた。
   He willingly helped me with my work.

5. *Kono tokei wa go-fun gurai susunde iru.*
   この時計は五分ぐらい進んでいる。
   This watch is about 5 minutes fast.

* As with other verbs indicating movement, *susumu* 進む may take a direct object, thus giving an idea of "going through a defined area." (See example 1.)

suteru すてる

捨てる to throw away, abandon, desert: (trans.)

		Affirmative	*Negative*
PLAIN FORM	PRESENT	suteru	sutenai
	PAST	suteta	sutenakatta
MASU FORM	PRESENT	sutemasu	sutemasen
	PAST	sutemashita	sutemasen deshita
TE FORM		sutete	sutenakute
CONDITIONAL	PLAIN	sutereba/suteta ra	sutenakereba/ sutenakatta ra
	FORMAL	sutemashita ra	sutemasen deshita ra
VOLITIONAL	PLAIN	suteyō	–
	FORMAL	sutemashō	–
IMPERATIVE		sutero	suteru na

	Affirmative		*Affirmative*
POTENTIAL	suterareru/sutereru	**CAUS. PASSIVE**	sutesaserareru
PASSIVE	suterareru	**HONORIFIC**	osute ni naru/suterareru
CAUSATIVE	sutesaseru	**HUMBLE**	osute suru

Examples:

1. *Dōro ni gomi o sutenaide kudasai.*
   道路にごみを捨てないでください。
   Please don't litter in the street.

2. *Hikkoshi no toki, iranai mono o takusan sutemashita.*
   引っ越しの時、要らない物をたくさん捨てました。
   When I was moving, I threw away many unwanted things.

3. *Furui shashin ya tegami wa nakanaka suterarenai.*
   古い写真や手紙はなかなか捨てられない。
   I just can't throw these old pictures and letters away.

4. *Kono hako wa sutete mo ii desu ka.*
   この箱は捨ててもいいですか。
   Do you mind if I throw away this box?

5. *Haha ni manga no hon o suterarete shimatta.*
   母に漫画の本を捨てられてしまった。
   My mother had my comic books thrown away.

suwaru すわる

GROUP 1

座る to sit down, take a seat: (intrans.)

		Affirmative	*Negative*
PLAIN FORM	PRESENT	suwaru	suwaranai
	PAST	suwatta	suwaranakatta
MASU FORM	PRESENT	suwarimasu	suwarimasen
	PAST	suwarimashita	suwarimasen deshita
TE FORM		suwatte	suwaranakute
CONDITIONAL	PLAIN	suwareba/suwatta ra	suwaranakereba/ suwaranakatta ra
	FORMAL	suwarimashita ra	suwarimasen deshita ra
VOLITIONAL	PLAIN	suwarō	–
	FORMAL	suwarimashō	–
IMPERATIVE		suware	suwaru na

	Affirmative		*Affirmative*
POTENTIAL	suwareru	**CAUS. PASSIVE**	suwaraserareru/ suwarasareru
PASSIVE	suwarareru	**HONORIFIC**	osuwari ni naru/ suwarareru
CAUSATIVE	suwaraseru	**HUMBLE**	(osuwari suru)

Examples:

1. *Dōzo koko ni suwatte kudasai.*
   どうぞここに座ってください。
   Please sit down here.

2. *Kono seki ni suwatte mo ii desu ka.*
   この席に座ってもいいですか。
   May I sit in this seat?

3. *Kodomo wa piano ni mukatte suwatta.*
   子供はピアノに向かって座った。
   The child sat down at the piano.

4. *Sensei wa gakusei o isu ni suwaraseta.*
   先生は学生をいすに座らせた。
   The teacher made his students sit down in their chairs.

5. *Kono zaseki ni wa futari shika suwarenai darō.*
   この座席には二人しか座れないだろう。
   Only two persons may sit in this seat.

taberu たべる

食べる to eat, to live on: (trans.)

		Affirmative	*Negative*
PLAIN FORM	PRESENT	taberu	tabenai
	PAST	tabeta	tabenakatta
MASU FORM	PRESENT	tabemasu	tabemasen
	PAST	tabemashita	tabemasen deshita
TE FORM		tabete	tabenakute
CONDITIONAL	PLAIN	tabereba/tabeta ra	tabenakereba/ tabenakatta ra
	FORMAL	tabemashita ra	tabemasen deshita ra
VOLITIONAL	PLAIN	tabeyō	–
	FORMAL	tabemashō	–
IMPERATIVE		tabero	taberu na

	Affirmative		*Affirmative*
POTENTIAL	taberareru/tabereru	**CAUS. PASSIVE**	tabesaserareru
PASSIVE	taberareru	**HONORIFIC**	meshiagaru/otabe ni naru/taberareru
CAUSATIVE	tabesaseru	**HUMBLE**	itadaku

Examples:

1. *Mō hiru-gohan o tabemashita ka. / Iie, mada tabete imasen.*
   もう昼御飯を食べましたか。/ いいえ、まだ食べていません。
   Have you had lunch yet? / No, I have not.

2. *Issho ni ban gohan o tabeyō.*
   一緒に晩御飯を食べよう。
   Let's have dinner together.

3. *Mō sukoshi okashi o meshiagarimasen ka. / Hai, itadakimasu.*
   もう少しお菓子を召し上がりませんか。/ はい、いただきます。
   Would you like to have some more cakes? / Yes, please.

4. *Kanojo wa nama no sakana ga taberaremasen.*
   彼女は生の魚が食べられません。
   She cannot eat raw fish.

5. *Kodomo no toki, haha ni yasai o tabesaserareta.*
   子どもの時、母に野菜を食べさせられた。
   When I was a child, my mother made me eat vegetables.

tamaru たまる

GROUP 1

たまる to be saved, accumulated, piled up: (intrans.)

		Affirmative	Negative
PLAIN FORM	PRESENT	tamaru	tamaranai
	PAST	tamatta	tamaranakatta
MASU FORM	PRESENT	tamarimasu	tamarimasen
	PAST	tamarimashita	tamarimasen deshita
TE FORM		tamatte	tamaranakute
CONDITIONAL	PLAIN	tamareba/tamatta ra	tamaranakereba/ tamaranakatta ra
	FORMAL	tamarimashita ra	tamarimasen deshita ra
VOLITIONAL	PLAIN	tamarō	–
	FORMAL	tamarimashō	–
IMPERATIVE		tamare	tamaru na

	Affirmative		Affirmative
POTENTIAL	tamareru	**CAUS. PASSIVE**	tamaraserareru/ tamarasareru
PASSIVE	tamarareru	**HONORIFIC**	otamari ni naru/ tamarareru
CAUSATIVE	tamaraseru	**HUMBLE**	(otamari suru)

Examples:

1. *Ginkō no kōza ni gojūman-en tamatta.*
   銀行の口座に五十万円たまった。
   There is 500,000 yen saved in my bank account.

2. *Tsukue no ue ni hokori ga tamatte iru.*
   机の上にほこりがたまっている。
   Dust has accumulated on the desk.

3. *Yachin no shiharai ga nika-getsu bun tamatte iru.*
   家賃の支払いが二か月分たまっている。
   I am two months behind in my rent.

4. *Kare wa kanari sutoresu ga tamatte iru yō da.*
   彼はかなりストレスがたまっているようだ。
   He seems to be under a lot of stress.

5. *Shigoto ga tamatte ita node, pātii ni ikanakatta.*
   仕事がたまっていたので、パーティーに行かなかった。
   I had so much work left to do that I didn't go to the party.

tameru ためる

ためる to save, store up, accumulate: (trans.)

		Affirmative	Negative
PLAIN FORM	PRESENT	tameru	tamenai
	PAST	tameta	tamenakatta
MASU FORM	PRESENT	tamemasu	tamemasen
	PAST	tamemashita	tamemasen deshita
TE FORM		tamete	tamenakute
CONDITIONAL	PLAIN	tamereba/tameta ra	tamenakereba/ tamenakatta ra
	FORMAL	tamemashita ra	tamemasen deshita ra
VOLITIONAL	PLAIN	tameyō	–
	FORMAL	tamemashō	–
IMPERATIVE		tamero	tameru na

	Affirmative		Affirmative
POTENTIAL	tamerareru/ tamereru	CAUS. PASSIVE	tamesaserareru
PASSIVE	tamerareru	HONORIFIC	otame ni naru/ tamerareru
CAUSATIVE	tamesaseru	HUMBLE	(otame suru)

Examples:

1. *Atarashii terebi o kau temeni, okane o tamete imasu.*
   新しいテレビを買うために、お金をためています。
   I am saving money to buy a new TV.

2. *Kono chihō de wa amamizu o tamete, sore o inryō-sui ni tsukau.*
   この地方では雨水をためて、それを飲料水に使う。
   In this area they save rainwater and use it for drinking water.

3. *Tsukare o tamenai yō ni, tokidoki yasunda hō ga ii.*
   疲れをためないように、時々休んだほうがいい。
   You should take a rest occasionally, so you don't become fatigued.

4. *Kono kādo no pointo o tamereba, shōhin to kōkan dekiru.*
   このカードのポイントをためれば、賞品と交換できる。
   Points accumulated on this card can be traded for a prize.

5. *Shukudai o tamete shimatte, sensei ni shikarareta.*
   宿題をためてしまって、先生に叱られた。
   I was scolded by my teacher for leaving my homework undone.

tamesu ためす

ためす to test, try: (trans.)

		Affirmative	Negative
PLAIN FORM	PRESENT	tamesu	tamesanai
	PAST	tameshita	tamesanakatta
MASU FORM	PRESENT	tameshimasu	tameshimasen
	PAST	tameshimashita	tameshimasen deshita
TE FORM		tameshite	tamesanakute
CONDITIONAL	PLAIN	tameseba/tameshita ra	tamesanakereba/ tamesanakatta ra
	FORMAL	tameshimashita ra	tameshimasen deshita ra
VOLITIONAL	PLAIN	tamesō	–
	FORMAL	tameshimashō	–
IMPERATIVE		tamese	tamesu na

	Affirmative		Affirmative
POTENTIAL	tameseru	**CAUS. PASSIVE**	tamesaserareru
PASSIVE	tamesareru	**HONORIFIC**	otameshi ni naru/ tamesareru
CAUSATIVE	tamesaseru	**HUMBLE**	otameshi suru

Examples:

1. *Atarashii shōhin o tameshite mita.*
   新しい商品を試してみた。
   I tried a new product.

2. *Jibun no chikara o tamesu tame ni, shiken o ukete mita.*
   自分の力を試すために、試験を受けてみた。
   I took an exam in order to test my ability.

3. *Kono kikai ga ugoku ka dō ka, tameshite miyō.*
   この機械が動くかどうか、試してみよう。
   Let's test this machine to see whether it works or not.

4. *Nando mo tameshite mite, yatto seikō shita.*
   何度も試してみて、やっと成功した。
   After trying it out many times, I succeeded at last.

5. *Donata demo go-jiyū ni otameshi kudasai.*
   どなたでもご自由にお試しください。
   We would like anyone to have a free try.

tanomu たのむ

頼む to ask a person to do, reserve (tickets), to rely on: (trans.)

		Affirmative	Negative
PLAIN FORM	PRESENT	tanomu	tanomanai
	PAST	tanonda	tanomanakatta
MASU FORM	PRESENT	tanomimasu	tanomimasen
	PAST	tanomimashita	tanomimasen deshita
TE FORM		tanonde	tanomanakute
CONDITIONAL	PLAIN	tanomeba/tanonda ra	tanomanakereba/ tanomanakatta ra
	FORMAL	tanomimashita ra	tanomimasen deshita ra
VOLITIONAL	PLAIN	tanomō	–
	FORMAL	tanomimashō	–
IMPERATIVE		tanome	tanomu na

	Affirmative		Affirmative
POTENTIAL	tanomeru	**CAUS. PASSIVE**	tanomaserareru/ tanomasareru
PASSIVE	tanomareru	**HONORIFIC**	otanomi ni naru/ tanomareru
CAUSATIVE	tanomaseru	**HUMBLE**	otanomi suru

Examples:

1. *Chichi ni kūkō made okutte kureru yō ni tanonda.*
   父に空港まで送ってくれるように頼んだ。
   I asked my father to take me to the airport.

2. *Haha ni kaimono o tanomaremashita.*
   母に買い物を頼まれました。
   I was asked to go shopping by my mother.

3. *Kare ni tanomeba, tetsudatte kureru deshō.*
   彼に頼めば、手伝ってくれるでしょう。
   He will help you if you ask him.

4. *Nomimono wa nani o tanomimashō ka.*
   飲み物は何を頼みましょうか。
   What shall we get to drink?

5. *Tanomu kara, kono koto wa himitsu ni shite kudasai.*
   頼むから、この事は秘密にしてください。
   Please, I beg you to keep this matter secret.

tanoshimu たのしむ

楽しむ to enjoy oneself, take pleasure in, have a good time: (trans.)

		Affirmative	*Negative*
PLAIN FORM	PRESENT	tanoshimu	tanoshimanai
	PAST	tanoshinda	tanoshimanakatta
MASU FORM	PRESENT	tanoshimimasu	tanoshimimasen
	PAST	tanoshimimashita	tanoshimimasen deshita
TE FORM		tanoshinde	tanoshimanakute
CONDITIONAL	PLAIN	tanoshimeba/ tanoshinda ra	tanoshimanakereba/ tanoshimanakatta ra
	FORMAL	tanoshimimashita ra	tanoshimimasen deshita ra
VOLITIONAL	PLAIN	tanoshimō	–
	FORMAL	tanoshimimashō	–
IMPERATIVE		tanoshime	tanoshimu na

	Affirmative		*Affirmative*
POTENTIAL	tanoshimeru	**CAUS. PASSIVE**	tanoshimaserareru/ tanoshimasareru
PASSIVE	tanoshimareru	**HONORIFIC**	otanoshimi ni naru/ tanoshimareru
CAUSATIVE	tanoshimaseru	**HUMBLE**	(otanoshimi suru)

Examples:

1. *Shigoto no koto wa wasurete, tanoshimimashō.*
   仕事のことは忘れて、楽しみましょう。
   Let's forget what happened at work and enjoy ourselves.

2. *Nichiyōbi ni doraibu o tanoshimō to omotte imasu.*
   日曜日にドライブを楽しもうと思っています。
   I think I will enjoy my driving on Sunday.

3. *Okinawa de wa ichinen-jū kirei na umi ga tanoshimemasu.*
   沖縄では一年中きれいな海が楽しめます。
   You can enjoy the beautiful sea all year round in Okinawa.

4. *Saikin isogashikute, shumi no tsuri o tanoshimu jikan ga nai.*
   最近忙しくて、趣味の釣りを楽しむ時間がない。
   Since I have been busy recently, I don't even have the time to enjoy my hobby, fishing.

5. *Imōto wa gakusei seikatsu o tanoshinde iru yō da.*
   妹は学生生活を楽しんでいるようだ。
   My younger sister seems to be enjoying the student life.

taoreru たおれる

倒れる to fall down, collapse: (intrans.)

		Affirmative	Negative
PLAIN FORM	PRESENT	taoreru	taorenai
	PAST	taoreta	taorenakatta
MASU FORM	PRESENT	taoremasu	taoremasen
	PAST	taoremashita	taoremasen deshita
TE FORM		taorete	taorenakute
CONDITIONAL	PLAIN	taorereba/taoreta ra	taorenakereba/ taorenakatta ra
	FORMAL	taoremashita ra	taoremasen deshita ra
VOLITIONAL	PLAIN	taoreyō	–
	FORMAL	taoremashō	–
IMPERATIVE		taorero	taoreru na

	Affirmative		Affirmative
POTENTIAL	taorerareru/taorereru	**CAUS. PASSIVE**	taoresaserareru
PASSIVE	taorerareru	**HONORIFIC**	otaore ni naru/ taorerareru
CAUSATIVE	taoresaseru	**HUMBLE**	(otaore suru)

Examples:

1. *Kanojo wa ki o ushinatte, yuka ni taoremashita.*
   彼女は気を失って、床に倒れました。
   She lost consciousness and fell to the floor.

2. *Taifū de kōen no ki ga taoremashita.*
   台風で公園の木が倒れました。
   The trees in the park were knocked down by the typhoon.

3. *Ki no ne ni tsumazuite, taore sō ni natta.*
   木の根につまずいて、倒れそうになった。
   I tripped on a tree root and almost fell down.

4. *Kare wa karō de taorete, nyūin shita.*
   彼は過労で倒れて、入院した。
   He collapsed from overwork and was hospitalized.

5. *Hondana ga taorenai yō ni, kabe ni kotei shita.*
   本棚が倒れないように、壁に固定した。
   I fixed the bookshelf to the wall so that it would not fall over.

taosu たおす

倒す to throw down, knock down, defeat: (trans.)

		Affirmative	Negative
PLAIN FORM	PRESENT	taosu	taosanai
	PAST	taoshita	taosanakatta
MASU FORM	PRESENT	taoshimasu	taoshimasen
	PAST	taoshimashita	taoshimasen deshita
TE FORM		taoshite	taosanakute
CONDITIONAL	PLAIN	taoseba/taoshita ra	taosanakereba/ taosanakatta ra
	FORMAL	taoshimashita ra	taoshimasen deshita ra
VOLITIONAL	PLAIN	taosō	–
	FORMAL	taoshimashō	–
IMPERATIVE		taose	taosu na

	Affirmative		Affirmative
POTENTIAL	taoseru	**CAUS. PASSIVE**	taosaserareru
PASSIVE	taosareru	**HONORIFIC**	otaoshi ni naru/taosareru
CAUSATIVE	taosaseru	**HUMBLE**	(otaoshi suru)

Examples:

1. *Sōji o shite ite, ukkari shite kabin o taoshite shimatta.*
   掃除をしていて、うっかりして花瓶を倒してしまった。
   I carelessly knocked over the vase while cleaning.

2. *Gurasu o taosanai yō ni shite kudasai.*
   グラスを倒さないようにしてください。
   Please be careful not to knock over the glass.

3. *Kare wa tenisu no shiai de kyōteki o taoshita.*
   彼はテニスの試合で強敵を倒した。
   In the tennis match, he defeated a powerful opponent.

4. *Gen-naikaku o taosu beki da to kare wa shuchō shita.*
   現内閣を倒すべきだと彼は主張した。
   He insisted that the present Cabinet be overthrown.

5. *Chanpion wa chōsensha ni taosareta.*
   チャンピオンは挑戦者に倒された。
   The champion was defeated by the challenger.

tariru たりる

足りる to be enough, be sufficient, suffice: (intrans.)

		Affirmative	Negative
PLAIN FORM	PRESENT	tariru	tarinai
	PAST	tarita	tarinakatta
MASU FORM	PRESENT	tarimasu	tarimasen
	PAST	tarimashita	tarimasen deshita
TE FORM		tarite	tarinakute
CONDITIONAL	PLAIN	tarireba/tarita ra	tarinakereba/ tarinakatta ra
	FORMAL	tarimashita ra	tarimasen deshita ra
VOLITIONAL	PLAIN	tariyō	–
	FORMAL	tarimashō	–
IMPERATIVE		tariro	tariru na

	Affirmative		Affirmative
POTENTIAL	(tarirareru)	**CAUS. PASSIVE**	tarisaserareru
PASSIVE	(tarirareru)	**HONORIFIC**	otari ni naru/tarirareru
CAUSATIVE	tarisaseru	**HUMBLE**	(otari suru)

Examples:

1. *Kono resutoran no shiharai wa ichi-man en areba tariru deshō.*
   このレストランの支払いは一万円あれば足りるでしょう。
   10,000 yen should be enough to pay this restaurant bill.

2. *Okane ga ichi-man en tarimasen.*
   お金が一万円足りません。
   I am 10,000 yen short.

3. *Buhin ga tarinakute, kikai no shūri ga dekinai.*
   部品が足りなくて、機械の修理ができない。
   We don't have enough parts to repair this machine.

4. *Motto benkyō shitai ga, jikan ga tarinai.*
   もっと勉強したいが、時間が足りない。
   I want to study some more, but I don't have enough time.

5. *Kono shigoto o suru ni wa kare wa keiken ga tarimasen.*
   この仕事をするには彼は経験が足りません。
   He doesn't have enough experience to do this work.

tashikameru たしかめる

確かめる to make sure, check, verify: (trans.)

		Affirmative	Negative
PLAIN FORM	PRESENT	tashikameru	tashikamenai
	PAST	tashikameta	tashikamenakatta
MASU FORM	PRESENT	tashikamemasu	tashikamemasen
	PAST	tashikamemashita	tashikamemasen deshita
TE FORM		tashikamete	tashikamenakute
CONDITIONAL	PLAIN	tashikamereba/ tashikameta ra	tashikamenakereba/ tashikamenakatta ra
	FORMAL	tashikamemashita ra	tashikamemasen deshita ra
VOLITIONAL	PLAIN	tashikameyō	–
	FORMAL	tashikamemashō	–
IMPERATIVE		tashikamero	tashikameru na

	Affirmative		Affirmative
POTENTIAL	tashikamerareru/ tashikamereru	**CAUS. PASSIVE**	tashikamesaserareru
PASSIVE	tashikamerareru	**HONORIFIC**	otashikame ni naru/ tashikamerareru
CAUSATIVE	tashikamesaseru	**HUMBLE**	otashikame suru

Examples:

1. *Hikōki no tōchaku jikan o denwa de tashikamemashita.*
   飛行機の到着時間を電話で確かめました。
   I telephoned and verified the arrival time of the plane.

2. *Kore ga tadashii ka dō ka tashikamete kudasai.*
   これが正しいかどうか確かめてください。
   Please check to see whether this is correct or not.

3. *Yotei o tashikamete kara, odenwa shimasu.*
   予定を確かめてから、お電話します。
   I will call you after checking the schedule.

4. *Pātii ni shusseki suru hito no kazu o tashikamenakereba naranai.*
   パーティーに出席する人の数を確かめなければならない。
   We must check the number of participants for the party.

5. *Sore ga hontō da to iu koto ga tashikamerareta.*
   それが本当だということが確かめられた。
   It was verified and found to be true.

tasukaru たすかる

助かる to be saved, rescued, spared: (intrans.)

		Affirmative	*Negative*
PLAIN FORM	PRESENT	tasukaru	tasukaranai
	PAST	tasukatta	tasukaranakatta
MASU FORM	PRESENT	tasukarimasu	tasukarimasen
	PAST	tasukarimashita	tasukarimasen deshita
TE FORM		tasukatte	tasukaranakute
CONDITIONAL	PLAIN	tasukareba/tasukatta ra	tasukaranakereba/ tasukaranakatta ra
	FORMAL	tasukarimashita ra	tasukarimasen deshita ra
VOLITIONAL	PLAIN	tasukarō	–
	FORMAL	tasukarimashō	–
IMPERATIVE		tasukare	tasukaru na

	Affirmative		*Affirmative*
POTENTIAL	tasukareru	**CAUS. PASSIVE**	tasukaraserareru/ tasukarasareru
PASSIVE	tasukarareru	**HONORIFIC**	otasukari ni naru/ tasukarareru
CAUSATIVE	tasukaraseru	**HUMBLE**	(otasukari suru)

Examples:

1. *Shōnen ga kawa ni ochita ga, tasukatta.*
   少年が川に落ちたが、助かった。
   The boy fell into the river but was rescued.

2. *Sono jiko de untenshu wa kisekiteki ni tasukatta sō da.*
   その事故で運転手は奇跡的に助かったそうだ。
   I hear that the driver was miraculously rescued from the accident.

3. *Tomodachi ni hikkoshi o tetsudatte moratte, tasukatta.*
   友達に引っ越しを手伝ってもらって、助かった。
   Thankfully, my friend helped me move.

4. *Teinei ni oshiete kudasatte, taihen tasukarimashita.*
   丁寧に教えてくださって、大変助かりました。
   I was very happy that you taught me so nicely.

5. *Atarashii basu ga tōtta ra, jūmin wa totemo tasukaru darō.*
   新しいバスが通ったら、住民はとても助かるだろう。
   Once the new bus route is introduced here, the inhabitants will be very much delighted.

tasukeru たすける

GROUP 2

助ける to help, save, rescue: (trans.)

		Affirmative	Negative
PLAIN FORM	PRESENT	tasukeru	tasukenai
	PAST	tasuketa	tasukenakatta
MASU FORM	PRESENT	tasukemasu	tasukemasen
	PAST	tasukemashita	tasukemasen deshita
TE FORM		tasukete	tasukenakute
CONDITIONAL	PLAIN	tasukereba/tasuketa ra	tasukenakereba/ tasukenakatta ra
	FORMAL	tasukemashita ra	tasukemasen deshita ra
VOLITIONAL	PLAIN	tasukeyō	–
	FORMAL	tasukemashō	–
IMPERATIVE		tasukero	tasukeru na

	Affirmative		Affirmative
POTENTIAL	tasukerareru/ tasukereru	**CAUS. PASSIVE**	tasukesaserareru
PASSIVE	tasukerareru	**HONORIFIC**	otasuke ni naru/ tasukerareru
CAUSATIVE	tasukesaseru	**HUMBLE**	otasuke suru

Examples:

1. *Kare wa umi de oboresō na kodomo o tasukemashita.*
   彼は海でおぼれそうな子供を助けました。
   He rescued the child who nearly drowned in the sea.

2. *Haha ga watashi no shukudai o tasukete kuremashita.*
   母が私の宿題を助けてくれました。
   My mother helped me with my homework.

3. *"Tasukete!" to iu koe ga dokoka kara kikoeta.*
   「助けて」という声がどこかから聞こえた。
   I heard the voice of somebody screaming "Help me!" coming from somewhere.

4. *Isha wa sono kanja o tasukeru koto ga dekinakatta.*
   医者はその患者を助けることができなかった。
   The doctor could not save his patient.

5. *Mawari no hito ni tasukerarete, purojekuto o seikō saseta.*
   周りの人に助けられて、プロジェクトを成功させた。
   The project succeeded with the help of my acquaintances.

tateru たてる

立てる to stand, to erect, raise, establish; 建てる to build: (both trans.)

		Affirmative	*Negative*
PLAIN FORM	PRESENT	tateru	tatenai
	PAST	tateta	tatenakatta
MASU FORM	PRESENT	tatemasu	tatemasen
	PAST	tatemashita	tatemasen deshita
TE FORM		tatete	tatenakute
CONDITIONAL	PLAIN	tatereba/tateta ra	tatenakereba/ tatenakatta ra
	FORMAL	tatemashita ra	tatemasen deshita ra
VOLITIONAL	PLAIN	tateyō	–
	FORMAL	tatemashō	–
IMPERATIVE		tatero	tateru na

	Affirmative		*Affirmative*
POTENTIAL	taterareru/tatereru	**CAUS. PASSIVE**	tatesaserareru
PASSIVE	taterareru	**HONORIFIC**	otate ni naru/taterareru
CAUSATIVE	tatesaseru	**HUMBLE**	otate suru

Examples:

1. *Mise no mae ni ōkina kanban o tateta*
   店の前に大きな看板を立てた。
   We put up a big signboard in front of our shop.

2. *Natsuyasumi no keikaku o tatemashō.*
   夏休みの計画を立てましょう。
   Let's make a plan for summer vacation.

3. *Eki mae ni kōsō biru o tateru keikaku ga aru sō da.*
   駅前に高層ビルを建てる計画があるそうだ。
   I hear that there is a plan to build a high-rise building in front of
   the station.

4. *Yoshida-san wa saikin ie o tatemashita.*
   吉田さんは最近家を建てました。
   Mr. Yoshida recently built his house.

5. *Sono otera wa hasseiki goro taterareta.*
   そのお寺は八世紀ごろ建てられた。
   That temple was built around the 8th century.

tatsu たつ

立つ to stand, rise; 建つ to be built;* たつ to pass, elapse:* (all intrans.)

		Affirmative	*Negative*
PLAIN FORM	PRESENT	tatsu	tatanai
	PAST	tatta	tatanakatta
MASU FORM	PRESENT	tachimasu	tachimasen
	PAST	tachimashita	tachimasen deshita
TE FORM		tatte	tatanakute
CONDITIONAL	PLAIN	tateba/tatta ra	tatanakereba/ tatanakatta ra
	FORMAL	tachimashita ra	tachimasen deshita ra
VOLITIONAL	PLAIN	tatō	–
	FORMAL	tachimashō	–
IMPERATIVE		tate	tatsu na

	Affirmative		*Affirmative*
POTENTIAL	tateru	**CAUS. PASSIVE**	tataserareru/tatasareru
PASSIVE	tatareru	**HONORIFIC**	otachi ni naru/tatareru
CAUSATIVE	tataseru	**HUMBLE**	otachi suru

Examples:

1. *Keikan ga machi-kado ni tatte iru.*
   警官が街角に立っている。
   A policeman is standing at the street corner.

2. *Ashi ga shibirete tatemasen.*
   足がしびれて、立てません。
   I can't stand up because my legs have gone to sleep.

3. *Basu ga kanzen ni tomaru made, seki o tatanaide kudasai.*
   バスが完全に止まるまで、席を立たないでください。
   Please do not leave your seat until the bus comes to a complete stop.

4. *Sensei wa shukudai o wasureta seito o tataseta.*
   先生は宿題を忘れた生徒を立たせた。
   The teacher made the students who didn't do their homework stand up.

5. *Kare ga koko ni kite kara go-nen ga tachimashita.*
   彼がここにきてから五年がたちました。
   Five years has passed since he came here.

* The verbs *tatsu* meaning "to be built" 建つ and "to pass, elapse" 経つ generally do not use the imperative, volitional, potential, honorific, humble, passive, causative, or causative passive forms.

tayoru たよる

頼る to depend on, rely on: (intrans.)*

		Affirmative	*Negative*
PLAIN FORM	PRESENT	tayoru	tayoranai
	PAST	tayotta	tayoranakatta
MASU FORM	PRESENT	tayorimasu	tayorimasen
	PAST	tayorimashita	tayorimasen deshita
TE FORM		tayotte	tayoranakute
CONDITIONAL	PLAIN	tayoreba/tayotta ra	tayoranakereba/ tayoranakatta ra
	FORMAL	tayorimashita ra	tayorimasen deshita ra
VOLITIONAL	PLAIN	tayorō	–
	FORMAL	tayorimashō	–
IMPERATIVE		tayore	tayoru na

	Affirmative		*Affirmative*
POTENTIAL	tayoreru	**CAUS. PASSIVE**	tayoraserareru/ tayorasareru
PASSIVE	tayorareru	**HONORIFIC**	otayori ni naru/tayorareru
CAUSATIVE	tayoraseru	**HUMBLE**	otayori suru

Examples:

1. *Kaisha ni haitta bakari na node, senpai ni tayotte shigoto o shite iru.*
   会社に入ったばかりなので、先輩に頼って仕事をしている。
   As I just joined this company, I have to rely on my seniors to get the job done.

2. *Hoka no hito ni tayoranaide, shukudai wa jibun de yatte kudasai.*
   ほかの人に頼らないで、宿題は自分でやってください。
   Please do your homework by yourself, without relying on other people.

3. *Kare wa tomodachi ni tayorareta ra, iya to wa ienai.*
   彼は友達に頼られたら、嫌とは言えない。
   When asked to do something by a friend, he cannot say "No."

4. *Kodomo no koro no kioku ni tayotte, origami o otte mita.*
   子供のころの記憶に頼って、折り紙を折ってみた。
   I tried making origami from my childhood memory.

5. *Kanojo wa ani o tayotte, Tōkyō ni kimashita.*
   彼女は兄を頼って、東京に来ました。
   She came to Tokyo by relying on her older brother's help.

---

* *Tayoru* 頼る is also used like a transitive verb. (See example 5.)

tazuneru たずねる

尋ねる to ask, look for, search; 訪ねる to visit: (both trans.)

		Affirmative	Negative
PLAIN FORM	PRESENT	tazuneru	tazunenai
	PAST	tazuneta	tazunenakatta
MASU FORM	PRESENT	tazunemasu	tazunemasen
	PAST	tazunemashita	tazunemasen deshita
TE FORM		tazunete	tazunenakute
CONDITIONAL	PLAIN	tazunereba/tazuneta ra	tazunenakereba/ tazunenakatta ra
	FORMAL	tazunemashita ra	tazunemasen deshita ra
VOLITIONAL	PLAIN	tazuneyō	–
	FORMAL	tazunemashō	–
IMPERATIVE		tazunero	tazuneru na

	Affirmative		Affirmative
POTENTIAL	tazunerareru/ tazunereru	**CAUS. PASSIVE**	tazunesaserareru
PASSIVE	tazunerareru	**HONORIFIC**	otazune ni naru/ tazunerareru
CAUSATIVE	tazunesaseru	**HUMBLE**	otazune suru

Examples:

1. *Anata ni tazune-tai koto ga arimasu.*
   あなたに尋ねたいことがあります。
   I have a question to ask you.

2. *Chotto otazune shimasu ga, eki wa dochira no hō deshō ka.*
   ちょっとお尋ねしますが、駅はどちらの方でしょうか。
   Excuse me, but could you please show me where the station is?

3. *Kuwashii koto wa tantōsha ni otazune kudasai.*
   詳しいことは担当者にお尋ねください。
   For further information, please ask the person in charge.

4. *Watashi wa Kyōto no o-tera ya jinja o tazunemashita.*
   私は京都のお寺や神社を訪ねました。
   I visited temples and shrines in Kyoto.

5. *Zehi ichido Kamakura o tazunete mite kudasai.*
   是非一度鎌倉を訪ねてみてください。
   You should visit Kamakura at least once.

tetsudau てつだう

手伝う to help, assist: (trans.)

		Affirmative	*Negative*
PLAIN FORM	PRESENT	tetsudau	tetsudawanai
	PAST	tetsudatta	tetsudawanakatta
MASU FORM	PRESENT	tetsudaimasu	tetsudaimasen
	PAST	tetsudaimashita	tetsudaimasen deshita
TE FORM		tetsudatte	tetsudawanakute
CONDITIONAL	PLAIN	tetsudaeba/tetsudatta ra	tetsudawanakereba/ tetsudawanakatta ra
	FORMAL	tetsudaimashita ra	tetsudaimasen deshita ra
VOLITIONAL	PLAIN	tetsudaō	–
	FORMAL	tetsudaimashō	–
IMPERATIVE		tetsudae	tetsudau na

	Affirmative		*Affirmative*
POTENTIAL	tetsudaeru	**CAUS. PASSIVE**	tetsudawaserareru/ tetsudawasareru
PASSIVE	tetsudawareru	**HONORIFIC**	otetsudai ni naru/ tetsudawareru
CAUSATIVE	tetsudawaseru	**HUMBLE**	otetsudai suru

Examples:

1. *Kono shigoto o tetsudatte kuremasen ka. / Yorokonde otetsudai shimasu.*
   この仕事を手伝ってくれませんか。/ 喜んでお手伝いします。
   Could you help with this job? / I would be glad to help you.

2. *Nani ka tetsudau koto ga arimasu ka.*
   何か手伝うことがありますか。
   Can I do anything to help you?

3. *Kono tsukue o hakobu no o tetsudatte kudasai.*
   この机を運ぶのを手伝ってください。
   Please help me move this desk.

4. *Chichi wa ani ni shigoto o tetsudawasete iru.*
   父は兄に仕事を手伝わせている。
   My father made my older brother help with his work.

5. *Haha ni niwa no sōji o tetsudawasareta.*
   母に庭の掃除を手伝わされた。
   I was forced to help my mother clean the garden.

tobasu とばす

飛ばす to let fly, to skip (over), jump, hurry: (trans.)

		Affirmative	Negative
PLAIN FORM	PRESENT	tobasu	tobasanai
	PAST	tobashita	tobasanakatta
MASU FORM	PRESENT	tobashimasu	tobashimasen
	PAST	tobashimashita	tobashimasen deshita
TE FORM		tobashite	tobasanakute
CONDITIONAL	PLAIN	tobaseba/tobashita ra	tobasanakereba/ tobasanakatta ra
	FORMAL	tobashimashita ra	tobashimasen deshita ra
VOLITIONAL	PLAIN	tobasō	–
	FORMAL	tobashimashō	–
IMPERATIVE		tobase	tobasu na

	Affirmative		Affirmative
POTENTIAL	tobaseru	**CAUS. PASSIVE**	tobasaserareru
PASSIVE	tobasareru	**HONORIFIC**	otobashi ni naru/ tobasareru
CAUSATIVE	tobasaseru	**HUMBLE**	otobashi suru

Examples:

1. *Sono otoko no ko wa kami-hikōki o tōku e tobashita.*
   その男の子は紙飛行機を遠くへ飛ばした。
   The boy let fly a paper airplane.

2. *Kaze de bōshi ga tobasareta.*
   風で帽子が飛ばされた。
   My hat was blown off by the wind.

3. *Kare wa byōin made kuruma o tobashita.*
   彼は病院まで車を飛ばした。
   He drove his car quickly to the hospital.

4. *Sonna ni tobasanaide kudasai. Supiido no dashi-sugi desu.*
   そんなに飛ばさないでください。スピードの出し過ぎです。
   Please watch your speed. You drive too fast.

5. *Kyōmi ga nai pēji o tobashite, zasshi o yonda.*
   興味がないページを飛ばして、雑誌を読んだ。
   I read the magazine, skipping the pages that did not interest me.

tobu とぶ

飛ぶ to fly, take to the air ; 跳ぶ to jump, leap (intrans.)*

		Affirmative	Negative
PLAIN FORM	PRESENT	tobu	tobanai
	PAST	tonda	tobanakatta
MASU FORM	PRESENT	tobimasu	tobimasen
	PAST	tobimashita	tobimasen deshita
TE FORM		tonde	tobanakute
CONDITIONAL	PLAIN	tobeba/tonda ra	tobanakereba/ tobanakatta ra
	FORMAL	tobimashita ra	tobimasen deshita ra
VOLITIONAL	PLAIN	tobō	–
	FORMAL	tobimashō	–
IMPERATIVE		tobe	tobu na

	Affirmative		*Affirmative*
POTENTIAL	toberu	**CAUS. PASSIVE**	tobaserareru/tobasareru
PASSIVE	tobareru	**HONORIFIC**	otobi ni naru/tobareru
CAUSATIVE	tobaseru	**HUMBLE**	(otobi suru)

Examples:

1. *Shiroi tori ga umi no ue o tonde imasu.*
   白い鳥が海の上を飛んでいます。
   A white bird is flying over the ocean.

2. *Kare wa hashiri-takatobi de ni-mētoru tonda.*
   彼は走り高跳びで2メートル跳んだ。
   He leaped two meters in the high jump.

3. *Kare wa tadachi ni Pari e tonda.*
   彼は直ちにパリへ飛んだ。
   He flew immediately to Paris.

4. *Kare wa shigoto ga owaru to, ie e tonde kaetta.*
   彼は仕事が終わると、家へ飛んで帰った。
   When he finished working, he hurried home.

5. *Kono hon wa tobu yō ni urete iru.*
   この本は飛ぶように売れている。
   This book is selling like hot cakes.

* As with other verbs indicating movement, *tobu* 飛ぶ may take a direct object, thus giving an idea of "going through a defined area." (See example 1.)

todokeru とどける

届ける to report, notify, send, deliver: (trans.)

		Affirmative	Negative
PLAIN FORM	PRESENT	todokeru	todokenai
	PAST	todoketa	todokenakatta
MASU FORM	PRESENT	todokemasu	todokemasen
	PAST	todokemashita	todokemasen deshita
TE FORM		todokete	todokenakute
CONDITIONAL	PLAIN	todokereba/todoketa ra	todokenakereba/todokenakatta ra
	FORMAL	todokemashita ra	todokemasen deshita ra
VOLITIONAL	PLAIN	todokeyō	–
	FORMAL	todokemashō	–
IMPERATIVE		todokero	todokeru na

	Affirmative		Affirmative
POTENTIAL	todokerareru/todokereru	**CAUS. PASSIVE**	todokesaserareru
PASSIVE	todokerareru	**HONORIFIC**	otodoke ni naru/todokerareru
CAUSATIVE	todokesaseru	**HUMBLE**	otodoke suru

Examples:

1. *Kono shorui o buchō ni todokete kudasai.*
   この書類を部長に届けてください。
   Please deliver this document to the director.

2. *Michi de kaban o hirotta node, kōban ni todoketa.*
   道でかばんを拾ったので、交番に届けた。
   I picked up a bag on the street and sent it to the police box.

3. *Jūsho ga kawatta ra, shiyakusho ni todokenakereba naranai.*
   住所が変わったら、市役所に届けなければならない。
   Whenever you change your address, you must report it to City Hall.

4. *Okaiage no shōhin wa mikka inai ni otodoke shimasu.*
   お買い上げの商品は三日以内にお届けします。
   We will deliver your purchase within 3 days.

5. *Shinbun wa maiasa roku-ji goro todokerareru.*
   新聞は毎朝六時ごろ届けられる。
   The newspaper is delivered around 6 o'clock every morning.

todoku とどく

届く to reach, arrive: (intrans.)

		Affirmative	Negative
PLAIN FORM	PRESENT	todoku	todokanai
	PAST	todoita	todokanakatta
MASU FORM	PRESENT	todokimasu	todokimasen
	PAST	todokimashita	todokimasen deshita
TE FORM		todoite	todokanakute
CONDITIONAL	PLAIN	todokeba/todoita ra	todokanakereba/ todokanakatta ra
	FORMAL	todokimashita ra	todokimasen deshita ra
VOLITIONAL	PLAIN	todokō	–
	FORMAL	todokimashō	–
IMPERATIVE		todoke	todoku na

	Affirmative		Affirmative
POTENTIAL	todokeru	**CAUS. PASSIVE**	todokaserareru/ todokasareru
PASSIVE	todokareru	**HONORIFIC**	otodoki ni naru/ todokareru
CAUSATIVE	todokaseru	**HUMBLE**	(otodoki suru)

Examples:

1. *Anata no tegami ga kinō todokimashita.*
   あなたの手紙が昨日届きました。
   Your letter reached me yesterday.

2. *Hayaku todoku yō ni, shorui o sokutatsu de okutta.*
   早く届くように、書類を速達で送った。
   I sent the documents by Express Mail so that they would be delivered soon.

3. *Kono kusuri wa kodomo no te ga todokanai tokoro ni shimatte kudasai.*
   この薬は子供の手が届かない所にしまってください。
   Please keep this medicine out of reach by children.

4. *Chūmon shita shinamono ga mada todoite inai.*
   注文した品物がまだ届いていない。
   My order has not arrived yet.

5. *Nimotsu ga todoita ka dō ka, kakunin shite kudasai.*
   荷物が届いたかどうか、確認してください。
   Please check to see if the baggage has arrived or not.

tokeru とける

解ける to become untied, be solved; 溶ける to dissolve, melt: (both intrans.)

		Affirmative	*Negative*
PLAIN FORM	PRESENT	tokeru	tokenai
	PAST	toketa	tokenakatta
MASU FORM	PRESENT	tokemasu	tokemasen
	PAST	tokemashita	tokemasen deshita
TE FORM		tokete	tokenakute
CONDITIONAL	PLAIN	tokereba/toketa ra	tokenakereba/ tokenakatta ra
	FORMAL	tokemashita ra	tokemasen deshita ra
VOLITIONAL	PLAIN	tokeyō	–
	FORMAL	tokemashō	–
IMPERATIVE		tokero	tokeru na

	Affirmative		*Affirmative*
POTENTIAL	(tokerareru)	**CAUS. PASSIVE**	tokesaserareru
PASSIVE	(tokerareru)	**HONORIFIC**	otoke ni naru/tokerareru
CAUSATIVE	tokesaseru	**HUMBLE**	(otoke suru)

Examples:

1. *Kono mondai wa nakanaka tokenai.*
   この問題は、なかなか解けない。
   We cannot easily solve this problem.

2. *Kutsuhimo ga tokete iru.*
   靴ひもが解けている。
   My shoelaces have become loose.

3. *Himo ga tokenai yō ni, kataku musunda.*
   ひもが解けないように、固く結んだ。
   I tied the strings tightly so that they would not come undone.

4. *Kinō futta yuki ga mada tokete imasen.*
   昨日降った雪がまだ溶けていません。
   Yesterday's snow has not melted yet.

5. *Aisukuriimu ga toke sō desu.*
   アイスクリームが溶けそうです。
   The ice cream looks as if it is about to melt.

toku とく

GROUP 1

解く to untie, unfasten, solve, to relieve of a post; 溶く to dissolve: (both trans.)

		Affirmative	Negative
PLAIN FORM	PRESENT	toku	tokanai
	PAST	toita	tokanakatta
MASU FORM	PRESENT	tokimasu	tokimasen
	PAST	tokimashita	tokimasen deshita
TE FORM		toite	tokanakute
CONDITIONAL	PLAIN	tokeba/toita ra	tokanakereba/ tokanakatta ra
	FORMAL	tokimashita ra	tokimasen deshita ra
VOLITIONAL	PLAIN	tokō	–
	FORMAL	tokimashō	–
IMPERATIVE		toke	toku na

	Affirmative		Affirmative
POTENTIAL	tokeru	**CAUS. PASSIVE**	tokaserareru/tokasareru
PASSIVE	tokareru	**HONORIFIC**	otoki ni naru/tokareru
CAUSATIVE	tokaseru	**HUMBLE**	otoki suru

Examples:

1. *Musunde atta himo o toite, hako o aketa.*
   結んであったひもを解いて、箱を開けた。
   I undid the strings tied around the box and opened it.

2. *Yatto sūgaku no mondai ga toketa.*
   やっと数学の問題が解けた。
   I finally managed to solve the math problem.

3. *Kare no gokai o toku no ni kurō shimashita.*
   彼の誤解を解くのに苦労しました。
   We had difficulty convincing him otherwise. (*lit.*,untie his misunderstanding)

4. *Kona miruku o oyu de toite, akachan ni nomaseta.*
   粉ミルクをお湯で溶いて、赤ちゃんに飲ませた。
   I dissolved powder milk in hot water and gave it to my baby.

5. *Tamago o toite, gyūnyū to mazete kudasai.*
   卵を溶いて、牛乳と混ぜてください。
   Please beat an egg, and then mix it with milk.

tomaru とまる

止まる to stop, halt; 泊まる to stay the night, lodge; 留まる to fasten: (all intrans.)

			Affirmative	*Negative*
PLAIN FORM		PRESENT	tomaru	tomaranai
		PAST	tomatta	tomaranakatta
MASU FORM		PRESENT	tomarimasu	tomarimasen
		PAST	tomarimashita	tomarimasen deshita
TE FORM			tomatte	tomaranakute
CONDITIONAL		PLAIN	tomareba/tomatta ra	tomaranakereba/ tomaranakatta ra
		FORMAL	tomarimashita ra	tomarimasen deshita ra
VOLITIONAL		PLAIN	tomarō	–
		FORMAL	tomarimashō	–
IMPERATIVE			tomare	tomaru na

	Affirmative		*Affirmative*
POTENTIAL	tomareru	**CAUS. PASSIVE**	tomaraserareru/ tomarasareru
PASSIVE	tomarareru	**HONORIFIC**	otomari ni naru/ tomarareru
CAUSATIVE	tomaraseru	**HUMBLE**	otomari suru

Examples:

1. *Watashi no uchi no mae de akai kuruma ga tomatta.*
   私のうちの前で赤い車が止まった。
   A red car stopped in front of my house.

2. *Ano tokei wa tomatte imasu.*
   あの時計は止まっています。
   That watch has stopped.

3. *Jiko de densha ga tomarimashita.*
   事故で電車が止まりました。
   An accident caused the train to stop.

4. *Ima itoko ga watashi no ie ni tomatte imasu.*
   今いとこが私の家に泊まっています。
   My cousin is staying at my home now.

5. *Ryokan ni tomatta koto ga arimasu ka.*
   旅館に泊まったことがありますか。
   Have you ever stayed at a *ryokan* (Japanese inn)?

tomeru

止める to stop, park; 泊める to give lodging; 留める to fasten, fix, attach to: (all trans.)

		Affirmative	*Negative*
PLAIN FORM	PRESENT	tomeru	tomenai
	PAST	tometa	tomenakatta
MASU FORM	PRESENT	tomemasu	tomemasen
	PAST	tomemashita	tomemasen deshita
TE FORM		tomete	tomenakute
CONDITIONAL	PLAIN	tomereba/tometa ra	tomenakereba/ tomenakatta ra
	FORMAL	tomemashita ra	tomemasen deshita ra
VOLITIONAL	PLAIN	tomeyō	–
	FORMAL	tomemashō	–
IMPERATIVE		tomero	tomeru na

	Affirmative		*Affirmative*
POTENTIAL	tomerareru/ tomereru	**CAUS. PASSIVE**	tomesaserareru
PASSIVE	tomerareru	**HONORIFIC**	otome ni naru/ tomerareru
CAUSATIVE	tomesaseru	**HUMBLE**	otome suru

Examples:

1. *Tsugi no kōsaten de kuruma o tomete kudasai.*
   次の交差点で車を止めてください。
   Please stop the car at the next intersection.

2. *Ano chūshajō ni kuruma o tomete okimashō.*
   あの駐車場に車を止めておきましょう。
   Let's park our car at that parking lot.

3. *Futari no kenka o tomeyō to shita ga, tomerarenakatta.*
   二人のけんかを止めようとしたが、止められなかった。
   I tried to stop the two from fighting, but could not.

4. *Yūjin o hito-ban tomete ageta.*
   友人を一晩泊めてあげた。
   I let my friend stay at my house for a night.

5. *Sono chizu o kabe ni shikkari tomete oite kudasai.*
   その地図を壁にしっかり留めておいてください。
   Please attach that map firmly to the wall.

toreru とれる

取れる to come off, be able to catch; 撮れる be taken (a photo): (both intrans.)

		Affirmative	Negative
PLAIN FORM	PRESENT	toreru	torenai
	PAST	toreta	torenakatta
MASU FORM	PRESENT	toremasu	toremasen
	PAST	toremashita	toremasen deshita
TE FORM		torete	torenakute
CONDITIONAL	PLAIN	torereba/toreta ra	torenakereba/torenakatta ra
	FORMAL	toremashita ra	toremasen deshita ra
VOLITIONAL	PLAIN	toreyō	–
	FORMAL	toremashō	–
IMPERATIVE		torero	toreru na

	Affirmative		Affirmative
POTENTIAL	(torerareru)	**CAUS. PASSIVE**	(toresaserareru)
PASSIVE	(torerareru)	**HONORIFIC**	otore ni naru/torerareru
CAUSATIVE	(toresaseru)	**HUMBLE**	(otore suru)

Examples:

1. *Uwagi no botan ga toreta.*
   上着のボタンが取れた。
   A button has come off my coat.

2. *Nabe no totte ga tore-sō da.*
   鍋の取っ手が取れそうだ。
   The handle of the pan is about to come off.

3. *Inku no shimi wa nakanaka torenai.*
   インクのしみはなかなか取れない。
   Ink stains do not come off easily.

4. *Kyonen wa tenkō ga yokute, kome ga takusan toreta.*
   去年は天候が良くて、米がたくさん取れた。
   Because the weather was fine last year, a lot of rice was harvested.

5. *Shashin ga yoku toreta ra, ichi-mai agemasu yo.*
   写真が良く撮れたら、一枚あげますよ。
   If the picture comes out well, I'll give you a copy.

toru とる

取る to get, take, steal ; 撮る to take a picture; 捕る to catch: (all trans.)

		Affirmative	*Negative*
PLAIN FORM	PRESENT	toru	toranai
	PAST	totta	toranakatta
MASU FORM	PRESENT	torimasu	torimasen
	PAST	torimashita	torimasen deshita
TE FORM		totte	toranakute
CONDITIONAL	PLAIN	toreba/totta ra	toranakereba/ toranakatta ra
	FORMAL	torimashita ra	torimasen deshita ra
VOLITIONAL	PLAIN	torō	–
	FORMAL	torimashō	–
IMPERATIVE		tore	toru na

	Affirmative		*Affirmative*
POTENTIAL	toreru	**CAUS. PASSIVE**	toraserareru/torasareru
PASSIVE	torareru	**HONORIFIC**	otori ni naru/torareru
CAUSATIVE	toraseru	**HUMBLE**	otori suru

Examples:

1. *Sono hon o totte kudasai.*
   その本を取ってください。
   Please take that book (for me).

2. *Nihon de wa jūhassai ni nattara, kuruma no menkyo ga toreru.*
   日本では十八歳になったら、車の免許が取れる。
   In Japan, persons 18 years and above can obtain a driver's license.

3. *Suri ni saifu o toraremashita.*
   すりに財布を取られました。
   My wallet was pickpocketed.

4. *Shashin o totte mo ii desu ka. / Hai, dōzo totte kudasai.*
   写真を撮ってもいいですか。 / はい、どうぞ撮ってください。
   May I take your picture? / Yes, you may.

5. *Watashi-tachi wa kawa de sakana o takusan torimashita.*
   私たちは川で魚をたくさん捕りました。
   We caught many fishes in the river.

tōru とおる

通る to pass, pass through: (intrans.)*

		Affirmative	*Negative*
PLAIN FORM	PRESENT	tōru	tōranai
	PAST	tōtta	tōranakatta
MASU FORM	PRESENT	tōrimasu	tōrimasen
	PAST	tōrimashita	tōrimasen deshita
TE FORM		tōtte	tōranakute
CONDITIONAL	PLAIN	tōreba/tōtta ra	tōranakereba/ tōranakatta ra
	FORMAL	tōrimashita ra	tōrimasen deshita ra
VOLITIONAL	PLAIN	tōrō	–
	FORMAL	tōrimashō	–
IMPERATIVE		tōre	tōru na

	Affirmative		*Affirmative*
POTENTIAL	tōreru	**CAUS. PASSIVE**	tōraserareru/tōrasareru
PASSIVE	tōrareru	**HONORIFIC**	otōri ni naru/tōrareru
CAUSATIVE	tōraseru	**HUMBLE**	(otōri suru)

Examples:

1. *Kono basu wa Meguro-eki o tōrimasu ka.*
   このバスは目黒駅を通りますか。
   Does this bus go by Meguro Station?

2. *Kare no ie e iku ni wa, semai michi o tōranakereba naranai.*
   彼の家へ行くには、狭い道を通らなければならない。
   I have to pass through a narrow street to get to his house.

3. *Kono michi o tōreba, gakkō made 2, 3 pun de tsukimasu.*
   この道を通れば、学校まで2，3分で着きます。
   If you go along this street, you will arrive at the school in two or
   three minutes.

4. *Sumimasen ga, chotto tōrasete kudasai.*
   すみませんが、ちょっと通らせてください。
   Excuse me, but please let me pass.

5. *Kanojo no koe wa tōku made yoku tōru.*
   彼女の声は遠くまでよく通る。
   Her voice carries far.

---

* As with other verbs indicating movement, *tōru* 通る may take a direct object, thus giving an idea of "going through a defined area." (See examples 1, 2 and 3.)

tsūjiru つうじる

通じる to make oneself understood, to lead to, be well informed, connect with (telephone): (intrans.)

		Affirmative	*Negative*
PLAIN FORM	PRESENT	tsūjiru	tsūjinai
	PAST	tsūjita	tsūjinakatta
MASU FORM	PRESENT	tsūjimasu	tsūjimasen
	PAST	tsūjimashita	tsūjimasen deshita
TE FORM		tsūjite	tsūjinakute
CONDITIONAL	PLAIN	tsūjireba/tsūjita ra	tsūjinakereba/ tsūjinakatta ra
	FORMAL	tsūjimashita ra	tsūjimasen deshita ra
VOLITIONAL	PLAIN	tsūjiyō	–
	FORMAL	tsūjimashō	–
IMPERATIVE		tsūjiro	tsūjiru na

	Affirmative		*Affirmative*
POTENTIAL	tsūjirareru/tsūjireru	**CAUS. PASSIVE**	tsūjisaserareru
PASSIVE	tsūjirareru	**HONORIFIC**	otsūji ni naru/tsūjirareru
CAUSATIVE	tsūjisaseru	**HUMBLE**	(otsūji suru)

Examples:

1. *Furansu-go de hanashita ga, karera ni wa tsūjinakatta.*
   フランス語で話したが、彼らには通じなかった。
   I spoke in French, but couldn't make myself understood to them.

2. *Kare ni wa jōdan ga tsujimasen.*
   彼には冗談が通じません。
   He doesn't understand jokes.

3. *Yamada-san to wa yūjin o tsūjite shiriaimashita.*
   山田さんとは友人を通じて知り合いました。
   I am acquainted with Mr. Yamada through my friend.

4. *Kare wa Nihon no koten bungaku ni tsūjite iru.*
   彼は日本の古典文学に通じている。
   He is well informed about Japanese classic literature.

5. *Nando kaketemo hanashi-chū de, denwa ga tsūjinai.*
   何度かけても話し中で、電話が通じない。
   No matter how many times I called, the call would not go through.

tsukamaeru つかまえる

捕まえる to catch, take hold of, arrest: (trans.)

		Affirmative	*Negative*
PLAIN FORM	PRESENT	*tsukamaeru*	*tsukamaenai*
	PAST	*tsukamaeta*	*tsukamaenakatta*
MASU FORM	PRESENT	*tsukamaemasu*	*tsukamaemasen*
	PAST	*tsukamaemashita*	*tsukamaemasen deshita*
TE FORM		*tsukamaete*	*tsukamaenakute*
CONDITIONAL	PLAIN	*tsukamaereba/ tsukamaeta ra*	*tsukamaenakereba/ tsukamaenakatta ra*
	FORMAL	*tsukamaemashita ra*	*tsukamaemasen deshita ra*
VOLITIONAL	PLAIN	*tsukamaeyō*	–
	FORMAL	*tsukamaemashō*	–
IMPERATIVE		*tsukamaero*	*tsukamaeru na*

	Affirmative		*Affirmative*
POTENTIAL	*tsukamaerareru/ tsukamaereru*	**CAUS. PASSIVE**	*tsukamaesaserareru*
PASSIVE	*tsukamaerareru*	**HONORIFIC**	*otsukamae ni naru/ tsukamaerareru*
CAUSATIVE	*tsukamaesaseru*	**HUMBLE**	*otsukamae suru*

Examples:

1. *Keisatsu wa dorobō o tsukamaemashita.*
   警察は泥棒を捕まえました。
   The police caught the robber.

2. *Kare wa ima isogashikute, nakanaka tsukamaerarenai.*
   彼は今忙しくて、なかなか捕まえられない。
   He is so busy now that we cannot catch hold of him.

3. *Kodomo ga chōchō o tsukamae yō to shite iru.*
   子供が蝶々を捕まえようとしている。
   The child is trying to catch butterflies.

4. *Ishogashi-sō na ueitā o tsukamaete, yatto nomimono o chūmon shita.*
   忙しそうなウェイターを捕まえて、やっと飲み物を注文した。
   I caught hold of the busy waiter and ordered some drinks at last.

5. *Yonaka ni takushii o tsukamaeru no wa muzukashii.*
   夜中にタクシーを捕まえるのは難しい。
   It's difficult to catch a taxi late at night.

tsukamu つかむ

つかむ to catch, grasp, take hold of: (trans.)

		Affirmative	Negative
PLAIN FORM	PRESENT	tsukamu	tsukamanai
	PAST	tsukanda	tsukamanakatta
MASU FORM	PRESENT	tsukamimasu	tsukamimasen
	PAST	tsukamimashita	tsukamimasen deshita
TE FORM		tsukande	tsukamanakute
CONDITIONAL	PLAIN	tsukameba/tsukanda ra	tsukamanakereba/ tsukamanakatta ra
	FORMAL	tsukamimashita ra	tsukamimasen deshita ra
VOLITIONAL	PLAIN	tsukamō	–
	FORMAL	tsukamimashō	–
IMPERATIVE		tsukame	tsukamu na

	Affirmative		Affirmative
POTENTIAL	tsukameru	CAUS. PASSIVE	tsukamaserareru/ tsukamasareru
PASSIVE	tsukamareru	HONORIFIC	otsukami ni naru/ tsukamareru
CAUSATIVE	tsukamaseru	HUMBLE	otsukami suru

Examples:

1. *Kare wa tonde kita bōru o ryōte de tsukanda.*
   彼は飛んできたボールを両手でつかんだ。
   He caught the ball in the air with both hands.

2. *Sono onna no ko wa okāsan no fuku o tsukande hanasanakatta.*
   その女の子はお母さんの服をつかんで放さなかった。
   The girl grabbed her mother by her clothes and did not let go.

3. *Dōmo kare no hanashi wa imi ga tsukamenai.*
   どうも彼の話は意味がつかめない。
   I cannot grasp the meaning of his story for some reason.

4. *Keisatsu wa nani ka atarashii jōhō o tsukanda rashii.*
   警察は何か新しい情報をつかんだらしい。
   The police seem to have gotten hold of some new information.

5. *Kaidan kara ochi-sō ni natte, awatete tesuri o tsukanda.*
   階段から落ちそうになって、慌てて手すりをつかんだ。
   I was about to fall down the stairs so I hurriedly grabbed the handrail.

tsukareru つかれる

疲れる to be tired, be weary: (intrans.)

		Affirmative	Negative
PLAIN FORM	PRESENT	tsukareru	tsukarenai
	PAST	tsukareta	tsukarenakatta
MASU FORM	PRESENT	tsukaremasu	tsukaremasen
	PAST	tsukaremashita	tsukaremasen deshita
TE FORM		tsukarete	tsukarenakute
CONDITIONAL	PLAIN	tsukarereba/tsukareta ra	tsukarenakereba/ tsukarenakatta ra
	FORMAL	tsukaremashita ra	tsukaremasen deshita ra
VOLITIONAL	PLAIN	tsukareyō	–
	FORMAL	tsukaremashō	–
IMPERATIVE		tsukarero	tsukareru na

	Affirmative		Affirmative
POTENTIAL	tsukarerareru/ tsukarereru	**CAUS. PASSIVE**	tsukaresaserareru
PASSIVE	(tsukarerareru)	**HONORIFIC**	otsukare ni naru/ tsukarerareru
CAUSATIVE	tsukaresaseru	**HUMBLE**	(otsukare suru)

Examples:

1. *Amari tsukarete ita node, nani mo taberaremasen deshita.*
   あまり疲れていたので、何も食べられませんでした。
   I was too tired to eat anything.

2. *Kare wa tsukareta kao de uchi ni kaette kita.*
   彼は疲れた顔でうちに帰ってきた。
   He came home looking tired.

3. *Kodomo-tachi wa asobi-tsukareta rashii.*
   子供達は遊び疲れたらしい。
   The children seem to be tired from playing.

4. *Nagai aida pasokon no shigoto o suru to, me ga tsukareru.*
   長い間パソコンの仕事をすると、目が疲れる。
   When I do work on the PC for long periods of time, my eyes get tired.

5. *Tsukareta ra, sukoshi yasunda hō ga ii.*
   疲れたら、少し休んだほうがいい。
   When you are tired, you should rest for a while.

tsukau つかう

使う to use, handle, employ: (trans.)

		Affirmative	Negative
PLAIN FORM	PRESENT	tsukau	tsukawanai
	PAST	tsukatta	tsukawanakatta
MASU FORM	PRESENT	tsukaimasu	tsukaimasen
	PAST	tsukaimashita	tsukaimasen deshita
TE FORM		tsukatte	tsukawanakute
CONDITIONAL	PLAIN	tsukaeba/tsukatta ra	tsukawanakereba/ tsukawanakatta ra
	FORMAL	tsukaimashita ra	tsukaimasen deshita ra
VOLITIONAL	PLAIN	tsukaō	–
	FORMAL	tsukaimashō	–
IMPERATIVE		tsukae	tsukau na

	Affirmative		Affirmative
POTENTIAL	tsukaeru	**CAUS. PASSIVE**	tsukawaserareru/ tsukawasareru
PASSIVE	tsukawareru	**HONORIFIC**	otsukai ni naru/ tsukawareru
CAUSATIVE	tsukawaseru	**HUMBLE**	otsukai suru

Examples:

1. *Denwa o tsukatte mo ii desu ka.*
   電話を使ってもいいですか。
   May I use your telephone?

2. *Ei-go wa kokusai-go to shite tsukawarete iru.*
   英語は国際語として使われている。
   English is used as an international language.

3. *Bāgen ni itte, takusan okane o tsukatte shimatta.*
   バーゲンに行って、たくさんお金を使ってしまった。
   I regretfully spent a lot of money at the sale.

4. *Sono fakkusu wa koshō shite ite, tsukaemasen.*
   そのファックスは故障していて、使えません。
   That fax machine is out of order. We cannot use it.

5. *Buchō wa hito o tsukau no ga umai.*
   部長は人を使うのがうまい。
   My manager is good at managing people.

tsukeru つける

付ける or 着ける put on, fix; つける to switch on: (all trans.)

		Affirmative	Negative
PLAIN FORM	PRESENT	tsukeru	tsukenai
	PAST	tsuketa	tsukenakatta
MASU FORM	PRESENT	tsukemasu	tsukemasen
	PAST	tsukemashita	tsukemasen deshita
TE FORM		tsukete	tsukenakute
CONDITIONAL	PLAIN	tsukereba/tsuketa ra	tsukenakereba/ tsukenakatta ra
	FORMAL	tsukemashita ra	tsukemasen deshita ra
VOLITIONAL	PLAIN	tsukeyō	–
	FORMAL	tsukemashō	–
IMPERATIVE		tsukero	tsukeru na

	Affirmative		Affirmative
POTENTIAL	tsukerareru/ tsukereru	**CAUS. PASSIVE**	tsukesaserareru
PASSIVE	tsukerareru	**HONORIFIC**	otsuke ni naru/ tsukerareru
CAUSATIVE	tsukesaseru	**HUMBLE**	otsuke suru

Examples:

1. *Kaban ni nafuda o tsukemashita.*
   かばんに名札を付けました。
   I attached my name card to my bag.

2. *Atsukereba, eakon o tsukemashō.*
   暑ければ、エアコンをつけましょう。
   If it is hot, let's switch on the air conditioner.

3. *Kega o shita ashi ni kusuri o tsukemashita.*
   けがをした足に薬を付けました。
   I put the medicine on my injured leg.

4. *Heya no denki o tsukete kudasai.*
   部屋の電気をつけてください。
   Please switch on the room light.

5. *Terebi o tsukete mo ii desu ka. / Iie, tsukenaide kudasai.*
   テレビをつけてもいいですか。/ いいえ、つけないでください。
   May I turn on the TV? / I would prefer you not.

tsuku つく

着く to arrive; 付く to stick to, attend; つく to be lighted: (all intrans.)*

		Affirmative	Negative
PLAIN FORM	PRESENT	tsuku	tsukanai
	PAST	tsuita	tsukanakatta
MASU FORM	PRESENT	tsukimasu	tsukimasen
	PAST	tsukimashita	tsukimasen deshita
TE FORM		tsuite	tsukanakute
CONDITIONAL	PLAIN	tsukeba/tsuita ra	tsukanakereba/tsukanakatta ra
	FORMAL	tsukimashita ra	tsukimasen deshita ra
VOLITIONAL	PLAIN	tsukō	–
	FORMAL	tsukimashō	–
IMPERATIVE		tsuke	tsuku na

	Affirmative		Affirmative
POTENTIAL	tsukeru	**CAUS. PASSIVE**	tsukaserareru/tsukasareru
PASSIVE	tsukareru	**HONORIFIC**	otsuki ni naru/tsukareru
CAUSATIVE	tsukaseru	**HUMBLE**	(otsuki suru)

Examples:

1. *Sono hikōki wa nan-ji ni tsukimasu ka.*
   その飛行機は何時に着きますか。
   What time will the plane arrive?

2. *Eki ni tsuita ra, denwa shite kudasai.*
   駅に着いたら、電話してください。
   When you arrive at the station, please call me.

3. *Kono kaban wa poketto ga takusan tsuite ite, benri desu.*
   このかばんはポケットがたくさん付いていて、便利です。
   This bag has many pockets so it is convenient.

4. *Terebi ga tsukanai'n desu ga, dō sureba ii desu ka.*
   テレビがつかないんですが、どうすればいいですか。
   The TV is not on, so what shall I do?

5. *Kare no heya ni akari ga tsuite iru.*
   彼の部屋に明かりがついている。
   The light is on in his room.

* The verb *tsuku* つく meaning "to be lighted" generally does not use the imperative, volitional, potential, passive, humble, causative, or causative passive forms.

tsukuru つくる

作る or 造る to make, create, produce: (trans.)

		Affirmative	Negative
PLAIN FORM	PRESENT	tsukuru	tsukuranai
	PAST	tsukutta	tsukuranakatta
MASU FORM	PRESENT	tsukurimasu	tsukurimasen
	PAST	tsukurimashita	tsukurimasen deshita
TE FORM		tsukutte	tsukuranakute
CONDITIONAL	PLAIN	tsukureba/tsukutta ra	tsukuranakereba/ tsukuranakatta ra
	FORMAL	tsukurimashita ra	tsukurimasen deshita ra
VOLITIONAL	PLAIN	tsukurō	–
	FORMAL	tsukurimashō	–
IMPERATIVE		tsukure	tsukuru na

	Affirmative		Affirmative
POTENTIAL	tsukureru	**CAUS. PASSIVE**	tsukuraserareru/ tsukurasareru
PASSIVE	tsukurareru	**HONORIFIC**	otsukuri ni naru/ tsukurareru
CAUSATIVE	tsukuraseru	**HUMBLE**	otsukuri suru

Examples:

1. *Ane wa fuku ya kaban o tsukuru no ga jōzu da.*
   姉は服やかばんを作るのが上手だ。
   My older sister is good at making clothes and bags.

2. *Tanjōbi ni tomodachi ga kēki o tsukutte kureta.*
   誕生日に友達がケーキを作ってくれた。
   My friend made me a cake for my birthday.

3. *Nihon ryōri ga tsukuremasu ka. / Iie. Tsukutta koto mo arimasen.*
   日本料理が作れますか。/ いいえ。作ったこともありません。
   Can you cook Japanese food? / No, I have never even tried.

4. *Shōrai jibun no kaisha o tsukurō to omotte imasu.*
   将来自分の会社を作ろうと思っています。
   I intend to start my own company in the near future.

5. *Kansai kokusai kūkō wa Ōsaka-wan no naka ni tsukurareta.*
   関西国際空港は大阪湾の中に造られた。
   The Kansai International Airport was built in the middle of the Osaka Bay.

tsutaeru つたえる

伝える to tell, report, introduce, transmit: (trans.)

		Affirmative	*Negative*
PLAIN FORM	PRESENT	tsutaeru	tsutaenai
	PAST	tsutaeta	tsutaenakatta
MASU FORM	PRESENT	tsutaemasu	tsutaemasen
	PAST	tsutaemashita	tsutaemasen deshita
TE FORM		tsutaete	tsutaenakute
CONDITIONAL	PLAIN	tsutaereba/tsutaeta ra	tsutaenakereba/ tsutaenakatta ra
	FORMAL	tsutaemashita ra	tsutaemasen deshita ra
VOLITIONAL	PLAIN	tsutaeyō	–
	FORMAL	tsutaemashō	–
IMPERATIVE		tsutaero	tsutaeru na

	Affirmative		*Affirmative*
POTENTIAL	tsutaerareru/ tsutaereru	**CAUS. PASSIVE**	tsutaesaserareru
PASSIVE	tsutaerareru	**HONORIFIC**	otsutae ni naru/ tsutaerareru
CAUSATIVE	tsutaesaseru	**HUMBLE**	otsutae suru

Examples:

1. *Ato de anata ni denwa suru yō ni kare ni tsutaete okimasu.*
   後であなたに電話するように彼に伝えておきます。
   I will tell him to phone you later.

2. *Buchō ni kaigi wa ni-ji kara da to tsutaete itadakemasen ka.*
   部長に会議は二時からだと伝えていただけませんか。
   Could you please inform your manager that the meeting will start at 2 o'clock?

3. *Tanaka-san ni yoroshiku otsutae kudasai.*
   田中さんによろしくお伝えください。
   Could you please give my best regards to Mr. Tanaka?

4. *Bukkyō wa Chūgoku kara Nihon ni tsutaerareta.*
   仏教は中国から日本に伝えられた。
   Buddhism was introduced to Japan from China.

5. *Dentō wa sedai kara sedai e to tsutaerarete iru.*
   伝統は世代から世代へと伝えられている。
   The tradition has been passed down from generation to generation.

tsutawaru つたわる

伝わる to be handed down, be transmitted, be introduced: (intrans.)

		Affirmative	*Negative*
PLAIN FORM	PRESENT	tsutawaru	tsutawaranai
	PAST	tsutawatta	tsutawaranakatta
MASU FORM	PRESENT	tsutawarimasu	tsutawarimasen
	PAST	tsutawarimashita	tsutawarimasen deshita
TE FORM		tsutawatte	tsutawaranakute
CONDITIONAL	PLAIN	tsutawareba/ tsutawatta ra	tsutawaranakereba/ tsutawaranakatta ra
	FORMAL	tsutawarimashita ra	tsutawarimasen deshita ra
VOLITIONAL	PLAIN	tsutawarō	–
	FORMAL	tsutawarimashō	–
IMPERATIVE		tsutaware	tsutawaru na

	Affirmative		*Affirmative*
POTENTIAL	tsutawareru	**CAUS. PASSIVE**	tsutawaraserareru/ tsutawarasareru
PASSIVE	tsutawarareru	**HONORIFIC**	otsutawari ni naru/ tsutawarareru
CAUSATIVE	tsutawaraseru	**HUMBLE**	(otsutawari suru)

Examples:

1. *Kono katana wa sofu no dai kara tsutawatta.*
   この刀は祖父の代から伝わった。
   This sword has been handed down from my grandfather's time.

2. *Sono nyūsu wa atto iu ma ni sekai-jū ni tsutawatta.*
   そのニュースはあっという間に世界中に伝わった。
   That news was transmitted to the entire world in no time.

3. *Kare no kinchō ga watashi-tachi ni made tsutawatte kita.*
   彼の緊張が私達にまで伝わってきた。
   Even we could feel his tension.

4. *Sono minwa wa watashi no kokyō ni furuku kara tsutawatte iru.*
   その民話は私の故郷に古くから伝わっている。
   That folktale has been passed down in my hometown since ancient time.

5. *Kare ni dengon o nokoshita ga, tsutawaranakatta yō da.*
   彼に伝言を残したが、伝わらなかったようだ。
   I left a message for him but it seems not to have reached him.

tsutsumu つつむ

GROUP 1

包む to wrap, veil, envelop in: (trans.)

		Affirmative	Negative
PLAIN FORM	PRESENT	tsutsumu	tsutsumanai
	PAST	tsutsunda	tsutsumanakatta
MASU FORM	PRESENT	tsutsumimasu	tsutsumimasen
	PAST	tsutsumimashita	tsutsumimasen deshita
TE FORM		tsutsunde	tsutsumanakute
CONDITIONAL	PLAIN	tsutsumeba/tsutsunda ra	tsutsumanakereba/ tsutsumanakatta ra
	FORMAL	tsutsumimashita ra	tsutsumimasen deshita ra
VOLITIONAL	PLAIN	tsutsumō	–
	FORMAL	tsutsumimashō	–
IMPERATIVE		tsutsume	tsutsumu na

	Affirmative		Affirmative
POTENTIAL	tsutsumeru	**CAUS. PASSIVE**	tsutsumaserareru/ tsutsumasareru
PASSIVE	tsutsumareru	**HONORIFIC**	otsutsumi ni naru/ tsutsumareru
CAUSATIVE	tsutsumaseru	**HUMBLE**	otsutsumi suru

Examples:

1. *Kore o kami ni tsutsunde kudasai.*
   これを紙に包んでください。
   Please wrap this up in paper.

2. *Ehon o katte, purezento yō ni tsutsunde moratta.*
   絵本を買って、プレゼント用に包んでもらった。
   I bought a picture book and asked to have it gift-wrapped.

3. *Ware-yasui mono wa yawarakai nuno de tsutsunda hō ga ii.*
   割れやすい物は柔らかい布で包んだほうがいい。
   Fragile goods should be wrapped up in a soft coth.

4. *Sanchō wa kiri ni tsutsumarete ita.*
   山頂は霧に包まれていた。
   The mountain top was covered in mist.

5. *Sono sakka no shōtai wa nazo ni tsutsumarete iru.*
   その作家の正体は謎に包まれている。
   The writer's true colors are cloaked in a veil of mystery.

tsuzukeru つづける

GROUP 2

続ける to continue, go on, proceed, carry on: (trans.)

		Affirmative	*Negative*
PLAIN FORM	PRESENT	*tsuzukeru*	*tsuzukenai*
	PAST	*tsuzuketa*	*tsuzukenakatta*
MASU FORM	PRESENT	*tsuzukemasu*	*tsuzukemasen*
	PAST	*tsuzukemashita*	*tsuzukemasen deshita*
TE FORM		*tsuzukete*	*tsuzukenakute*
CONDITIONAL	PLAIN	*tsuzukereba/ tsuzuketa ra*	*tsuzukenakereba/ tsuzukenakatta ra*
	FORMAL	*tsuzukemashita ra*	*tsuzukemasen deshita ra*
VOLITIONAL	PLAIN	*tsuzukeyō*	–
	FORMAL	*tsuzukemashō*	–
IMPERATIVE		*tsuzukero*	*tsuzukeru na*

	Affirmative		*Affirmative*
POTENTIAL	*tsuzukerareru/ tsuzukereru*	**CAUS. PASSIVE**	*tsuzukesaserareru*
PASSIVE	*tsuzukerareru*	**HONORIFIC**	*otsuzuke ni naru/ tsuzukerareru*
CAUSATIVE	*tsuzukesaseru*	**HUMBLE**	*otsuzuke suru*

Examples:

1. *Chichi wa mō sankagetsu gurai asa no jogingu o tsuzukete iru.*
   父はもう三か月ぐらい朝のジョギングを続けている。
   My father has been maintaining his morning jog for about three months now.

2. *Kono kōsu ga owatte mo, benkyō o tsuzukeyō to omotte imasu.*
   このコースが終わっても、勉強を続けようと思っています。
   I intend to continue my studies even after finishing this course.

3. *Karera wa yonaka made hanashi-tsuzukemashita.*
   彼らは夜中まで話し続けました。
   They kept talking until late at night.

4. *Gakkō ga isogashiku natta node, baito ga tsuzukerarenai.*
   学校が忙しくなったので、バイトが続けられない。
   I am too busy at school to continue my part-time job.

5. *Hanashi-ai wa yoru osoku made tsuzukerareta.*
   話し合いは夜遅くまで続けられた。
   The discussion carried on until late that night.

tsuzuku つづく

続く to continue, last, lead to, follow: (intrans.)

		Affirmative	Negative
PLAIN FORM	PRESENT	tsuzuku	tsuzukanai
	PAST	tsuzuita	tsuzukanakatta
MASU FORM	PRESENT	tsuzukimasu	tsuzukimasen
	PAST	tsuzukimashita	tsuzukimasen deshita
TE FORM		tsuzuite	tsuzukanakute
CONDITIONAL	PLAIN	tsuzukeba/tsuzuita ra	tsuzukanakereba/ tsuzukanakatta ra
	FORMAL	tsuzukimashita ra	tsuzukimasen deshita ra
VOLITIONAL	PLAIN	tsuzukō	–
	FORMAL	tsuzukimashō	–
IMPERATIVE		tsuzuke	tsuzuku na

	Affirmative		Affirmative
POTENTIAL	tsuzukeru	**CAUS. PASSIVE**	tsuzukaserareru/ tsuzukasareru
PASSIVE	tsuzukareru	**HONORIFIC**	otsuzuki ni naru/ tsuzukareru
CAUSATIVE	tsuzukaseru	**HUMBLE**	(otsuzuki suru)

Examples:

1. *Tenki-yohō ni yoru to, konshū wa tenki no ii hi ga tsuzuku sō da.*
   天気予報によると、今週は天気のいい日が続くそうだ。
   According to the weather forecast, the weather will continue to be good this week.

2. *Sono pātii wa yoru osoku made tsuzuita.*
   そのパーティーは夜遅くまで続いた。
   That party lasted until late that night.

3. *Zutsū ni tsuzuite, netsu mo dete kita yō da.*
   頭痛に続いて、熱も出てきたようだ。
   After the headache, it seems like I also got a fever.

4. *Kaiten o matsu hito no retsu wa nan-jū mētoru mo tsuzuite ita.*
   開店を待つ人の列は何十メートルも続いていた。
   The line of the people waiting for the opening sale stretched for miles.

5. *Yūbe kara ame ga furi-tsuzuite imasu.*
   ゆうべから雨が降り続いています。
   It has been raining since last night.

ugokasu うごかす

動かす to move, operate, influence: (trans.)

		Affirmative	Negative
PLAIN FORM	PRESENT	ugokasu	ugokasanai
	PAST	ugokashita	ugokasanakatta
MASU FORM	PRESENT	ugokashimasu	ugokashimasen
	PAST	ugokashimashita	ugokashimasen deshita
TE FORM		ugokashite	ugokasanakute
CONDITIONAL	PLAIN	ugokaseba/ ugokashita ra	ugokasanakereba/ ugokasanakatta ra
	FORMAL	ugokashimashita ra	ugokashimasen deshita ra
VOLITIONAL	PLAIN	ugokasō	–
	FORMAL	ugokashimashō	–
IMPERATIVE		ugokase	ugokasu na

	Affirmative		Affirmative
POTENTIAL	ugokaseru	**CAUS. PASSIVE**	ugokasaserareru
PASSIVE	ugokasareru	**HONORIFIC**	ougokashi ni naru/ ugokasareru
CAUSATIVE	ugokasaseru	**HUMBLE**	ougokashi suru

Examples:

1. *Kono tēburu o sukoshi migi ni ugokashite kudasai.*
   このテーブルを少し右に動かしてください。
   Please move this table a little farther to the right.

2. *Piano o ugokasu no o tetsudatte kuremasen ka.*
   ピアノを動かすのを手伝ってくれませんか。
   Will you please help me move the piano?

3. *Ano hako ga jama nan desu ga, chotto ugokashite mo ii desu ka.*
   あの箱が邪魔なんですが、ちょっと動かしてもいいですか。
   Is it all right if I move this box out of the way?

4. *Tama ni wa karada o ugokashita hō ga ii desu yo.*
   たまには体を動かしたほうがいいですよ。
   You should sometimes move your body.

5. *Watashi wa kare no kotoba ni kokoro o ugokasareta.*
   私は彼の言葉に心を動かされた。
   I was deeply moved by his words.

ugoku うごく

動く to move, change, run (intrans.)

		Affirmative	*Negative*
PLAIN FORM	PRESENT	ugoku	ugokanai
	PAST	ugoita	ugokanakatta
MASU FORM	PRESENT	ugokimasu	ugokimasen
	PAST	ugokimashita	ugokimasen deshita
TE FORM		ugoite	ugokanakute
CONDITIONAL	PLAIN	ugokeba/ugoita ra	ugokanakereba/ ugokanakatta ra
	FORMAL	ugokimashita ra	ugokimasen deshita ra
VOLITIONAL	PLAIN	ugokō	–
	FORMAL	ugokimashō	–
IMPERATIVE		ugoke	ugoku na

	Affirmative		*Affirmative*
POTENTIAL	ugokeru	**CAUS. PASSIVE**	ugokaserareru/ ugokasareru
PASSIVE	ugokareru	**HONORIFIC**	ougoki ni naru/ ugokareru
CAUSATIVE	ugokaseru	**HUMBLE**	(ougoki suru)

Examples:

1. *Kono omocha wa denchi de ugokimasu.*
   このおもちゃは電池で動きます。
   This toy runs on batteries.

2. *Kono tsukue wa omokute, oshitemo ugokimasen.*
   この机は重くて、押しても動きません。
   This desk is so heavy that it doesn't move even when pushed.

3. *Ashi ga shibirete shimatte, ugokemasen.*
   足がしびれてしまって、動けません。
   My feet are asleep so I cannot move.

4. *Sekai jōsei wa tsune ni ugoite imasu.*
   世界情勢は常に動いています。
   The state of affairs in the world is always changing.

5. *Kaminoke o kiru aida, ugokanaide kudasai ne.*
   髪の毛を切る間、動かないでくださいね。
   Please do not move while I am cutting your hair.

ukabu うかぶ

浮かぶ float, rise to the surface: (intrans.)

		Affirmative	*Negative*
PLAIN FORM	PRESENT	ukabu	ukabanai
	PAST	ukanda	ukabanakatta
MASU FORM	PRESENT	ukabimasu	ukabimasen
	PAST	ukabimashita	ukabimasen deshita
TE FORM		ukande	ukabanakute
CONDITIONAL	PLAIN	ukabeba/ukanda ra	ukabanakereba/ ukabanakatta ra
	FORMAL	ukabimashita ra	ukabimasen deshita ra
VOLITIONAL	PLAIN	ukabō	–
	FORMAL	ukabimashō	–
IMPERATIVE		ukabe	ukabu na

	Affirmative		*Affirmative*
POTENTIAL	ukaberu	**CAUS. PASSIVE**	ukabaserareru/ ukabasareru
PASSIVE	ukabareru	**HONORIFIC**	oukabi ni naru/ukabareru
CAUSATIVE	ukabaseru	**HUMBLE**	(oukabi suru)

Examples:

1. *Fune ga umi ni ukande iru.*
   船が海に浮かんでいる。
   A ship is floating in the sea.

2. *Shiroi kumo ga sora ni ukande imasu.*
   白い雲が空に浮かんでいます。
   White clouds are floating in the sky.

3. *Kare no kao ni wa fuan no iro ga ukanda.*
   彼の顔には不安の色が浮かんだ。
   A look of uneasiness appeared on his face.

4. *Kanojo no me ni namida ga ukabimashita.*
   彼女の目に涙が浮かびました。
   Tears welled up in her eyes.

5. *Meian ga ukanda.*
   名案が浮かんだ。
   A good idea occurred to me.

umareru うまれる

生まれる or 産まれる to be born, arise: (intrans.)

		Affirmative	*Negative*
PLAIN FORM	PRESENT	umareru	umarenai
	PAST	umareta	umarenakatta
MASU FORM	PRESENT	umaremasu	umaremasen
	PAST	umaremashita	umaremasen deshita
TE FORM		umarete	umarenakute
CONDITIONAL	PLAIN	umarereba/umareta ra	umarenakereba/ umarenakatta ra
	FORMAL	umaremashita ra	umaremasen deshita ra
VOLITIONAL	PLAIN	umareyō	–
	FORMAL	umaremashō	–
IMPERATIVE		umarero	umareru na

	Affirmative		*Affirmative*
POTENTIAL	umarerareru/ umarereru	**CAUS. PASSIVE**	umaresaserareru
PASSIVE	umarerareru	**HONORIFIC**	oumare ni naru/ umarerareru
CAUSATIVE	umaresaseru	**HUMBLE**	(oumare suru)

Examples:

1. *Watashi wa Tōkyō de umaremashita.*
   私は東京で生まれました。
   I was born in Tokyo.

2. *Yamada-san no tokoro ni onna no ko ga umaremashita.*
   山田さんのところに女の子が生まれました。
   A baby girl was born to Mr. Yamada.

3. *Raigetsu ane ni kodomo ga umareru yotei da.*
   来月姉に子供が生まれる予定だ。
   My sister is expecting a baby next month.

4. *Kono aida, umarete hajimete hikōki ni notta.*
   この間、生まれて初めて飛行機に乗った。
   I boarded an airplane for the first time in my life the other day.

5. *Kanojo wa joyū ni naru tame ni umarete kita yō da.*
   彼女は女優になるために生まれてきたようだ。
   She was born to be an actress.

umu うむ

生む or 産む to give birth, produce, yield: (trans.)

		Affirmative	Negative
PLAIN FORM	PRESENT	umu	umanai
	PAST	unda	umanakatta
MASU FORM	PRESENT	umimasu	umimasen
	PAST	umimashita	umimasen deshita
TE FORM		unde	umanakute
CONDITIONAL	PLAIN	umeba/unda ra	umanakereba/ umanakatta ra
	FORMAL	umimashita ra	umimasen deshita ra
VOLITIONAL	PLAIN	umō	–
	FORMAL	umimashō	–
IMPERATIVE		ume	umu na

	Affirmative		Affirmative
POTENTIAL	umeru	**CAUS. PASSIVE**	umaserareru/umasareru
PASSIVE	umareru	**HONORIFIC**	oumi ni naru/umareru
CAUSATIVE	umaseru	**HUMBLE**	oumi suru

Examples:

1. *Katte iru inu ga koinu o san-biki umimashita.*
   飼っている犬が子犬を三匹産みました。
   My dog gave birth to three puppies.

2. *Kono niwatori wa mainichi tamago o umu.*
   この鶏は毎日卵を産む。
   This hen lays eggs every day.

3. *Kare wa Nihon ga unda idai na kagakusha no hitori da.*
   彼は日本が生んだ偉大な科学者の一人だ。
   He is one of the great scientists to come out of Japan.

4. *Sono tōshi wa ōkina rieki o unde iru.*
   その投資は大きな利益を生んでいる。
   That investiment yields a big profit.

5. *Kare no hatsugen wa gokai o umi-yasui.*
   彼の発言は誤解を生みやすい。
   His remarks are easily misunderstood.

uru うる

売る to sell: (trans.)

		Affirmative	*Negative*
PLAIN FORM	PRESENT	uru	uranai
	PAST	utta	uranakatta
MASU FORM	PRESENT	urimasu	urimasen
	PAST	urimashita	urimasen deshita
TE FORM		utte	uranakute
CONDITIONAL	PLAIN	ureba/utta ra	uranakereba/ uranakatta ra
	FORMAL	urimashita ra	urimasen deshita ra
VOLITIONAL	PLAIN	urō	–
	FORMAL	urimashō	–
IMPERATIVE		ure	uru na

	Affirmative		*Affirmative*
POTENTIAL	ureru	**CAUS. PASSIVE**	uraserareru/urasareru
PASSIVE	urareru	**HONORIFIC**	ouri ni naru/urareru
CAUSATIVE	uraseru	**HUMBLE**	ouri suru

Examples:

1. *Kono jisho wa eki-mae no hon-ya de utte imasu.*
   この辞書は駅前の本屋で売っています。
   This dictionary is sold at the bookstore in front of the station.

2. *Suzuki-san ga ichi-man-en de gitā o utte kureta.*
   鈴木さんが一万円でギターを売ってくれた。
   Mr. Suzuki sold me his guitar for 10,000 yen.

3. *Tanaka-san wa ie o utte, Ōsaka ni hikkoshita sō da.*
   田中さんは家を売って、大阪に引っ越したそうだ。
   I heard that Mr. Tanaka sold his house and moved to Osaka.

4. *Kono seihin wa zenkoku no yakkyoku de urarete iru.*
   この製品は全国の薬局で売られている。
   This product is sold at drugstores nationwide.

5. *Kono kuruma wa furu-sugite, mō urenai darō.*
   この車は古すぎて、もう売れないだろう。
   This car is likely to be too old to be saleable.

utagau

疑う to doubt, suspect: (trans.)

		Affirmative	Negative
PLAIN FORM	PRESENT	utagau	utagawanai
	PAST	utagatta	utagawanakatta
MASU FORM	PRESENT	utagaimasu	utagaimasen
	PAST	utagaimashita	utagaimasen deshita
TE FORM		utagatte	utagawanakute
CONDITIONAL	PLAIN	utagaeba utagatta ra	utagawanakereba/ utagawanakatta ra
	FORMAL	utagaimashita ra	utagaimasen deshita ra
VOLITIONAL	PLAIN	utagaō	–
	FORMAL	utagaimashō	–
IMPERATIVE		utagae	utagau na

	Affirmative		Affirmative
POTENTIAL	utagaeru	**CAUS. PASSIVE**	utagawaserareru/ utagawasareru
PASSIVE	utagawareru	**HONORIFIC**	outagai ni naru/ utagawareru
CAUSATIVE	utagawaseru	**HUMBLE**	outagai suru

Examples:

1. *Sono hanashi ga hontō ka dō ka, utagatte imasu.*
   その話が本当かどうか、疑っています。
   I doubt that that story is true.

2. *Kare wa jibun no seikō o shinjite utagawanai.*
   彼は自分の成功を信じて疑わない。
   He believes in his success and never doubts himself.

3. *Tomodachi ni utagawarete, shokku datta.*
   友達に疑われて、ショックだった。
   I was shocked that my friend doubted me.

4. *Kare no kotoba o utagawazaru o enai.*
   彼の言葉を疑わざるをえない。
   I can't help but be doubtful of his words.

5. *Sono hanashi o kiite, jibun no mimi o utagatta.*
   その話を聞いて、自分の耳を疑った。
   After hearing the story, I could hardly believe my ears.

utau うたう

歌う to sing (trans.)

		Affirmative	Negative
PLAIN FORM	PRESENT	utau	utawanai
	PAST	utatta	utawanakatta
MASU FORM	PRESENT	utaimasu	utaimasen
	PAST	utaimashita	utaimasen deshita
TE FORM		utatte	utawanakute
CONDITIONAL	PLAIN	utaeba/utatta ra	utawanakereba/ utawanakatta ra
	FORMAL	utaimashita ra	utaimasen deshita ra
VOLITIONAL	PLAIN	utaō	–
	FORMAL	utaimashō	–
IMPERATIVE		utae	utau na

	Affirmative		Affirmative
POTENTIAL	utaeru	**CAUS. PASSIVE**	utawaserareru/ utawasareru
PASSIVE	utawareru	**HONORIFIC**	outai ni naru/utawareru
CAUSATIVE	utawaseru	**HUMBLE**	outai suru

Examples:

1. *Imōto wa uta o utau no ga suki da.*
   妹は歌を歌うのが好きだ。
   My younger sister likes to sing.

2. *Motto ōkii koe de utatte kudasai.*
   もっと大きい声で歌ってください。
   Please sing more loudly.

3. *Kanojo wa piano o hiki-nagara utatta.*
   彼女はピアノを弾きながら歌った。
   She sang while playing the piano.

4. *Nihon no uta ga utaemasu ka.*
   日本の歌が歌えますか。
   Can you sing any Japanese songs?

5. *Uta ga heta na noni, minna no mae de utawasareta.*
   歌が下手なのに、みんなの前で歌わされた。
   Even though I am poor at it, I was made to sing in front of everyone.

utsu うつ

打つ to beat, strike, hit; 撃つ to shoot: (both trans.)

		Affirmative	Negative
PLAIN FORM	PRESENT	utsu	utanai
	PAST	utta	utanakatta
MASU FORM	PRESENT	uchimasu	uchimasen
	PAST	uchimashita	uchimasen deshita
TE FORM		utte	utanakute
CONDITIONAL	PLAIN	uteba/utta ra	utanakereba/ utanakatta ra
	FORMAL	uchimashita ra	uchimasen deshita ra
VOLITIONAL	PLAIN	utō	–
	FORMAL	uchimashō	–
IMPERATIVE		ute	utsu na

	Affirmative		Affirmative
POTENTIAL	uteru	**CAUS. PASSIVE**	utaserareru/utasareru
PASSIVE	utareru	**HONORIFIC**	ouchi ni naru/utareru
CAUSATIVE	utaseru	**HUMBLE**	ouchi suru

Examples:

1. *Tsukue no kado de hiji o utte shimatta.*
   机の角で肘を打ってしまった。
   I hit my elbow on the corner of the table.

2. *Kanojo wa mēru o utsu no ga hayai.*
   彼女はメールを打つのが速い。
   She types her emails fast.

3. *Kabe ni kugi o utte, e o kaketa.*
   壁にくぎを打って、絵を掛けた。
   I hammered a nail into the wall and hung the picture.

4. *Keikan wa hannin ni ashi o utarete, kega o shita.*
   警官は犯人に足を撃たれて、けがをした。
   The policeman was injured by a gunshot to the leg from a criminal.

5. *Kare no supiichi wa chōshū no kokoro o utta.*
   彼のスピーチは聴衆の心を打った。
   His speech played on the audience's heartstrings.

utsuru うつる

移る to move, transfer; 映る to be reflected; 写る to photograph: (all intrans.)*

		Affirmative	*Negative*
PLAIN FORM	PRESENT	utsuru	utsuranai
	PAST	utsutta	utsuranakatta
MASU FORM	PRESENT	utsurimasu	utsurimasen
	PAST	utsurimashita	utsurimasen deshita
TE FORM		utsutte	utsuranakute
CONDITIONAL	PLAIN	utsureba/utsutta ra	utsuranakereba/ utsuranakatta ra
	FORMAL	utsurimashita ra	utsurimasen deshita ra
VOLITIONAL	PLAIN	utsurō	–
	FORMAL	utsurimashō	–
IMPERATIVE		utsure	utsuru na

	Affirmative		*Affirmative*
POTENTIAL	utsureru	**CAUS. PASSIVE**	utsuraserareru/ utsurasareru
PASSIVE	utsurareru	**HONORIFIC**	outsuri ni naru/utsurareru
CAUSATIVE	utsuraseru	**HUMBLE**	outsuri suru

Examples:

1. *Jimusho ga biru no ni-kai kara yon-kai ni utsurimashita.*
   事務所がビルの二階から四階に移りました。
   My office moved to the 4th floor from the 2nd floor.

2. *Tomodachi no kaze ga utsutte shimatta.*
   友達の風邪がうつってしまった。
   I caught a cold from my friend.

3. *Tanaka-san wa jinji-bu ni utsurimashita.*
   田中さんは人事部に移りました。
   Mr. Tanaka moved to the personnel department.

4. *Sakura no hana ga mizu ni utsutte imasu.*
   桜の花が水に映っています。
   The cherry blossoms are reflected in the water.

5. *Kono shashin no mannaka ni utsutte iru no wa watashi no ane desu.*
   この写真の真ん中に写っているのは私の姉です。
   The one in the center of the photo is my elder sister.

* In general, the verbs *utsuru* 映る meaning "to be reflected" and 写る meaning "to photograph" do not use the imperative, volitional, potential, or passive forms.

utsusu うつす

移す to move to, transfer; 写す to copy; 映す to reflect: (all trans.)

		Affirmative	*Negative*
PLAIN FORM	PRESENT	utsusu	utsusanai
	PAST	utsushita	utsusanakatta
MASU FORM	PRESENT	utsushimasu	utsushimasen
	PAST	utsushimashita	utsushimasen deshita
TE FORM		utsushite	utsusanakute
CONDITIONAL	PLAIN	utsuseba/utsushita ra	utsusanakereba/ utsusanakatta ra
	FORMAL	utsushimashita ra	utsushimasen deshita ra
VOLITIONAL	PLAIN	utsusō	–
	FORMAL	utsushimashō	–
IMPERATIVE		utsuse	utsusu na

	Affirmative		*Affirmative*
POTENTIAL	utsuseru	**CAUS. PASSIVE**	utsusaserareru
PASSIVE	utsusareru	**HONORIFIC**	outsushi ni naru/ utsusareru
CAUSATIVE	utsusaseru	**HUMBLE**	outsushi suru

Examples:

1. *Sono kaisha wa honsha o Ōsaka kara Tōkyō e utsushita.*
   その会社は本社を大阪から東京へ移した。
   That company moved its main office to Tokyo from Osaka.

2. *Hoka no hito ni kaze o utsusanai yō ni, masuku o shite iru.*
   ほかの人に風邪をうつさないように、マスクをしている。
   I wear a mask so I don't pass my cold to other people.

3. *Kare wa shi-gatsu kara eigyō-bu ni utsusareru sō da.*
   彼は四月から営業部に移されるそうだ。
   I hear that he will be transferred to the sales department in April.

4. *Kokuban no bunshō o nōto ni utsushite kudasai.*
   黒板の文章をノートに写してください。
   Please copy the sentences on the blackboard into your notebook.

5. *Dekakeru mae ni, jibun no sugata o kagami ni utsushite mita.*
   出かける前に、自分の姿を鏡に映してみた。
   I looked at my reflection in the mirror before going out.

wakareru わかれる

分かれる or 別れる to part, separate from, be divided: (intrans.)

		Affirmative	Negative
PLAIN FORM	PRESENT	wakareru	wakarenai
	PAST	wakareta	wakarenakatta
MASU FORM	PRESENT	wakaremasu	wakaremasen
	PAST	wakaremashita	wakaremasen deshita
TE FORM		wakarete	wakarenakute
CONDITIONAL	PLAIN	wakarereba/wakareta ra	wakarenakereba/ wakarenakatta ra
	FORMAL	wakaremashita ra	wakaremasen deshita ra
VOLITIONAL	PLAIN	wakareyō	–
	FORMAL	wakaremashō	–
IMPERATIVE		wakarero	wakareru na

	Affirmative		Affirmative
POTENTIAL	wakarerareru/ wakarereru	**CAUS. PASSIVE**	wakaresaserareru
PASSIVE	wakarerareru	**HONORIFIC**	owakare ni naru/ wakarerareru
CAUSATIVE	wakaresaseru	**HUMBLE**	owakare suru

Examples:

1. *Watashi wa kanojo to eki mae de wakaremashita.*
   私は彼女と駅前で別れました。
   I parted from her in front of the station.

2. *Kare wa shigoto no tsugō de kazoku to wakarete sunde iru.*
   彼は仕事の都合で家族と別れて住んでいる。
   He lives away from his family because of his business.

3. *Kanojo wa otto to wakareta sō desu.*
   彼女は夫と別れたそうです。
   I hear that she is separated from her husband.

4. *Gakkō wa hachi kurasu ni wakarete imasu.*
   学校はハクラスに分かれています。
   Our school is divided into eight classes.

5. *Sono mondai ni tsuite wa iken ga wakarete shimatta.*
   その問題については意見が分かれてしまった。
   Opinions about that matter were divided.

wakaru わかる

分かる to understand, know, find out: (intrans.)

		Affirmative	*Negative*
PLAIN FORM	PRESENT	wakaru	wakaranai
	PAST	wakatta	wakaranakatta
MASU FORM	PRESENT	wakarimasu	wakarimasen
	PAST	wakarimashita	wakarimasen deshita
TE FORM		wakatte	wakaranakute
CONDITIONAL	PLAIN	wakareba/wakatta ra	wakaranakereba/ wakaranakatta ra
	FORMAL	wakarimashita ra	wakarimasen deshita ra
VOLITIONAL	PLAIN	wakarō	–
	FORMAL	wakarimashō	–
IMPERATIVE		wakare	wakaru na

	Affirmative		*Affirmative*
POTENTIAL	(wakareru)	**CAUS. PASSIVE**	wakaraserareru/ wakarasareru
PASSIVE	(wakarareru)	**HONORIFIC**	owakari ni naru/ wakarareru
CAUSATIVE	wakaraseru	**HUMBLE**	(owakari suru)

Examples:

1. *Kono kopii-ki no tsukai-kata ga wakarimasu ka.*
   このコピー機の使い方が分かりますか。
   Do you know how to use this copier?

2. *Kotoba no imi ga wakaranakereba, jisho de shirabete kudasai.*
   言葉の意味が分からなければ、辞書で調べてください。
   If you do not understand the meaning of a word, please check the dictionary.

3. *Watashi wa chūgoku-go ga zenzen wakarimasen.*
   私は中国語が全然分かりません。
   I do not understand Chinese at all.

4. *Shiken no kekka wa mada wakatte imasen.*
   試験の結果はまだ分かっていません。
   The results of the exam have not come out yet.

5. *Kono sankōsho wa setsumei ga teinei de, wakari-yasui.*
   この参考書は説明が丁寧で、分かりやすい。
   The explanations in this reference book are carefully written and easy to understand.

wakeru わける

分ける to divide, separate, classify: (trans.)

		Affirmative	Negative
PLAIN FORM	PRESENT	wakeru	wakenai
	PAST	waketa	wakenakatta
MASU FORM	PRESENT	wakemasu	wakemasen
	PAST	wakemashita	wakemasen deshita
TE FORM		wakete	wakenakute
CONDITIONAL	PLAIN	wakereba/waketa ra	wakenakereba/ wakenakatta ra
	FORMAL	wakemashita ra	wakemasen deshita ra
VOLITIONAL	PLAIN	wakeyō	–
	FORMAL	wakemashō	–
IMPERATIVE		wakero	wakeru na

	Affirmative		Affirmative
POTENTIAL	wakerareru/ wakereru	**CAUS. PASSIVE**	wakesaserareru
PASSIVE	wakerareru	**HONORIFIC**	owake ni naru/ wakerareru
CAUSATIVE	wakesaseru	**HUMBLE**	owake suru

Examples:

1. *Kanojo wa kēki o itsutsu ni waketa.*
   彼女はケーキを五つに分けた。
   She divided the cake into five pieces.

2. *Sono chokoreto o sukoshi wakete kuremasen ka.*
   そのチョコレートを少し分けてくれませんか。
   Would you please share some of your chocolate with me?

3. *Kādo wa arufabetto-jun ni wakerarete iru.*
   カードはアルファベット順に分けられている。
   The cards are classified by alphabetical order.

4. *Sono futatsu no mondai wa wakete kangaeta hō ga ii.*
   その二つの問題は分けて考えたほうがいい。
   You should consider those two problems separately.

5. *Zaisan o dō wakeru ka, hanashi-atta.*
   財産をどう分けるか、話し合った。
   We discussed how we would distribute our property.

warau わらう

笑う to laugh, smile (intrans. and trans.)

		Affirmative	Negative
PLAIN FORM	PRESENT	warau	warawanai
	PAST	waratta	warawanakatta
MASU FORM	PRESENT	waraimasu	waraimasen
	PAST	waraimashita	waraimasen deshita
TE FORM		waratte	warawanakute
CONDITIONAL	PLAIN	waraeba/waratta ra	warawanakereba/ warawanakatta ra
	FORMAL	waraimashita ra	waraimasen deshita ra
VOLITIONAL	PLAIN	waraō	–
	FORMAL	waraimashō	–
IMPERATIVE		warae	warau na

	Affirmative		Affirmative
POTENTIAL	waraeru	**CAUS. PASSIVE**	warawaserareru/ warawasareru
PASSIVE	warawareru	**HONORIFIC**	owarai ni naru/ warawareru
CAUSATIVE	warawaseru	**HUMBLE**	(owarai suru)

Examples:

1. *Otōto wa manga o yomi-nagara, ōkii koe de waratte iru.*
   弟は漫画を読みながら、大きい声で笑っている。
   My younger brother is having a good laugh at the comic book.

2. *Kanojo wa kodomo-tachi ga asobu no o mite, nikkori waratta.*
   彼女は子供達が遊ぶのを見て、にっこり笑った。
   She smiled as she watched the children playing.

3. *Warai-sugite, onaka ga itaku natta.*
   笑いすぎて、おなかが痛くなった。
   I laughed so much that my stomach hurt.

4. *Sonna koto o shita ra, warawareru yo.*
   そんなことをしたら、笑われるよ。
   You'll be laughed at if you do such a thing.

5. *Kare wa itsumo jōdan o itte, minna o warawaseru.*
   彼はいつも冗談を言って、みんなを笑わせる。
   He always jokes and makes everybody laugh.

wareru われる

割れる to break, be divided, split: (intrans.)

		Affirmative	Negative
PLAIN FORM	PRESENT	wareru	warenai
	PAST	wareta	warenakatta
MASU FORM	PRESENT	waremasu	waremasen
	PAST	waremashita	waremasen deshita
TE FORM		warete	warenakute
CONDITIONAL	PLAIN	warereba/wareta ra	warenakereba/ warenakatta ra
	FORMAL	waremashita ra	waremasen deshita ra
VOLITIONAL	PLAIN	wareyō	–
	FORMAL	waremashō	–
IMPERATIVE		warero	wareru na

	Affirmative		Affirmative
POTENTIAL	(warerareru)	**CAUS. PASSIVE**	waresaserareru
PASSIVE	(warerareru)	**HONORIFIC**	oware ni naru/warerareru
CAUSATIVE	waresaseru	**HUMBLE**	(oware suru)

Examples:

1. *Bōru ga atatte, mado garasu ga wareta.*
   ボールが当たって、窓ガラスが割れた。
   The ball shattered the window on impact.

2. *Kono shokki wa jōbu de, kantan ni wa warenai darō.*
   この食器は丈夫で、簡単には割れないだろう。
   This tableware is durable and will not break easily.

3. *Kono gurasu wa ware-yasui node, ki o tsukete kudasai.*
   このグラスは割れやすいので、気を付けてください。
   Please take care when handling this glass because it is easily broken.

4. *Hyaku wa go de waremasu.*
   百は五で割れます。
   One hundred can be divided by five.

5. *Iken no chigai de, tō wa futatsu no ha ni wareta.*
   意見の違いで、党は二つの派に割れた。
   The political party split into two factions because of divergent opinions.

waru わる

割る to break, divide: (trans.)

			Affirmative	Negative
PLAIN FORM		PRESENT	waru	waranai
		PAST	watta	waranakatta
MASU FORM		PRESENT	warimasu	warimasen
		PAST	warimashita	warimasen deshita
TE FORM			watte	waranakute
CONDITIONAL		PLAIN	wareba/watta ra	waranakereba/ waranakatta ra
		FORMAL	warimashita ra	warimasen deshita ra
VOLITIONAL		PLAIN	warō	–
		FORMAL	warimashō	–
IMPERATIVE			ware	waru na

	Affirmative		Affirmative
POTENTIAL	wareru	**CAUS. PASSIVE**	waraserareru/warasareru
PASSIVE	warareru	**HONORIFIC**	owari ni naru/warareru
CAUSATIVE	waraseru	**HUMBLE**	(owari suru)

Examples:

1. *Koppu o otoshite, watte shimatta.*
   コップを落として、割ってしまった。
   I accidentally dropped the cup and broke it.

2. *Chokorēto o hanbun ni watte, futari de tabeta.*
   チョコレートを半分に割って、二人で食べた。
   We divided the chocolate into two and ate it together.

3. *Jū o ni de waru to, go ni naru.*
   十を二で割ると、五になる。
   Ten divided by two equals five.

4. *Kono kōri wa katakute, warenai.*
   この氷は硬くて割れない。
   This ice is too hard to break.

5. *Uisukii o mizu de watte nonda.*
   ウィスキーを水で割って飲んだ。
   I mixed whiskey with water and drank it.

wasureru わすれる

忘れる to forget, leave a thing behind: (trans.)

		Affirmative	*Negative*
PLAIN FORM	PRESENT	wasureru	wasurenai
	PAST	wasureta	wasurenakatta
MASU FORM	PRESENT	wasuremasu	wasuremasen
	PAST	wasuremashita	wasuremasen deshita
TE FORM		wasurete	wasurenakute
CONDITIONAL	PLAIN	wasurereba/wasureta ra	wasurenakereba/ wasurenakatta ra
	FORMAL	wasuremashita ra	wasuremasen deshita ra
VOLITIONAL	PLAIN	wasureyō	–
	FORMAL	wasuremashō	–
IMPERATIVE		wasurero	wasureru na

	Affirmative		*Affirmative*
POTENTIAL	wasurerareru/ wasurereru	**CAUS. PASSIVE**	wasuresaserareru
PASSIVE	wasurerareru	**HONORIFIC**	owasure ni naru/ wasurerareru
CAUSATIVE	wasuresaseru	**HUMBLE**	(owasure suru)

Examples:

1. *Kare no namae o wasuremashita.*
   彼の名前を忘れました。
   I forgot his name.

2. *Densha ni kasa o wasurete shimatta.*
   電車に傘を忘れてしまった。
   I forgot my umbrella in the train.

3. *Yakusoku no jikan o wasurenai yō ni, memo shite oita.*
   約束の時間を忘れないように、メモしておいた。
   I made a note of the appointment so I would not forget it.

4. *Ashita, wasurezu ni repōto o teishutsu shite kudasai.*
   明日、忘れずにレポートを提出してください。
   Please do not forget to submit your report tomorrow.

5. *Ginkō ni iku no o wasurete imashita.*
   銀行に行くのを忘れていました。
   I forgot to go to the bank.

wataru わたる

渡る to cross*, be brought over; わたる to range (from ~), cover: (both intrans.)

		Affirmative	*Negative*
PLAIN FORM	PRESENT	*wataru*	*wataranai*
	PAST	*watatta*	*wataranakatta*
MASU FORM	PRESENT	*watarimasu*	*watarimasen*
	PAST	*watarimashita*	*watarimasen deshita*
TE FORM		*watatte*	*wataranakute*
CONDITIONAL	PLAIN	*watareba/watatta ra*	*wataranakereba/ wataranakatta ra*
	FORMAL	*watarimashita ra*	*watarimasen deshita ra*
VOLITIONAL	PLAIN	*watarō*	–
	FORMAL	*watarimashō*	–
IMPERATIVE		*watare*	*wataru na*

	Affirmative		*Affirmative*
POTENTIAL	*watareru*	**CAUS. PASSIVE**	*wataraserareru/ watarasareru*
PASSIVE	*watarareru*	**HONORIFIC**	*owatari ni naru/ watarareru*
CAUSATIVE	*wataraseru*	**HUMBLE**	*(owatari suru)*

Examples:

1. *Ano hashi o wataru to, migigawa ni chūshajō ga arimasu.*
   あの橋を渡ると、右側に駐車場があります。
   When you cross that bridge, you will find a parking lot.

2. *Dōro no mukō-gawa ni watarimashō.*
   道路の向こう側に渡りましょう。
   Let's go over to the other side of the road.

3. *Kōsaten o watatte kara, kuruma o tomete kudasai.*
   交差点を渡ってから、車を止めてください。
   Please stop the car after crossing the intersection.

4. *Kaigi wa mikka-kan ni watatte okonawareru.*
   会議は三日間にわたって行われる。
   The meeting will be held for three days.

5. *Kare no kenkyū wa hiroi han'i ni watatte imasu.*
   彼の研究は広い範囲にわたっています。
   His studies cover a wide field of topics.

---

* As with other verbs indicating movement, *wataru* 渡る meaning "to cross" may take a direct object, thus giving an idea of "going through a defined area."

watasu わたす

渡す to hand, give, transfer: (trans.)

		Affirmative	Negative
PLAIN FORM	PRESENT	watasu	watasanai
	PAST	watashita	watasanakatta
MASU FORM	PRESENT	watashimasu	watashimasen
	PAST	watashimashita	watashimasen deshita
TE FORM		watashite	watasanakute
CONDITIONAL	PLAIN	wataseba/watashita ra	watasanakereba/ watasanakatta ra
	FORMAL	watashimashita ra	watashimasen deshita ra
VOLITIONAL	PLAIN	watasō	–
	FORMAL	watashimashō	–
IMPERATIVE		watase	watasu na

	Affirmative		Affirmative
POTENTIAL	wataseru	**CAUS. PASSIVE**	watasaserareru
PASSIVE	watasareru	**HONORIFIC**	owatashi ni naru/ watasareru
CAUSATIVE	watasaseru	**HUMBLE**	owatashi suru

Examples:

1. *Kono tegami o kare ni watashite kudasai.*
   この手紙を彼に渡してください。
   Please hand him this letter.

2. *Supiido ihan o shite, kippu o watasareta.*
   スピード違反をして、切符を渡された。
   As a result of my violation of the speed limit, I was handed a ticket.

3. *Sono shima e hashi o watasu keikaku ga aru.*
   その島へ橋を渡す計画がある。
   There is a plan to construct a bridge to that island.

4. *Kare wa ie o musuko ni watashita.*
   彼は家を息子に渡した。
   He gave his house to his son.

5. *Sūtsu wa reshiito to hikikae ni owatashi shimasu.*
   スーツはレシートと引き換えにお渡しします。
   We will give you your suit in exchange for the receipt.

yabureru やぶれる

破れる to tear, break;* 敗れる to lose a game, be defeated: (both intrans.)

		Affirmative	*Negative*
PLAIN FORM	PRESENT	yabureru	yaburenai
	PAST	yabureta	yaburenakatta
MASU FORM	PRESENT	yaburemasu	yaburemasen
	PAST	yaburemashita	yaburemasen deshita
TE FORM		yaburete	yaburenakute
CONDITIONAL	PLAIN	yaburereba/yabureta ra	yaburenakereba/ yaburenakatta ra
	FORMAL	yaburemashita ra	yaburemasen deshita ra
VOLITIONAL	PLAIN	yabureyō	–
	FORMAL	yaburemashō	–
IMPERATIVE		yaburero	yabureru na

	Affirmative		*Affirmative*
POTENTIAL	yaburerareru/ yaburereru	**CAUS. PASSIVE**	yaburesaserareru
PASSIVE	yaburerareru	**HONORIFIC**	oyabure ni naru/ yaburerareru
CAUSATIVE	yaburesaseru	**HUMBLE**	(oyabure suru)

Examples:

1. *Sono fukuro wa yaburete imasu.*
   その袋は破れています。
   That bag is torn.

2. *Uwagi ga kugi ni hikkakatte, yabureta.*
   上着がくぎに引っかかって、破れた。
   My jacket caught on a nail and tore.

3. *Kaimono bukuro ga yabure-sō desu.*
   買い物袋が破れそうです。
   My shopping bag is about to tear.

4. *Kono shorui wa oretari yaburetari shinai yō ni shite kudasai.*
   この書類は折れたり破れたりしないようにしてください。
   Please make sure that this document is not folded or torn.

5. *Karera wa shiai ni yaburete, kuyashi-sō datta.*
   彼らは試合に敗れて、悔しそうだった。
   They seem to be disappointed after losing the game.

---

* The verb *yabureru* 破れる meaning "to tear, break" does not generally use the imperative, volitional, potential, or passive forms.

yaburu やぶる

破る to tear, break; 敗る to beat, defeat: (both trans.)

		Affirmative	Negative
PLAIN FORM	PRESENT	yaburu	yaburanai
	PAST	yabutta	yaburanakatta
MASU FORM	PRESENT	yaburimasu	yaburimasen
	PAST	yaburimashita	yaburimasen deshita
TE FORM		yabutte	yaburanakute
CONDITIONAL	PLAIN	yabureba/yabutta ra	yaburanakereba/ yaburanakatta ra
	FORMAL	yaburimashita ra	yaburimasen deshita ra
VOLITIONAL	PLAIN	yaburō	–
	FORMAL	yaburimashō	–
IMPERATIVE		yabure	yaburu na

	Affirmative		Affirmative
POTENTIAL	yabureru	**CAUS. PASSIVE**	yaburaserareru/ yaburasareru
PASSIVE	yaburareru	**HONORIFIC**	oyaburi ni naru/ yaburareru
CAUSATIVE	yaburaseru	**HUMBLE**	(oyaburi suru)

Examples:

1. *Kanojo wa sono tegami o komakaku yabutte suteta.*
   彼女はその手紙を細かく破って捨てた。
   She tore the letter into small pieces and threw them away.

2. *Kare wa yakusoku o yabutta koto ga nai.*
   彼は約束を破ったことがない。
   He has never broken his promises.

3. *Sono dorobō wa sekyuritii shisutemu o yabutte, shinnyū shita.*
   その泥棒はセキュリティーシステムを破って、侵入した。
   That thief sneaked in after breaking through the security system.

4. *Kare no kiroku wa dare ni mo yaburarenai darō.*
   彼の記録は誰にも破られないだろう。
   His record is not likely to be broken by anybody.

5. *Kanojo wa tenisu no shiai de kyōteki o yaburimashita.*
   彼女はテニスの試合で強敵を敗りました。
   She beat a powerful opponent in the tennis match.

yakeru やける

焼ける to be burned, grilled; やける to be jealous: (both intrans.)

		Affirmative	*Negative*
PLAIN FORM	PRESENT	*yakeru*	*yakenai*
	PAST	*yaketa*	*yakenakatta*
MASU FORM	PRESENT	*yakemasu*	*yakemasen*
	PAST	*yakemashita*	*yakemasen deshita*
TE FORM		*yakete*	*yakenakute*
CONDITIONAL	PLAIN	*yakereba/yaketa ra*	*yakenakereba/ yakenakatta ra*
	FORMAL	*yakemashita ra*	*yakemasen deshita ra*
VOLITIONAL	PLAIN	*yakeyō*	–
	FORMAL	*yakemashō*	–
IMPERATIVE		*yakero*	*yakeru na*

	Affirmative		*Affirmative*
POTENTIAL	*yakerareru/yakereru*	**CAUS. PASSIVE**	*yakesaserareru*
PASSIVE	*yakerareru*	**HONORIFIC**	*oyake ni naru/yakerareru*
CAUSATIVE	*yakesaseru*	**HUMBLE**	*(oyake suru)*

Examples:

1. *Kaji de ie ga san-gen yaketa.*
   火事で家が三軒焼けた。
   Three houses were burnt down by a fire.

2. *Kono niku wa yoku yakete inai.*
   この肉はよく焼けていない。
   This meat is undercooked.

3. *Sakana ga yakeru nioi ga shimasu.*
   魚が焼けるにおいがします。
   I smell a fish being grilled.

4. *Kanojo no hada wa hi ni yakete, komugi-iro ni natta.*
   彼女の肌は日に焼けて、小麦色になった。
   Her skin tanned and became a golden-brown.

5. *Kare no kōun ni wa mattaku yakeru.*
   彼の幸運には全くやける。
   I am really envious of his good luck.

yaku やく

焼く to burn, grill; やく to be jealous of, envy: (both trans.)

		Affirmative	Negative
PLAIN FORM	PRESENT	yaku	yakanai
	PAST	yaita	yakanakatta
MASU FORM	PRESENT	yakimasu	yakimasen
	PAST	yakimashita	yakimasen deshita
TE FORM		yaite	yakanakute
CONDITIONAL	PLAIN	yakeba/yaita ra	yakanakereba/ yakanakatta ra
	FORMAL	yakimashita ra	yakimasen deshita ra
VOLITIONAL	PLAIN	yakō	–
	FORMAL	yakimashō	–
IMPERATIVE		yake	yaku na

	Affirmative		Affirmative
POTENTIAL	yakeru	**CAUS. PASSIVE**	yakaserareru/yakasareru
PASSIVE	yakareru	**HONORIFIC**	oyaki ni naru/yakareru
CAUSATIVE	yakaseru	**HUMBLE**	oyaki suru

Examples:

1. *Watashi wa kēki o yaku no ga suki desu.*
   私はケーキを焼くのが好きです。
   I like baking cakes.

2. *Asa-gohan ni pan o ichi-mai yaite tabeta.*
   朝御飯にパンを一枚焼いて食べた。
   I toasted a slice of bread and ate it for breakfast.

3. *Niku wa mō sukoshi yaita hō ga ii desu.*
   肉はもう少し焼いたほうがいいです。
   You should grill the meat a little more.

4. *Biichi de hada o yakimashita.*
   ビーチで肌を焼きました。
   I got a suntan at the beach.

5. *Kare wa dōryō no shōshin o yaite iru yō da.*
   彼は同僚の昇進をやいているようだ。
   He seems jealous of his co-worker's promotion.

yameru やめる

やめる to stop doing, abandon; 辞める to resign, retire: (both trans.)

		Affirmative	Negative
PLAIN FORM	PRESENT	yameru	yamenai
	PAST	yameta	yamenakatta
MASU FORM	PRESENT	yamemasu	yamemasen
	PAST	yamemashita	yamemasen deshita
TE FORM		yamete	yamenakute
CONDITIONAL	PLAIN	yamereba/yameta ra	yamenakereba/ yamenakatta ra
	FORMAL	yamemashita ra	yamemasen deshita ra
VOLITIONAL	PLAIN	yameyō	–
	FORMAL	yamemashō	–
IMPERATIVE		yamero	yameru na

	Affirmative		Affirmative
POTENTIAL	yamerareru/ yamereru	**CAUS. PASSIVE**	yamesaserareru
PASSIVE	yamerareru	**HONORIFIC**	oyame ni naru/ yamerareru
CAUSATIVE	yamesaseru	**HUMBLE**	(oyame suru)

Examples:

1. *Tsukareta kara, kaimono ni iku no o yamemashita.*
   疲れたから、買い物に行くのをやめました。
   Because I was tired, I decided not to go shopping.

2. *Tabako o yameta hō ga ii yo.*
   たばこをやめたほうがいいよ。
   You'd better quit smoking.

3. *Supōtsu kurabu o yameyō to omotte imasu.*
   スポーツクラブをやめようと思っています。
   I intend to quit my gym.

4. *Koko de sawagu no wa yamete kudasai.*
   ここで騒ぐのはやめてください。
   Please stop making noises here.

5. *Kare wa kaisha o yamesaserareta.*
   彼は会社を辞めさせられた。
   He was forced to resign from his company.

yaru やる

やる to do, to give, send:* (trans.)

		Affirmative	*Negative*
PLAIN FORM	PRESENT	yaru	yaranai
	PAST	yatta	yaranakatta
MASU FORM	PRESENT	yarimasu	yarimasen
	PAST	yarimashita	yarimasen deshita
TE FORM		yatte	yaranakute
CONDITIONAL	PLAIN	yareba/yatta ra	yaranakereba/ yaranakatta ra
	FORMAL	yarimashita ra	yarimasen deshita ra
VOLITIONAL	PLAIN	yarō	–
	FORMAL	yarimashō	–
IMPERATIVE		yare	yaru na

	Affirmative		*Affirmative*
POTENTIAL	yareru	**CAUS. PASSIVE**	yaraserareru/yarasareru
PASSIVE	yarareru	**HONORIFIC**	nasaru/oyari ni naru/ yarareru
CAUSATIVE	yaraseru	**HUMBLE**	itasu

Examples:

1. *Kare wa ima shukudai o yatte iru.*
   彼は今、宿題をやっている。
   He is doing his homework now.

2. *Otōsan wa nani o nasatte imasu ka. / Hon'ya o yatte imasu.*
   お父さんは何をなさっていますか。/ 本屋をやっています。
   What does your father do? / He runs a bookstore.

3. *Tenisu demo yaranai? / Un, yarō.*
   テニスでもやらない。/ うん、やろう。
   Shall we play tennis? / Yeah, cool.

4. *Maiasa inu ni esa o yarimasu.*
   毎朝犬に餌をやります。
   I feed my dog every morning.

5. *Musuko no tanjōbi ni, jitensha o katte yatta.*
   息子の誕生日に、自転車を買ってやった。
   I bought him a bicycle for his birthday.

* The verb *yaru* やる meaning "to give, send" generally does not use the honorific or humble forms.

yaseru やせる

やせる to lose weight, become thin, become infertile: (intrans.)

		Affirmative	Negative
PLAIN FORM	PRESENT	yaseru	yasenai
	PAST	yaseta	yasenakatta
MASU FORM	PRESENT	yasemasu	yasemasen
	PAST	yasemashita	yasemasen deshita
TE FORM		yasete	yasenakute
CONDITIONAL	PLAIN	yasereba/yaseta ra	yasenakereba/ yasenakatta ra
	FORMAL	yasemashita ra	yasemasen deshita ra
VOLITIONAL	PLAIN	yaseyō	–
	FORMAL	yasemashō	–
IMPERATIVE		yasero	yaseru na

	Affirmative		Affirmative
POTENTIAL	yaserareru/yasereru	**CAUS. PASSIVE**	yasesaserareru
PASSIVE	yaserareru	**HONORIFIC**	oyase ni naru/yaserareru
CAUSATIVE	yasesaseru	**HUMBLE**	(oyase suru)

Examples:

1. *Koko sanka-getsu de, go kiro yaseta.*
   ここ三か月で、五キロやせた。
   I have lost five kilograms these past three months.

2. *Kanojo wa totemo yasete iru.*
   彼女はとてもやせている。
   She is skinny.

3. *Ato san kiro gurai yasenakereba naranai.*
   あと三キロぐらいやせなければならない。
   I need to lose around three more kilograms.

4. *Amai mono ga suki da kara, nakanaka yaserarenai.*
   甘い物が好きだから、なかなかやせられない。
   Because I like sweets, I cannot easily lose weight.

5. *Kono tochi wa hidoku yasete iru.*
   この土地はひどくやせている。
   This soil is terribly infertile.

yasumu やすむ

休む to take a rest, sleep, be absent from, take a vacation: (intrans.)

		Affirmative	Negative
PLAIN FORM	PRESENT	yasumu	yasumanai
	PAST	yasunda	yasumanakatta
MASU FORM	PRESENT	yasumimasu	yasumimasen
	PAST	yasumimashita	yasumimasen deshita
TE FORM		yasunde	yasumanakute
CONDITIONAL	PLAIN	yasumeba/yasunda ra	yasumanakereba/ yasumanakatta ra
	FORMAL	yasumimashita ra	yasumimasen deshita ra
VOLITIONAL	PLAIN	yasumō	–
	FORMAL	yasumimashō	–
IMPERATIVE		yasume	yasumu na

	Affirmative		Affirmative
POTENTIAL	yasumeru	**CAUS. PASSIVE**	yasumaserareru/ yasumasareru
PASSIVE	yasumareru	**HONORIFIC**	oyasumi ni naru/ yasumareru
CAUSATIVE	yasumaseru	**HUMBLE**	(oyasumi suru)

Examples:

1. *Kare wa kinō byōki de gakkō o yasunda.*
   彼は昨日病気で学校を休んだ。
   He was absent from school yesterday because of illness.

2. *Kusuri o nonde yukkuri yasumeba, kaze wa naoru deshō.*
   薬を飲んでゆっくり休めば、風邪は治るでしょう。
   If you take medicine and get enough rest, you will recover from your cold.

3. *Chotto yasumō.*
   ちょっと休もう。
   Let's take a break.

4. *Sakuya wa yoku oyasumi ni naremashita ka.*
   昨夜はよくお休みになれましたか。
   Were you able to sleep well last night?

5. *Ashita yōji ga aru node, shigoto o yasumasete itadakemasen ka.*
   明日用事があるので、仕事を休ませていただけませんか。
   May I take tomorrow off to attend to a personal matter?

yatou やとう

雇う to employ, hire: (trans.)

		Affirmative	Negative
PLAIN FORM	PRESENT	yatou	yatowanai
	PAST	yatotta	yatowanakatta
MASU FORM	PRESENT	yatoimasu	yatoimasen
	PAST	yatoimashita	yatoimasen deshita
TE FORM		yatotte	yatowanakute
CONDITIONAL	PLAIN	yatoeba/yatotta ra	yatowanakereba/ yatowanakatta ra
	FORMAL	yatoimashita ra	yatoimasen deshita ra
VOLITIONAL	PLAIN	yatoō	–
	FORMAL	yatoimashō	–
IMPERATIVE		yatoe	yatou na

	Affirmative		Affirmative
POTENTIAL	yatoeru	**CAUS. PASSIVE**	yatowaserareru/ yatowasareru
PASSIVE	yatowareru	**HONORIFIC**	oyatoi ni naru/ yatowareru
CAUSATIVE	yatowaseru	**HUMBLE**	(oyatoi suru)

Examples:

1. *Sono kaisha wa sen-nin rōdōsha o yatotte iru.*
   その会社は千人労働者を雇っている。
   That company employs 1,000 workers.

2. *Kare wa kaisha ni untenshu to shite yatowarete imasu.*
   彼は会社に運転手として雇われています。
   He is employed as a driver in the firm.

3. *Uekiya o ichi-nichi yatoimashita.*
   植木屋を一日雇いました。
   We hired a gardener for a day.

4. *Dareka senmonka o yatotta hō ga ii.*
   誰か専門家を雇ったほうがいい。
   We should employ a specialist.

5. *Isogashii kara, arubaito o yatoō to omotte imasu.*
   忙しいから、アルバイトを雇おうと思っています。
   We intend to employ a part-timer since we are busy.

yobu よぶ

呼ぶ to call, invite, attract (customers): (trans.)

		Affirmative	Negative
PLAIN FORM	PRESENT	yobu	yobanai
	PAST	yonda	yobanakatta
MASU FORM	PRESENT	yobimasu	yobimasen
	PAST	yobimashita	yobimasen deshita
TE FORM		yonde	yobanakute
CONDITIONAL	PLAIN	yobeba/yonda ra	yobanakereba/ yobanakatta ra
	FORMAL	yobimashita ra	yobimasen deshita ra
VOLITIONAL	PLAIN	yobō	–
	FORMAL	yobimashō	–
IMPERATIVE		yobe	yobu na

	Affirmative		Affirmative
POTENTIAL	yoberu	**CAUS. PASSIVE**	yobaserareru/yobasareru
PASSIVE	yobareru	**HONORIFIC**	oyobi ni naru/yobareru
CAUSATIVE	yobaseru	**HUMBLE**	oyobi suru

Examples:

1. *Satō-san ga anata o yonde imasu yo.*
   佐藤さんがあなたを呼んでいますよ。
   Mr. Sato is calling for you.

2. *Kare o shokuji ni yobimashō.*
   彼を食事に呼びましょう。
   Let's invite him for a meal.

3. *Denwa de takushii o yonde kudasai.*
   電話でタクシーを呼んでください。
   Please call a taxi.

4. *Anata o nan to yobeba ii desu ka. / Tarō to yonde kudasai.*
   あなたを何と呼べばいいですか。／太郎と呼んでください。
   What shall I call you? / Please call me Taro.

5. *Namae o yobareta ra, henji o shite kudasai.*
   名前を呼ばれたら、返事をしてください。
   If your name is called, please answer.

yomu よむ

読む to read: (trans.)

		Affirmative	Negative
PLAIN FORM	PRESENT	yomu	yomanai
	PAST	yonda	yomanakatta
MASU FORM	PRESENT	yomimasu	yomimasen
	PAST	yomimashita	yomimasen deshita
TE FORM		yonde	yomanakute
CONDITIONAL	PLAIN	yomeba/yonda ra	yomanakereba/ yomanakatta ra
	FORMAL	yomimashita ra	yomimasen deshita ra
VOLITIONAL	PLAIN	yomō	–
	FORMAL	yomimashō	–
IMPERATIVE		yome	yomu na

	Affirmative		Affirmative
POTENTIAL	yomeru	**CAUS. PASSIVE**	yomaserareru/ yomasareru
PASSIVE	yomareru	**HONORIFIC**	oyomi ni naru
CAUSATIVE	yomaseru	**HUMBLE**	oyomi suru

Examples:

1. *Maiasa ie o deru mae ni, shinbun o yomimasu.*
   毎朝家を出る前に、新聞を読みます。
   I read the newspaper every morning before leaving the house.

2. *Hiragana ga yomemasu ka. / Hai, yomeru yō ni narimashita.*
   ひらがなが読めますか。/ はい、読めるようになりました。
   Can you read hiragana? / Yes, I learned how to read it.

3. *Ano kanji wa nan to yomimasu ka. / Kin-en to yomimasu.*
   あの漢字は何と読みますか。/ きんえん（禁煙）と読みます。
   How do you pronounce that kanji? / We pronounce it "Kin-en"
   (No smoking).

4. *Kanojo wa kodomo ni dōwa o yonde yatta.*
   彼女は子供に童話を読んでやった。
   She read a nursery story to the children.

5. *Kono shōsetsu o oyomi ni narimashita ka.*
   この小説をお読みになりましたか。
   I was wondering if you have read this novel.

yorokobu よろこぶ

喜ぶ to be glad, be delighted: (intrans. and trans.)

		Affirmative	*Negative*
PLAIN FORM	PRESENT	yorokobu	yorokobanai
	PAST	yorokonda	yorokobanakatta
MASU FORM	PRESENT	yorokobimasu	yorokobimasen
	PAST	yorokobimashita	yorokobimasen deshita
TE FORM		yorokonde	yorokobanakute
CONDITIONAL	PLAIN	yorokobeba/ yorokonda ra	yorokobanakereba/ yorokobanakatta ra
	FORMAL	yorokobimashita ra	yorokobimasen deshita ra
VOLITIONAL	PLAIN	yorokobō	–
	FORMAL	yorokobimashō	–
IMPERATIVE		yorokobe	yorokobu na

	Affirmative		*Affirmative*
POTENTIAL	yorokoberu	**CAUS. PASSIVE**	yorokobaserareru/ yorokobasareru
PASSIVE	yorokobareru	**HONORIFIC**	oyorokobi ni naru/ yorokobareru
CAUSATIVE	yorokobaseru	**HUMBLE**	oyorokobi suru

Examples:

1. *Haha wa watashi no seikō o totemo yorokonde kureta.*
   母は私の成功をとても喜んでくれた。
   Mother was delighted with my success.

2. *Anata ga buji da to kiite, minna totemo yorokonde imasu.*
   あなたが無事だと聞いて、みんなとても喜んでいます。
   We were very glad to hear that you were safe.

3. *Kyū na henka o yorokobanai hito mo iru.*
   急な変化を喜ばない人もいる。
   There are some people who are not pleased with sudden changes.

4. *Watashi ni dekiru koto ga areba, yorokonde otetsudai shimashō.*
   私にできることがあれば、喜んでお手伝いしましょう。
   I would be glad to help with whatever I can.

5. *Sumimasen ga, chotto te o kashite kuremasen ka. / Hai, yorokonde.*
   すみませんが、ちょっと手を貸してくれませんか。/ はい、喜んで。
   Excuse me, but can you please give me a hand? / Yes, with pleasure.

yoru よる

寄る to draw near, drop in; よる or 因る to depend on, be due to: (both intrans.)

		Affirmative	Negative
PLAIN FORM	PRESENT	yoru	yoranai
	PAST	yotta	yoranakatta
MASU FORM	PRESENT	yorimasu	yorimasen
	PAST	yorimashita	yorimasen deshita
TE FORM		yotte	yoranakute
CONDITIONAL	PLAIN	yoreba/yotta ra	yoranakereba/ yoranakatta ra
	FORMAL	yorimashita ra	yorimasen deshita ra
VOLITIONAL	PLAIN	yorō	–
	FORMAL	yorimashō	–
IMPERATIVE		yore	yoru na

	Affirmative		Affirmative
POTENTIAL	yoreru	**CAUS. PASSIVE**	yoraserareru/yorasareru
PASSIVE	yorareru	**HONORIFIC**	oyori ni naru/yorareru
CAUSATIVE	yoraseru	**HUMBLE**	oyori suru

Examples:

1. *Ie e kaeru mae ni, konbini e yorimasita.*
   家へ帰る前に、コンビニへ寄りました。
   I dropped by a convenience store before going home.

2. *Ginkō ni yotte, okane o oroshimashita.*
   銀行に寄って、お金を下ろしました。
   I dropped into a bank and withdrew some money.

3. *Shashin o tori-tai kara, mannaka ni yotte kudasai.*
   写真を撮りたいから、真ん中に寄ってください。
   I want to take a picture so please move nearer the center.

4. *Shūkan wa kuni ni yotte chigaimasu.*
   習慣は国によって違います。
   Customs vary, depending on the country.

5. *Sono jiko wa kare no fuchūi unten ni yoru mono deshita.*
   その事故は彼の不注意運転に因るものでした。
   That accident was due to his careless driving.

you よう

酔う to get drunk, become intoxicated: (intrans.)

		Affirmative	*Negative*
PLAIN FORM	PRESENT	you	yowanai
	PAST	yotta	yowanakatta
MASU FORM	PRESENT	yoimasu	yoimasen
	PAST	yoimashita	yoimasen deshita
TE FORM		yotte	yowanakute
CONDITIONAL	PLAIN	yoeba/yotta ra	yowanakereba/ yowanakatta ra
	FORMAL	yoimashita ra	yoimasen deshita ra
VOLITIONAL	PLAIN	yoō	–
	FORMAL	yoimashō	–
IMPERATIVE		yoe	you na

	Affirmative		*Affirmative*
POTENTIAL	yoeru	**CAUS. PASSIVE**	yowaserareru/ yowasareru
PASSIVE	yowareru	**HONORIFIC**	oyoi ni naru/yowareru
CAUSATIVE	yowaseru	**HUMBLE**	(oyoi suru)

Examples:

1. *Yūbe osake o nomi-sugite, yotte shimaimashita.*
   ゆうべお酒を飲み過ぎて、酔ってしまいました。
   Last night I drank too much and got drunk.

2. *Kare wa ikura osake o nondemo, yowanai.*
   彼はいくらお酒を飲んでも、酔わない。
   No matter how much liquor he drinks, he does not get drunk.

3. *Watashi wa norimono ni yoi-yasui.*
   私は乗り物に酔いやすい。
   I get motion sickness easily.

4. *Kuruma ni yowanai yō ni, kusuri o nonde oita.*
   車に酔わないように、薬を飲んでおいた。
   To avoid getting carsick, I took medicine first.

5. *Kanojo no utsukushii koe wa chōshū o yowasemashita.*
   彼女の美しい声は聴衆を酔わせました。
   Her beautiful voice enchanted the audience.

yurusu ゆるす

許す to forgive, permit, allow, admit into: (trans.)

		Affirmative	Negative
PLAIN FORM	PRESENT	*yurusu*	*yurusanai*
	PAST	*yurushita*	*yurusanakatta*
MASU FORM	PRESENT	*yurushimasu*	*yurushimasen*
	PAST	*yurushimashita*	*yurushimasen deshita*
TE FORM		*yurushite*	*yurusanakute*
CONDITIONAL	PLAIN	*yuruseba/yurushita ra*	*yurusanakereba/ yurusanakatta ra*
	FORMAL	*yurushimashita ra*	*yurushimasen deshita ra*
VOLITIONAL	PLAIN	*yurusō*	–
	FORMAL	*yurushimashō*	–
IMPERATIVE		*yuruse*	*yurusu na*

	Affirmative		Affirmative
POTENTIAL	*yuruseru*	**CAUS. PASSIVE**	*yurusaserareru*
PASSIVE	*yurusareru*	**HONORIFIC**	*oyurushi ni naru/ yurusareru*
CAUSATIVE	*yurusaseru*	**HUMBLE**	*(oyurushi suru)*

Examples:

1. *Jōshi ga yurushite kureta ra, nagai yasumi ga toritai.*
上司が許してくれたら、長い休みが取りたい。
I want to take a long holiday if my boss allows it.

2. *Gomeiwaku o okake shimashita. Dōka oyurushi kudasai.*
ご迷惑をおかけしました。どうかお許しください。
I'm sorry to have troubled you. Please forgive me.

3. *Kyōshitu de no kitsuen wa yurusarete imasen.*
教室での喫煙は許されていません。
Smoking is not allowed in classrooms.

4. *Kare ga yakusoku o yabutta koto ga dōshitemo yurusenakatta.*
彼が約束を破ったことがどうしても許せなかった。
I have never been able to forgive him for breaking his promise.

5. *Chichi wa watashi ga kuruma no menkyo o toru no o yurushite kureta.*
父は私が車の免許を取るのを許してくれた。
My father permitted me to get a driver's license.

A LIST OF COMPOUND VERBS

Compound verbs are formed by adding a verb to the pre-*masu* form of another verb. Thus, the original meaning of the verb (in pre-*masu* form) is modified by the attached verb. Following are 14 common examples of such verbs:

~ akiru 飽きる : to be sick of, to be tired of
(often used with *tabe-, mi-, yomi-, kiki-, asobi-*)

> *Kono ryōri wa mō tabe-akimashita.*
> この料理は、もう食べ飽きました。
> I am sick of eating this food.

~ au 合う : (to do something) together or with/to each other
(often used with *hanashi-, tasuke-*)

> *Shūmatsu wa nani o suru ka, hanashi-aimashō.*
> 週末は何をするか、話し合いましょう。
> Let's discuss what we will do this weekend.

~ dasu 出す : to start (suddenly or nonvolitionally)
(often used with *furi-, hashiri-, naki-*)

> *Ame ga kyūni furi-dashimashita.*
> 雨が急に降り出しました。
> It started raining suddenly.

~ hajimeru 始める : to begin
(often used with *narai-, hataraki-, yomi-, kaki-*)

> *Sengetsu kara ikebana o narai-hajimemashita.*
> 先月から生け花を習い始めました。
> I started learning Ikebana last month.

~ kaeru 換える : to change, to switch
(often used with *nori-, kai-, kaki-*)

> *Shibuya-eki de chikatetsu ni nori-kaemasu.*
> 渋谷駅で地下鉄に乗り換えます。
> I will transfer to the subway at Shibuya Station.

~ kiru 切る : (to do something) to the end
(often used with *tsukai-, tsukare-, nige-, tabe-*)

Hamigakiko o tsukai-kitte shimatta.
歯磨き粉を使い切ってしまった。
I used up all of my toothpaste.

~ machigaeru 間違える : to mistake, to mis- (verb)
(often used with *kaki-, yomi-, kiki-, nori-*)

Kaki-machigaeta tokoro o keshigomu de keshimashita.
書き間違えた所を消しゴムで消しました。
I erased the spot that I miswrote with an eraser.

~ mawaru 回る : to (verb) around
(often used with *aruki-, hashiri-, tobi-, asobi-*)

Machi jū o aruki-mawatte, totemo tsukaremashita.
町中を歩き回って、とても疲れました。
I walked all around town, so I am very tired.

~ naosu 直す : to do over, to fix
(often used with *mi-, tsukuri-, kaki-, yomi-*)

Tesuto o dasu mae ni, mō ichido mi-naoshite kudasai.
テストを出す前に、もう一度見直してください。
Before you turn the test in, please look it over once again.

~ nareru 慣れる : to be used to
(often used with *tsukai-, haki-, sumi-, tsukuri-*)

Sumi-nareta machi o hanaretakunai.
住み慣れた町を離れたくない。
I have gotten used to living in this town, so I do not want to leave.

~ nokosu 残す : to leave undone
(often used with *yari-, tabe-*)

Yari-nokoshita shigoto o ie ni motte kaerimashita.
やり残した仕事を家に持って帰りました。
I brought my unfinished work home.

~ owaru 終わる : to finish
(often used with *yomi-, tsukuri-, kaki-, arai-*)

Sono hon wa mō yomi-owarimashita.
その本は、もう読み終わりました。
I have already finished reading that book.

~ tsuzukeru 続ける : to continue, to keep doing
(often used with *hataraki-, aruki-, hanashi-*)

> *Musume wa ichi-jikan mo denwa de hanashi-tsuzukete iru.*
> 娘は一時間も電話で話し続けている。
> My daughter has been talking on the phone for an hour.

~ wasureru 忘れる : to forget
(often used with *kake-, shime-, ake-, kaki-, keshi-*)

> *Heya no kagi o kake-wasuremashita.*
> 部屋の鍵を掛け忘れました。
> I forgot to lock the door to the room.

A LIST OF SURU VERBS

Many verbs simply consist of a noun followed by *suru*. The different forms of these verbs are made by conjugating the verb *suru* する; for instance, the present *masu* form of *annai suru* is *annai shimasu*, the causative form is *annai sasemasu*, and so forth. Following are 277 commonly used noun + *suru* verbs.

aiyō suru 愛用する (trans.) to use regularly, patronize

akusesu suru アクセスする (intrans.) to access (for Internet)

annai suru 案内する (trans.) to guide, lead

anshin suru 安心する (intrans.) to be relieved, feel secure

antei suru 安定する (intrans.) to be steady, stable

appu suru アップする (trans.) to upload (for Internet)

arenji suru アレンジする (trans.) to arrange

bakuhatsu suru 爆発する (intrans.) to explode, burst, blow up

bengo suru 弁護する (trans.) to defend, testify for

benkyō suru 勉強する (trans.) to study, to give a discount

benshō suru 弁償する (trans.) to compensate, repay for loss

bōshi suru 防止する (trans.) to prevent, keep in check

boshū suru 募集する (trans.) to recruit, collect

bunseki suru 分析する (trans.) to analyze, break down

charenji suru チャレンジする (intrans.) to challenge

chikoku suru 遅刻する (intrans.) to be late, tardy

chokin suru 貯金する (intrans.) to save money

chōsa suru 調査する (trans.) to investigate, inquire into, examine

chōsei suru 調整する (trans.) to regulate, adjust

chūcho suru ちゅうちょする (trans.) to hesitate, waver, vacillate

chūi suru 注意する (intrans.) to be careful of, pay attention to

chūkei suru 中継する (trans.) to relay (a broadcast)

chūkoku suru 忠告する (trans. or intrans.) to warn

chūmoku suru 注目する (trans. or intrans.) to observe, take notice of

chūmon suru 注文する (trans.) to order (food, goods)

chūshi suru 中止する (trans.) to stop, discontinue, call off

daunrōdo suru ダウンロードする (trans.) to download (for Internet)

dakyō suru 妥協する (intrans.) to compromise

dansu suru ダンスする (intrans.) to dance

denwa suru 電話する (intrans.) to make a telephone call

dokuritsu suru 独立する (intrans.) to become independent

dōi suru 同意する (intrans.) to agree, approve

dōnyū suru 導入する (trans.) to bring in, introduce

doraggu suru ドラッグする (trans.) to drag with a (computer) mouse

doryoku suru 努力する (intrans.) to make an effort, work hard

eigyō suru 営業する (trans. or intrans.) to do business, be open

eikyō suru 影響する (intrans.) to influence, affect

enchō suru 延長する (trans. or intrans.) to extend, lengthen

engi suru 演技する (intrans.) to act, perform

enjo suru 援助する (trans.) to assist, help, support, aid

enki suru 延期する (trans.) to postpone, put off

enryo suru 遠慮する (trans. or intrans.) to refrain, hold back

fakkusu suru ファックスする (trans.) to fax

forō suru フォローする (trans.) to follow on line

fukkatsu suru 復活する (trans. or intrans.) to revive, restore

fukushū suru 復習する (trans.) to review, go over

fukushū suru 復讐する (intrans.) to revenge

fukyū suru 普及する (trans. or intrans.) to spread, diffuse

funin suru 赴任する (intrans.) to leave for one's new post

fusoku suru 不足する (intrans.) to be short of, be lacking

futan suru 負担する (trans.) to bear the weight of

gaman suru 我慢する (trans.) to be patient, endure

genshō suru 減少する (intrans. or trans.) to decrease

gentei suru 限定する (trans.) to limit, restrict

giron suru 議論する (trans. or intrans.) to argue, discuss, debate

gokai suru 誤解する (trans.) to misunderstand

gōkaku suru 合格する (intrans.) to pass an examination

gōkei suru 合計する (trans.) to add up, total

hagu suru ハグする (trans.) to hug

haishi suru 廃止する (trans.) to abolish, do away with, repeal

haitatsu suru 配達する (trans.) to deliver

hakai suru 破壊する (trans, or intrans.) to destroy, break, ruin

hakkō suru 発行する (trans.) to publish, issue, bring out

han'ei suru 反映する (trans, or intrans.) to reflect

han'ei suru 繁栄する (intrans.) to prosper, flourish

handan suru 判断する (trans.) to judge, conclude

hansei suru 反省する (trans.) to reflect on oneself, reconsider

hantai suru 反対する (intrans.) to be against, be opposed

hatsubai suru 発売する (trans.) to begin selling, put on the market

hatsumei suru 発明する (trans.) to invent

hatten suru 発展する (intrans.) to develop, expand

heikin suru 平均する (trans. or intrans.) to average, balance

henka suru 変化する (intrans.) to change, alter, be transformed

henshū suru 編集する (trans.) to edit, compile

hihan suru 批判する (trans.) to criticize

hitei suru 否定する (trans.) to deny, negate

hon'yaku suru 翻訳する (trans.) to translate

hōkoku suru 報告する (trans.) to report, inform

hōmon suru 訪問する (trans.) to visit, call on, pay a visit

hoshō suru 保証する (trans.) to guarantee, warrant

hoshō suru 補償する (trans.) to compensate, make up for

hyōka suru 評価する (trans.) to appraise, value

ihan suru 違反する (intrans.) to violate

iji suru 維持する (trans.) to maintain, support, keep

intai suru 引退する (intrans.) to retire, give up one's position

irai suru 依頼する (trans.) to request, ask

itchi suru 一致する (intrans.) to agree with, be in unison

ito suru 意図する (trans.) to intend to do, make a goal

janpu suru ジャンプする (intrans.) to jump

jikken suru 実験する (trans.) to experiment

jikkō suru 実行する (trans.) to carry out, execute

jiman suru 自慢する (trans.) to be proud, boast of, take pride in

jiritsu suru 自立する (intrans.) to become independent

jishoku suru 辞職する (trans.) to resign

jitsugen suru 実現する (intrans. or trans.) to be realized, come true

jogingu suru ジョギングする (intrans.) to jog

jōei suru 上映する (trans.) to show a film

jōho suru 譲歩する (trans.) to concede, give way to

jōshō suru 上昇する (intrans.) to go up, rise, ascend

junbi suru 準備する (trans. or intrans.) to prepare

kaifuku suru 回復する (intrans. or trans.) to restore, recuperate

kaihatsu suru 開発する (trans.) to develop, exploit

kaihō suru 開放する (trans.) to open a place to the public

kaihō suru 解放する (trans.) to release, set a prisoner free

kaikaku suru 改革する (trans.) to reform, improve

kaiketsu suru 解決する (trans. or intrans.) to settle, resolve

kaisai suru 開催する (trans.) to hold (an event)

kaisei suru 改正する (trans.) to revise, amend, improve

kaishaku suru 解釈する (trans.) to interpret, explain

kaitaku suru 開拓する (trans.) to reclaim, exploit, develop

kakō suru 下降する (intrans.) to come down, descend, drop

kakō suru 加工する (trans.) to process, manufacture

kakudai suru 拡大する (trans. or intrans.) to magnify, enlarge, expand

kakunin suru 確認する (trans.) to confirm, ascertain

kankei suru 関係する (intrans.) to be related, have a relationship

kanri suru 管理する (trans.) to manage, control, administer

kansatsu suru 観察する (trans.) to observe, watch closely

kansei suru 完成する (intrans. or trans.) to finish, complete

kanshin suru 感心する (intrans.) to admire, be impressed

kanshō suru 観賞する　(trans.) to appreciate

katei suru 仮定する　(trans.) to assume, suppose

katsudō suru 活動する　(intrans.) to be active

katsuyaku suru 活躍する　(intrans.) be active in, take an active part

katto suru カットする　(trans.) to cut

keiei suru 経営する　(trans.) to manage, conduct, run (a business)

keika suru 経過する　(intrans.) to pass, elapse, expire

keikaku suru 計画する　(trans.) to plan

keiken suru 経験する　(trans.) to experience, undergo

keisan suru 計算する　(trans.) to count, calculate, sum up

keiyaku suru 契約する　(trans.) to contract, make a contract with

kekkon suru 結婚する　(intrans.) to marry

kenbutsu suru 見物する　(trans.) to go sightseeing

kenka suru けんかする　(intrans.) to quarrel, fight

kenkyū suru 研究する　(trans.) to study, research

kenshū suru 研修する　(trans.) to study, train, intern

kentō suru 検討する　(trans.) to examine, investigate, think over

kesseki suru 欠席する　(intrans.) to be absent

kesshin suru 決心する　(intrans.) to make up one's mind, decide

kettei suru 決定する　(trans. or intrans.) to decide, determine

kiipu suru キープする　(trans.) to keep

kikku suru キックする　(trans.) to kick

kinchō suru 緊張する　(intrans.) to be tense, nervous

kinen suru 記念する　(trans.) to commemorate

kiroku suru 記録する　(trans.) to record, write down

kisu suru キスする　(intrans.) to kiss

kitai suru 期待する　(trans.) to expect, hope

kōgeki suru 攻撃する　(trans.) to attack, charge, criticize

kōji suru 工事する　(intrans.) to construct

kōkai suru 後悔する　(trans. or intrans.) to regret, repent, be sorry

kōkan suru 交換する　(trans.) to exchange

konran suru 混乱する　(intrans.) to be confused, be in disorder

kontorōru suru コントロールする　(trans.) to control

kopii suru コピーする　(trans.) to make a copy

kōryo suru 考慮する　(trans.) to consider, think over

kōryū suru 交流する (intrans.) to exchange (ideas, culture)

koshō suru 故障する (intrans.) to break down

kōshō suru 交渉する (intrans.) to negotiate

kōtai suru 交代する (intrans.) to take turns, take a person's place

kurikku suru クリックする (trans.) to click with a mouse

kyanseru suru キャンセルする (trans.) to cancel

kyohi suru 拒否する (trans.) to refuse, reject, deny

kyōiku suru 教育する (trans.) to educate

kyoka suru 許可する (trans.) to permit

kyōkyū suru 供給する (trans.) to supply, furnish, provide

kyōsei suru 強制する (trans.) to compel, force a person to do

kyōsō suru 競争する (intrans.) to compete

kyūjo suru 救助する (trans.) to rescue, help

kyūkei suru 休憩する (intrans.) to rest, take a break

kyūshū suru 吸収する (trans.) to absorb

mēru suru メールする (intrans.) to send an email

meiwaku suru 迷惑する (intrans.) to be troubled/annoyed

mensetsu suru 面接する (intrans.) to interview

mikkusu suru ミックスする (trans.) to mix

misu suru ミスする (trans. or intrans.) to make a mistake, to miss

mokunin suru 黙認する (trans.) to permit or approve tacitly

mujun suru 矛盾する (intrans.) to be contradictory, to conflict

mushi suru 無視する (trans.) to ignore, disregard

nattoku suru 納得する (trans.) to be convinced

ninshiki suru 認識する (trans.) to recognize, realize, understand

nyūgaku suru 入学する (intrans.) to enter a school

nyūin suru 入院する (intrans.) to be hospitalized

ōen suru 応援する (trans.) to aid, support, encourage, cheer

ōfuku suru 往復する (intrans.) to go and return

ōyō suru 応用する (trans.) to apply, put into practice

pasu suru パスする (trans. or intrans.) to pass (mainly used in sports) *rakudai suru* 落第する (intrans.) to fail an exam, be rejected

rakusen suru 落選する (intrans.) to be defeated in an election

renraku suru 連絡する (intrans. or trans.) to contact, get in touch

renshū suru 練習する (trans.) to practice, exercise

riido suru リードする (trans. or intrans.) to lead

rikai suru 理解する (trans.) to understand, comprehend

rikon suru 離婚する (intrans.) to divorce

riyō suru 利用する (trans.) to make use of

rokku suru ロックする (trans.) to lock

rokuon suru 録音する (trans.) to record (sound)

rōhi suru 浪費する (trans.) to waste (money or time), throw away

ryokō suru 旅行する (intrans.) to travel

ryōri suru 料理する (trans.) to cook

ryūgaku suru 留学する (intrans.) to study abroad

saiban suru 裁判する (trans.) to hold a trial

saiyō suru 採用する (trans.) to employ, adopt (measures)

sanka suru 参加する (intrans.) to join, take part in

sanpo suru 散歩する (intrans.) to take a walk

sansei suru 賛成する (intrans.) to agree, approve

seikatsu suru 生活する (intrans.) to make a living, support oneself

seikō suru 成功する (intrans.) to succeed

seisan suru 生産する (trans.) to produce, manufacture

senkō suru 専攻する (trans.) to specialize, major in

senkyo suru 選挙する (trans.) to elect

sensō suru 戦争する (intrans.) to make war

sentaku suru 選択する (trans.) to choose, select

sentaku suru 洗濯する (trans.) to wash (clothes)

setsumei suru 説明する (trans.) to explain

setsuyaku suru 節約する (trans.) to economize, skimp, save

setto suru セットする (trans.) to set

settoku suru 説得する (trans.) to persuade

sewa suru 世話する (trans.) to take care of, look after (someone)

shidō suru 指導する (trans.) to lead, guide

shigeki suru 刺激する (trans.) to stimulate, irritate, excite *shihai suru* 支配する (trans.) to control, dominate

shiji suru 指示する (trans.) to instruct

shimei suru 指名する (trans.) to nominate, designate

shinpai suru 心配する (trans, or intrans.) to be anxious, feel uneasy

shinpo suru 進歩する (intrans.) to make progress, advance

shinryaku suru 侵略する (trans.) to invade

shinsei suru 申請する (trans.) to make out an application

shinyō suru 信用する (trans.) to trust, believe, place confidence in

shippai suru 失敗する (intrans.) to fail

shishutsu suru 支出する (trans.) to spend (expenditures)

shiteki suru 指摘する (trans.) to point out

shitsumon suru 質問する (trans. or intrans.) to ask a question

shiyō suru 使用する (trans.) to use, employ

shokuji suru 食事する (intrans.) to take a meal

shōhi suru 消費する (trans.) to consume, expend

shōkai suru 紹介する (trans.) to introduce, present

shōmei suru 証明する (trans.) to prove, testify, certify

shōshin suru 昇進する (intrans.) to be promoted

shōtai suru 招待する (trans.) to invite

shoyū suru 所有する (trans.) to own, possess

shozoku suru 所属する (intrans.) to belong to

shuchō suru 主張する (trans.) to insist on, assert, emphasize

shūchū suru 集中する (trans. or intrans.) to concentrate, centralize

shukushō suru 縮小する (trans. or intrans.) to reduce, cut, curtail

shuppan suru 出版する (trans.) to publish, issue

shuppatsu suru 出発する (intrans.) to leave for, depart

shūri suru 修理する (trans.) to repair, mend, fix

shūshoku suru 就職する (intrans.) to find employment

shusseki suru 出席する (intrans.) to attend

shutchō suru 出張する (intrans.) to go on a business trip

sōdan suru 相談する (trans. or intrans.) to consult, discuss

sōji suru 掃除する (trans.) to clean

sonzai suru 存在する (intrans.) to exist

sōsa suru 操作する (trans.) to operate, handle

soshiki suru 組織する (trans.) to organize, form

sotsugyō suru 卒業する (trans.) to graduate from

sōzō suru 想像する (trans.) to imagine, guess

suisen suru 推薦する (trans.) to recommend

sutāto suru スタートする (intrans.) to start

taiho suru 逮捕する (trans.) to arrest, apprehend

taiin suru 退院する (intrans.) to be released from a hospital

tairitsu suru 対立する (intrans.) to be opposed

tanken suru 探検する (trans.) to explore

tantō suru 担当する (trans.) to take charge of

tassei suru 達成する (trans.) to achieve, attain, accomplish

tacchi suru タッチする (intrans.) to touch

teian suru 提案する (trans.) to propose, suggest

teishutsu suru 提出する (trans.) to submit, present

tetsuya suru 徹夜する (intrans.) to work all night

tōchaku suru 到着する (intrans.) to arrive

tōhyō suru 投票する (intrans.) to vote, cast a ballot

tōitsu suru 統一する (trans.) to unify, unite

torihiki suru 取り引きする (trans. or intrans.) to have dealings with

tōsen suru 当選する (intrans.) to be elected

tōshi suru 投資する (intrans.)* to invest

tsūchi suru 通知する (trans.) to inform, give notice

tsuika suru 追加する (trans.) to supplement, add

tsūka suru 通過する (intrans.) to pass, go through without stopping

un'ei suru 運営する (trans.) to manage, run, administer

unten suru 運転する (trans. or intrans.) to drive, to manage (money)

wakai suru 和解する (intrans.) to be reconciled with

yakusoku suru 約束する (trans.) to promise

yobō suru 予防する (trans.) to prevent, protect

yōkyū suru 要求する (trans.) to demand, claim

---

* Classified as an intransitive, but often used like a transitive verb.

yōsei suru 養成する　(trans.) to train, develop (a person)

yoshū suru 予習する　(trans.) to study beforehand

yosō suru 予想する　(trans.) to predict, anticipate

yoyaku suru 予約する　(trans.) to reserve, book

yūkai suru 誘拐する　(trans.) to kidnap

yunyū suru 輸入する　(trans.) to import

yūshō suru 優勝する　(intrans.) to win a contest or championship

yushutsu suru 輸出する　(trans.) to export

yūsō suru 郵送する　(trans.) to send by mail

yūwaku suru 誘惑する　(trans.) to tempt, lure, entice

zetsubō suru 絶望する　(intrans.) to have no hope, be in despair

zōka suru 増加する　(trans. or intrans.) to increase, grow, augment